RED THORN

GLASGOW KISS

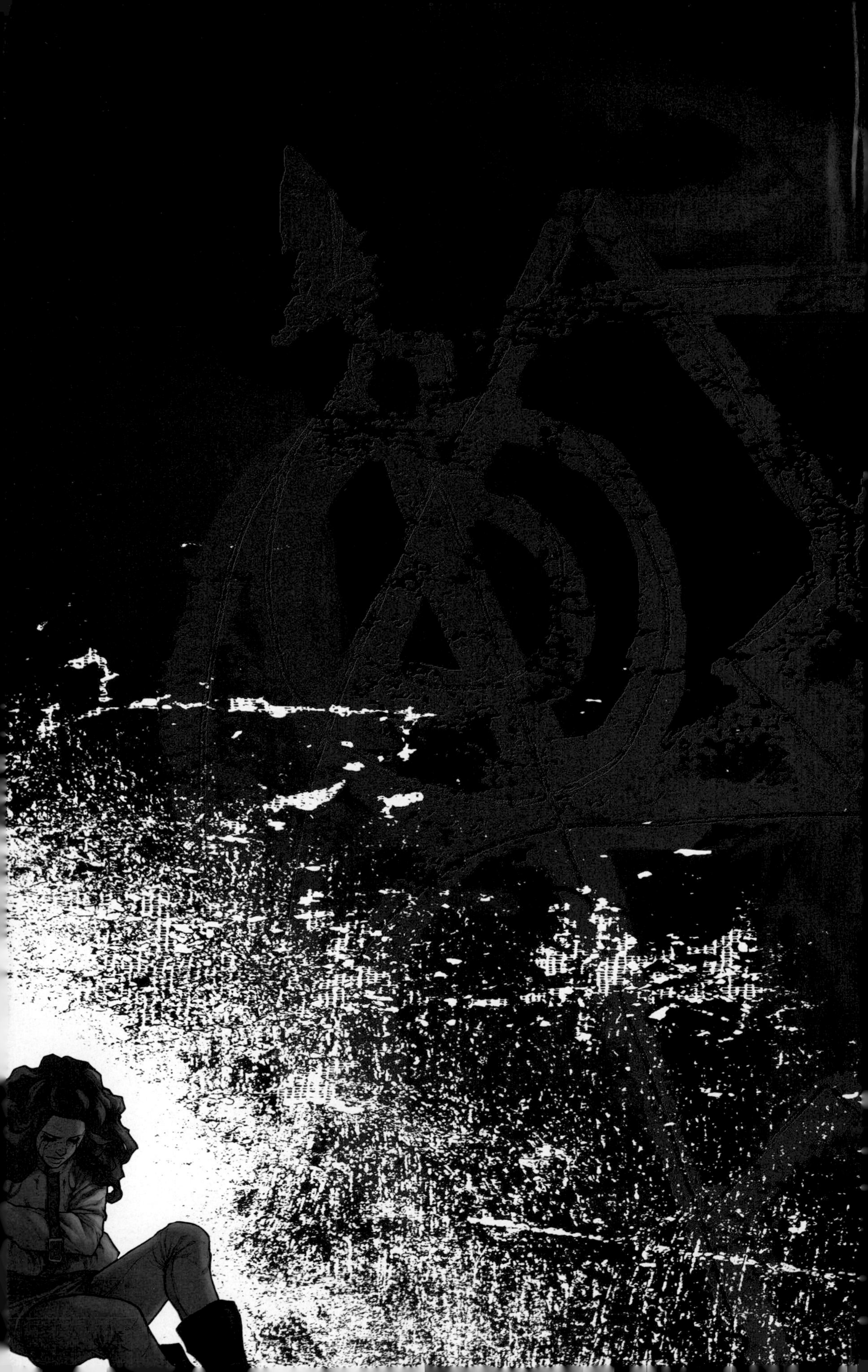

RED THORN GLASGOW KISS

DAVID BAILLIE WRITER
MEGHAN HETRICK ARTIST

STEVE PUGH GUEST ARTIST (ISSUE #7)

STEVE OLIFF (ISSUES #1-6)
NICK FILARDI (ISSUE #7) COLORISTS

TODD KLEIN LETTERER

CHOONG YOON COVER ART
AND ORIGINAL SERIES COVERS

SPECIAL THANKS TO
PETER GROSS AND MIKE CAREY

RED THORN CREATED BY
DAVID BAILLIE AND MEGHAN HETRICK

ROWENA YOW Editor – Original Series
JEB WOODARD Group Editor – Collected Editions
SCOTT NYBAKKEN Editor – Collected Edition
STEVE COOK Design Director – Books
LOUIS PRANDI Publication Design

SHELLY BOND VP & Executive Editor – Vertigo

DIANE NELSON President
DAN DIDIO AND JIM LEE Co-Publishers
GEOFF JOHNS Chief Creative Officer
AMIT DESAI Senior VP – Marketing & Global Franchise Management
NAIRI GARDINER Senior VP – Finance
SAM ADES VP – Digital Marketing
BOBBIE CHASE VP – Talent Development
MARK CHIARELLO Senior VP – Art, Design & Collected Editions
JOHN CUNNINGHAM VP – Content Strategy
ANNE DEPIES VP – Strategy Planning & Reporting
DON FALLETTI VP – Manufacturing Operations
LAWRENCE GANEM VP – Editorial Administration & Talent Relations
ALISON GILL Senior VP – Manufacturing & Operations
HANK KANALZ Senior VP – Editorial Strategy & Administration
JAY KOGAN VP – Legal Affairs
DEREK MADDALENA Senior VP – Sales & Business Development
JACK MAHAN VP – Business Affairs
DAN MIRON VP – Sales Planning & Trade Development
NICK NAPOLITANO VP – Manufacturing Administration
CAROL ROEDER VP – Marketing
EDDIE SCANNELL VP – Mass Account & Digital Sales
COURTNEY SIMMONS Senior VP – Publicity & Communications
JIM (SKI) SOKOLOWSKI VP – Comic Book Specialty & Newsstand Sales
SANDY YI Senior VP – Global Franchise Management

Logo design by Nancy Ogami

RED THORN VOL. 1: GLASGOW KISS

Published by DC Comics. Compilation and all new material Copyright ©
2016 David Baillie and Meghan Hetrick. All Rights Reserved.

Originally published in single magazine form as RED THORN 1-7.
Copyright © 2015, 2016 David Baillie and Meghan Hetrick. All Rights
Reserved. All characters, their distinctive likenesses and related
elements featured in this publication are trademarks of David Baillie
and Meghan Hetrick. VERTIGO is a trademark of DC Comics. The
stories, characters and incidents featured in this publication are
entirely fictional. DC Comics does not read or accept unsolicited
submissions of ideas, stories or artwork.

DC Comics
2900 West Alameda Avenue
Burbank, CA 91505
Printed in the USA. First Printing.
ISBN: 978-1-4012-6361-4

Library of Congress Cataloging-in-Publication Data

Names: Baillie, David (Freelance writer and artist), author. | Hetrick,
Meghan, illustrator. | Pugh, Steve, 1966- illustrator. | Oliff, Steve,
illustrator.
Title: Red Thorn. Volume 1, Glasgow kiss / David Baillie, Meghan Hetrick,
Steve Pugh, Steve Oliff.
Other titles: Glasgow kiss
Description: Burbank, CA : DC Comics/Vertigo, [2016] | "Originally
published in single magazine form as RED THORN 1-7"
Identifiers: LCCN 2016017544 | ISBN 9781401263614 (paperback)
Subjects: LCSH: Comic books, strips, etc. | BISAC: COMICS & GRAPHIC
NOVELS / Fantasy.
Classification: LCC PN6737.B24 R43 2016 | DDC 741.5/9411—dc23
LC record available at https://lccn.loc.gov/2016017544

PEFC Certified

Printed on paper from
sustainably managed
forests and controlled
sources

PEFC
PEFC/29-31-75   www.pefc.org

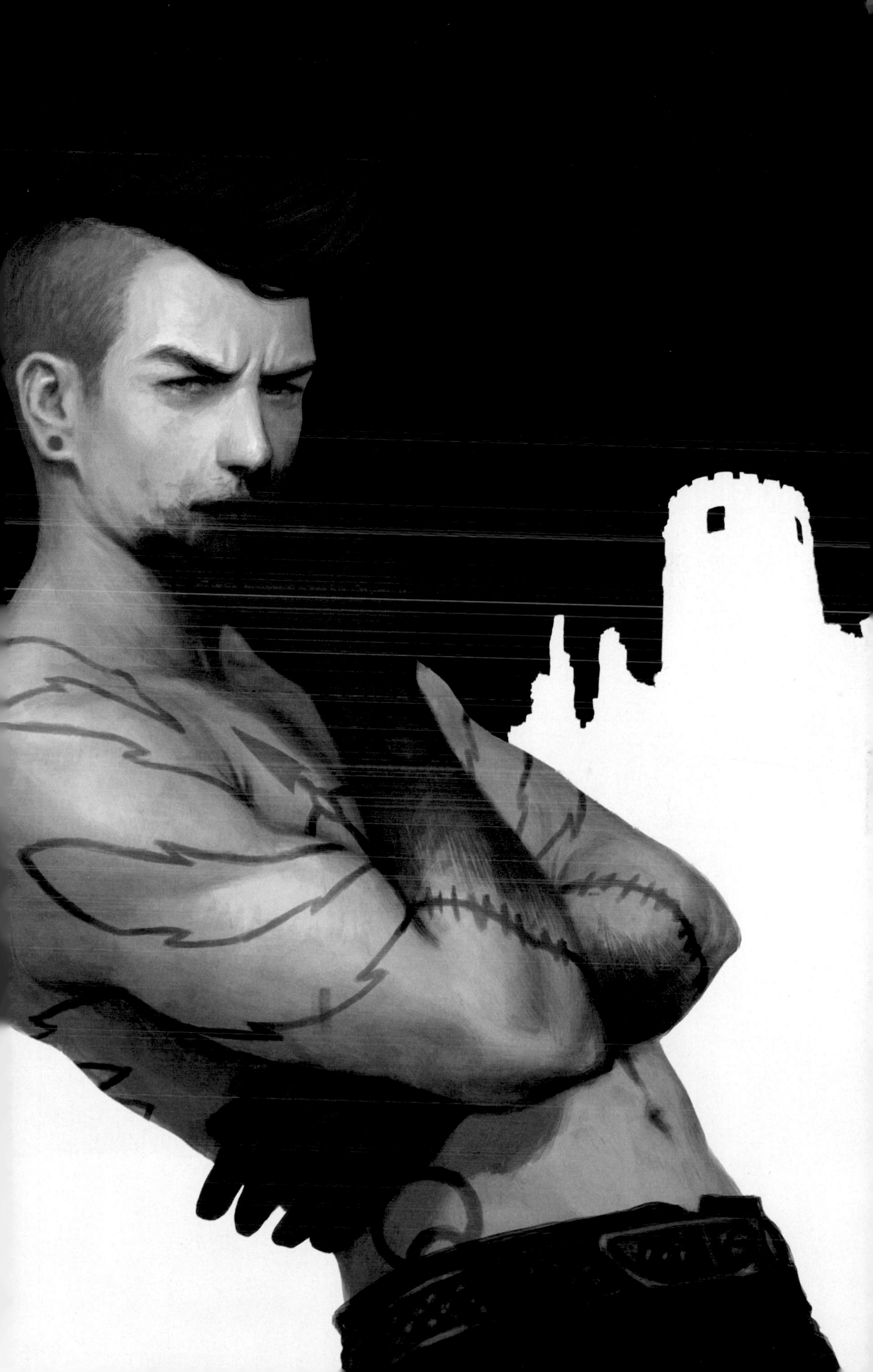

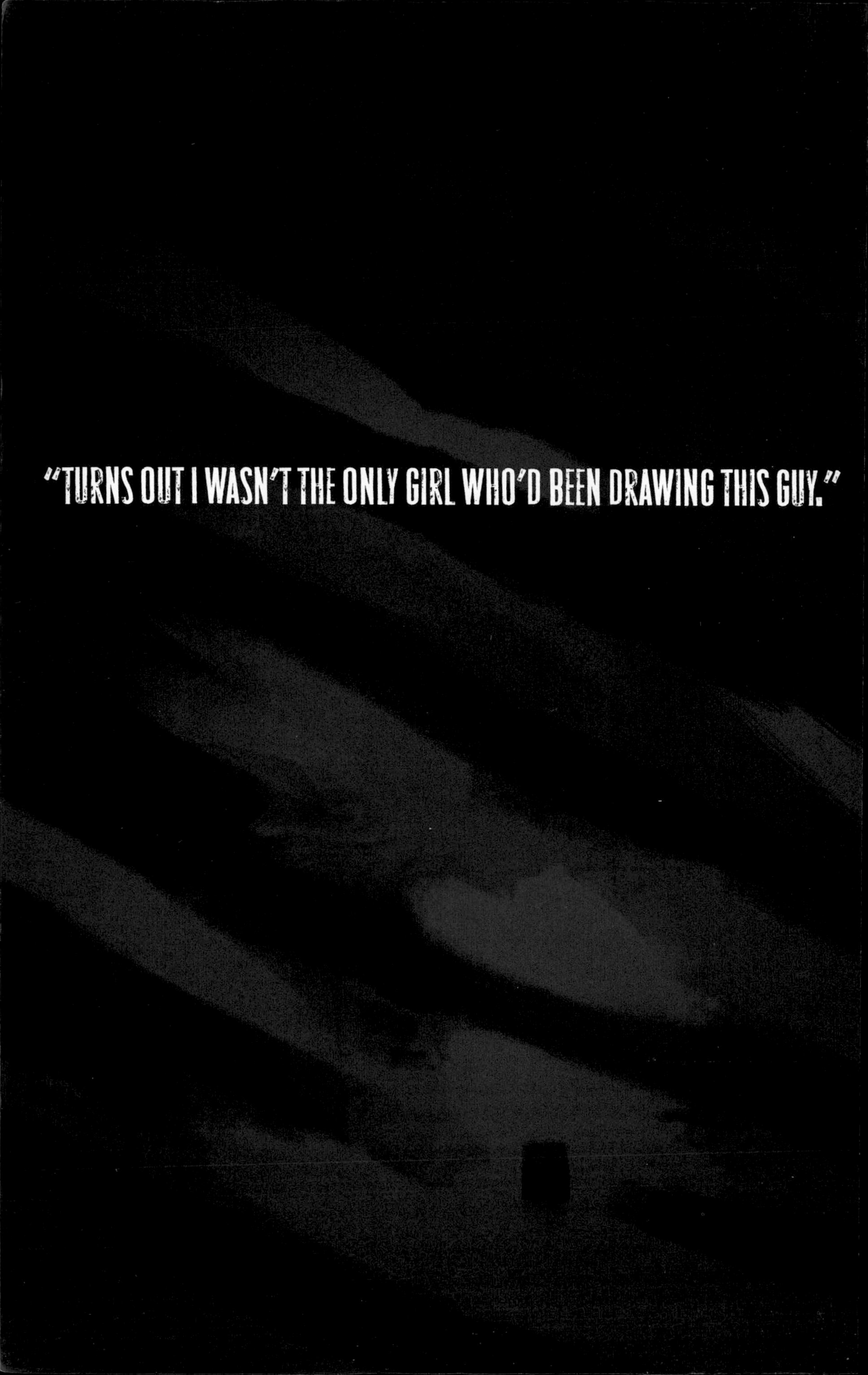
"TURNS OUT I WASN'T THE ONLY GIRL WHO'D BEEN DRAWING THIS GUY."

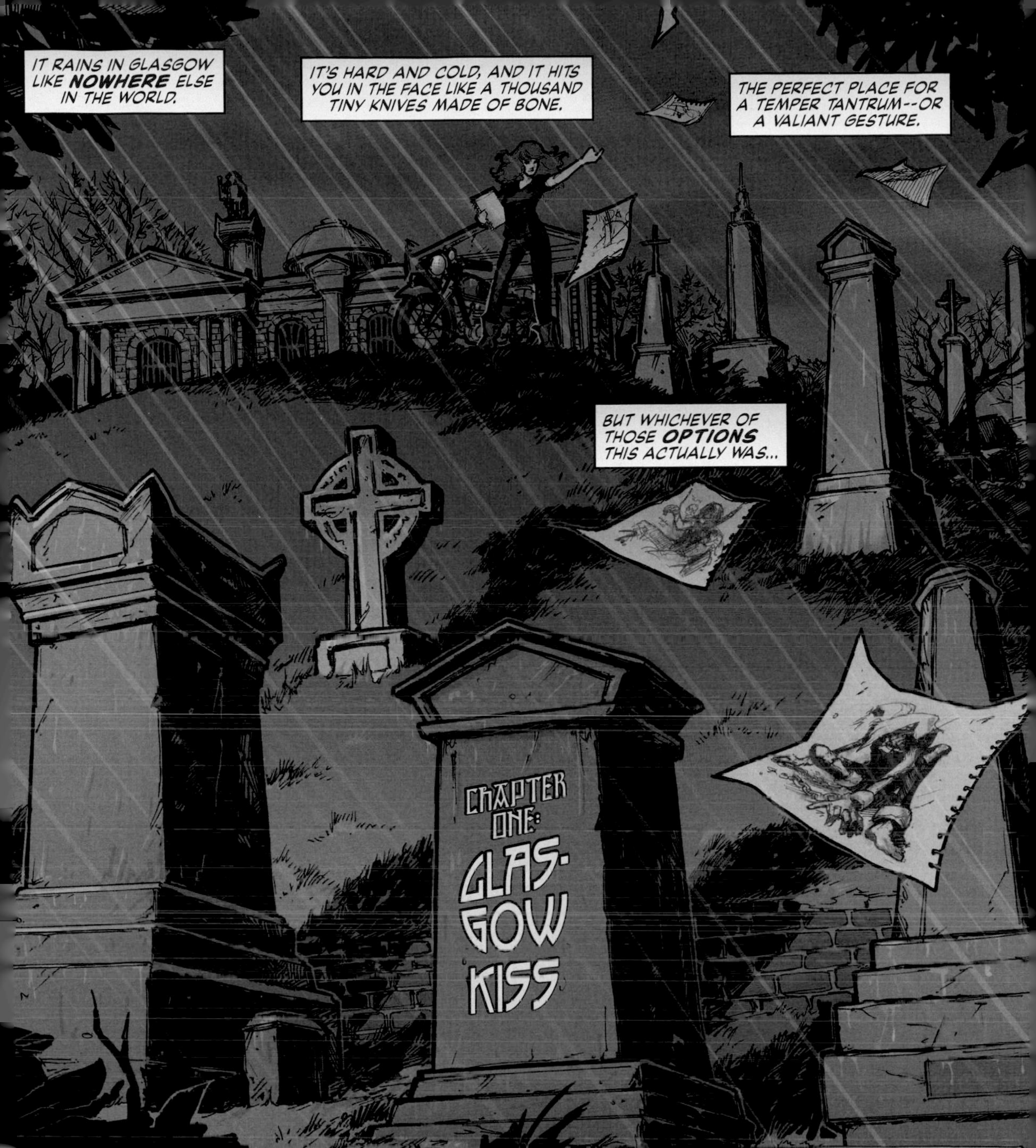
IT RAINS IN GLASGOW LIKE **NOWHERE** ELSE IN THE WORLD.
IT'S HARD AND COLD, AND IT HITS YOU IN THE FACE LIKE A THOUSAND TINY KNIVES MADE OF BONE.
THE PERFECT PLACE FOR A TEMPER TANTRUM--OR A VALIANT GESTURE.
BUT WHICHEVER OF THOSE **OPTIONS** THIS ACTUALLY WAS...
CHAPTER ONE:
GLAS-GOW KISS

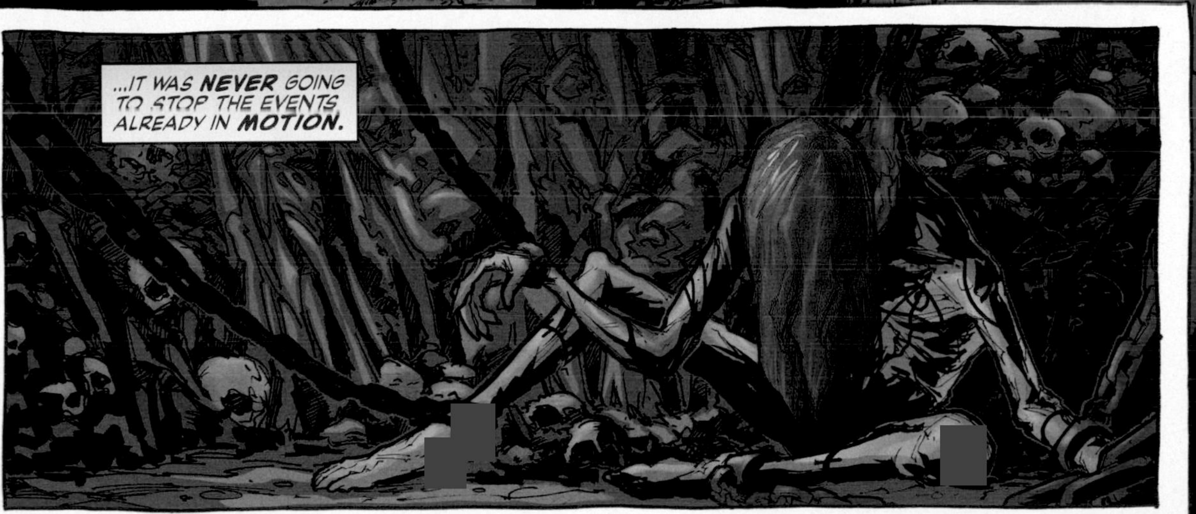
...IT WAS **NEVER** GOING TO STOP THE EVENTS ALREADY IN **MOTION**.

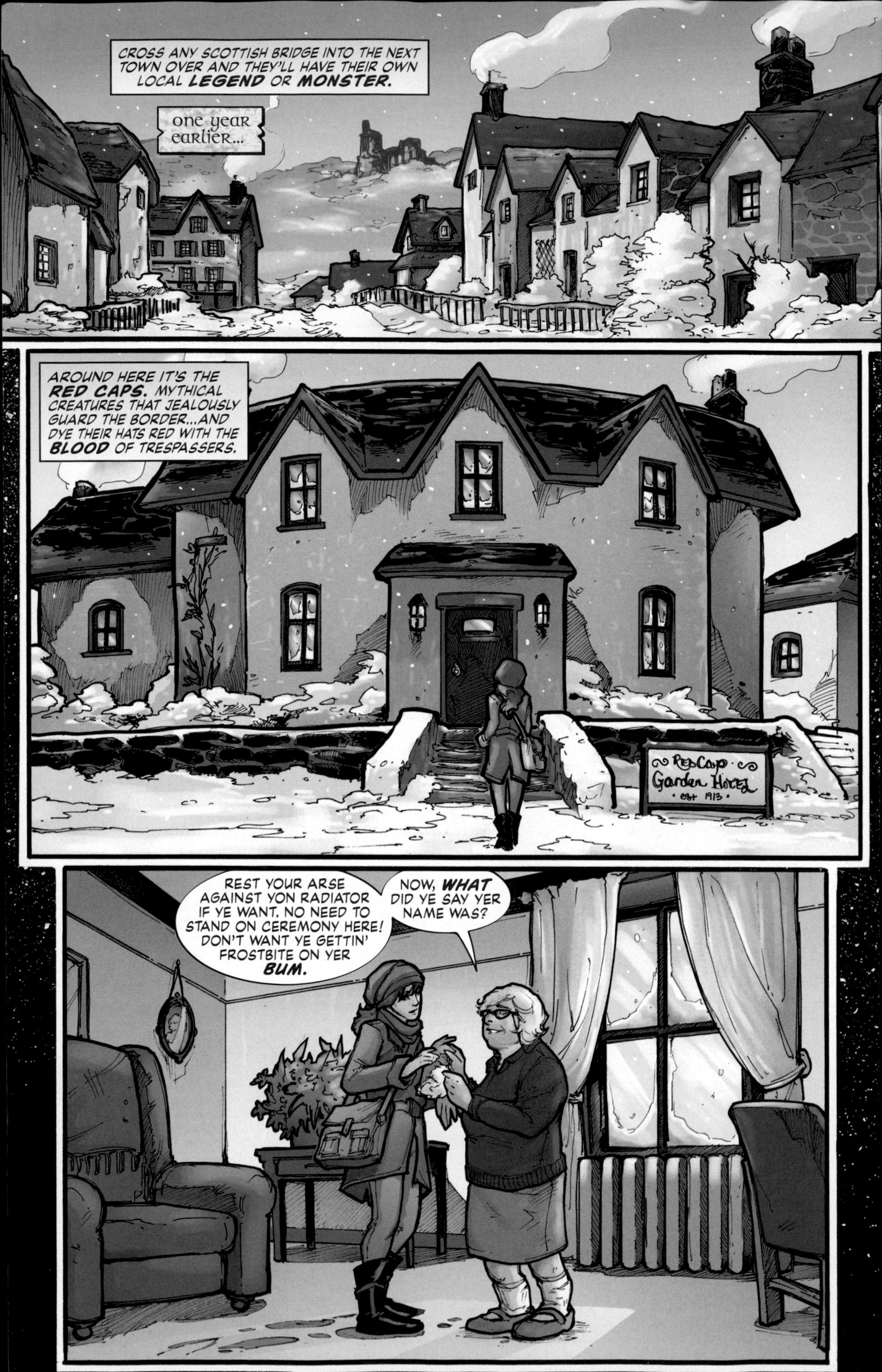
CROSS ANY SCOTTISH BRIDGE INTO THE NEXT TOWN OVER AND THEY'LL HAVE THEIR OWN LOCAL **LEGEND** OR **MONSTER.**
one year earlier...
AROUND HERE IT'S THE **RED CAPS.** MYTHICAL CREATURES THAT JEALOUSLY GUARD THE BORDER...AND DYE THEIR HATS RED WITH THE **BLOOD** OF TRESPASSERS.
RedCap Garden Hotel est 1913
REST YOUR ARSE AGAINST YON RADIATOR IF YE WANT. NO NEED TO STAND ON CEREMONY HERE! DON'T WANT YE GETTIN' FROSTBITE ON YER **BUM.**
NOW, **WHAT** DID YE SAY YER NAME WAS?

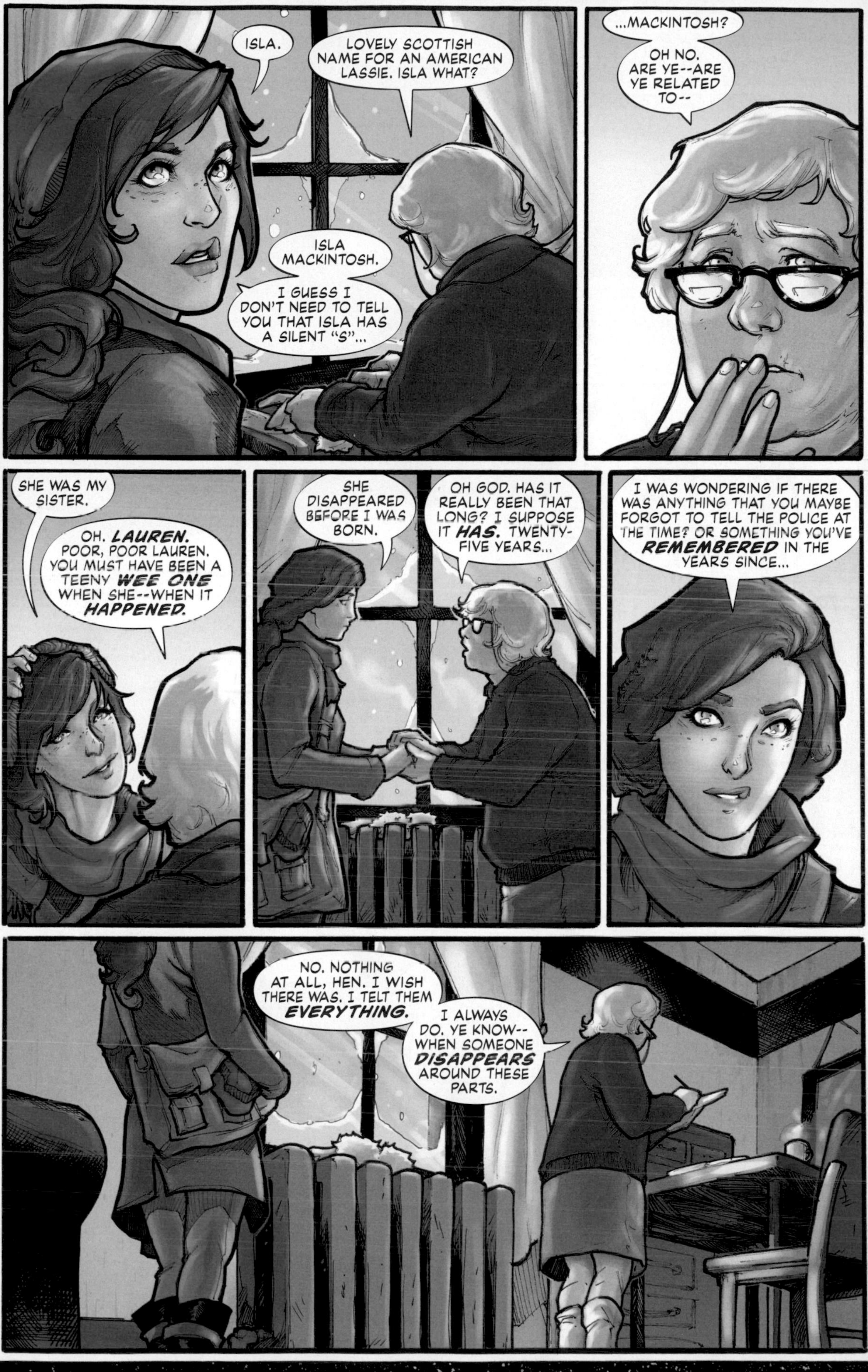
ISLA.
LOVELY SCOTTISH NAME FOR AN AMERICAN LASSIE. ISLA WHAT?
ISLA MACKINTOSH.
I GUESS I DON'T NEED TO TELL YOU THAT ISLA HAS A SILENT "S"...
...MACKINTOSH?
OH NO. ARE YE--ARE YE RELATED TO--
SHE WAS MY SISTER.
OH. LAUREN. POOR, POOR LAUREN. YOU MUST HAVE BEEN A TEENY WEE ONE WHEN SHE--WHEN IT HAPPENED.
SHE DISAPPEARED BEFORE I WAS BORN.
OH GOD. HAS IT REALLY BEEN THAT LONG? I SUPPOSE IT HAS. TWENTY-FIVE YEARS...
I WAS WONDERING IF THERE WAS ANYTHING THAT YOU MAYBE FORGOT TO TELL THE POLICE AT THE TIME? OR SOMETHING YOU'VE REMEMBERED IN THE YEARS SINCE...
NO. NOTHING AT ALL, HEN. I WISH THERE WAS. I TELT THEM EVERYTHING.
I ALWAYS DO. YE KNOW--WHEN SOMEONE DISAPPEARS AROUND THESE PARTS.

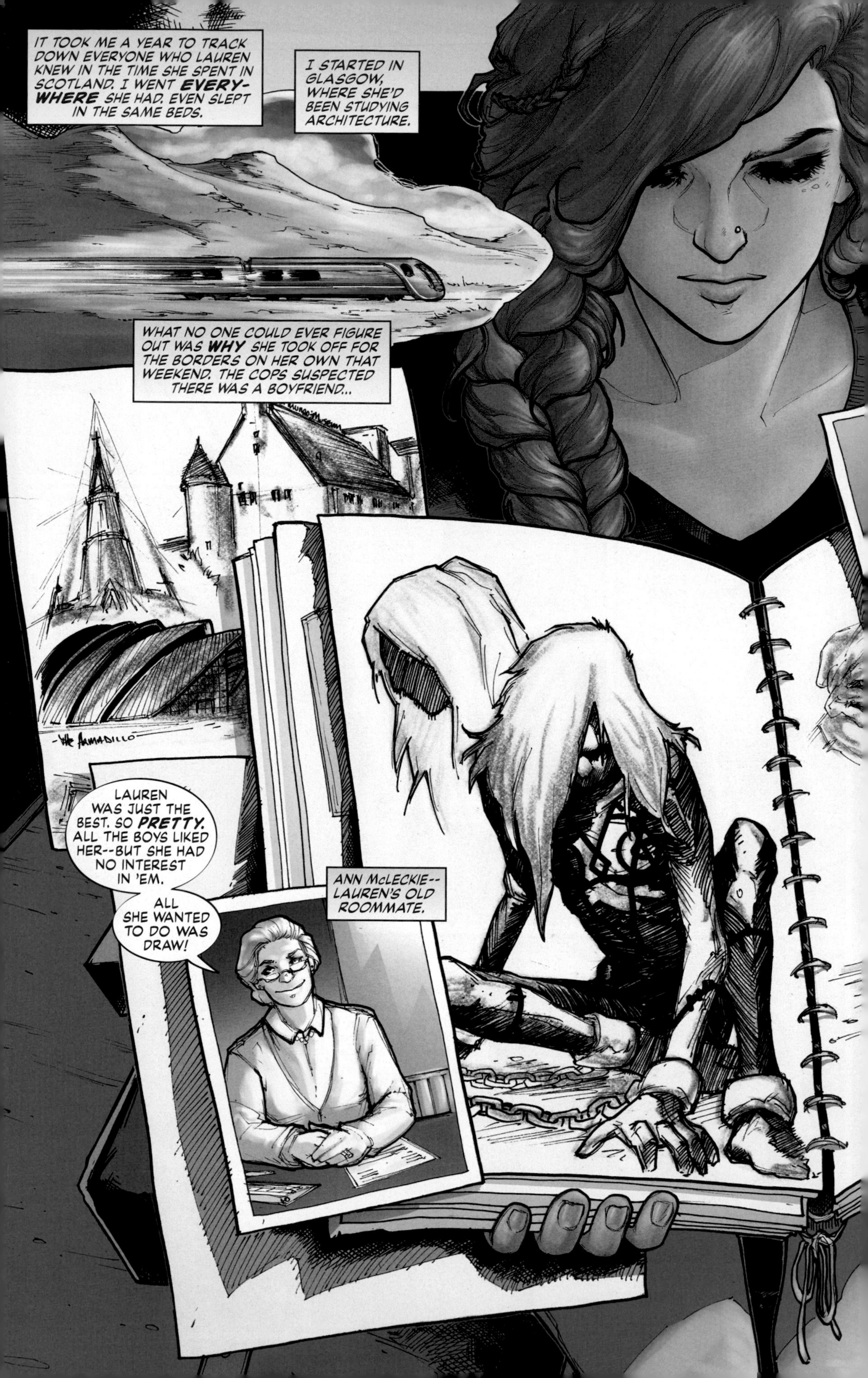
IT TOOK ME A YEAR TO TRACK DOWN EVERYONE WHO LAUREN KNEW IN THE TIME SHE SPENT IN SCOTLAND. I WENT EVERY-WHERE SHE HAD. EVEN SLEPT IN THE SAME BEDS.
I STARTED IN GLASGOW, WHERE SHE'D BEEN STUDYING ARCHITECTURE.
WHAT NO ONE COULD EVER FIGURE OUT WAS WHY SHE TOOK OFF FOR THE BORDERS ON HER OWN THAT WEEKEND. THE COPS SUSPECTED THERE WAS A BOYFRIEND...
LAUREN WAS JUST THE BEST. SO PRETTY. ALL THE BOYS LIKED HER--BUT SHE HAD NO INTEREST IN 'EM.
ALL SHE WANTED TO DO WAS DRAW!
ANN McLECKIE--LAUREN'S OLD ROOMMATE.

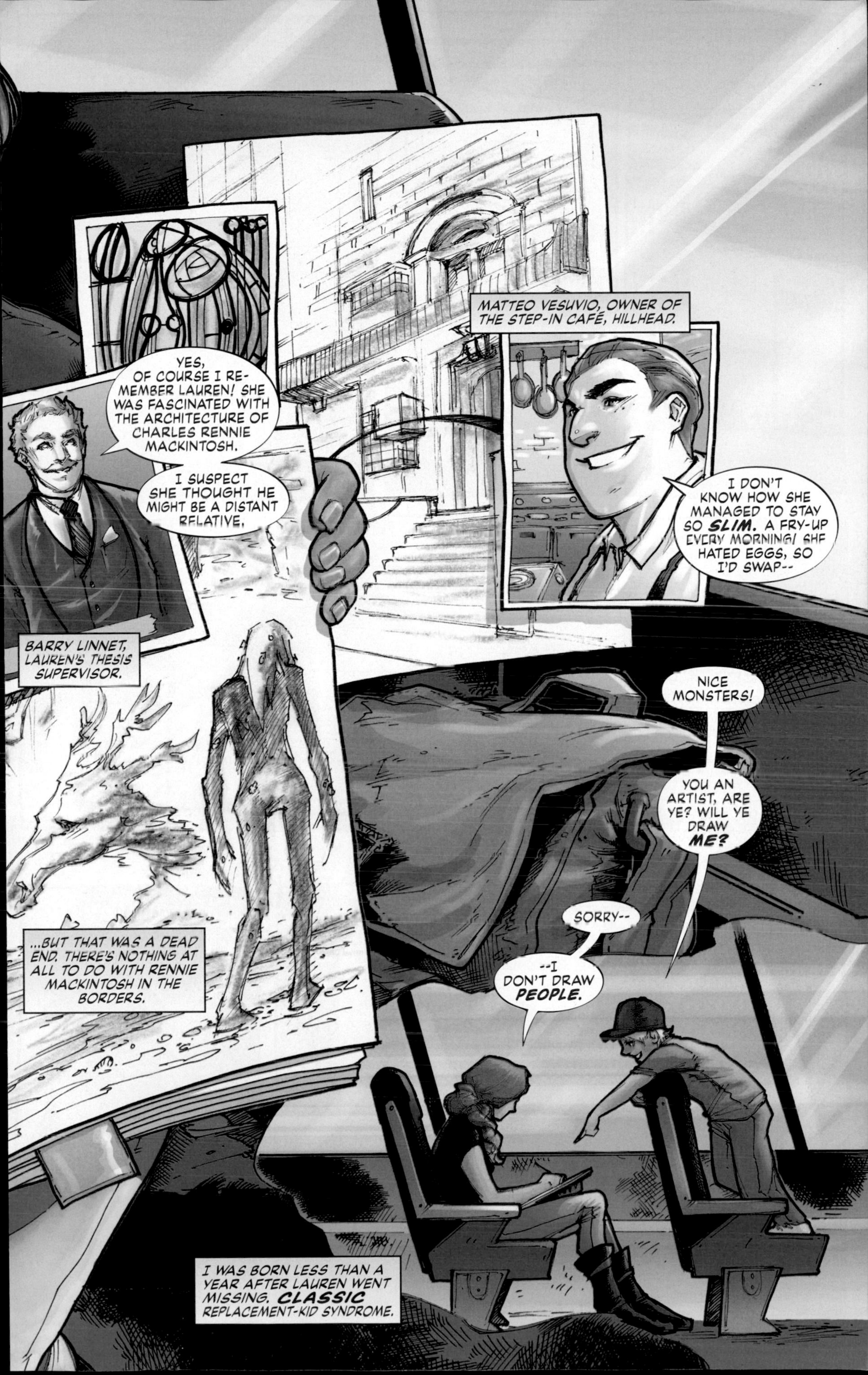

MATTEO VESUVIO, OWNER OF THE STEP-IN CAFÉ, HILLHEAD.
YES, OF COURSE I REMEMBER LAUREN! SHE WAS FASCINATED WITH THE ARCHITECTURE OF CHARLES RENNIE MACKINTOSH.
I SUSPECT SHE THOUGHT HE MIGHT BE A DISTANT RELATIVE.
I DON'T KNOW HOW SHE MANAGED TO STAY SO SLIM. A FRY-UP EVERY MORNING! SHE HATED EGGS, SO I'D SWAP--
BARRY LINNET, LAUREN'S THESIS SUPERVISOR.
NICE MONSTERS!
YOU AN ARTIST, ARE YE? WILL YE DRAW ME?
...BUT THAT WAS A DEAD END. THERE'S NOTHING AT ALL TO DO WITH RENNIE MACKINTOSH IN THE BORDERS.
SORRY--
--I DON'T DRAW PEOPLE.
I WAS BORN LESS THAN A YEAR AFTER LAUREN WENT MISSING. CLASSIC REPLACEMENT-KID SYNDROME.

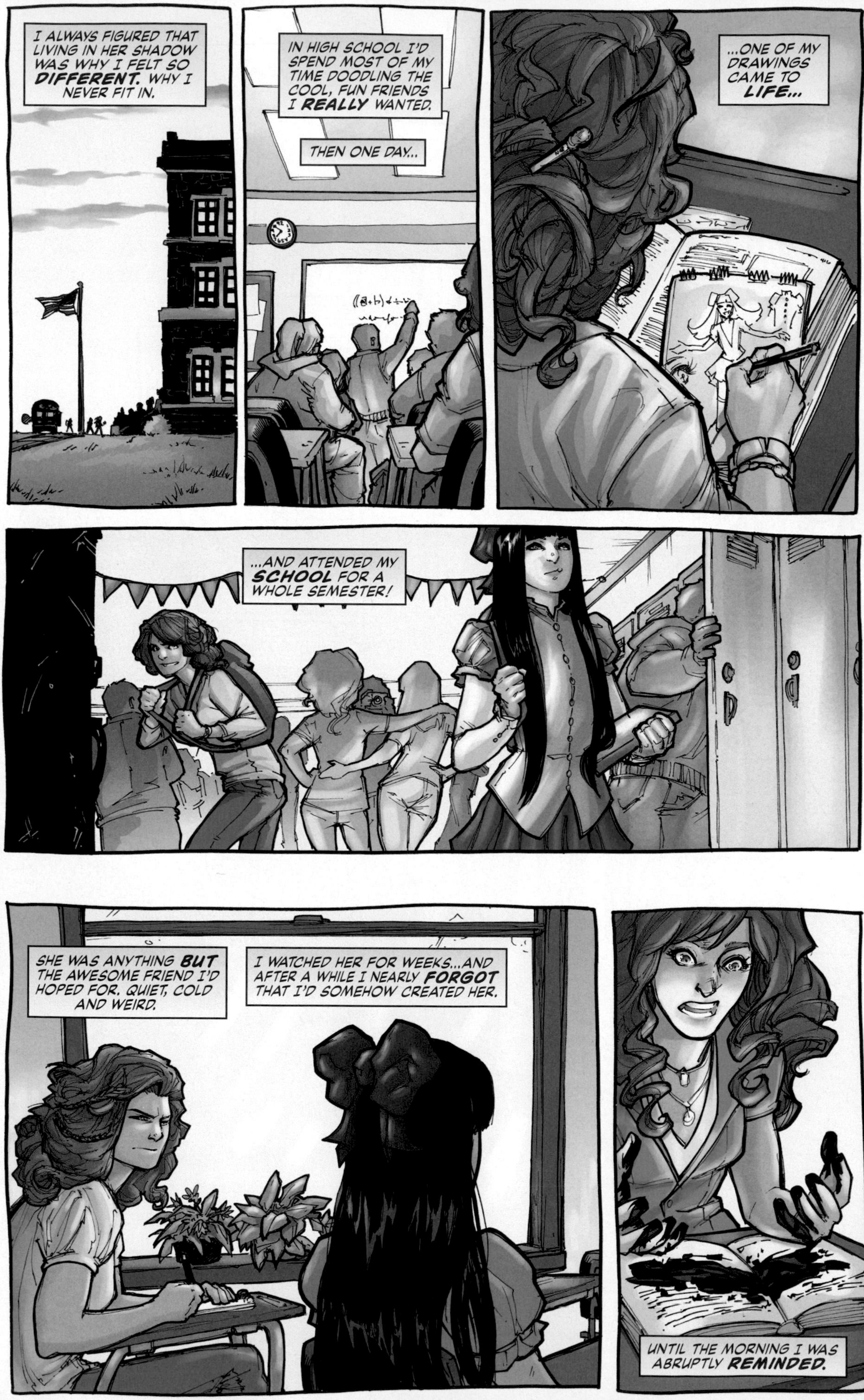

I ALWAYS FIGURED THAT LIVING IN HER SHADOW WAS WHY I FELT SO **DIFFERENT.** WHY I NEVER FIT IN.
IN HIGH SCHOOL I'D SPEND MOST OF MY TIME DOODLING THE COOL, FUN FRIENDS I **REALLY** WANTED.
THEN ONE DAY...
...ONE OF MY DRAWINGS CAME TO **LIFE...**
...AND ATTENDED MY **SCHOOL** FOR A WHOLE SEMESTER!
SHE WAS ANYTHING **BUT** THE AWESOME FRIEND I'D HOPED FOR. QUIET, COLD AND WEIRD.
I WATCHED HER FOR WEEKS...AND AFTER A WHILE I NEARLY **FORGOT** THAT I'D SOMEHOW CREATED HER.
UNTIL THE MORNING I WAS ABRUPTLY **REMINDED.**

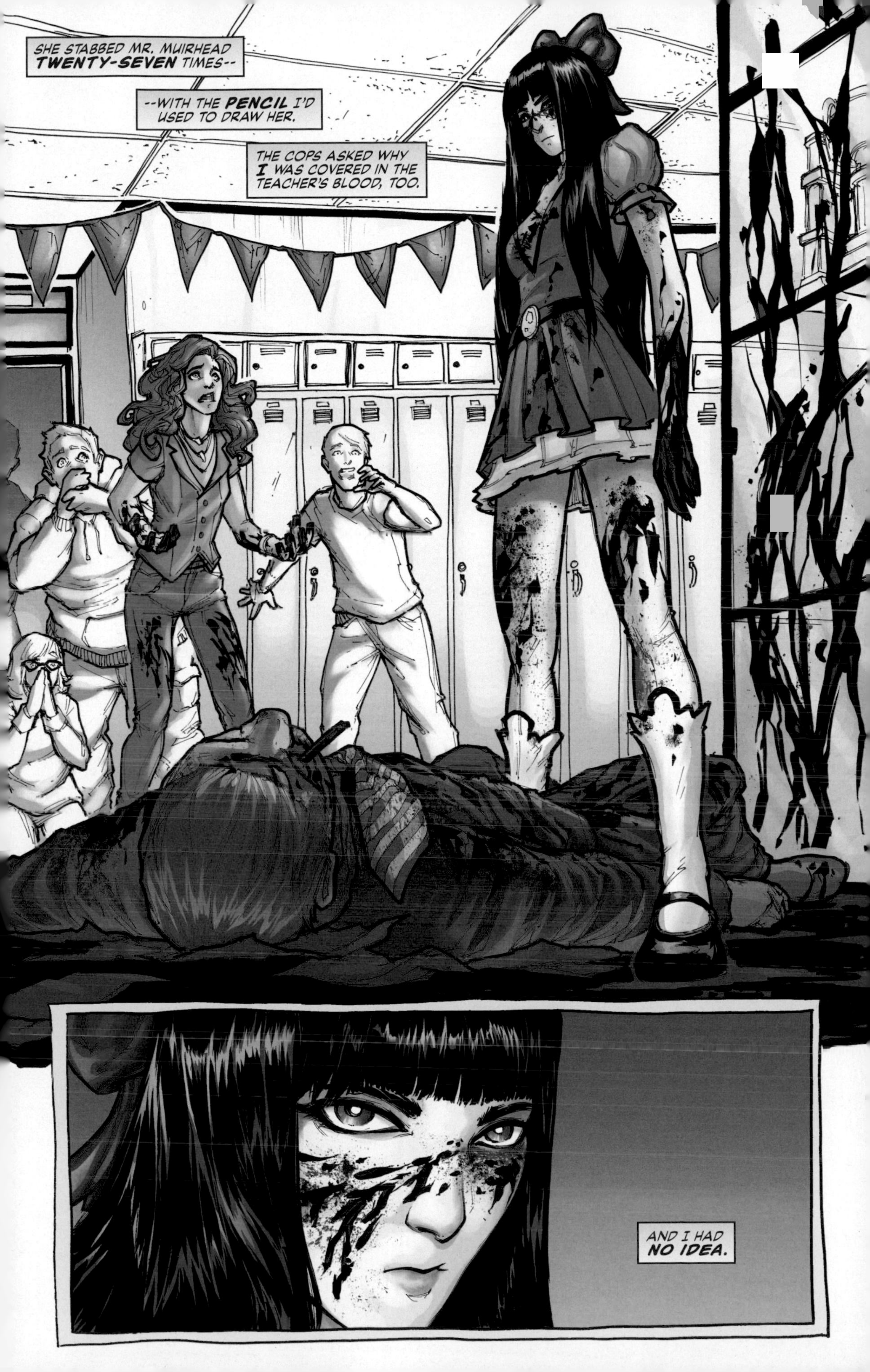
SHE STABBED MR. MUIRHEAD **TWENTY-SEVEN** TIMES--
--WITH THE **PENCIL** I'D USED TO DRAW HER.
THE COPS ASKED WHY **I** WAS COVERED IN THE TEACHER'S BLOOD, TOO.
AND I HAD **NO IDEA.**

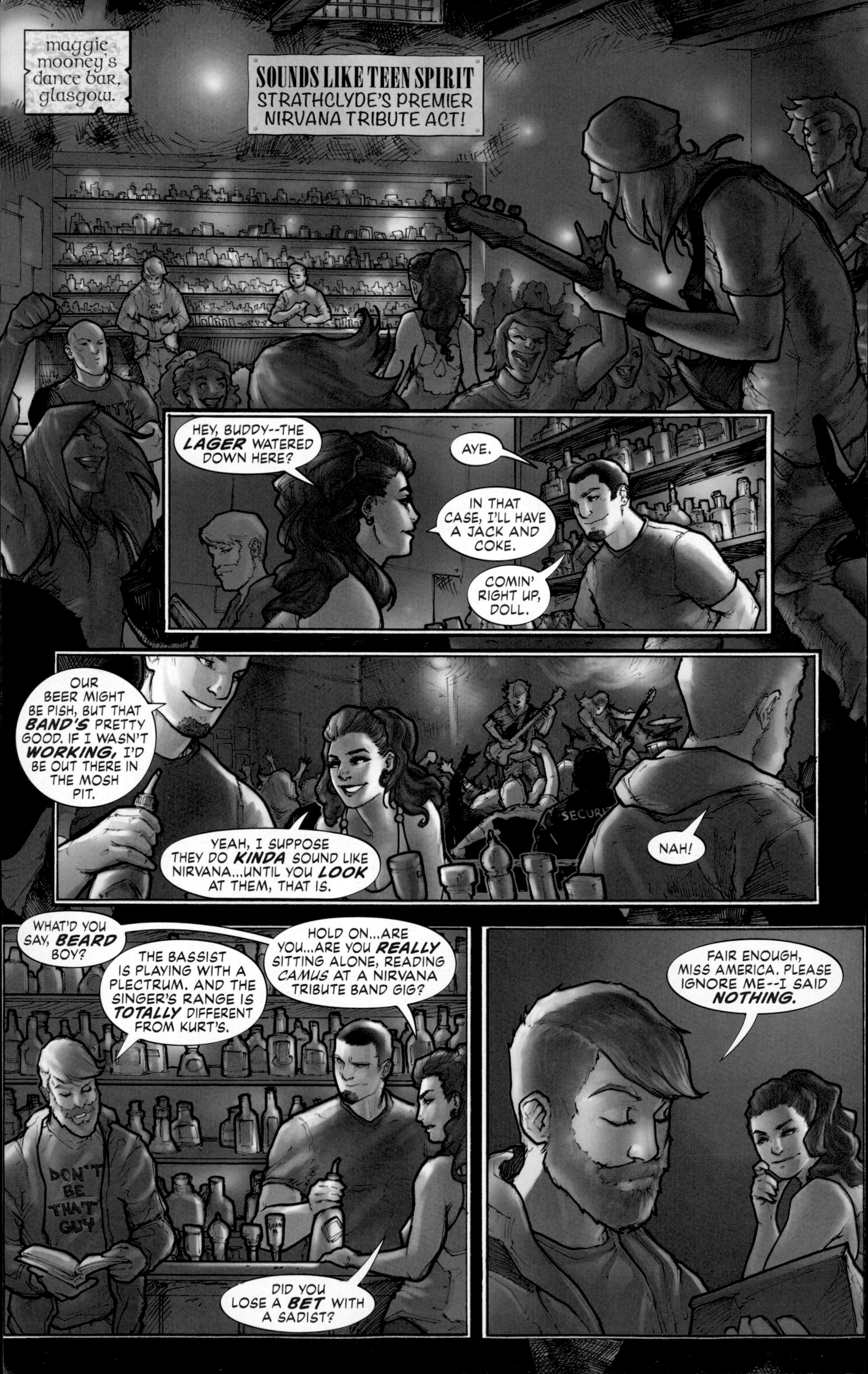
maggie mooney's dance bar, glasgow.
SOUNDS LIKE TEEN SPIRIT
STRATHCLYDE'S PREMIER NIRVANA TRIBUTE ACT!
HEY, BUDDY--THE LAGER WATERED DOWN HERE?
AYE.
IN THAT CASE, I'LL HAVE A JACK AND COKE.
COMIN' RIGHT UP, DOLL.
OUR BEER MIGHT BE PISH, BUT THAT BAND'S PRETTY GOOD. IF I WASN'T WORKING, I'D BE OUT THERE IN THE MOSH PIT.
YEAH, I SUPPOSE THEY DO KINDA SOUND LIKE NIRVANA...UNTIL YOU LOOK AT THEM, THAT IS.
NAH!
WHAT'D YOU SAY, BEARD BOY?
THE BASSIST IS PLAYING WITH A PLECTRUM. AND THE SINGER'S RANGE IS TOTALLY DIFFERENT FROM KURT'S.
HOLD ON...ARE YOU...ARE YOU REALLY SITTING ALONE, READING CAMUS AT A NIRVANA TRIBUTE BAND GIG?
DON'T BE THAT GUY
DID YOU LOSE A BET WITH A SADIST?
FAIR ENOUGH, MISS AMERICA. PLEASE IGNORE ME--I SAID NOTHING.

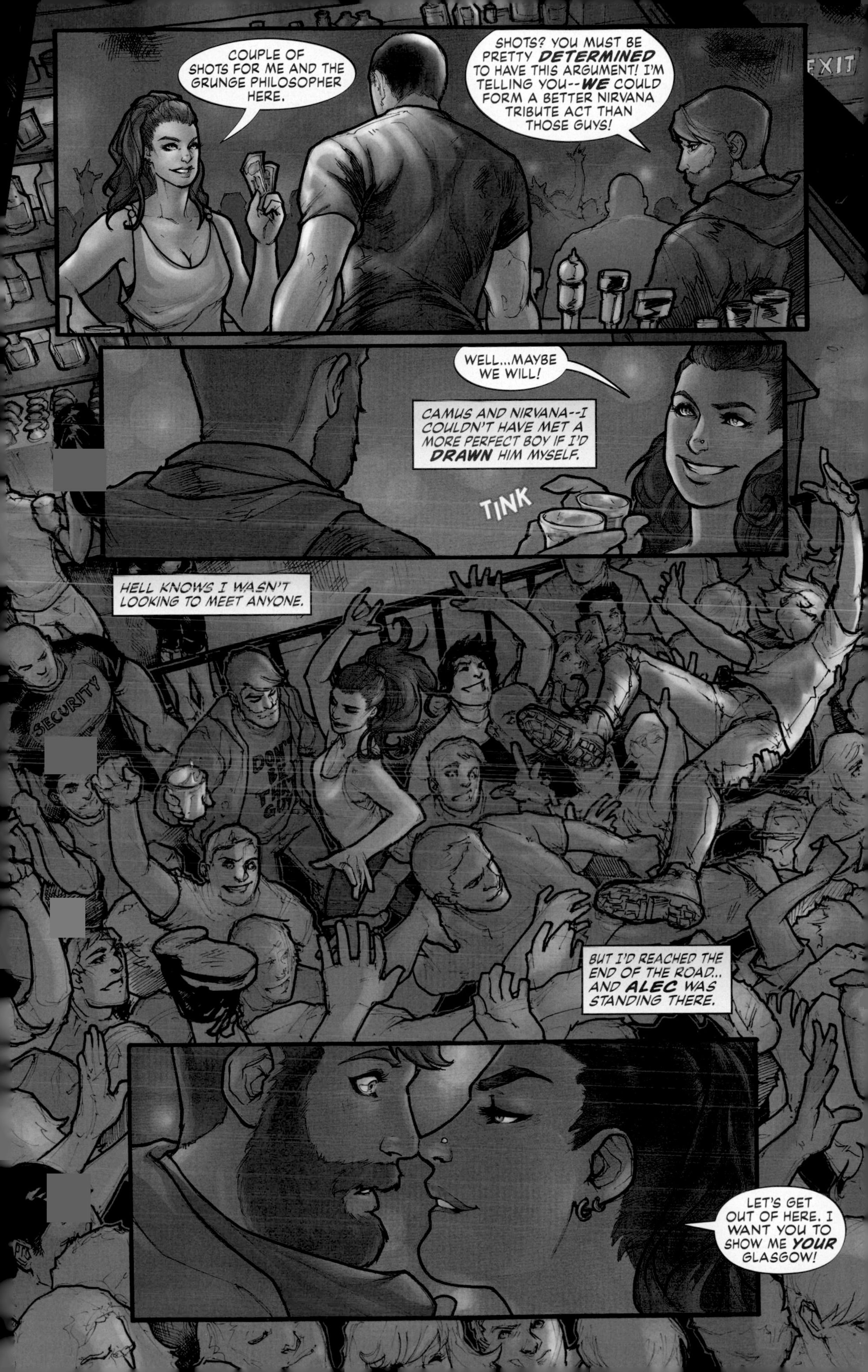
EXIT
COUPLE OF SHOTS FOR ME AND THE GRUNGE PHILOSOPHER HERE.
SHOTS? YOU MUST BE PRETTY DETERMINED TO HAVE THIS ARGUMENT! I'M TELLING YOU--WE COULD FORM A BETTER NIRVANA TRIBUTE ACT THAN THOSE GUYS!
WELL...MAYBE WE WILL!
CAMUS AND NIRVANA--I COULDN'T HAVE MET A MORE PERFECT BOY IF I'D DRAWN HIM MYSELF.
TINK
HELL KNOWS I WASN'T LOOKING TO MEET ANYONE.
SECURITY
BUT I'D REACHED THE END OF THE ROAD... AND ALEC WAS STANDING THERE.
LET'S GET OUT OF HERE. I WANT YOU TO SHOW ME YOUR GLASGOW!

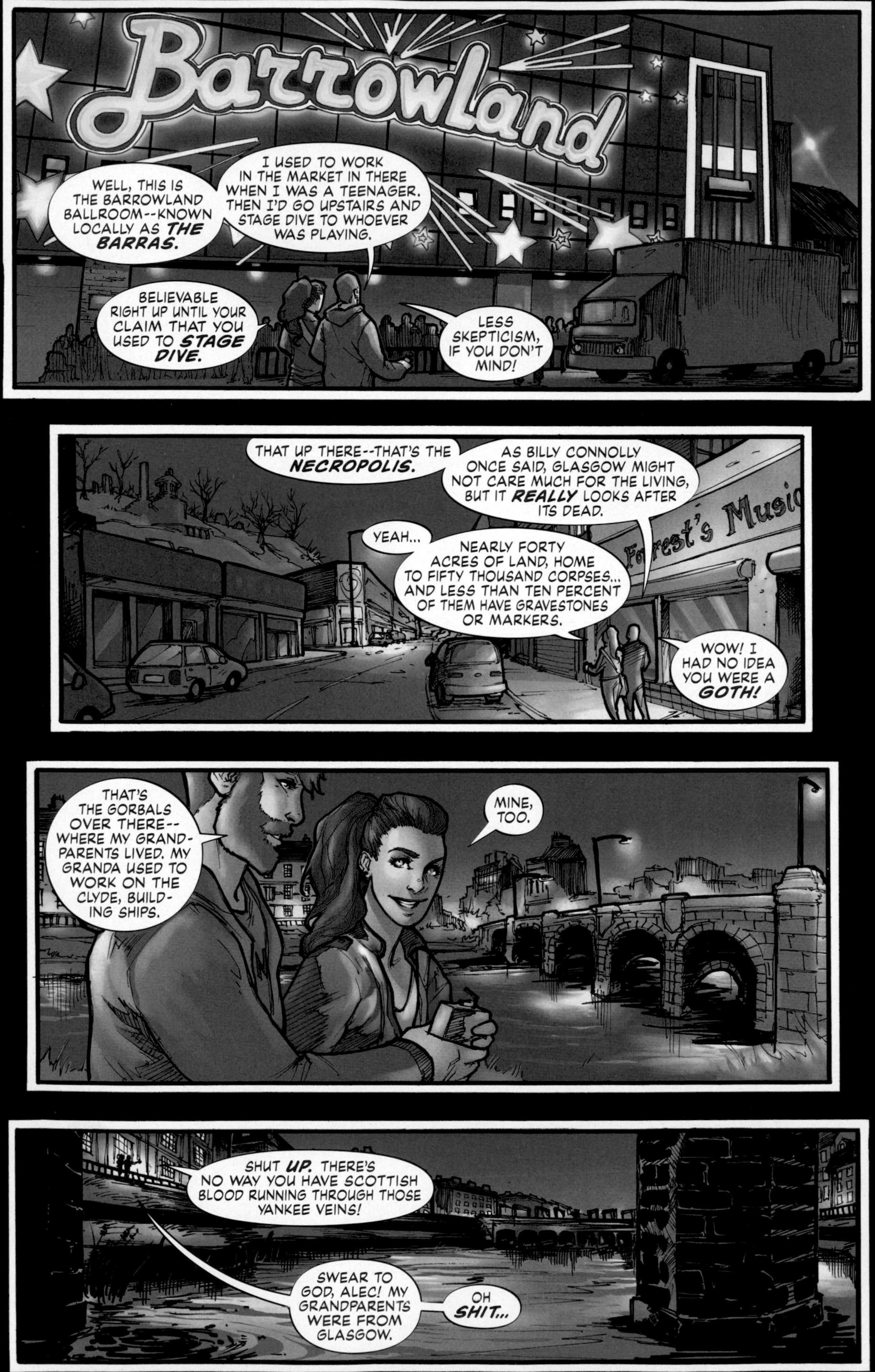
Barrowland
WELL, THIS IS THE BARROWLAND BALLROOM--KNOWN LOCALLY AS THE BARRAS.
I USED TO WORK IN THE MARKET IN THERE WHEN I WAS A TEENAGER. THEN I'D GO UPSTAIRS AND STAGE DIVE TO WHOEVER WAS PLAYING.
BELIEVABLE RIGHT UP UNTIL YOUR CLAIM THAT YOU USED TO STAGE DIVE.
LESS SKEPTICISM, IF YOU DON'T MIND!
THAT UP THERE--THAT'S THE NECROPOLIS.
AS BILLY CONNOLLY ONCE SAID, GLASGOW MIGHT NOT CARE MUCH FOR THE LIVING, BUT IT REALLY LOOKS AFTER ITS DEAD.
YEAH...
NEARLY FORTY ACRES OF LAND, HOME TO FIFTY THOUSAND CORPSES... AND LESS THAN TEN PERCENT OF THEM HAVE GRAVESTONES OR MARKERS.
WOW! I HAD NO IDEA YOU WERE A GOTH!
THAT'S THE GORBALS OVER THERE--WHERE MY GRAND-PARENTS LIVED. MY GRANDA USED TO WORK ON THE CLYDE, BUILD-ING SHIPS.
MINE, TOO.
SHUT UP. THERE'S NO WAY YOU HAVE SCOTTISH BLOOD RUNNING THROUGH THOSE YANKEE VEINS!
SWEAR TO GOD, ALEC! MY GRANDPARENTS WERE FROM GLASGOW.
OH SHIT...

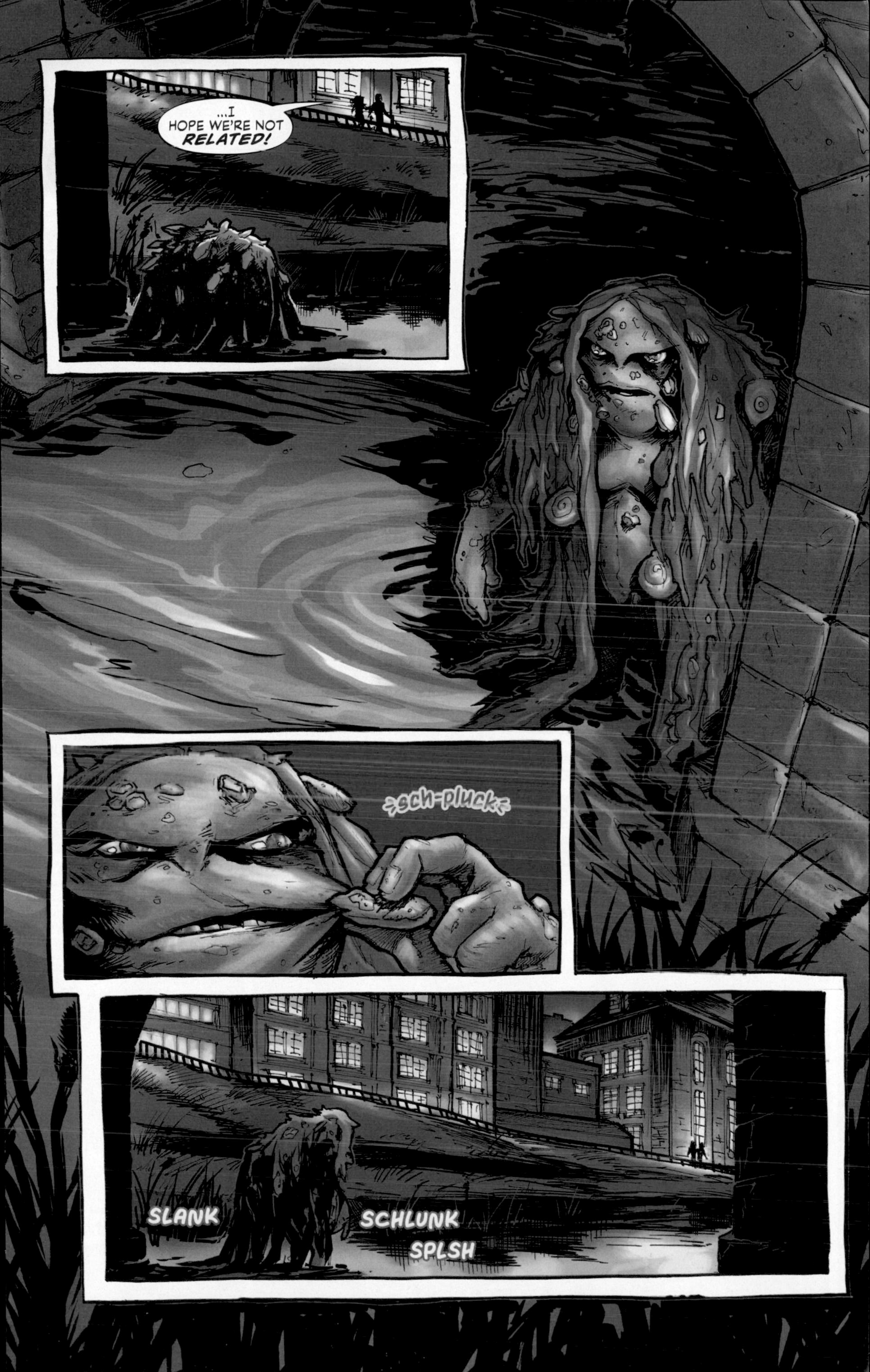
...I HOPE WE'RE NOT RELATED!
sch-pluck
SLANK
SCHLUNK
SPLSH

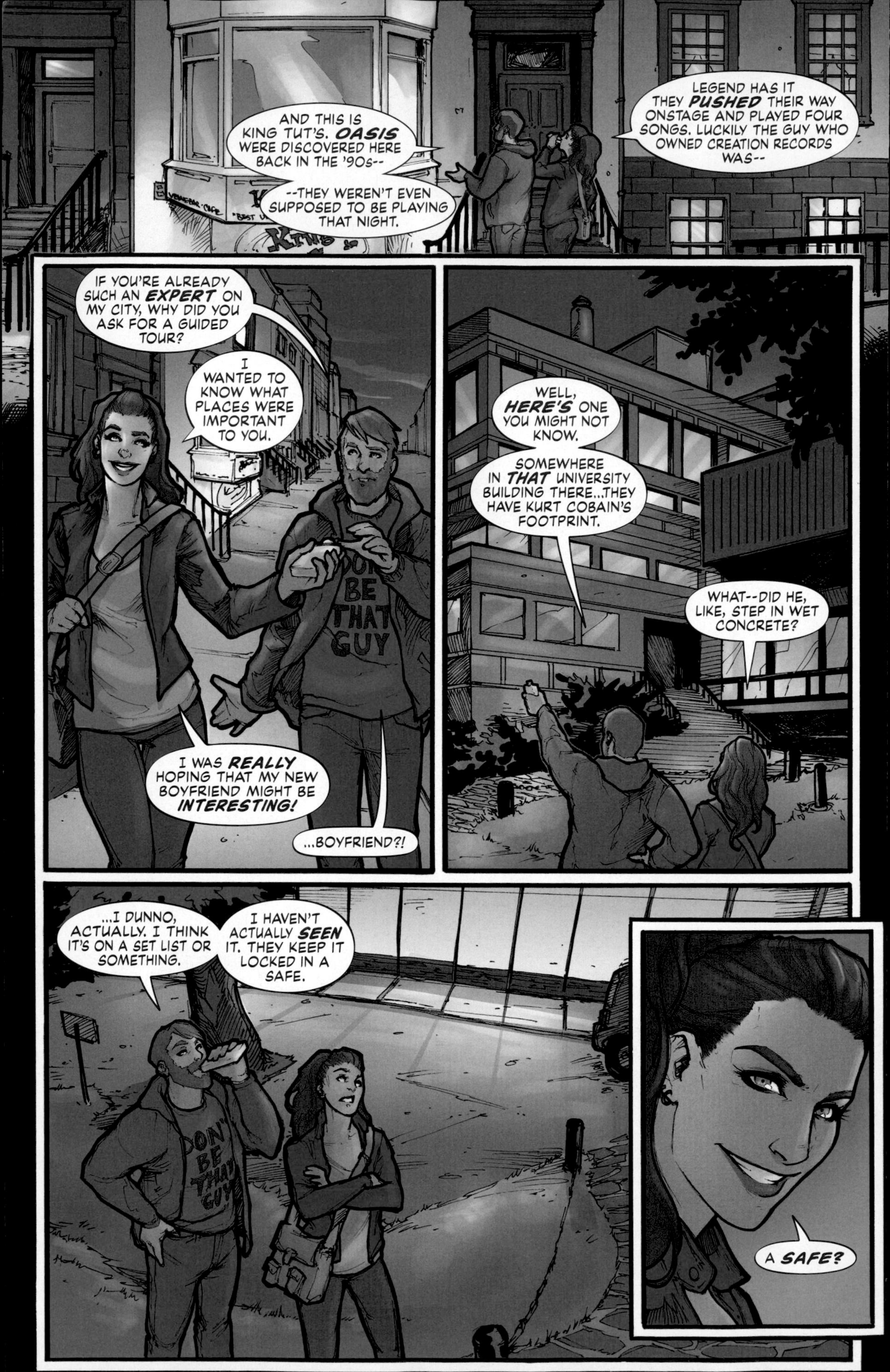
AND THIS IS KING TUT'S. OASIS WERE DISCOVERED HERE BACK IN THE '90s--
--THEY WEREN'T EVEN SUPPOSED TO BE PLAYING THAT NIGHT.
LEGEND HAS IT THEY PUSHED THEIR WAY ONSTAGE AND PLAYED FOUR SONGS. LUCKILY THE GUY WHO OWNED CREATION RECORDS WAS--
IF YOU'RE ALREADY SUCH AN EXPERT ON MY CITY, WHY DID YOU ASK FOR A GUIDED TOUR?
I WANTED TO KNOW WHAT PLACES WERE IMPORTANT TO YOU.
I WAS REALLY HOPING THAT MY NEW BOYFRIEND MIGHT BE INTERESTING!
...BOYFRIEND?!
DON'T BE THAT GUY
WELL, HERE'S ONE YOU MIGHT NOT KNOW.
SOMEWHERE IN THAT UNIVERSITY BUILDING THERE...THEY HAVE KURT COBAIN'S FOOTPRINT.
WHAT--DID HE, LIKE, STEP IN WET CONCRETE?
...I DUNNO, ACTUALLY. I THINK IT'S ON A SET LIST OR SOMETHING.
I HAVEN'T ACTUALLY SEEN IT. THEY KEEP IT LOCKED IN A SAFE.
A SAFE?

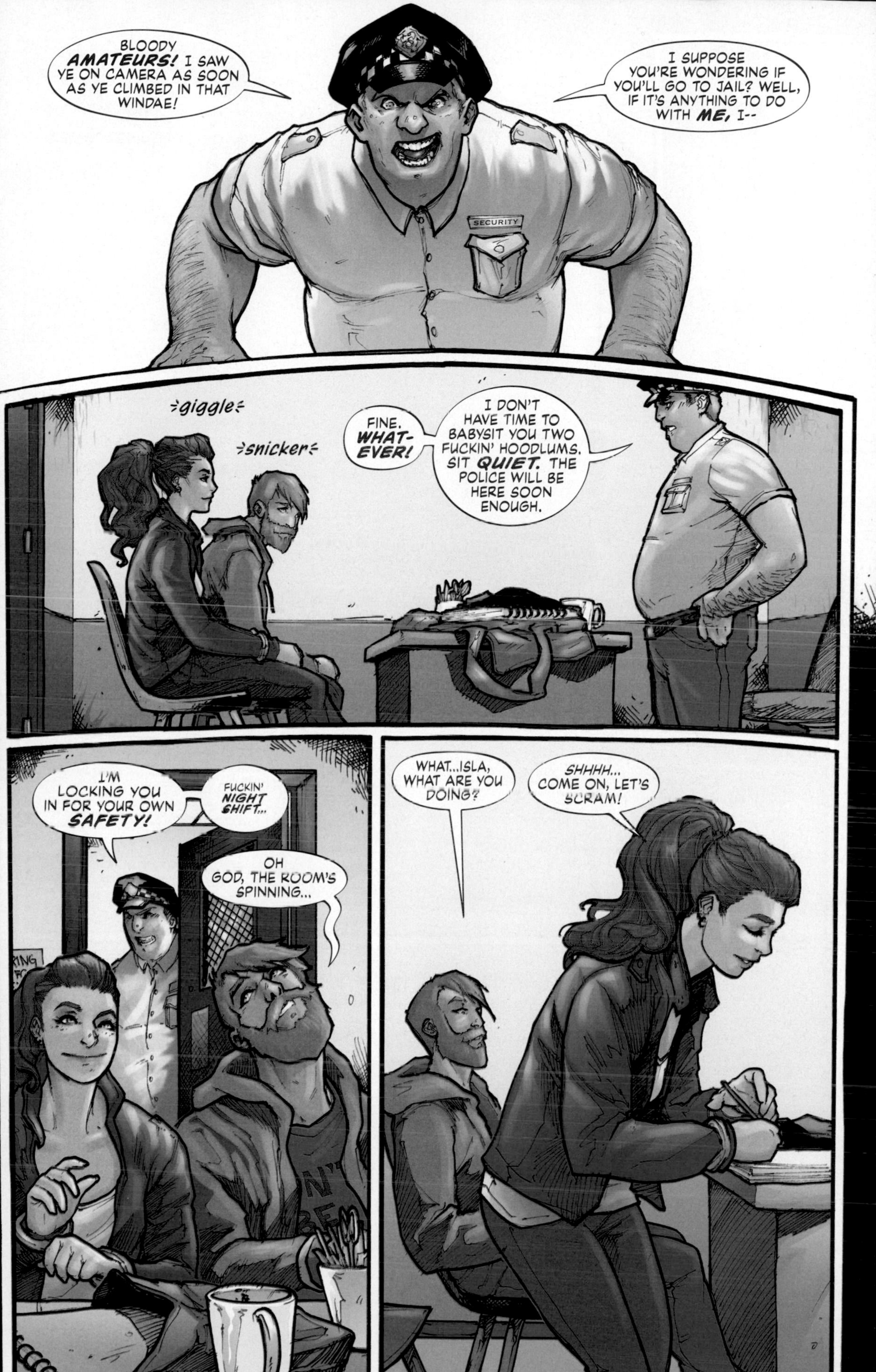

BLOODY AMATEURS! I SAW YE ON CAMERA AS SOON AS YE CLIMBED IN THAT WINDAE!
I SUPPOSE YOU'RE WONDERING IF YOU'LL GO TO JAIL? WELL, IF IT'S ANYTHING TO DO WITH ME, I--
giggle
snicker
FINE. WHATEVER!
I DON'T HAVE TIME TO BABYSIT YOU TWO FUCKIN' HOODLUMS. SIT QUIET. THE POLICE WILL BE HERE SOON ENOUGH.
I'M LOCKING YOU IN FOR YOUR OWN SAFETY!
FUCKIN' NIGHT SHIFT...
OH GOD, THE ROOM'S SPINNING...
WHAT...ISLA, WHAT ARE YOU DOING?
SHHHH... COME ON, LET'S SCRAM!

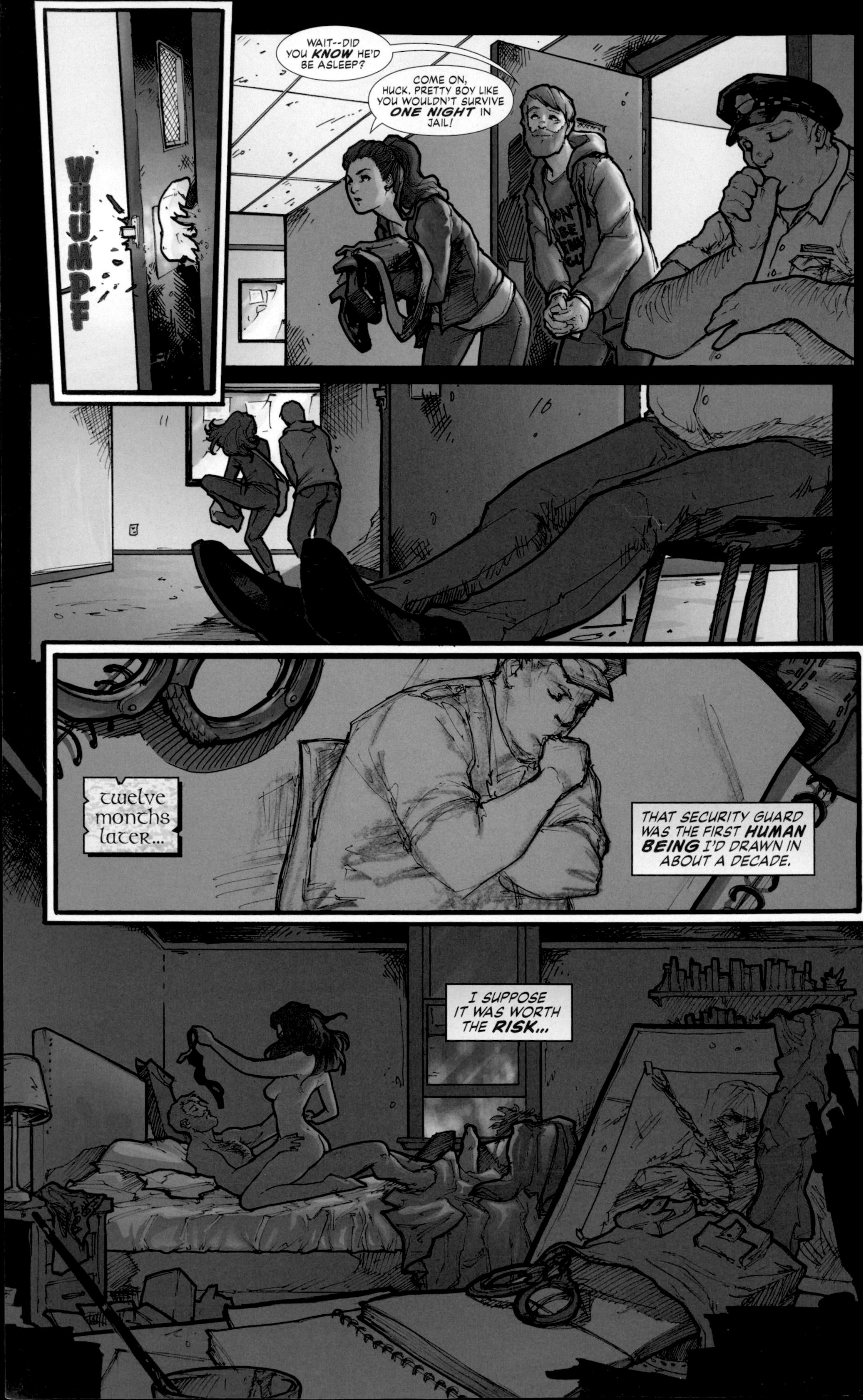
WHUMPF
WAIT--DID YOU KNOW HE'D BE ASLEEP?
COME ON, HUCK, PRETTY BOY LIKE YOU WOULDN'T SURVIVE ONE NIGHT IN JAIL!
twelve months later...
THAT SECURITY GUARD WAS THE FIRST HUMAN BEING I'D DRAWN IN ABOUT A DECADE.
I SUPPOSE IT WAS WORTH THE RISK...

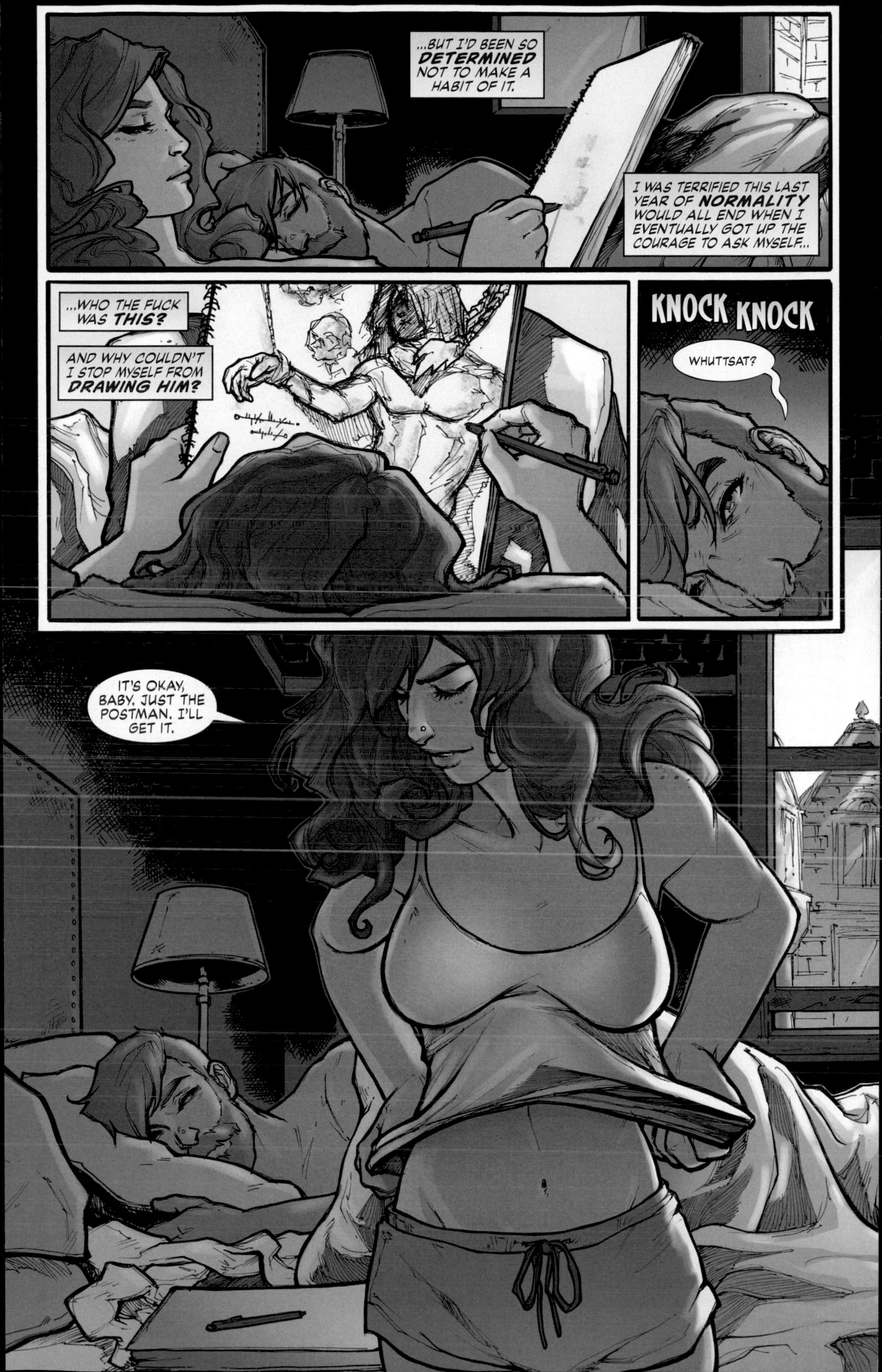
...BUT I'D BEEN SO DETERMINED NOT TO MAKE A HABIT OF IT.
I WAS TERRIFIED THIS LAST YEAR OF NORMALITY WOULD ALL END WHEN I EVENTUALLY GOT UP THE COURAGE TO ASK MYSELF...
...WHO THE FUCK WAS THIS?
AND WHY COULDN'T I STOP MYSELF FROM DRAWING HIM?
KNOCK KNOCK
WHUTTSAT?
IT'S OKAY, BABY. JUST THE POSTMAN. I'LL GET IT.

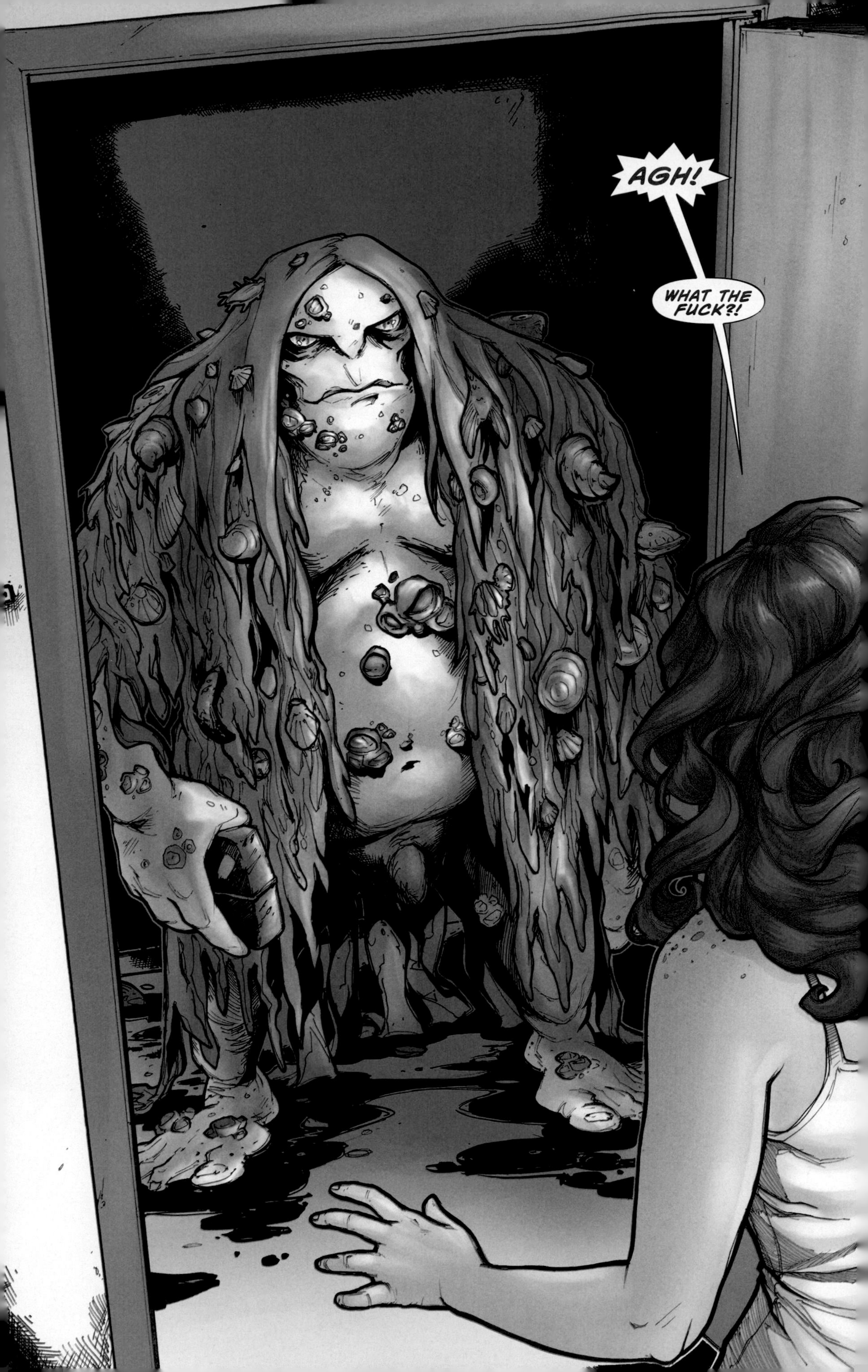
AGH!
WHAT THE FUCK?!

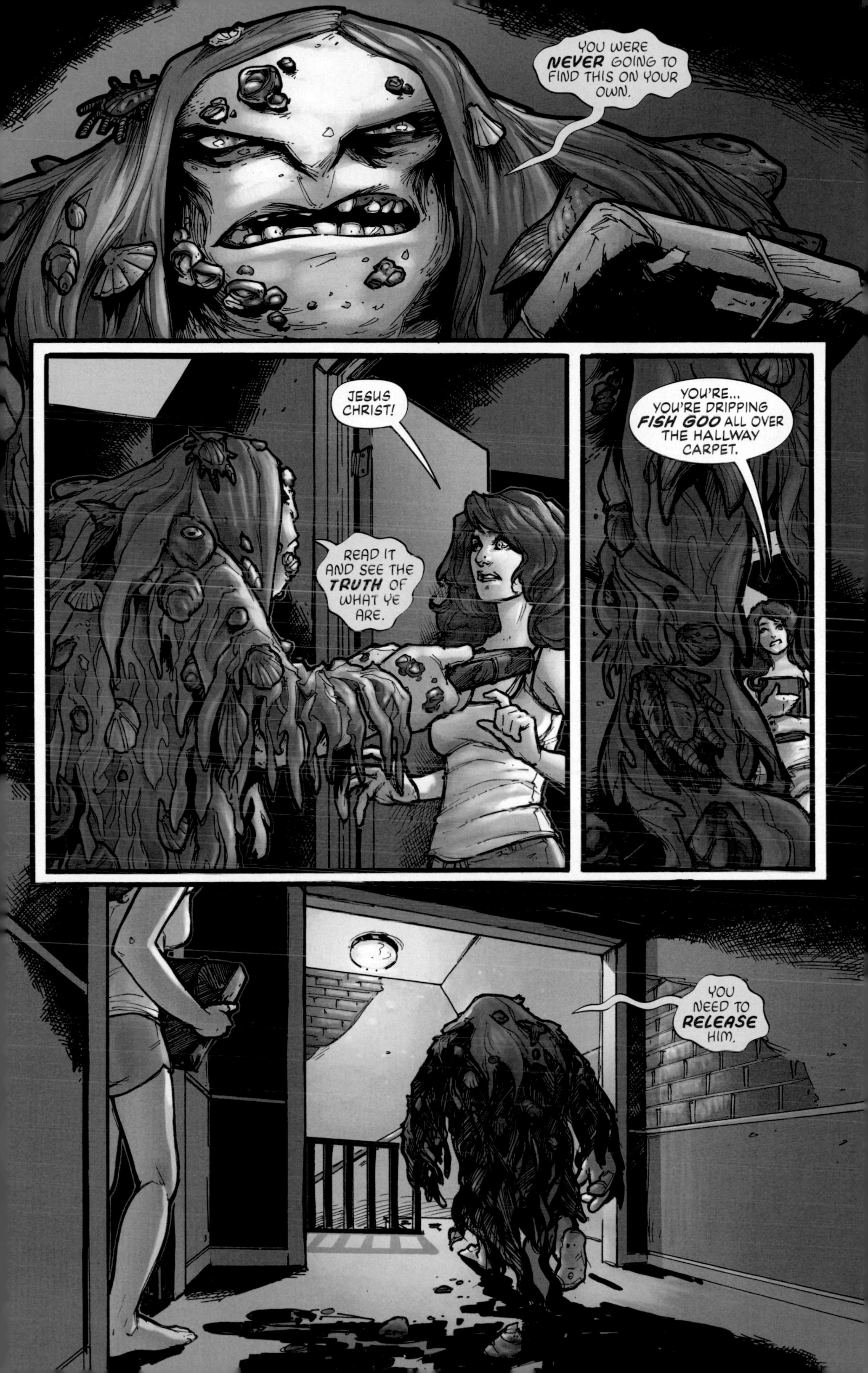
YOU WERE NEVER GOING TO FIND THIS ON YOUR OWN.
JESUS CHRIST!
READ IT AND SEE THE TRUTH OF WHAT YE ARE.
YOU'RE... YOU'RE DRIPPING FISH GOO ALL OVER THE HALLWAY CARPET.
YOU NEED TO RELEASE HIM.

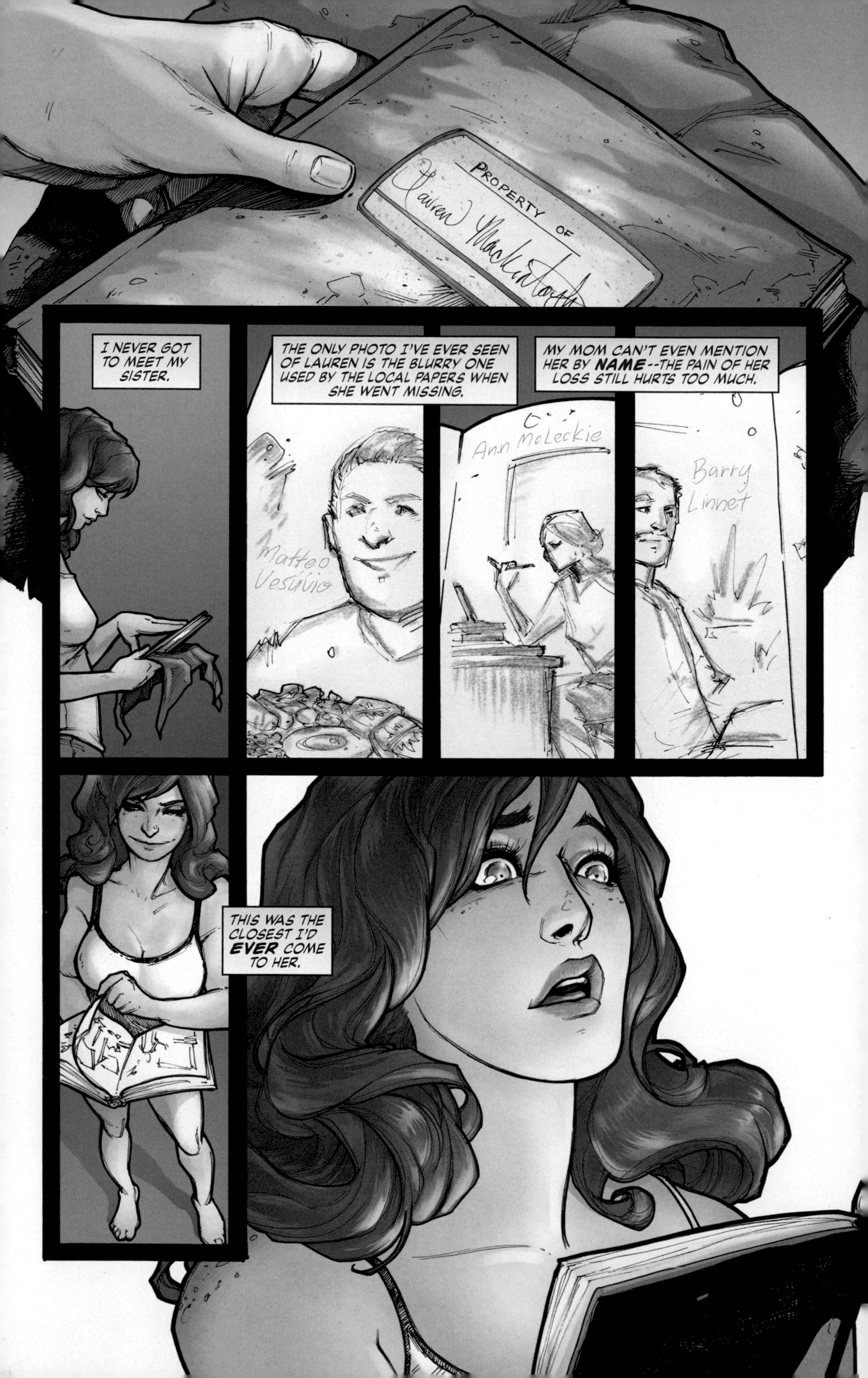
PROPERTY OF
Lauren MacIntosh
I NEVER GOT TO MEET MY SISTER.
THE ONLY PHOTO I'VE EVER SEEN OF LAUREN IS THE BLURRY ONE USED BY THE LOCAL PAPERS WHEN SHE WENT MISSING.
Matteo Vesuvio
Ann McLeckie
MY MOM CAN'T EVEN MENTION HER BY NAME--THE PAIN OF HER LOSS STILL HURTS TOO MUCH.
Barry Linnet
THIS WAS THE CLOSEST I'D EVER COME TO HER.

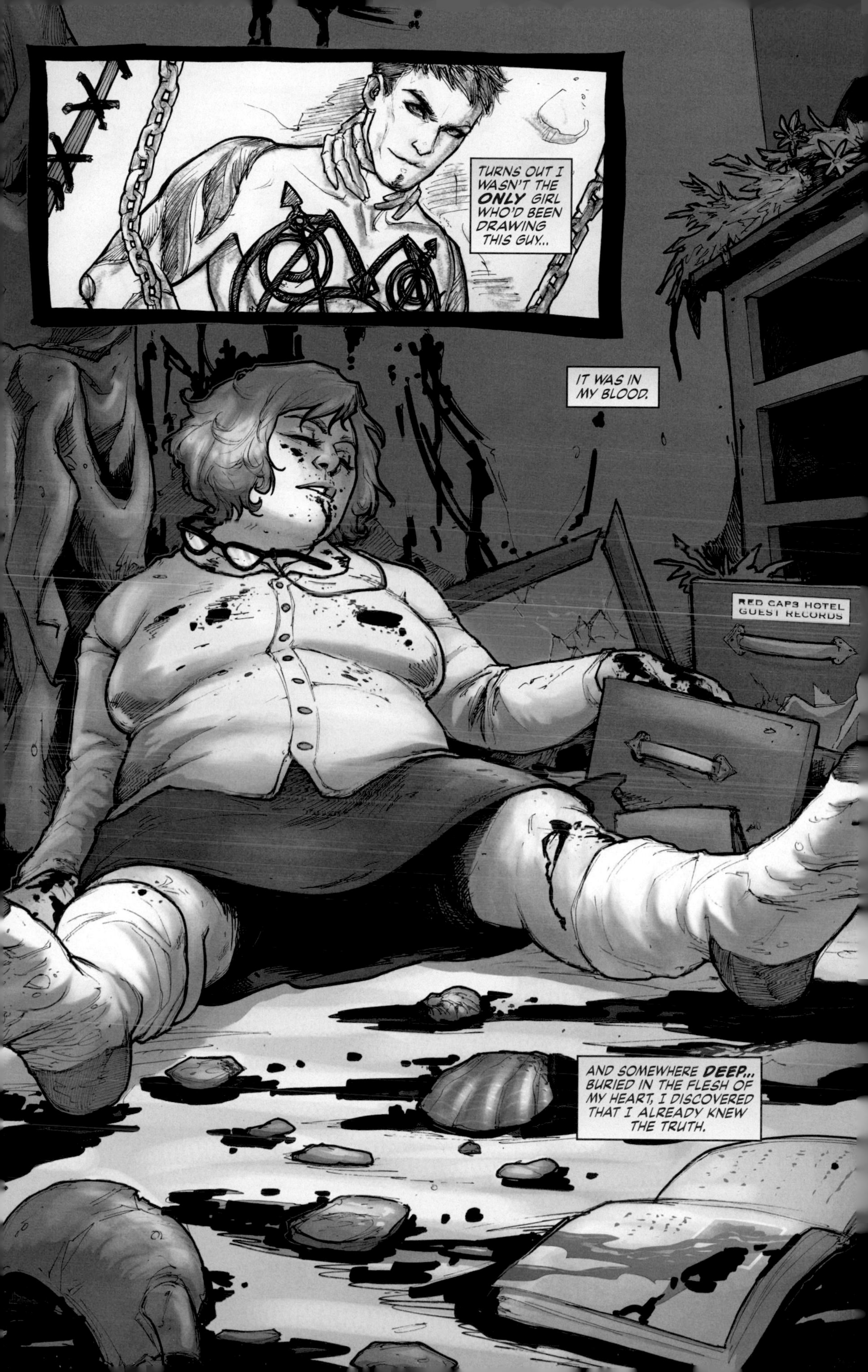
TURNS OUT I WASN'T THE **ONLY** GIRL WHO'D BEEN DRAWING THIS GUY...
IT WAS IN MY BLOOD.
RED CAPS HOTEL GUEST RECORDS
AND SOMEWHERE **DEEP**... BURIED IN THE FLESH OF MY HEART, I DISCOVERED THAT I ALREADY KNEW THE TRUTH.

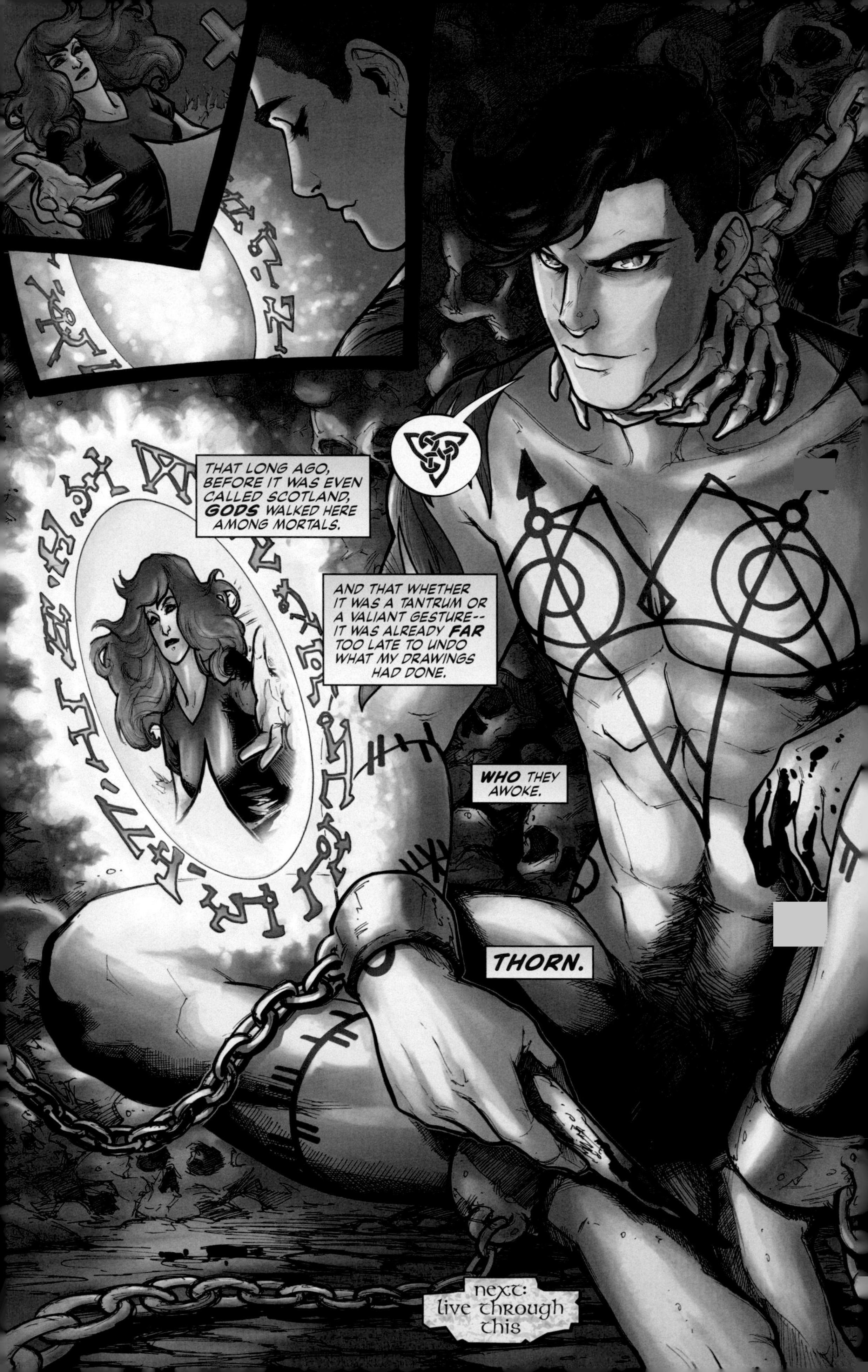

THAT LONG AGO, BEFORE IT WAS EVEN CALLED SCOTLAND, GODS WALKED HERE AMONG MORTALS.
AND THAT WHETHER IT WAS A TANTRUM OR A VALIANT GESTURE-- IT WAS ALREADY FAR TOO LATE TO UNDO WHAT MY DRAWINGS HAD DONE.
WHO THEY AWOKE.
THORN.
next: live through this

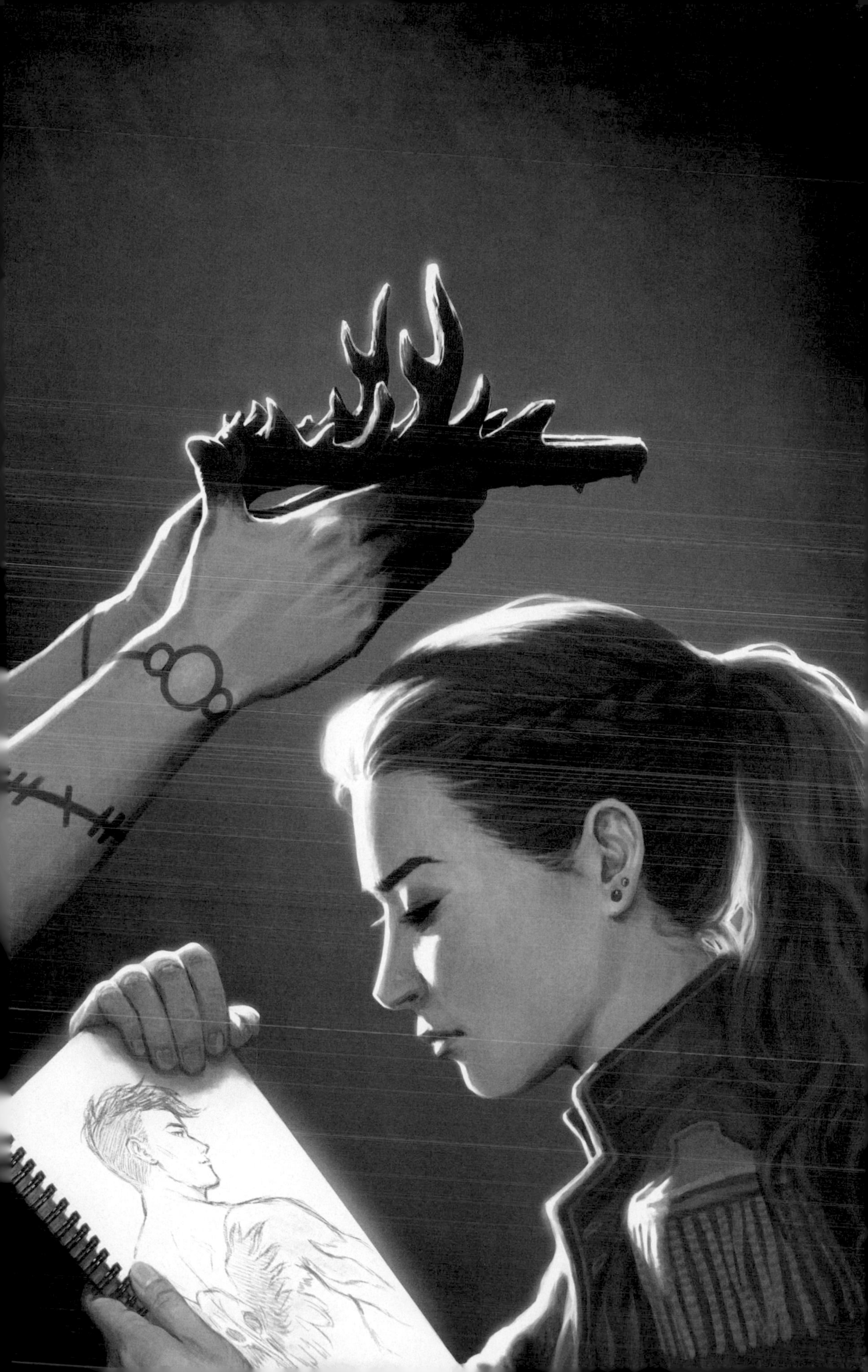

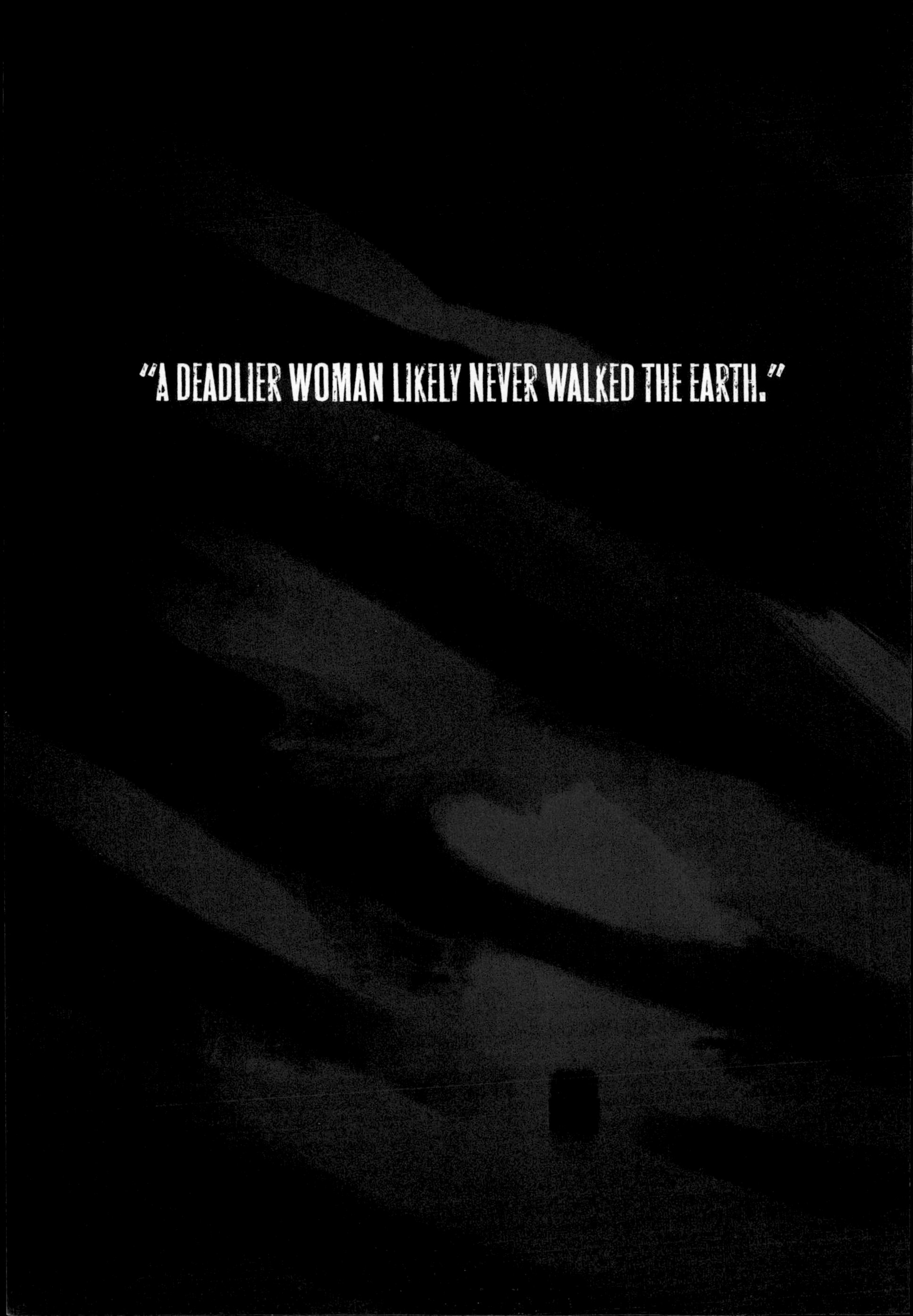
"A DEADLIER WOMAN LIKELY NEVER WALKED THE EARTH."

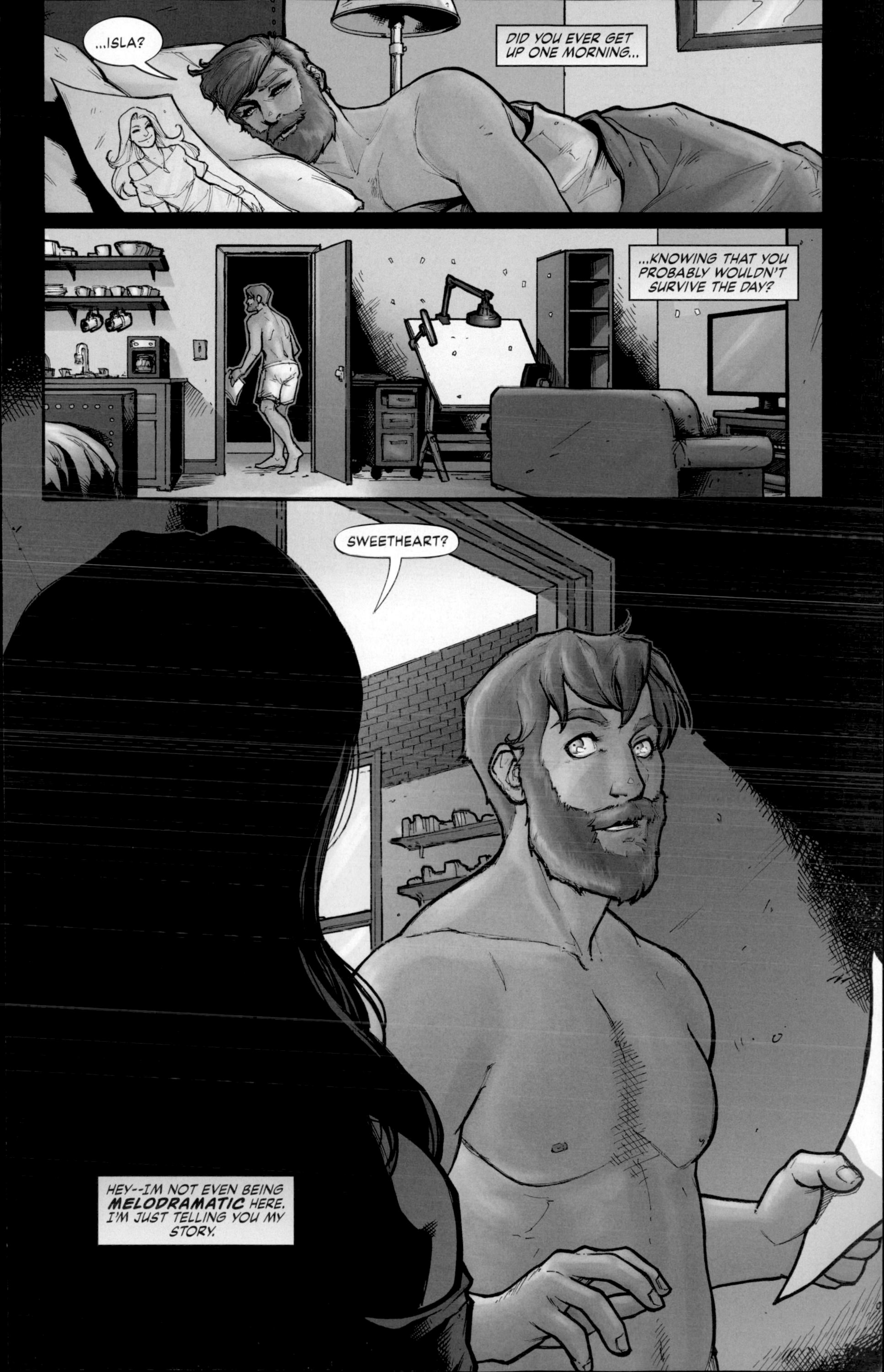

...ISLA?
DID YOU EVER GET UP ONE MORNING...
...KNOWING THAT YOU PROBABLY WOULDN'T SURVIVE THE DAY?
SWEETHEART?
HEY--I'M NOT EVEN BEING **MELODRAMATIC** HERE. I'M JUST TELLING YOU MY STORY.

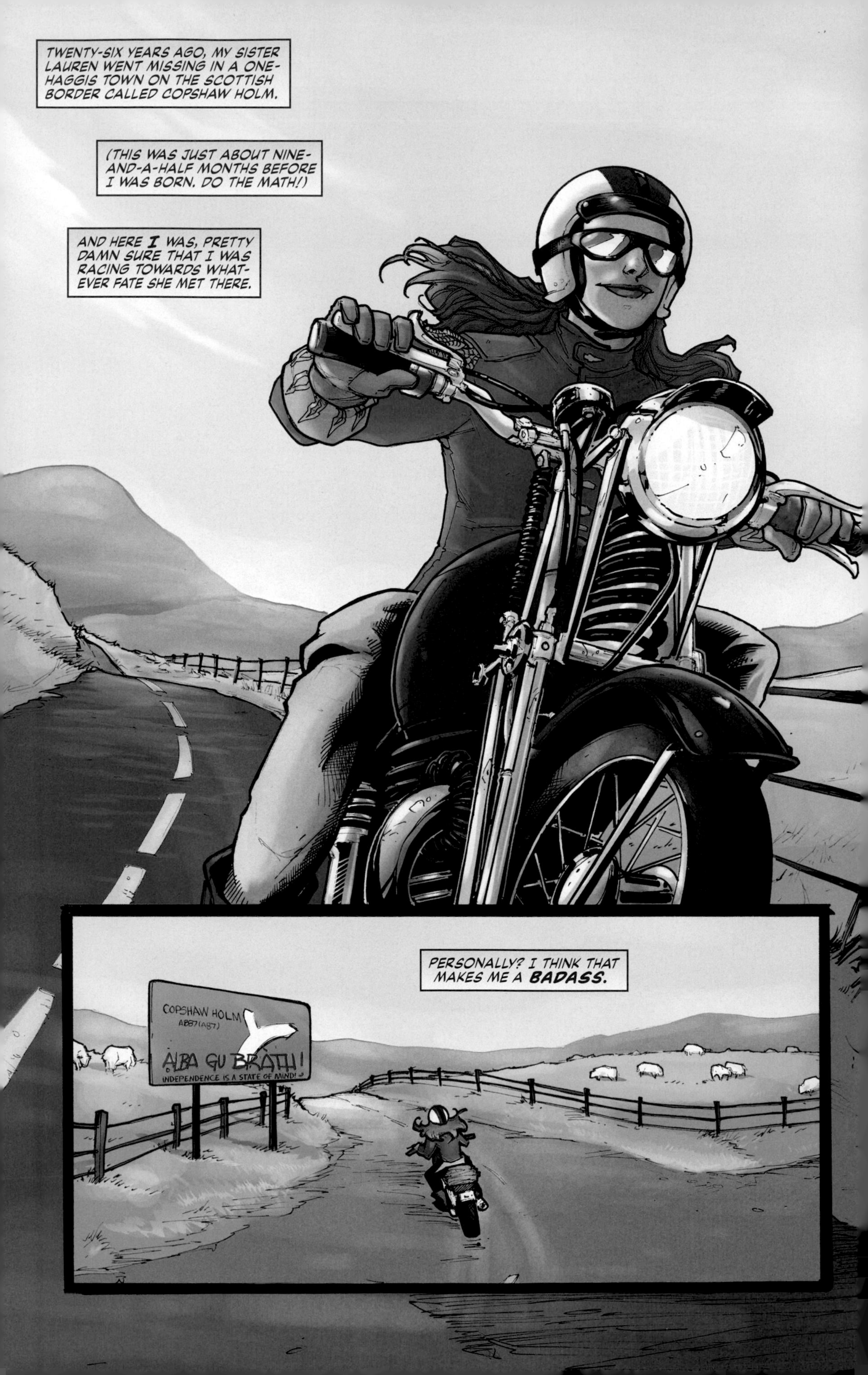
TWENTY-SIX YEARS AGO, MY SISTER LAUREN WENT MISSING IN A ONE-HAGGIS TOWN ON THE SCOTTISH BORDER CALLED COPSHAW HOLM.
(THIS WAS JUST ABOUT NINE-AND-A-HALF MONTHS BEFORE I WAS BORN. DO THE MATH!)
AND HERE I WAS, PRETTY DAMN SURE THAT I WAS RACING TOWARDS WHATEVER FATE SHE MET THERE.
PERSONALLY? I THINK THAT MAKES ME A BADASS.
COPSHAW HOLM
A887(A87)
ALBA GU BRATH!
INDEPENDENCE IS A STATE OF MIND!

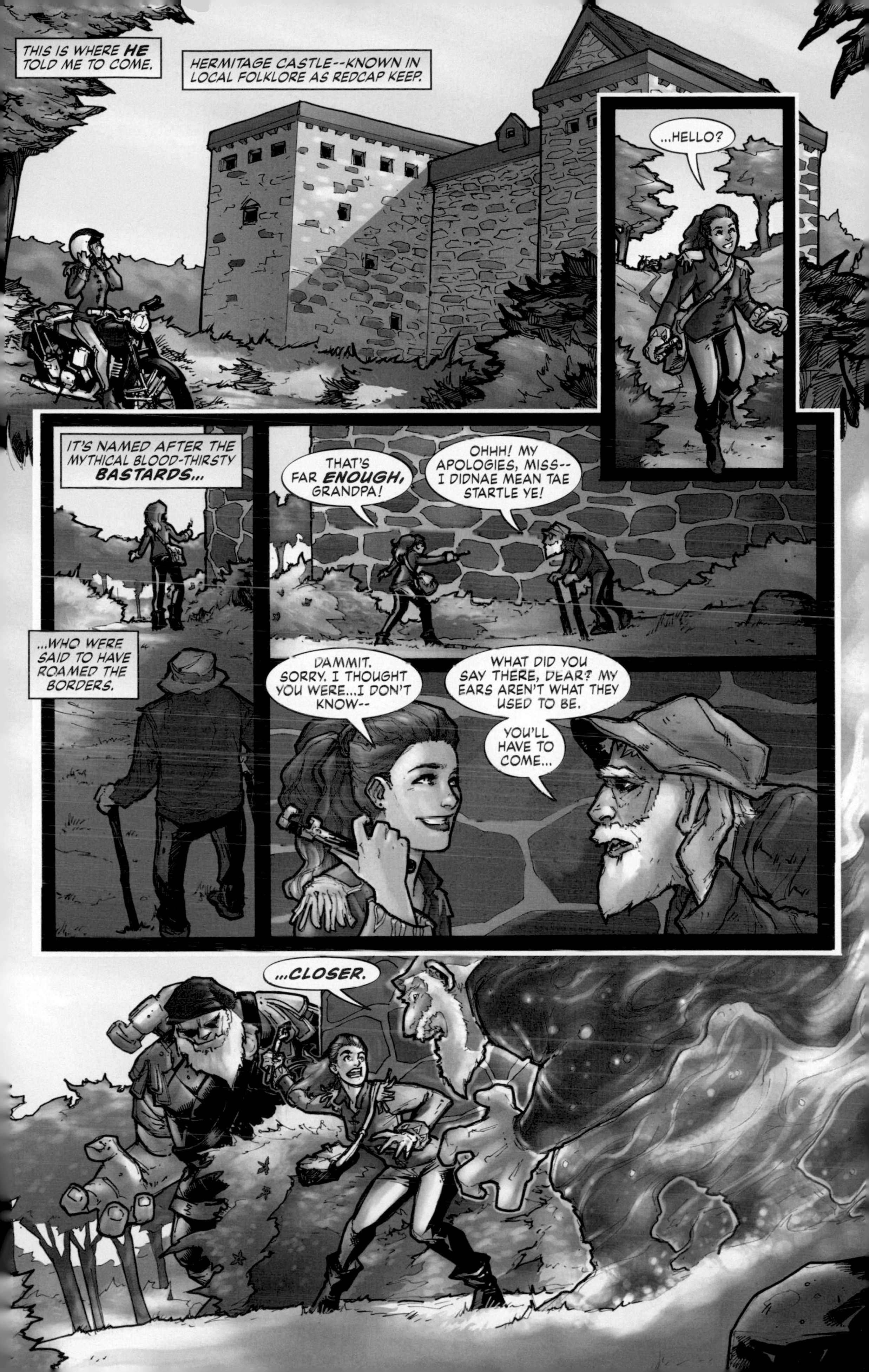
THIS IS WHERE **HE** TOLD ME TO COME.
HERMITAGE CASTLE--KNOWN IN LOCAL FOLKLORE AS REDCAP KEEP.
...HELLO?
IT'S NAMED AFTER THE MYTHICAL BLOOD-THIRSTY **BASTARDS...**
...WHO WERE SAID TO HAVE ROAMED THE BORDERS.
THAT'S FAR **ENOUGH,** GRANDPA!
OHHH! MY APOLOGIES, MISS-- I DIDNAE MEAN TAE STARTLE YE!
DAMMIT. SORRY. I THOUGHT YOU WERE...I DON'T KNOW--
WHAT DID YOU SAY THERE, DEAR? MY EARS AREN'T WHAT THEY USED TO BE.
YOU'LL HAVE TO COME...
...CLOSER.

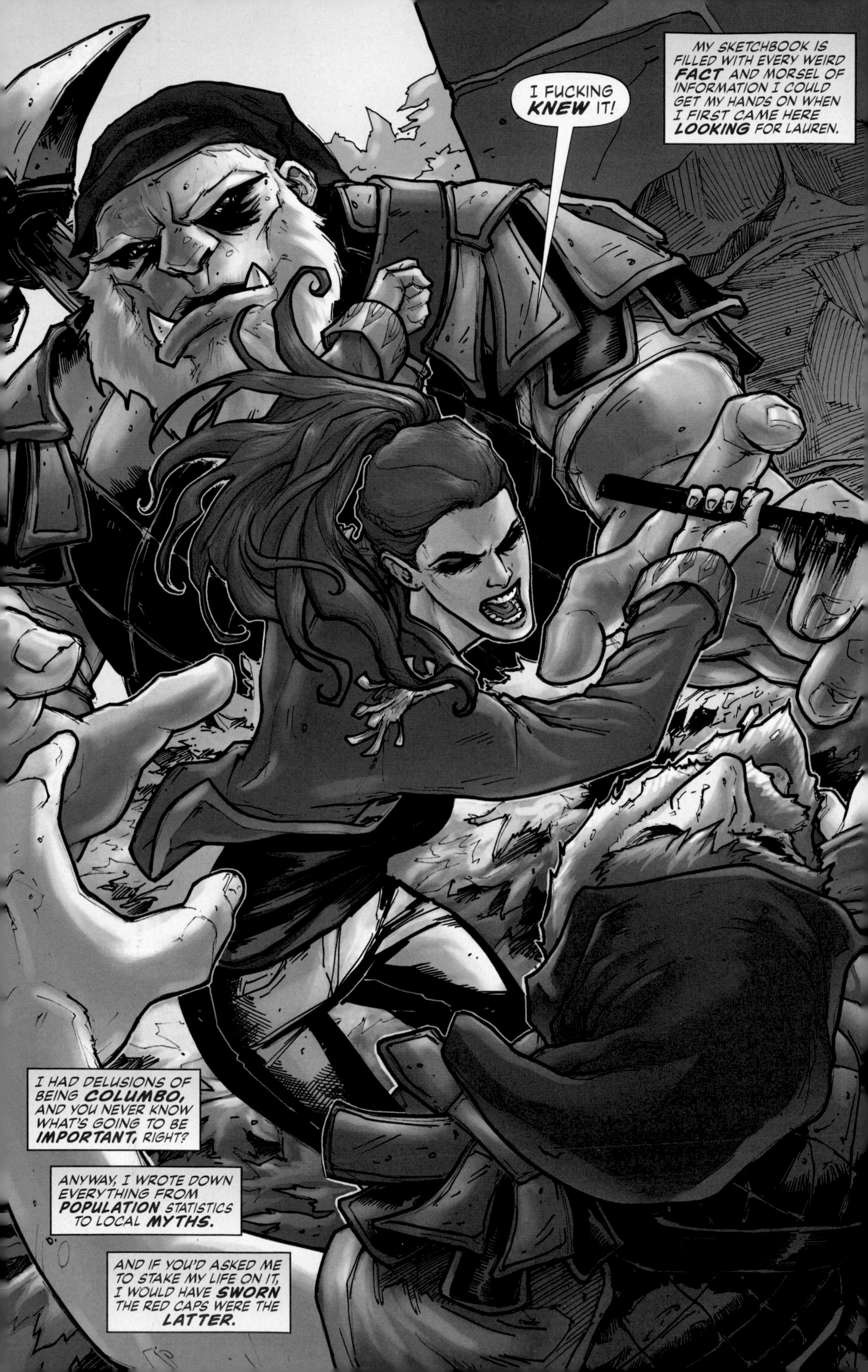
MY SKETCHBOOK IS FILLED WITH EVERY WEIRD FACT AND MORSEL OF INFORMATION I COULD GET MY HANDS ON WHEN I FIRST CAME HERE LOOKING FOR LAUREN.
I FUCKING KNEW IT!
I HAD DELUSIONS OF BEING COLUMBO, AND YOU NEVER KNOW WHAT'S GOING TO BE IMPORTANT, RIGHT?
ANYWAY, I WROTE DOWN EVERYTHING FROM POPULATION STATISTICS TO LOCAL MYTHS.
AND IF YOU'D ASKED ME TO STAKE MY LIFE ON IT, I WOULD HAVE SWORN THE RED CAPS WERE THE LATTER.

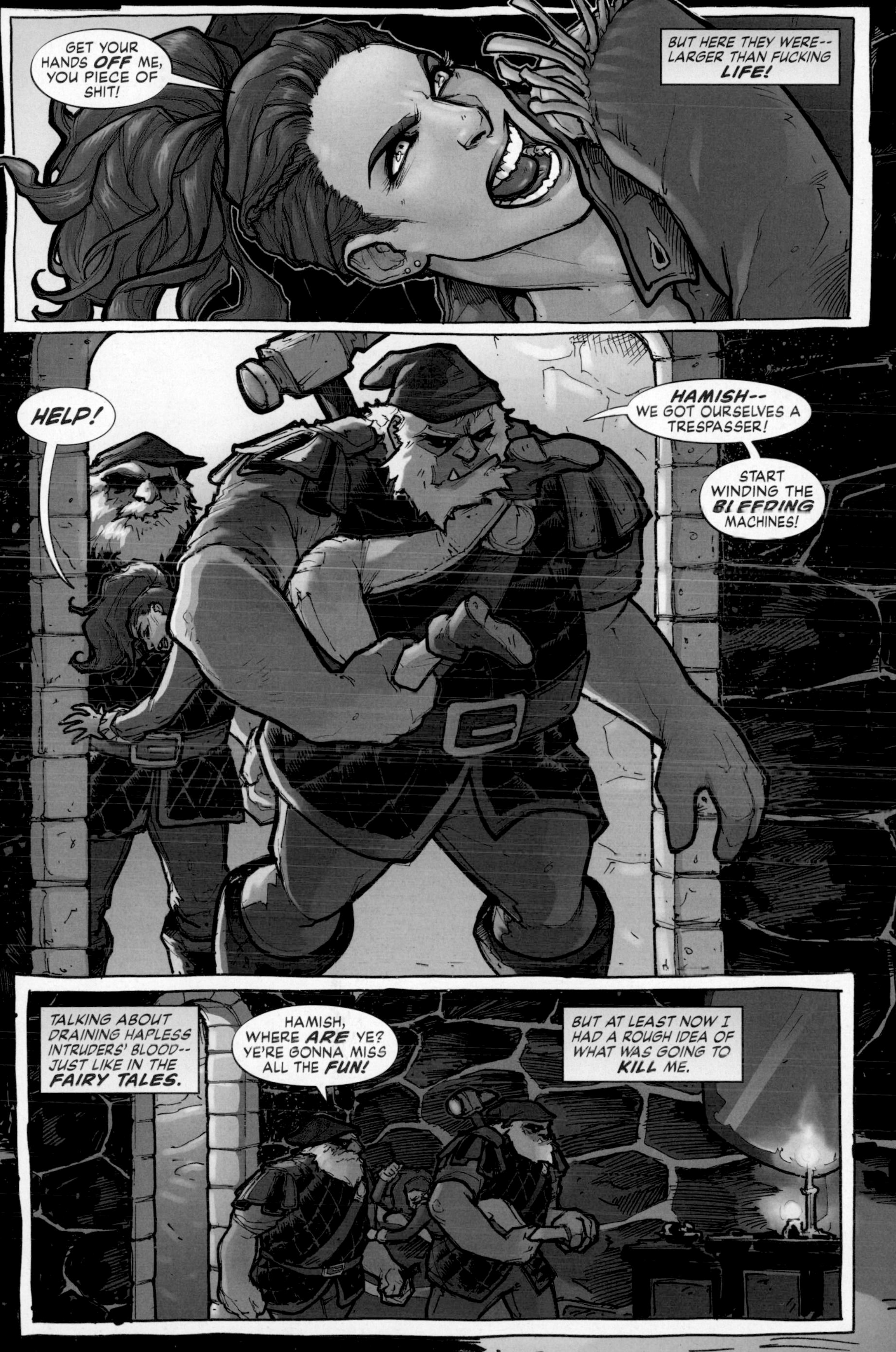
GET YOUR HANDS OFF ME, YOU PIECE OF SHIT!
BUT HERE THEY WERE-- LARGER THAN FUCKING LIFE!
HELP!
HAMISH-- WE GOT OURSELVES A TRESPASSER!
START WINDING THE BLEEDING MACHINES!
TALKING ABOUT DRAINING HAPLESS INTRUDERS' BLOOD-- JUST LIKE IN THE FAIRY TALES.
HAMISH, WHERE ARE YE? YE'RE GONNA MISS ALL THE FUN!
BUT AT LEAST NOW I HAD A ROUGH IDEA OF WHAT WAS GOING TO KILL ME.

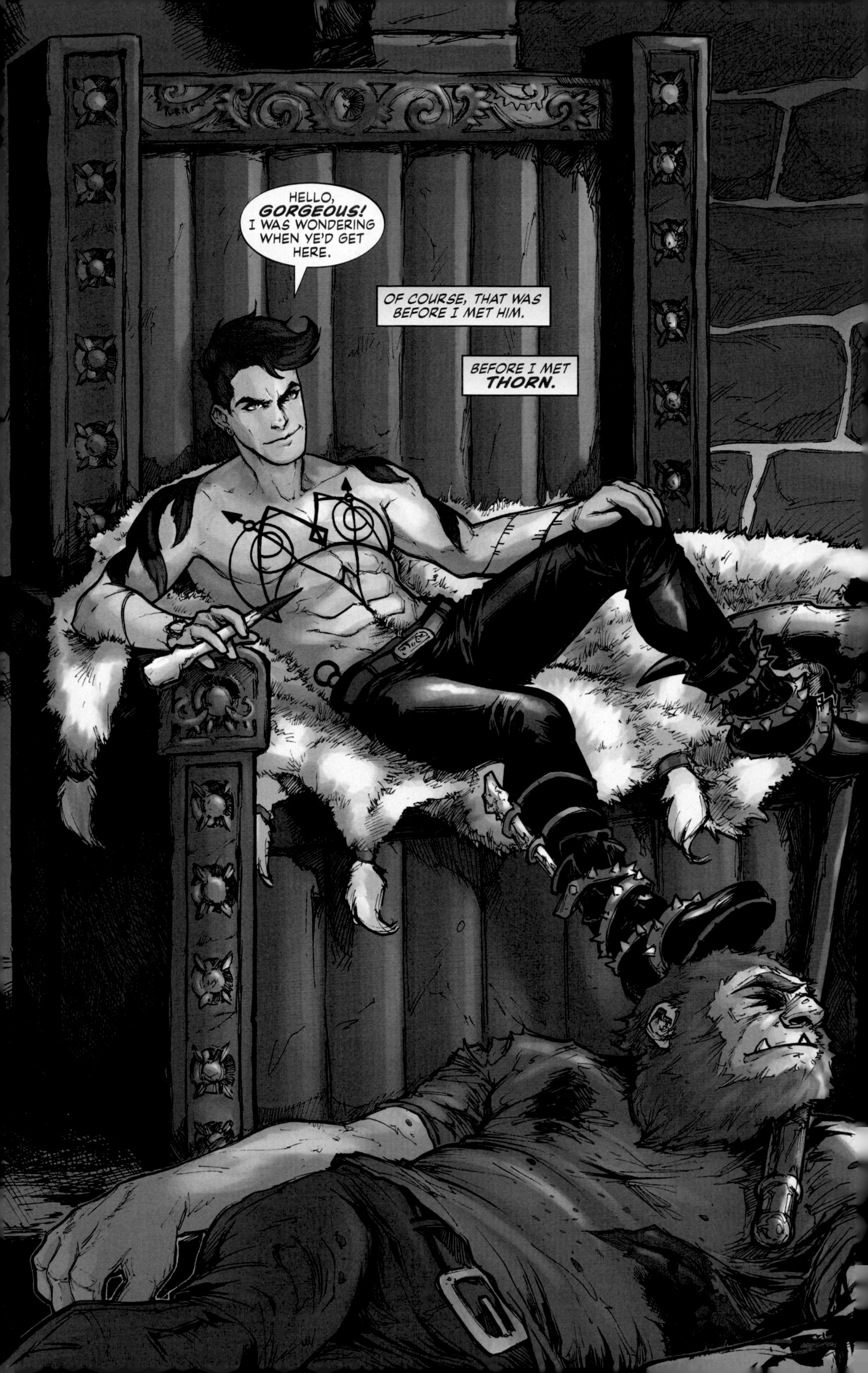
HELLO, GORGEOUS! I WAS WONDERING WHEN YE'D GET HERE.
OF COURSE, THAT WAS BEFORE I MET HIM.
BEFORE I MET THORN.

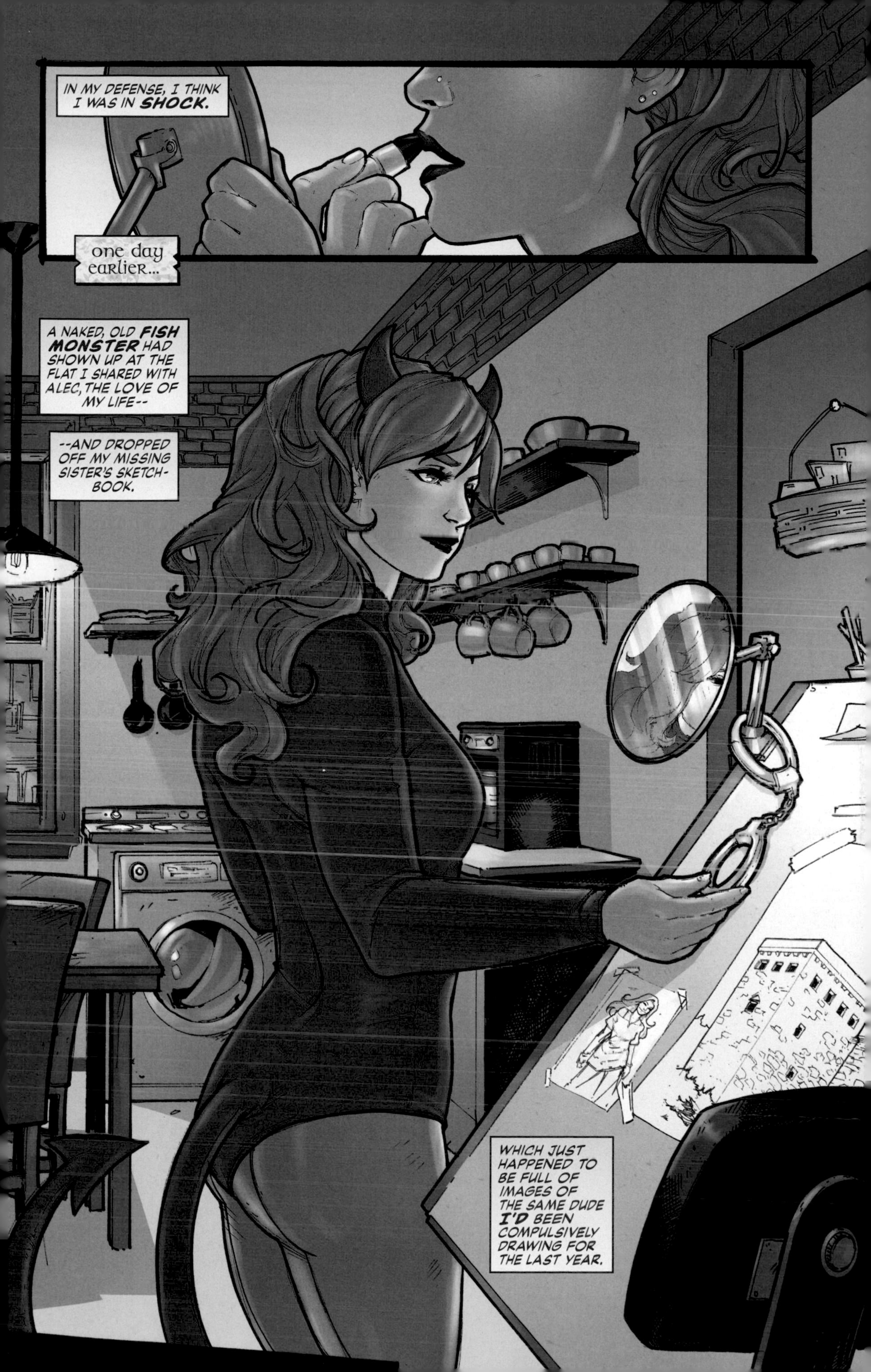
IN MY DEFENSE, I THINK I WAS IN **SHOCK.**
one day earlier...
A NAKED, OLD **FISH MONSTER** HAD SHOWN UP AT THE FLAT I SHARED WITH ALEC, THE LOVE OF MY LIFE--
--AND DROPPED OFF MY MISSING SISTER'S SKETCH-BOOK.
WHICH JUST HAPPENED TO BE FULL OF IMAGES OF THE SAME DUDE ***I'D*** BEEN COMPULSIVELY DRAWING FOR THE LAST YEAR.

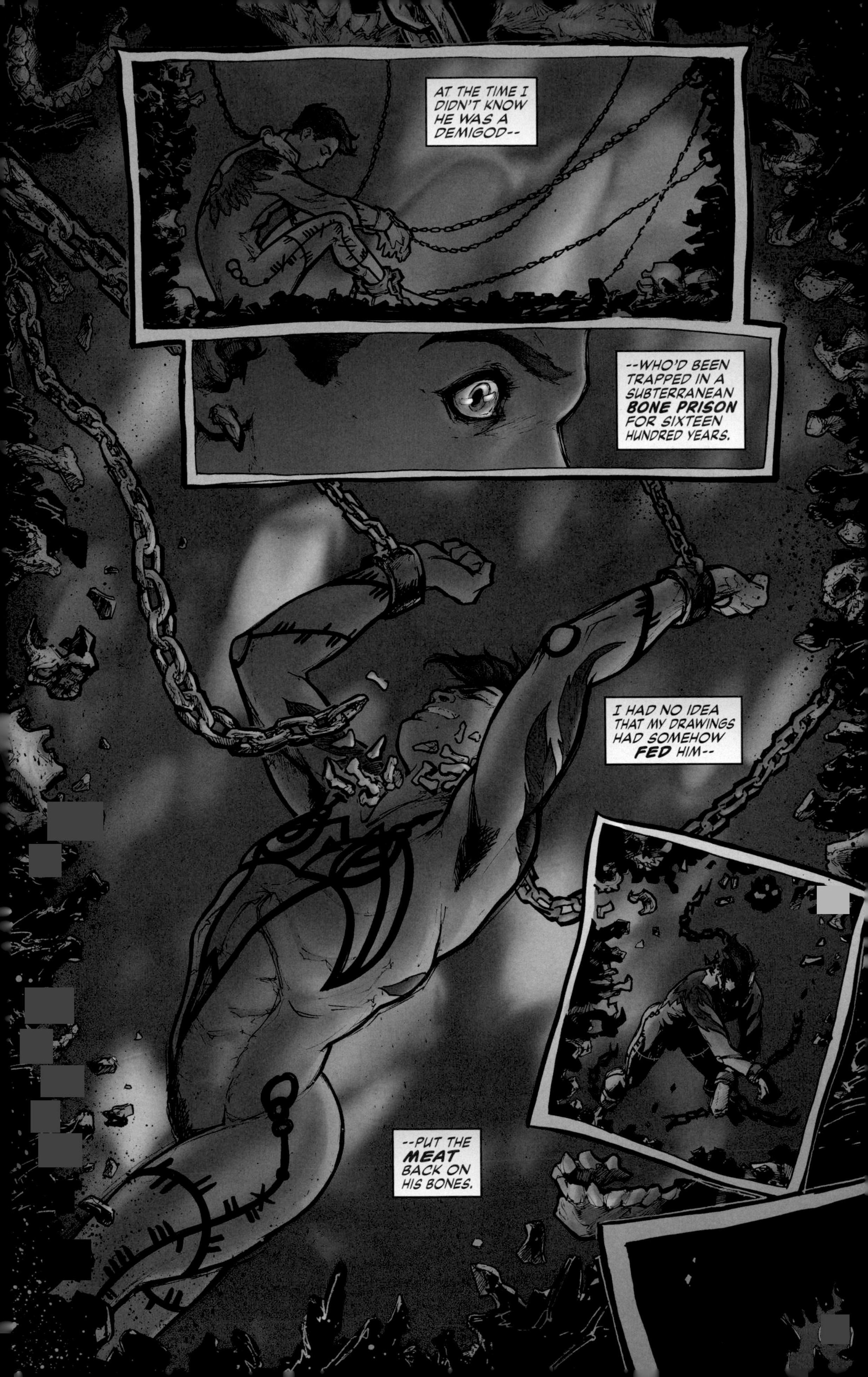
AT THE TIME I DIDN'T KNOW HE WAS A DEMIGOD--
--WHO'D BEEN TRAPPED IN A SUBTERRANEAN BONE PRISON FOR SIXTEEN HUNDRED YEARS.
I HAD NO IDEA THAT MY DRAWINGS HAD SOMEHOW FED HIM--
--PUT THE MEAT BACK ON HIS BONES.

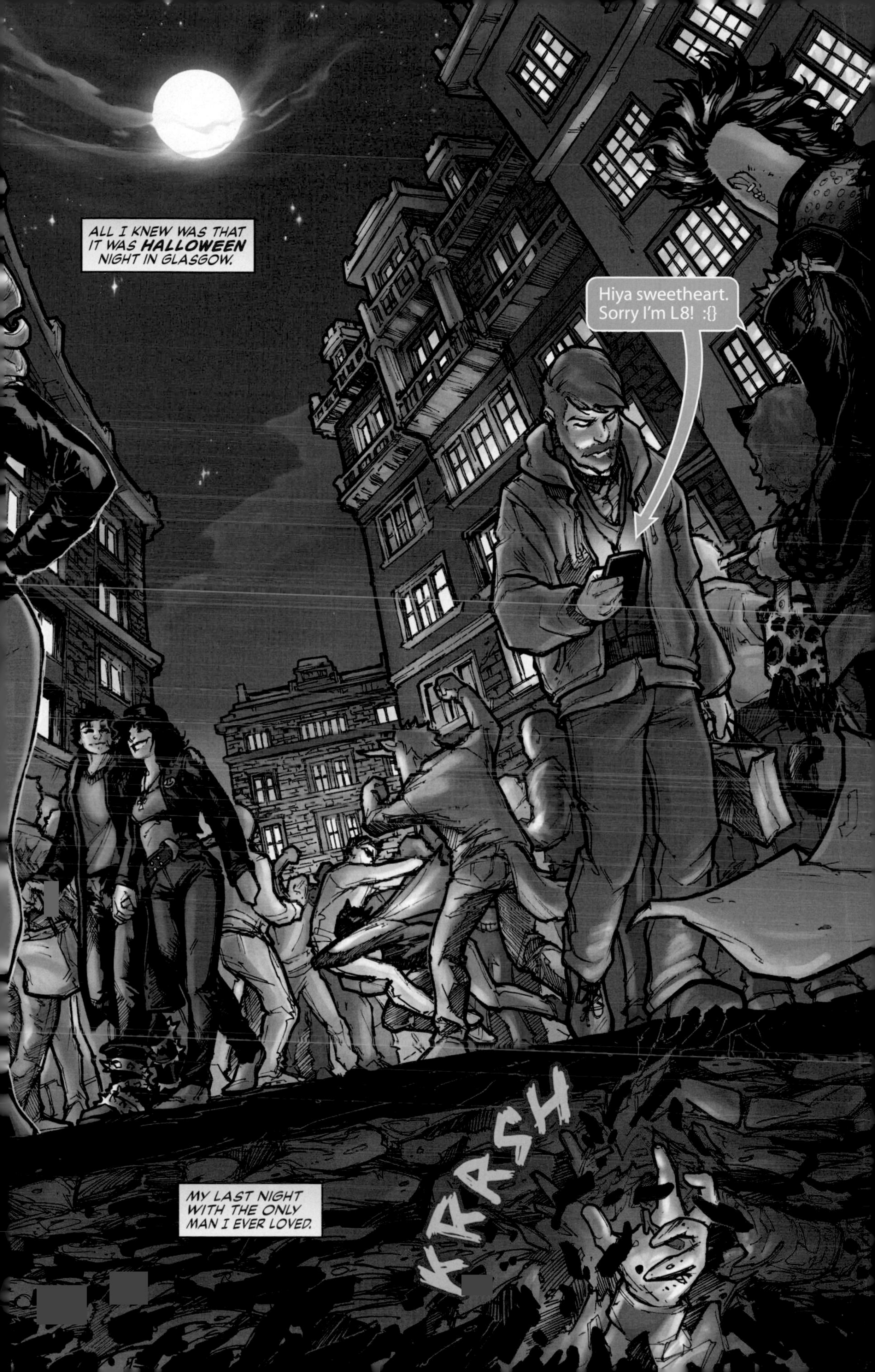
ALL I KNEW WAS THAT IT WAS **HALLOWEEN** NIGHT IN GLASGOW.
Hiya sweetheart. Sorry I'm L8! :{}
MY LAST NIGHT WITH THE ONLY MAN I EVER LOVED.
KRRSH

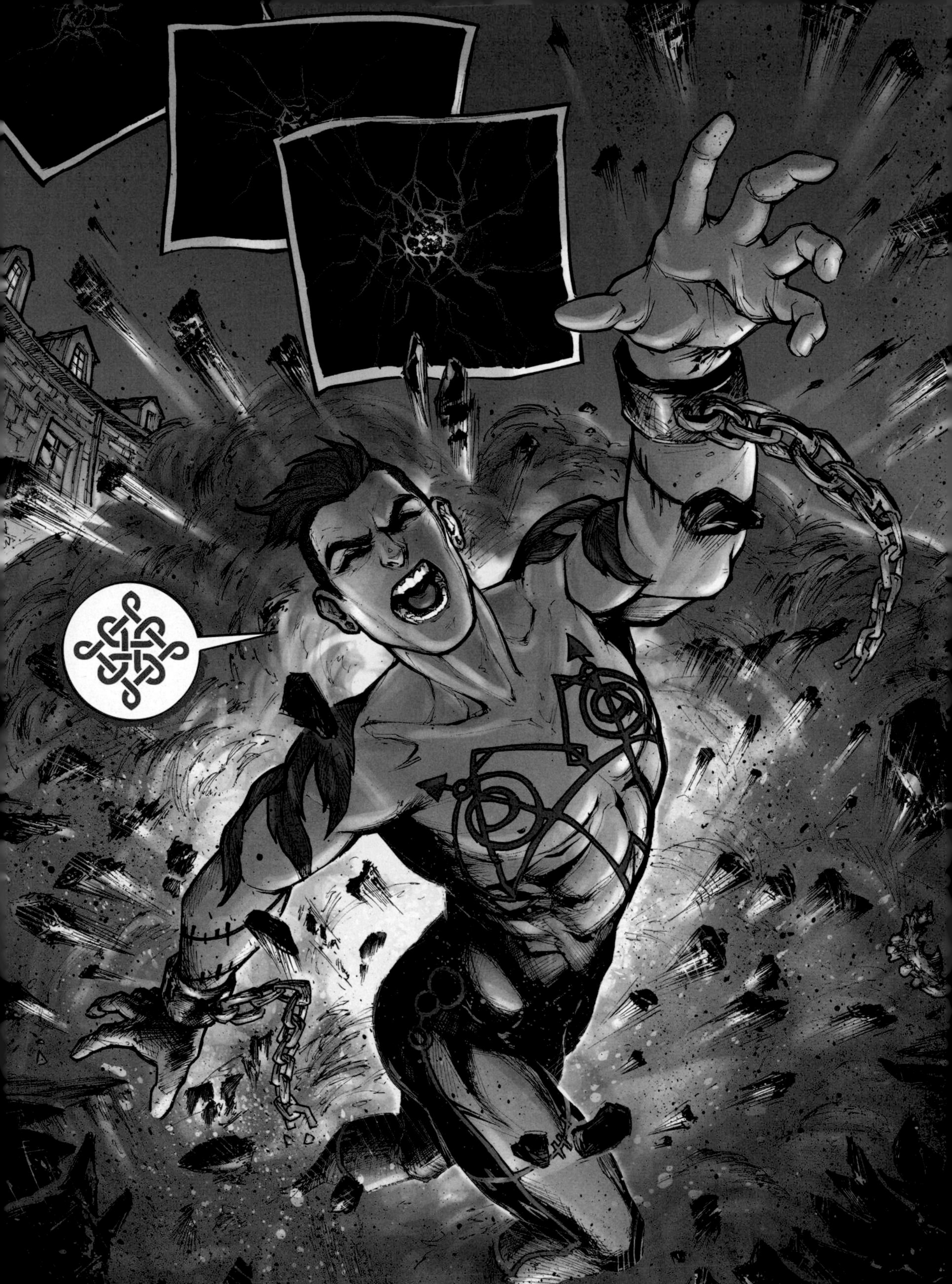

GLASGOW KISS CHAPTER TWO:
REBEL OF THE UNDERGROUND

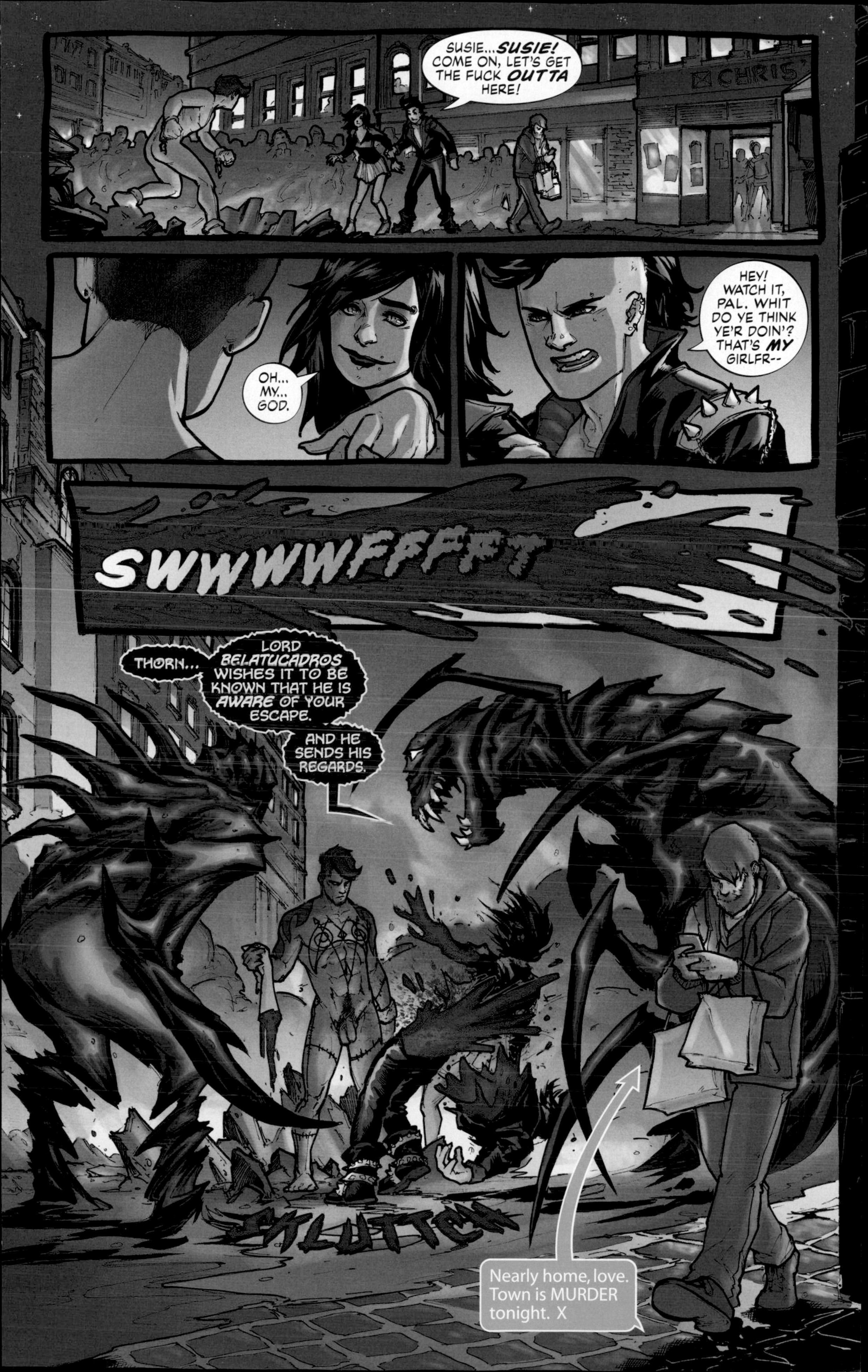
SUSIE...SUSIE! COME ON, LET'S GET THE FUCK OUTTA HERE!
CHRIS'
OH... MY... GOD.
HEY! WATCH IT, PAL. WHIT DO YE THINK YE'R DOIN'? THAT'S MY GIRLFR--
SWWWWFFFFT
THORN...
LORD BELATUCADROS WISHES IT TO BE KNOWN THAT HE IS AWARE OF YOUR ESCAPE.
AND HE SENDS HIS REGARDS.
SKLUTTCH
Nearly home, love. Town is MURDER tonight. X

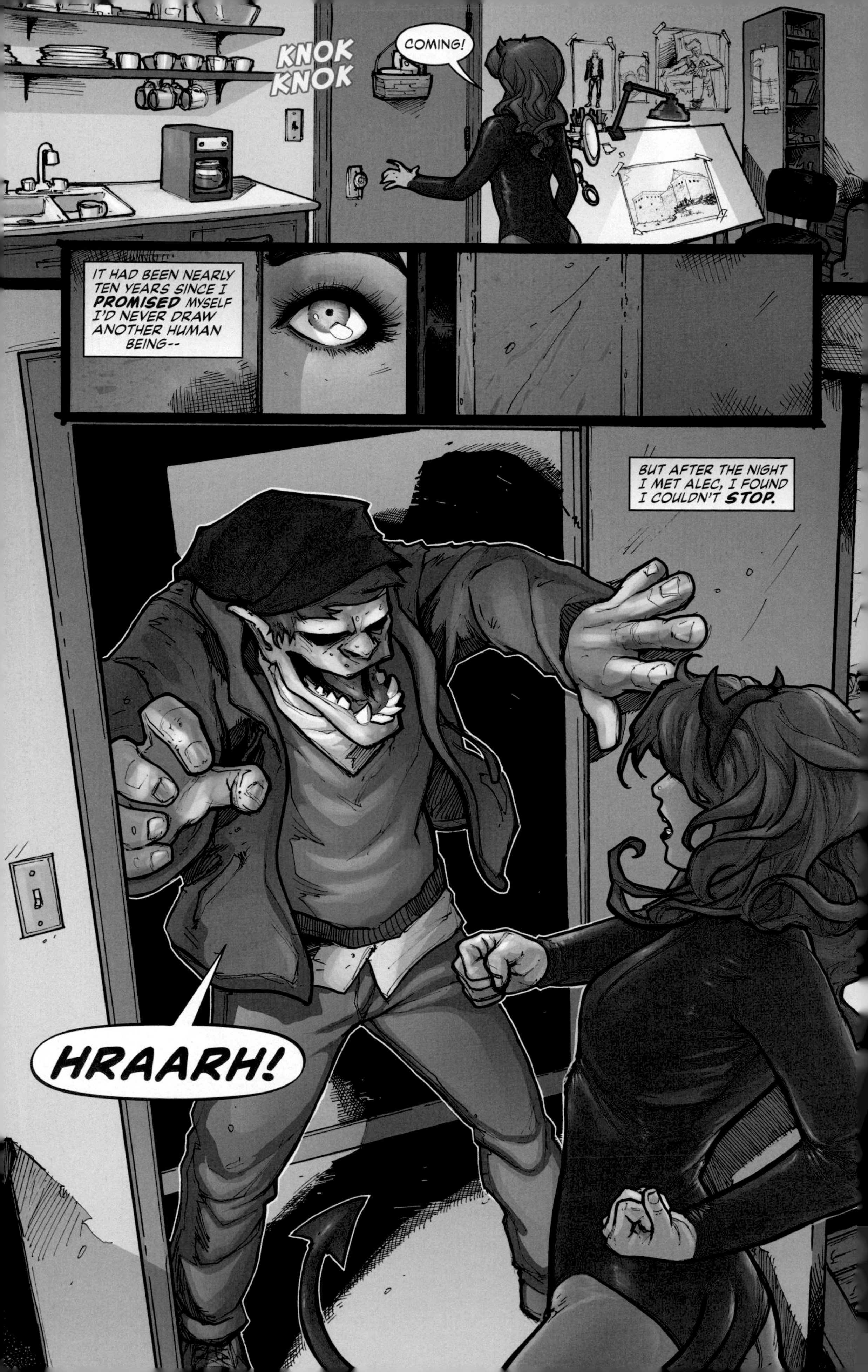
KNOK KNOK
COMING!
IT HAD BEEN NEARLY TEN YEARS SINCE I PROMISED MYSELF I'D NEVER DRAW ANOTHER HUMAN BEING--
BUT AFTER THE NIGHT I MET ALEC, I FOUND I COULDN'T STOP.
HRAARH!

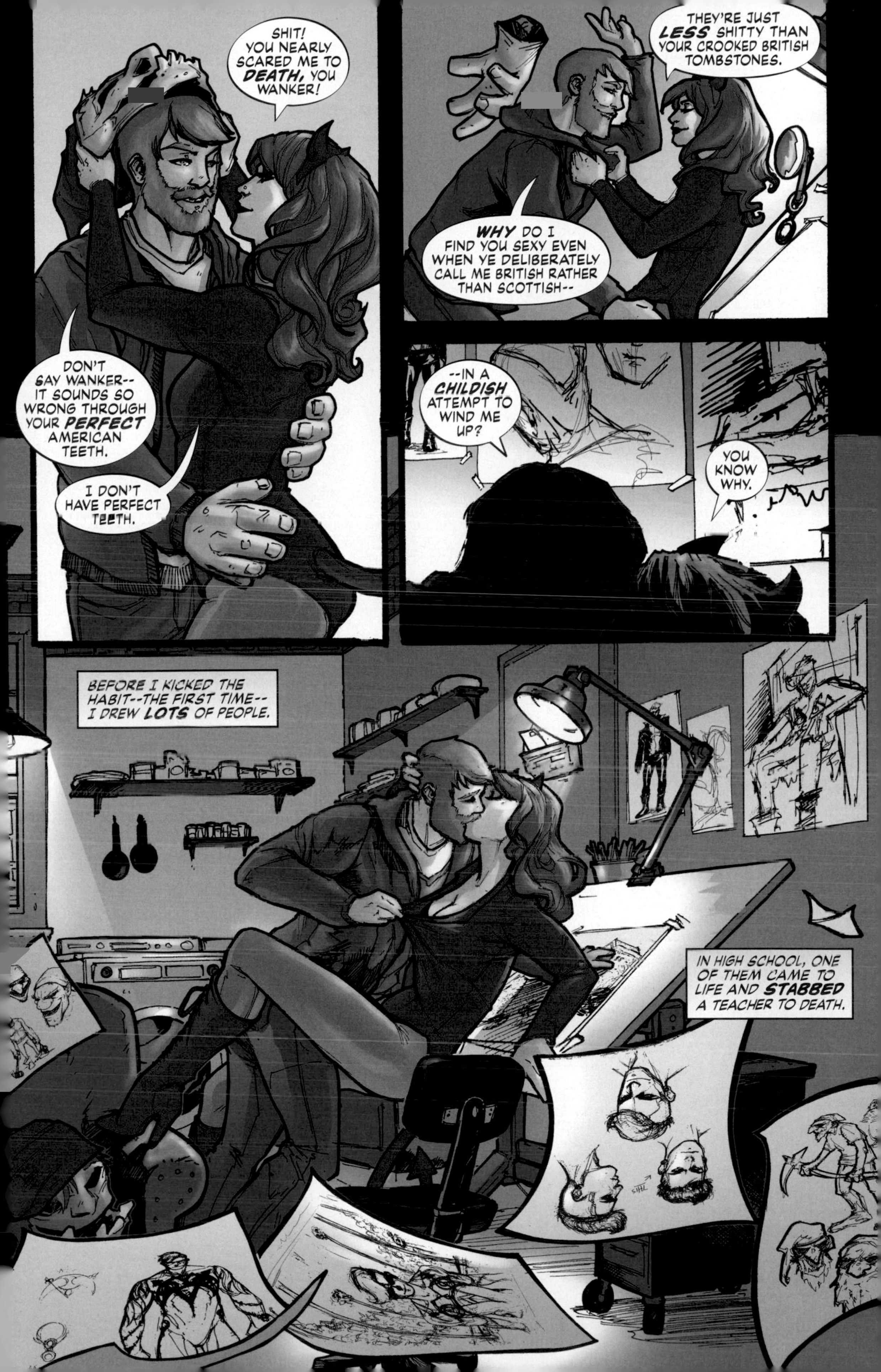
SHIT! YOU NEARLY SCARED ME TO DEATH, YOU WANKER!
DON'T SAY WANKER-- IT SOUNDS SO WRONG THROUGH YOUR PERFECT AMERICAN TEETH.
I DON'T HAVE PERFECT TEETH.
THEY'RE JUST LESS SHITTY THAN YOUR CROOKED BRITISH TOMBSTONES.
WHY DO I FIND YOU SEXY EVEN WHEN YE DELIBERATELY CALL ME BRITISH RATHER THAN SCOTTISH--
--IN A CHILDISH ATTEMPT TO WIND ME UP?
YOU KNOW WHY.
BEFORE I KICKED THE HABIT--THE FIRST TIME-- I DREW LOTS OF PEOPLE.
IN HIGH SCHOOL, ONE OF THEM CAME TO LIFE AND STABBED A TEACHER TO DEATH.

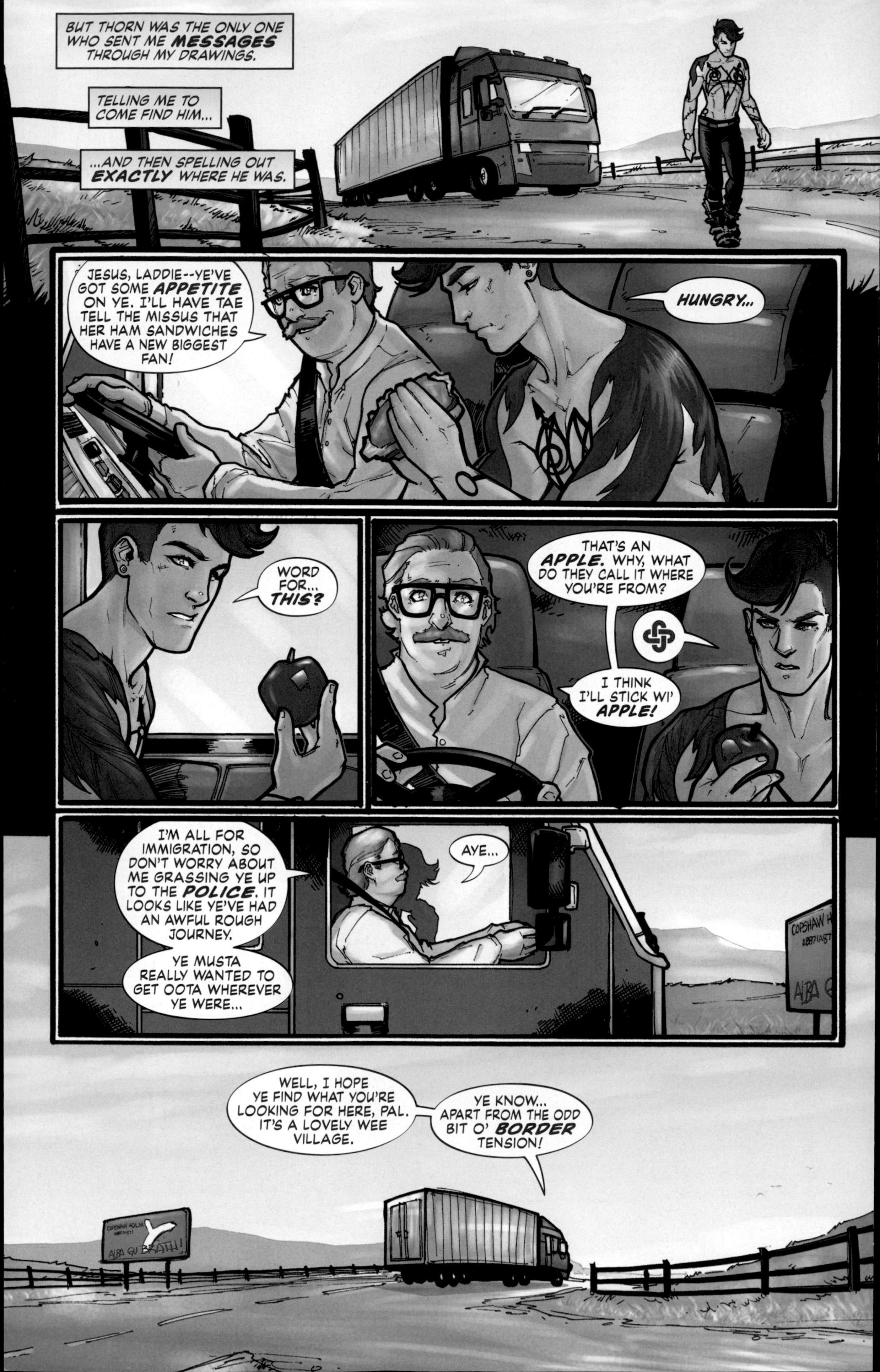
BUT THORN WAS THE ONLY ONE WHO SENT ME MESSAGES THROUGH MY DRAWINGS.
TELLING ME TO COME FIND HIM...
...AND THEN SPELLING OUT EXACTLY WHERE HE WAS.
JESUS, LADDIE--YE'VE GOT SOME APPETITE ON YE. I'LL HAVE TAE TELL THE MISSUS THAT HER HAM SANDWICHES HAVE A NEW BIGGEST FAN!
HUNGRY...
WORD FOR... THIS?
THAT'S AN APPLE. WHY, WHAT DO THEY CALL IT WHERE YOU'RE FROM?
I THINK I'LL STICK WI' APPLE!
I'M ALL FOR IMMIGRATION, SO DON'T WORRY ABOUT ME GRASSING YE UP TO THE POLICE. IT LOOKS LIKE YE'VE HAD AN AWFUL ROUGH JOURNEY.
AYE...
YE MUSTA REALLY WANTED TO GET OOTA WHEREVER YE WERE...
ALBA
WELL, I HOPE YE FIND WHAT YOU'RE LOOKING FOR HERE, PAL. IT'S A LOVELY WEE VILLAGE.
YE KNOW... APART FROM THE ODD BIT O' BORDER TENSION!
ALBA GU BRATH!

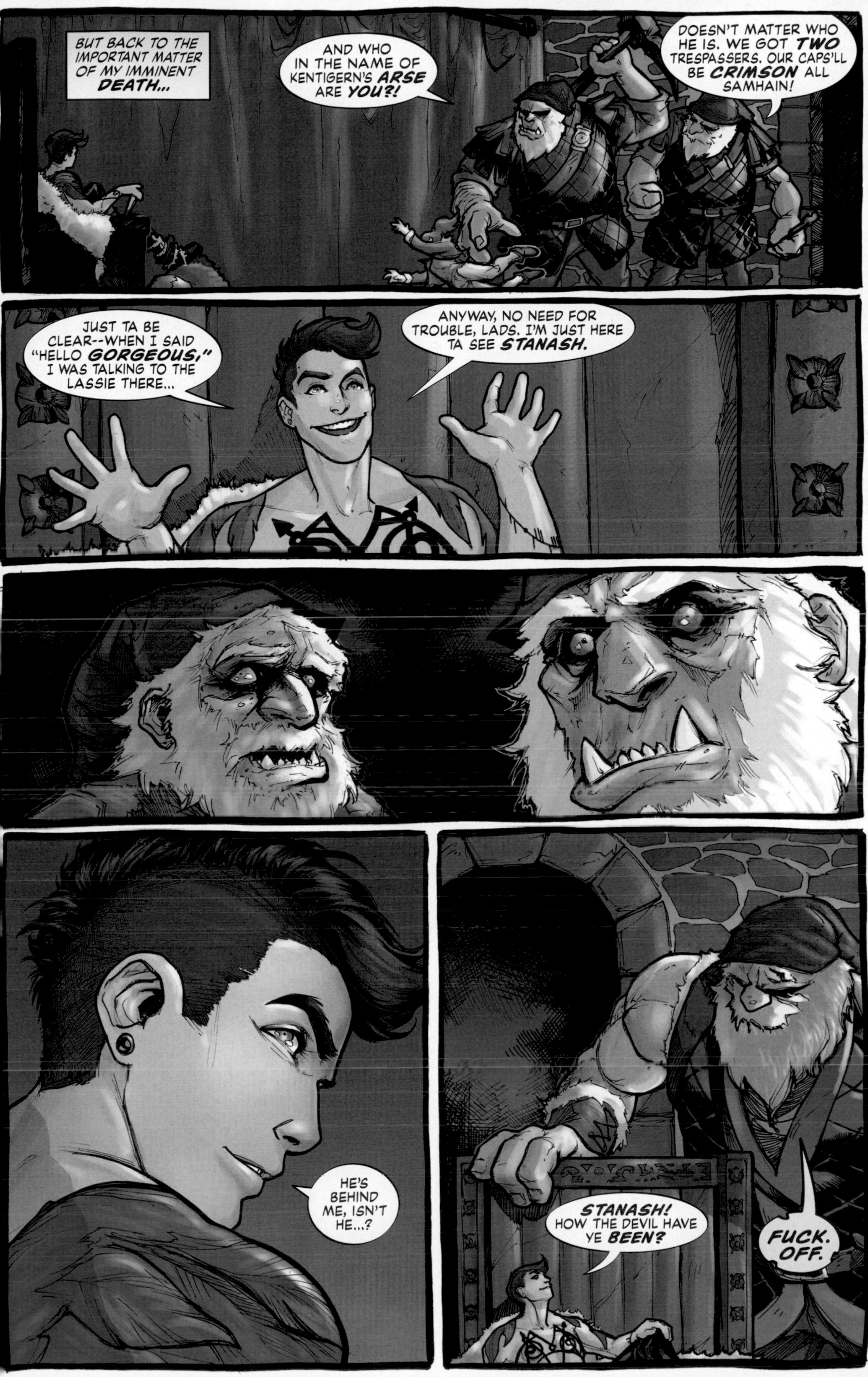
BUT BACK TO THE IMPORTANT MATTER OF MY IMMINENT DEATH...
AND WHO IN THE NAME OF KENTIGERN'S ARSE ARE YOU?!
DOESN'T MATTER WHO HE IS. WE GOT TWO TRESPASSERS. OUR CAPS'LL BE CRIMSON ALL SAMHAIN!
JUST TA BE CLEAR--WHEN I SAID "HELLO GORGEOUS," I WAS TALKING TO THE LASSIE THERE...
ANYWAY, NO NEED FOR TROUBLE, LADS. I'M JUST HERE TA SEE STANASH.
HE'S BEHIND ME, ISN'T HE...?
STANASH! HOW THE DEVIL HAVE YE BEEN?
FUCK. OFF.

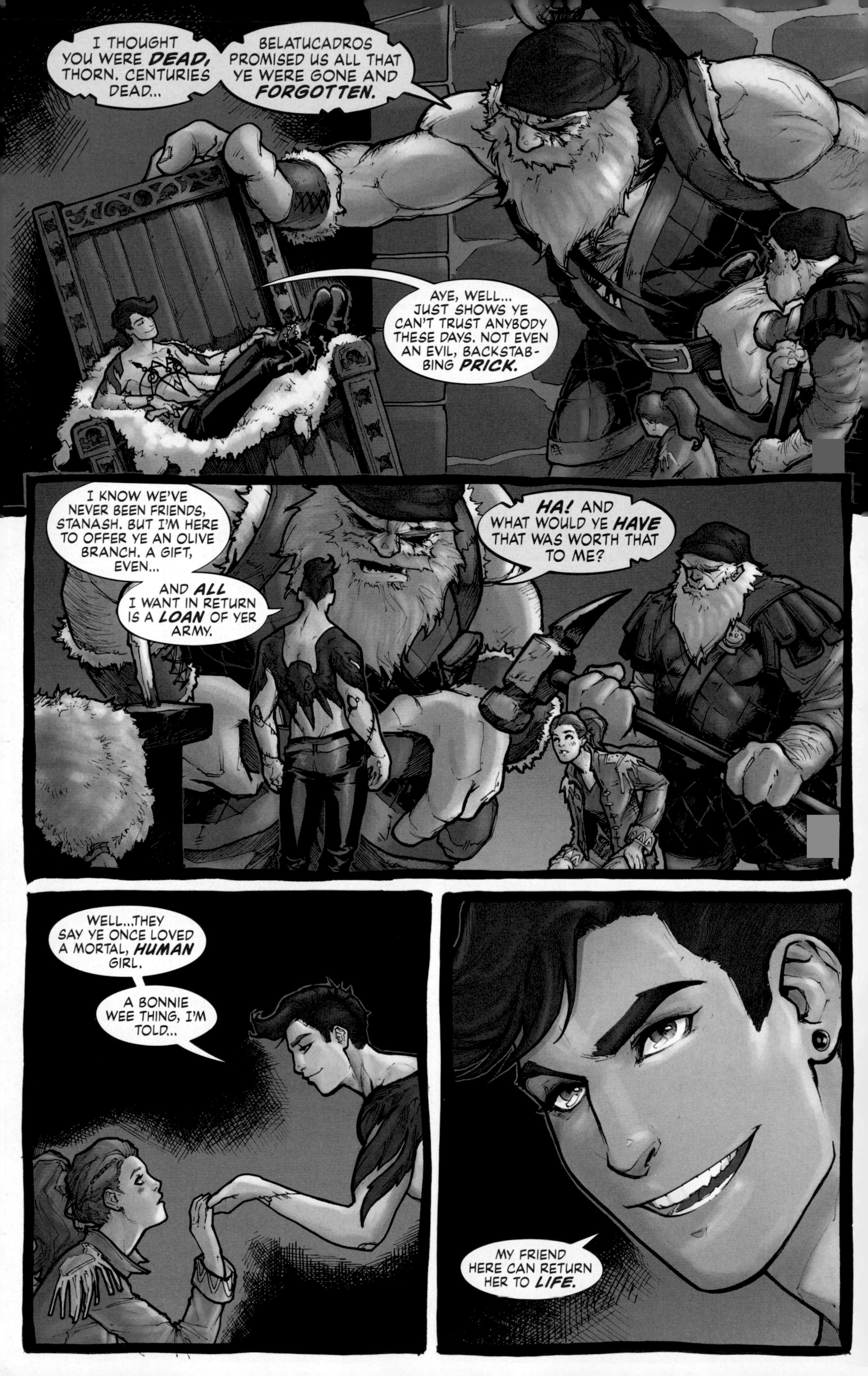
I THOUGHT YOU WERE DEAD, THORN. CENTURIES DEAD...
BELATUCADROS PROMISED US ALL THAT YE WERE GONE AND FORGOTTEN.
AYE, WELL... JUST SHOWS YE CAN'T TRUST ANYBODY THESE DAYS. NOT EVEN AN EVIL, BACKSTABBING PRICK.
I KNOW WE'VE NEVER BEEN FRIENDS, STANASH. BUT I'M HERE TO OFFER YE AN OLIVE BRANCH. A GIFT, EVEN...
AND ALL I WANT IN RETURN IS A LOAN OF YER ARMY.
HA! AND WHAT WOULD YE HAVE THAT WAS WORTH THAT TO ME?
WELL...THEY SAY YE ONCE LOVED A MORTAL, HUMAN GIRL.
A BONNIE WEE THING, I'M TOLD...
MY FRIEND HERE CAN RETURN HER TO LIFE.

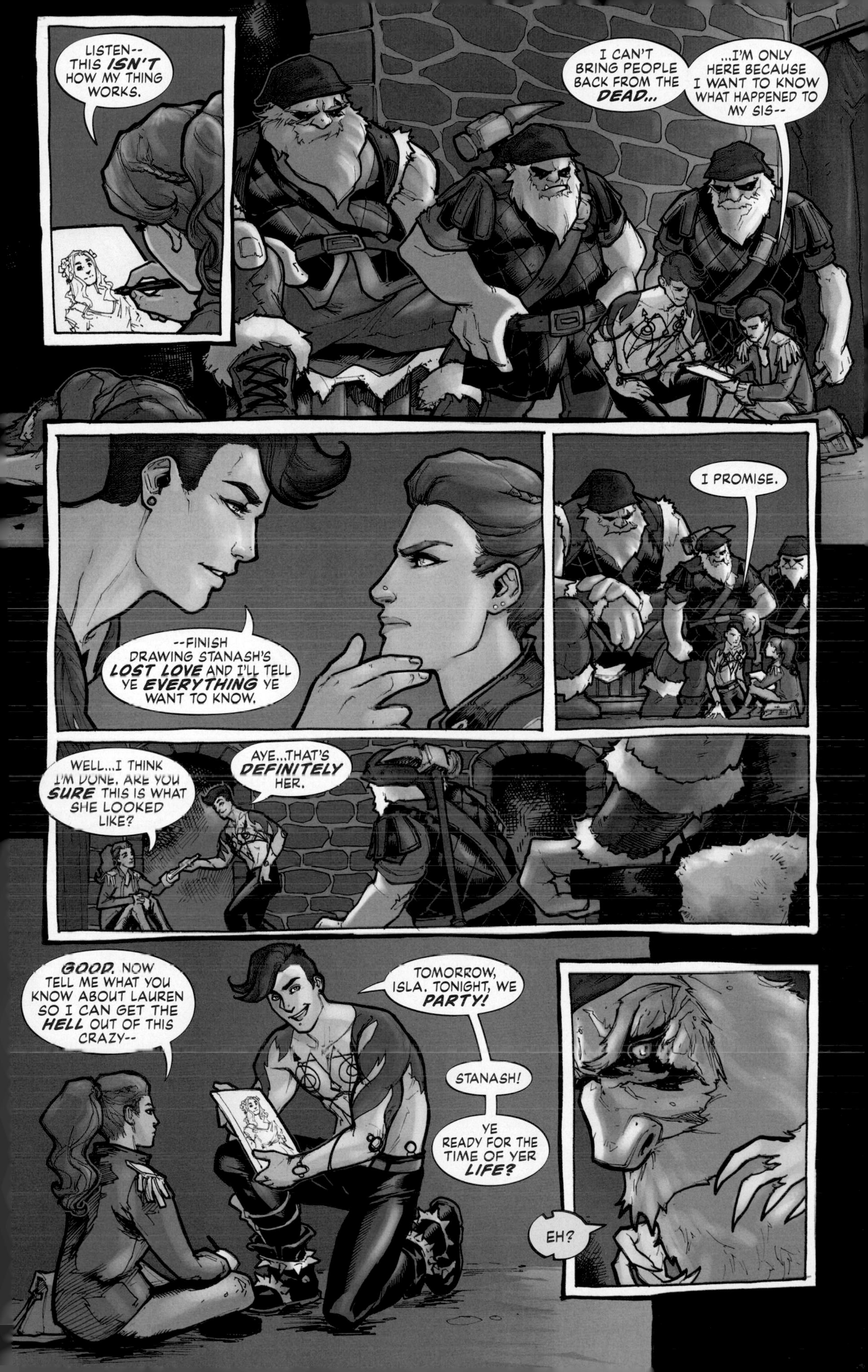
LISTEN-- THIS ISN'T HOW MY THING WORKS.
I CAN'T BRING PEOPLE BACK FROM THE DEAD...
...I'M ONLY HERE BECAUSE I WANT TO KNOW WHAT HAPPENED TO MY SIS--
--FINISH DRAWING STANASH'S LOST LOVE AND I'LL TELL YE EVERYTHING YE WANT TO KNOW.
I PROMISE.
WELL...I THINK I'M DONE. ARE YOU SURE THIS IS WHAT SHE LOOKED LIKE?
AYE...THAT'S DEFINITELY HER.
GOOD. NOW TELL ME WHAT YOU KNOW ABOUT LAUREN SO I CAN GET THE HELL OUT OF THIS CRAZY--
TOMORROW, ISLA. TONIGHT, WE PARTY!
STANASH!
YE READY FOR THE TIME OF YER LIFE?
EH?

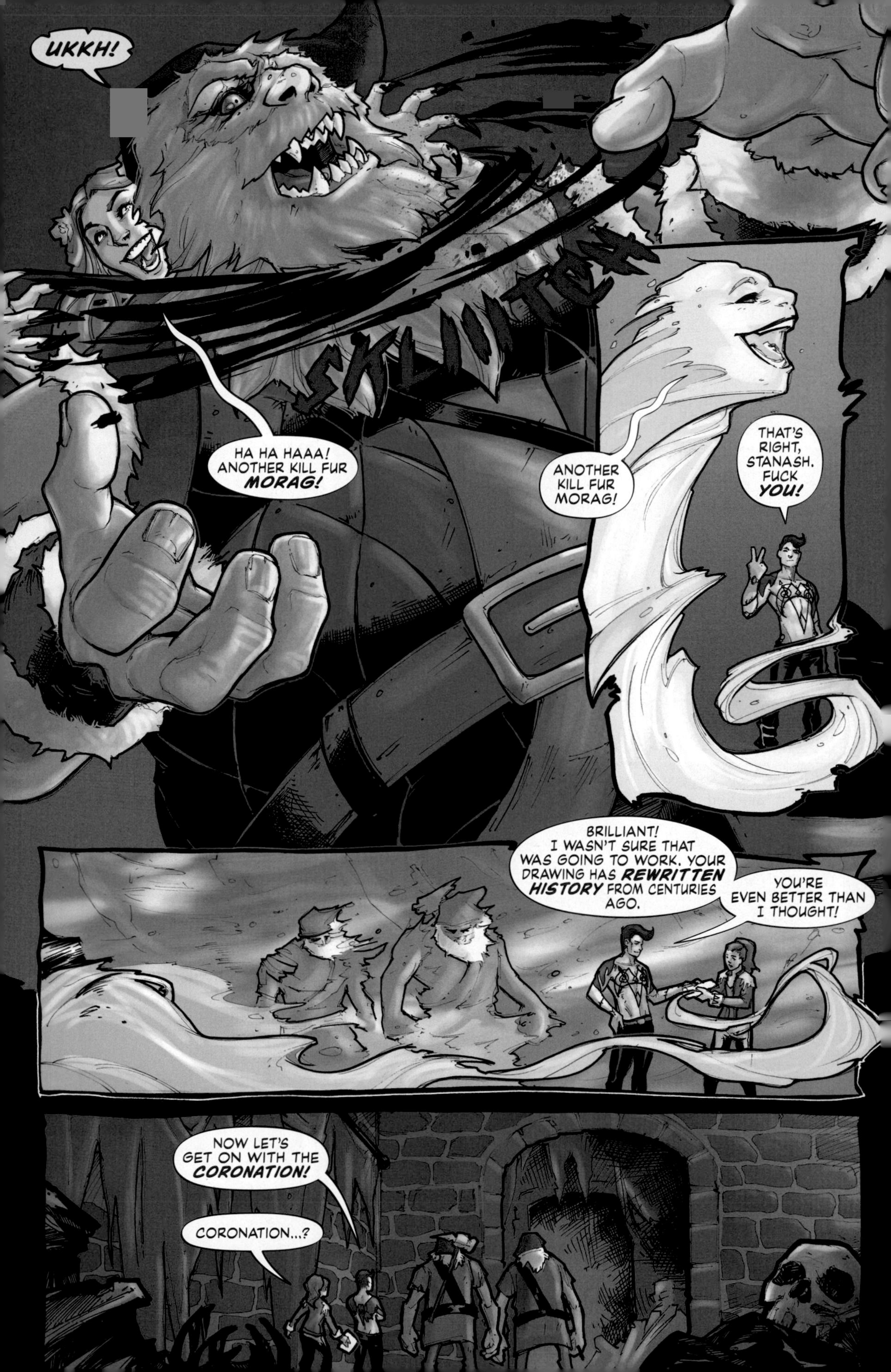
UKKH!
SKLIIITCH
HA HA HAAA! ANOTHER KILL FUR ***MORAG!***
ANOTHER KILL FUR MORAG!
THAT'S RIGHT, STANASH. FUCK ***YOU!***
BRILLIANT! I WASN'T SURE THAT WAS GOING TO WORK. YOUR DRAWING HAS ***REWRITTEN HISTORY*** FROM CENTURIES AGO.
YOU'RE EVEN BETTER THAN I THOUGHT!
NOW LET'S GET ON WITH THE ***CORONATION!***
CORONATION...?

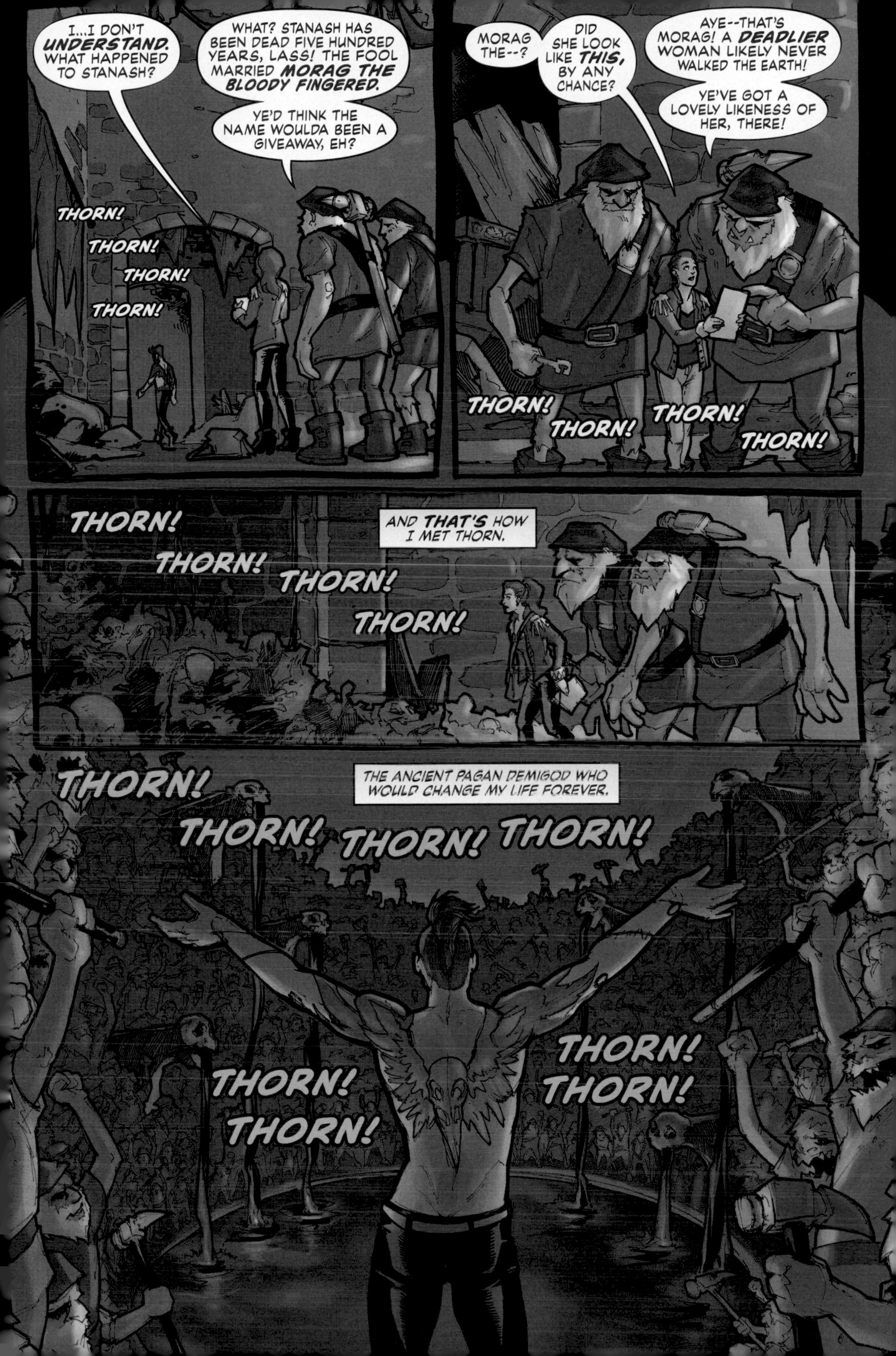
I...I DON'T UNDERSTAND. WHAT HAPPENED TO STANASH?
WHAT? STANASH HAS BEEN DEAD FIVE HUNDRED YEARS, LASS! THE FOOL MARRIED MORAG THE BLOODY FINGERED.
YE'D THINK THE NAME WOULDA BEEN A GIVEAWAY, EH?
THORN!
THORN!
THORN!
THORN!
MORAG THE--?
DID SHE LOOK LIKE THIS, BY ANY CHANCE?
AYE--THAT'S MORAG! A DEADLIER WOMAN LIKELY NEVER WALKED THE EARTH!
YE'VE GOT A LOVELY LIKENESS OF HER, THERE!
THORN!
THORN!
THORN!
THORN!
THORN!
THORN!
THORN!
THORN!
AND THAT'S HOW I MET THORN.
THE ANCIENT PAGAN DEMIGOD WHO WOULD CHANGE MY LIFE FOREVER.
THORN!
THORN!
THORN!
THORN!
THORN!
THORN!
THORN!
THORN!

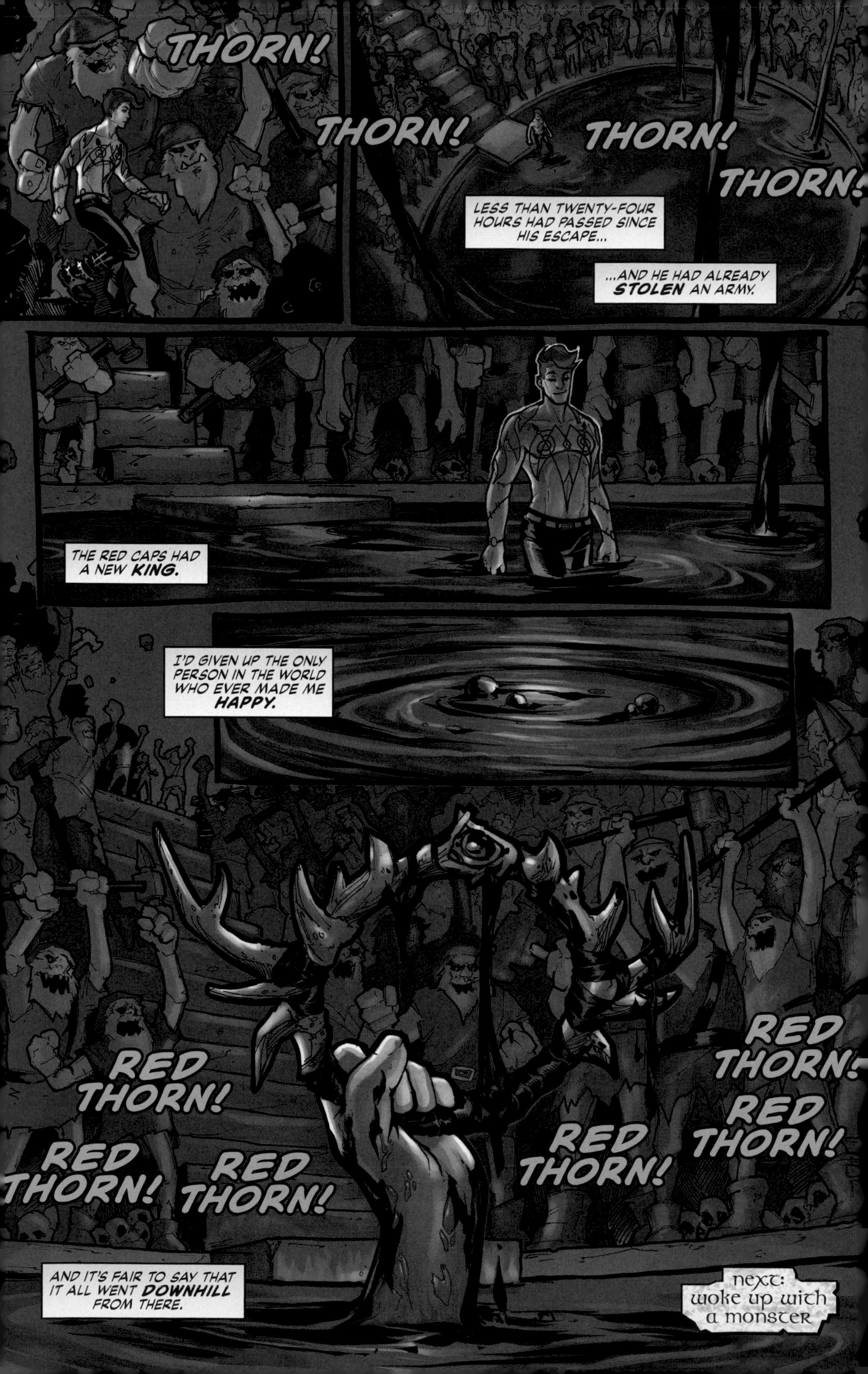
THORN!
THORN!
THORN!
THORN!
LESS THAN TWENTY-FOUR HOURS HAD PASSED SINCE HIS ESCAPE...
...AND HE HAD ALREADY STOLEN AN ARMY.
THE RED CAPS HAD A NEW KING.
I'D GIVEN UP THE ONLY PERSON IN THE WORLD WHO EVER MADE ME HAPPY.
RED THORN!
RED THORN!
RED THORN!
RED THORN!
RED THORN!
RED THORN!
AND IT'S FAIR TO SAY THAT IT ALL WENT DOWNHILL FROM THERE.
next: woke up with a monster

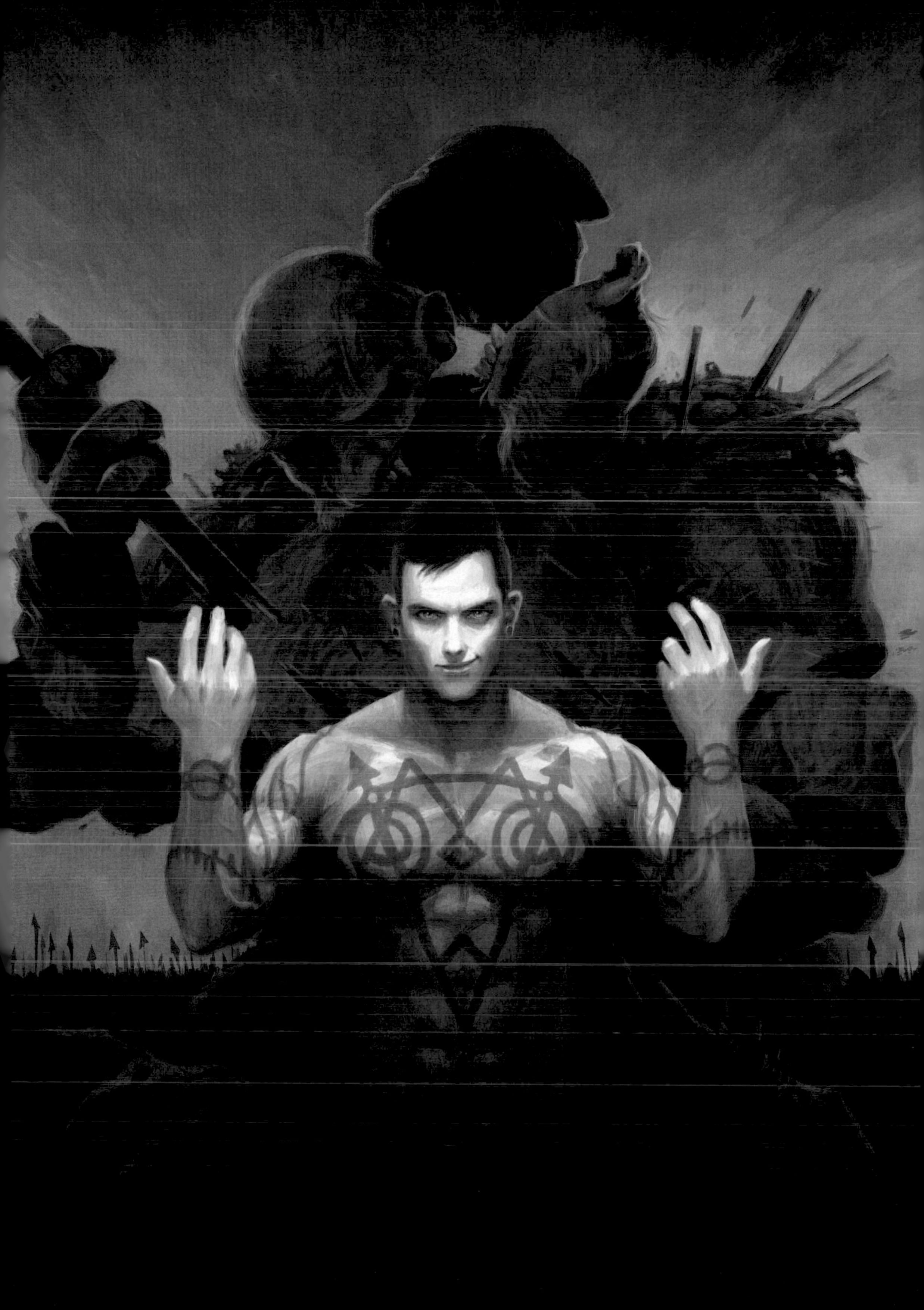

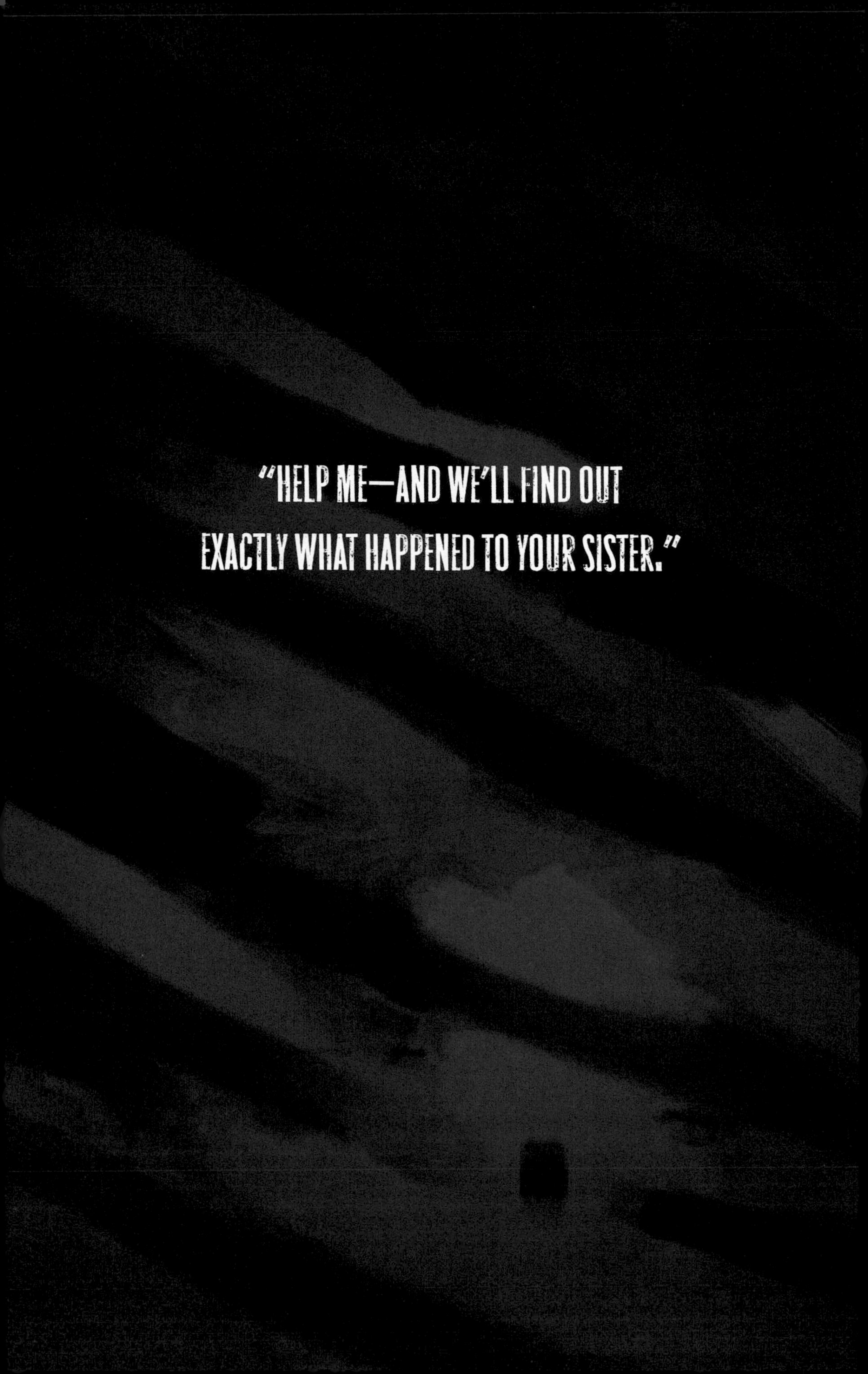
"HELP ME—AND WE'LL FIND OUT
EXACTLY WHAT HAPPENED TO YOUR SISTER."

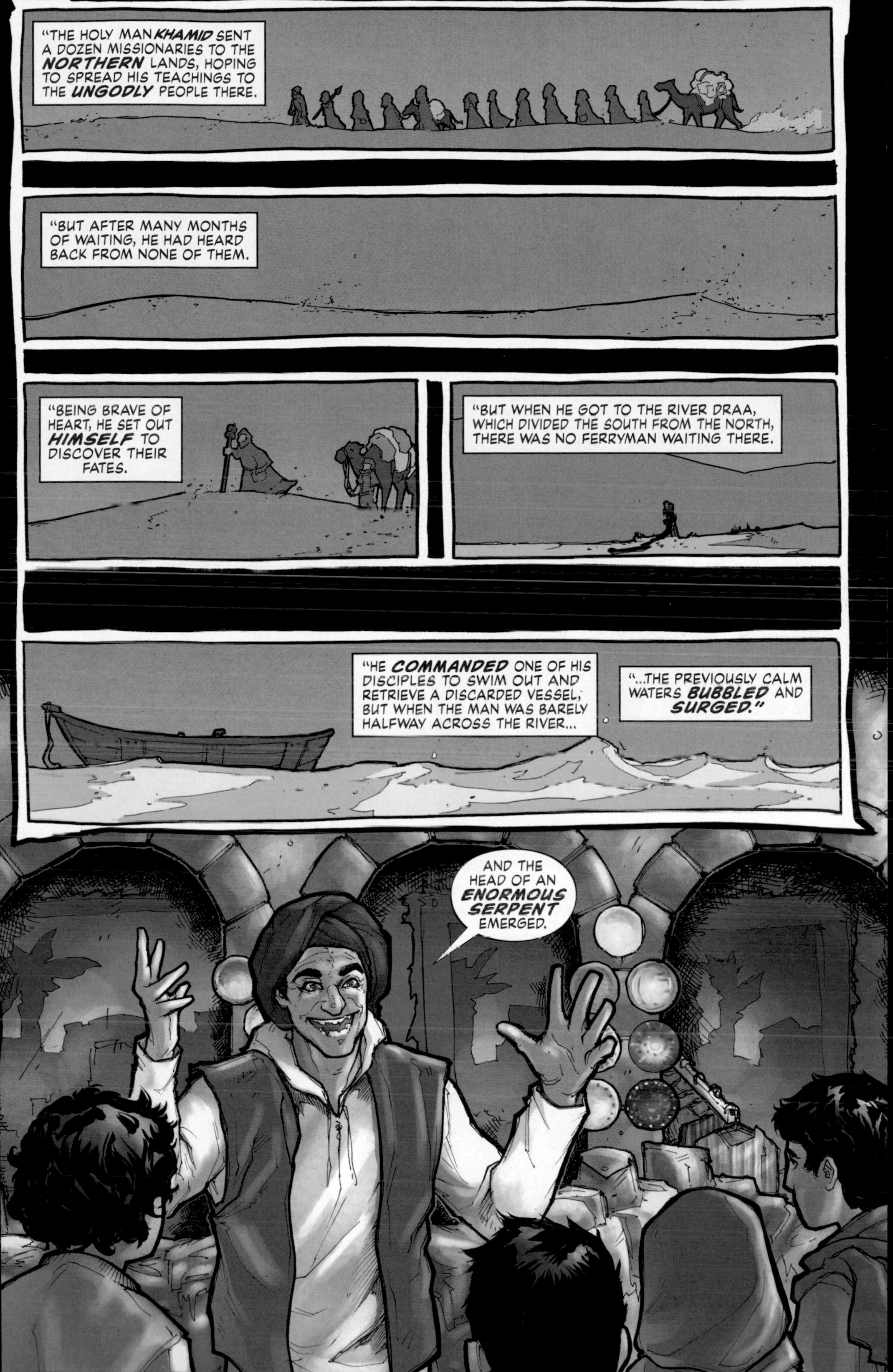
"THE HOLY MAN KHAMID SENT A DOZEN MISSIONARIES TO THE NORTHERN LANDS, HOPING TO SPREAD HIS TEACHINGS TO THE UNGODLY PEOPLE THERE.
"BUT AFTER MANY MONTHS OF WAITING, HE HAD HEARD BACK FROM NONE OF THEM.
"BEING BRAVE OF HEART, HE SET OUT HIMSELF TO DISCOVER THEIR FATES.
"BUT WHEN HE GOT TO THE RIVER DRAA, WHICH DIVIDED THE SOUTH FROM THE NORTH, THERE WAS NO FERRYMAN WAITING THERE.
"HE COMMANDED ONE OF HIS DISCIPLES TO SWIM OUT AND RETRIEVE A DISCARDED VESSEL, BUT WHEN THE MAN WAS BARELY HALFWAY ACROSS THE RIVER...
"...THE PREVIOUSLY CALM WATERS BUBBLED AND SURGED."
AND THE HEAD OF AN ENORMOUS SERPENT EMERGED.

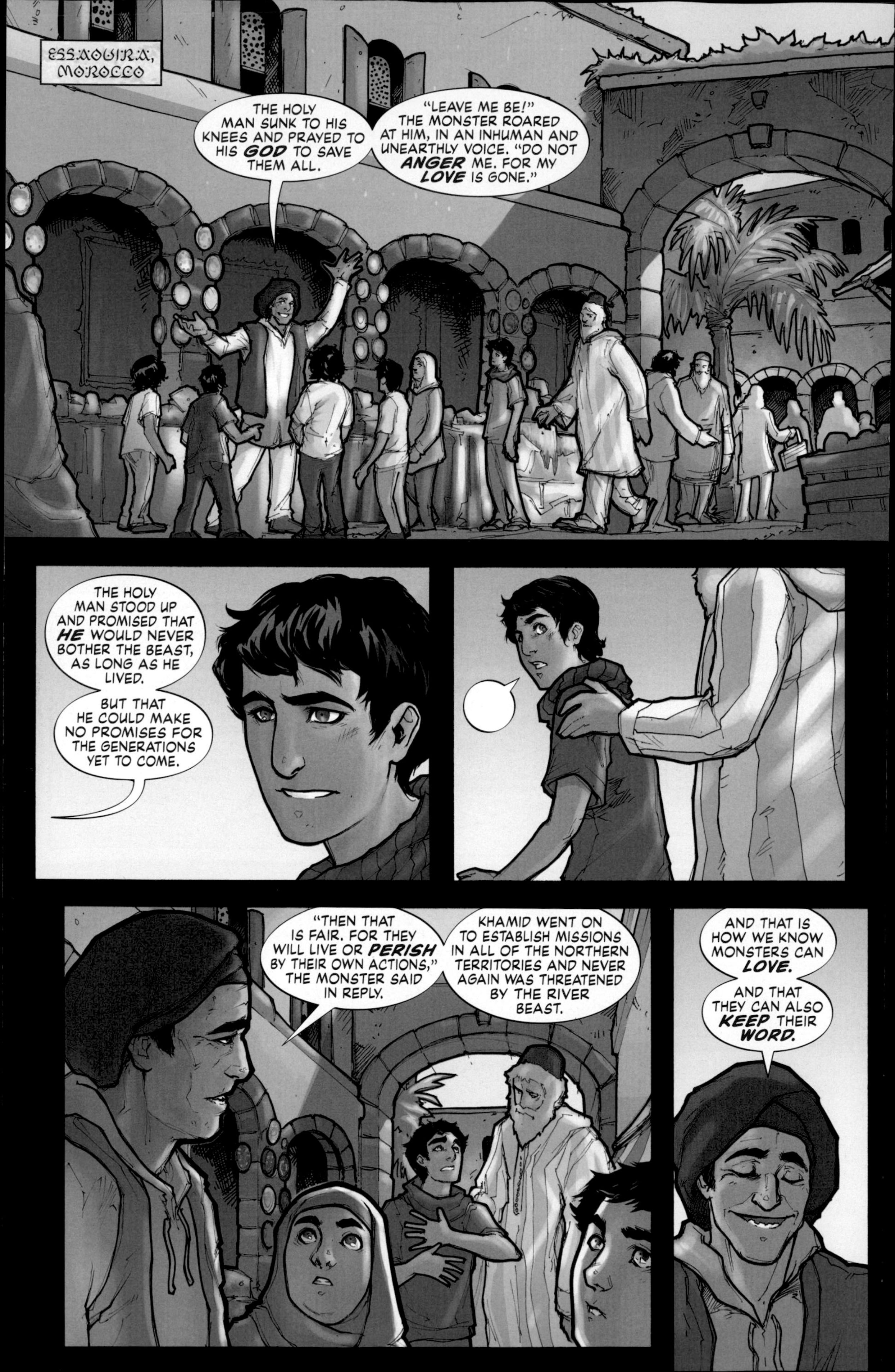
ESSAOUIRA, MOROCCO
THE HOLY MAN SUNK TO HIS KNEES AND PRAYED TO HIS GOD TO SAVE THEM ALL.
"LEAVE ME BE!" THE MONSTER ROARED AT HIM, IN AN INHUMAN AND UNEARTHLY VOICE. "DO NOT ANGER ME. FOR MY LOVE IS GONE."
THE HOLY MAN STOOD UP AND PROMISED THAT HE WOULD NEVER BOTHER THE BEAST, AS LONG AS HE LIVED.
BUT THAT HE COULD MAKE NO PROMISES FOR THE GENERATIONS YET TO COME.
"THEN THAT IS FAIR. FOR THEY WILL LIVE OR PERISH BY THEIR OWN ACTIONS," THE MONSTER SAID IN REPLY.
KHAMID WENT ON TO ESTABLISH MISSIONS IN ALL OF THE NORTHERN TERRITORIES AND NEVER AGAIN WAS THREATENED BY THE RIVER BEAST.
AND THAT IS HOW WE KNOW MONSTERS CAN LOVE.
AND THAT THEY CAN ALSO KEEP THEIR WORD.

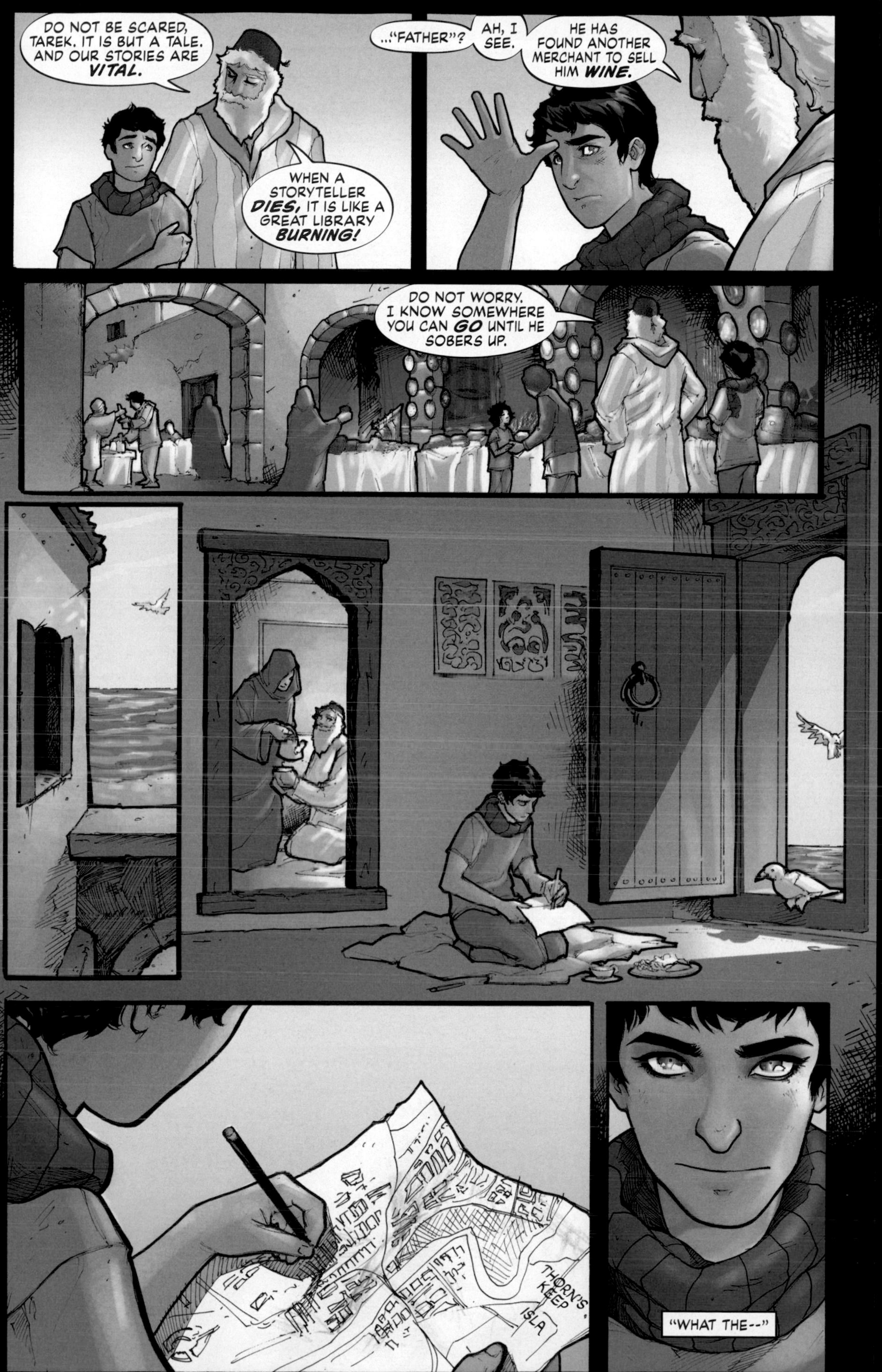
DO NOT BE SCARED, TAREK. IT IS BUT A TALE. AND OUR STORIES ARE VITAL.
WHEN A STORYTELLER DIES, IT IS LIKE A GREAT LIBRARY BURNING!
..."FATHER"?
AH, I SEE.
HE HAS FOUND ANOTHER MERCHANT TO SELL HIM WINE.
DO NOT WORRY. I KNOW SOMEWHERE YOU CAN GO UNTIL HE SOBERS UP.
THORN'S KEEP
ISLA
"WHAT THE--"

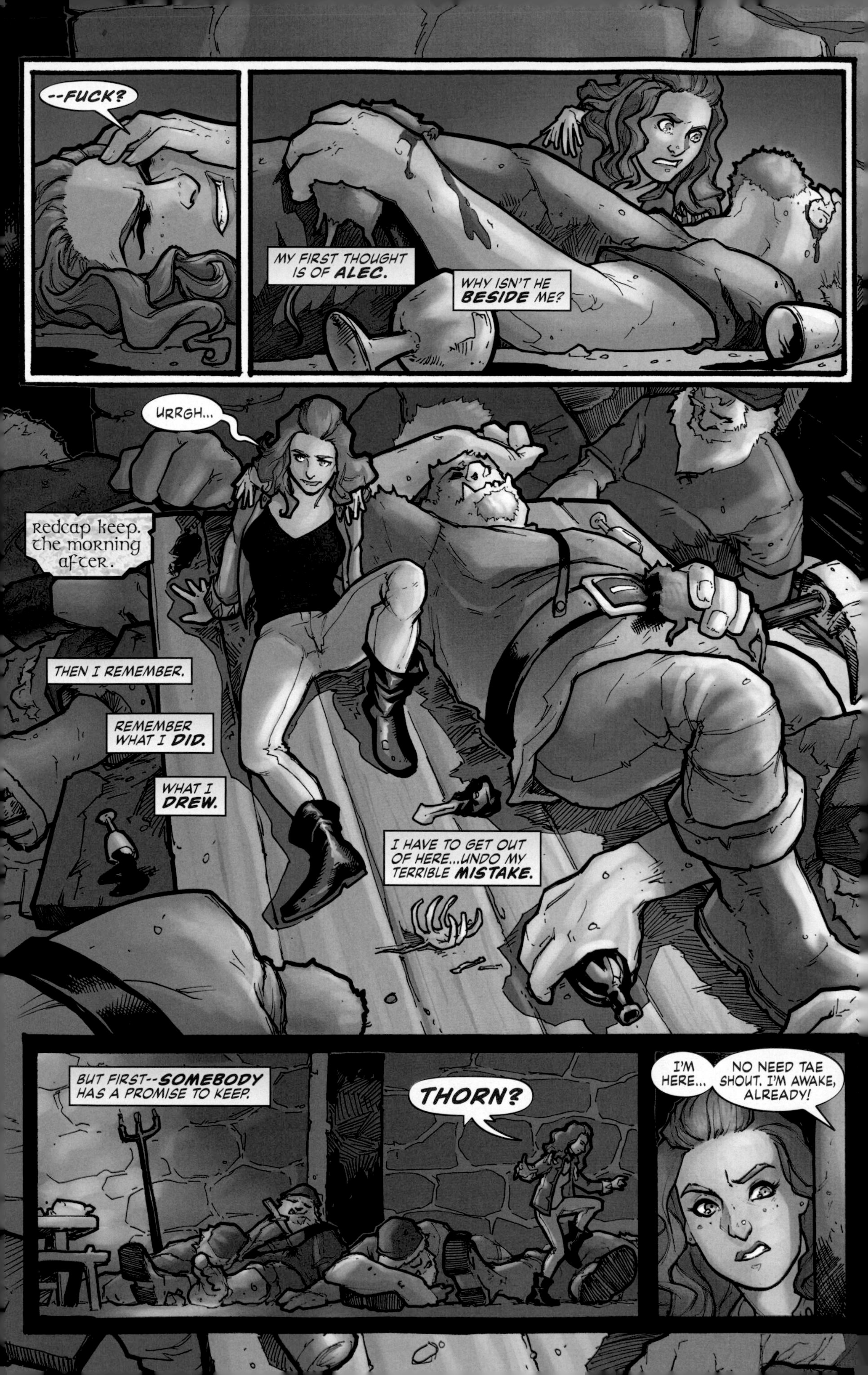
--FUCK?
MY FIRST THOUGHT IS OF ALEC.
WHY ISN'T HE BESIDE ME?
URRGH...
Redcap keep. the morning after.
THEN I REMEMBER.
REMEMBER WHAT I DID.
WHAT I DREW.
I HAVE TO GET OUT OF HERE...UNDO MY TERRIBLE MISTAKE.
BUT FIRST--SOMEBODY HAS A PROMISE TO KEEP.
THORN?
I'M HERE...
NO NEED TAE SHOUT. I'M AWAKE, ALREADY!

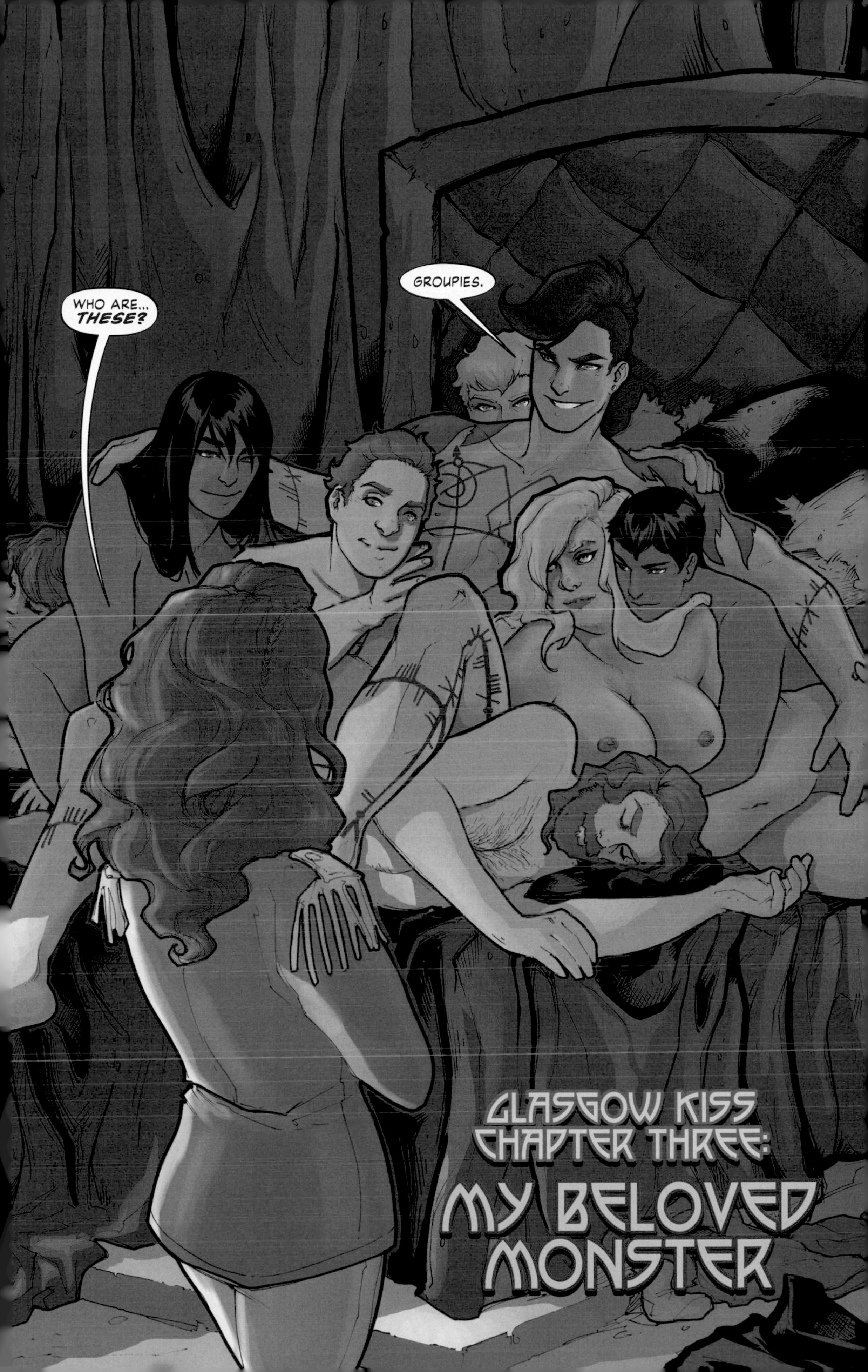
WHO ARE... THESE?
GROUPIES.
GLASGOW KISS CHAPTER THREE:
MY BELOVED MONSTER

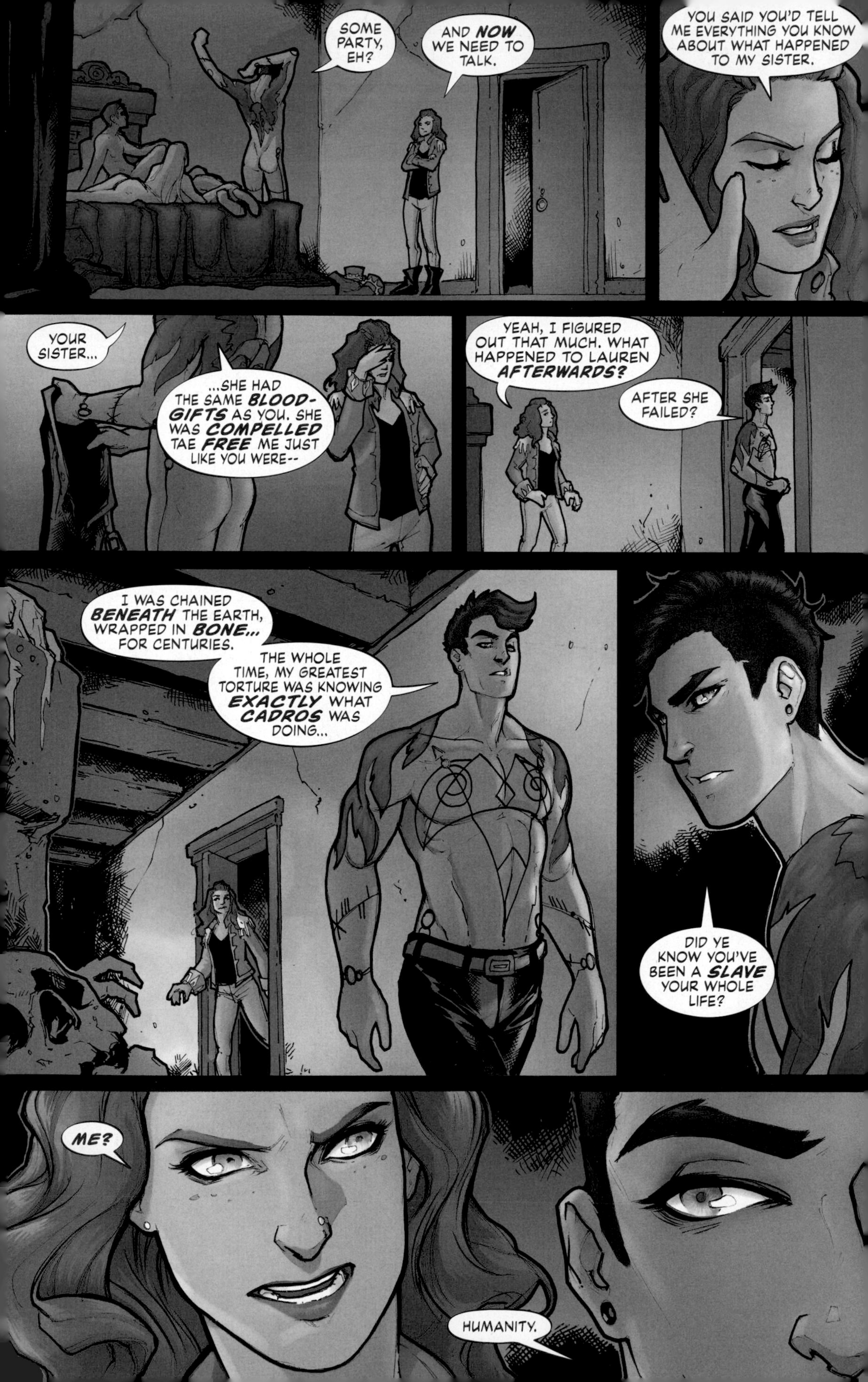
SOME PARTY, EH?
AND NOW WE NEED TO TALK.
YOU SAID YOU'D TELL ME EVERYTHING YOU KNOW ABOUT WHAT HAPPENED TO MY SISTER.
YOUR SISTER...
...SHE HAD THE SAME BLOOD-GIFTS AS YOU. SHE WAS COMPELLED TAE FREE ME JUST LIKE YOU WERE--
YEAH, I FIGURED OUT THAT MUCH. WHAT HAPPENED TO LAUREN AFTERWARDS?
AFTER SHE FAILED?
I WAS CHAINED BENEATH THE EARTH, WRAPPED IN BONE... FOR CENTURIES.
THE WHOLE TIME, MY GREATEST TORTURE WAS KNOWING EXACTLY WHAT CADROS WAS DOING...
DID YE KNOW YOU'VE BEEN A SLAVE YOUR WHOLE LIFE?
ME?
HUMANITY.

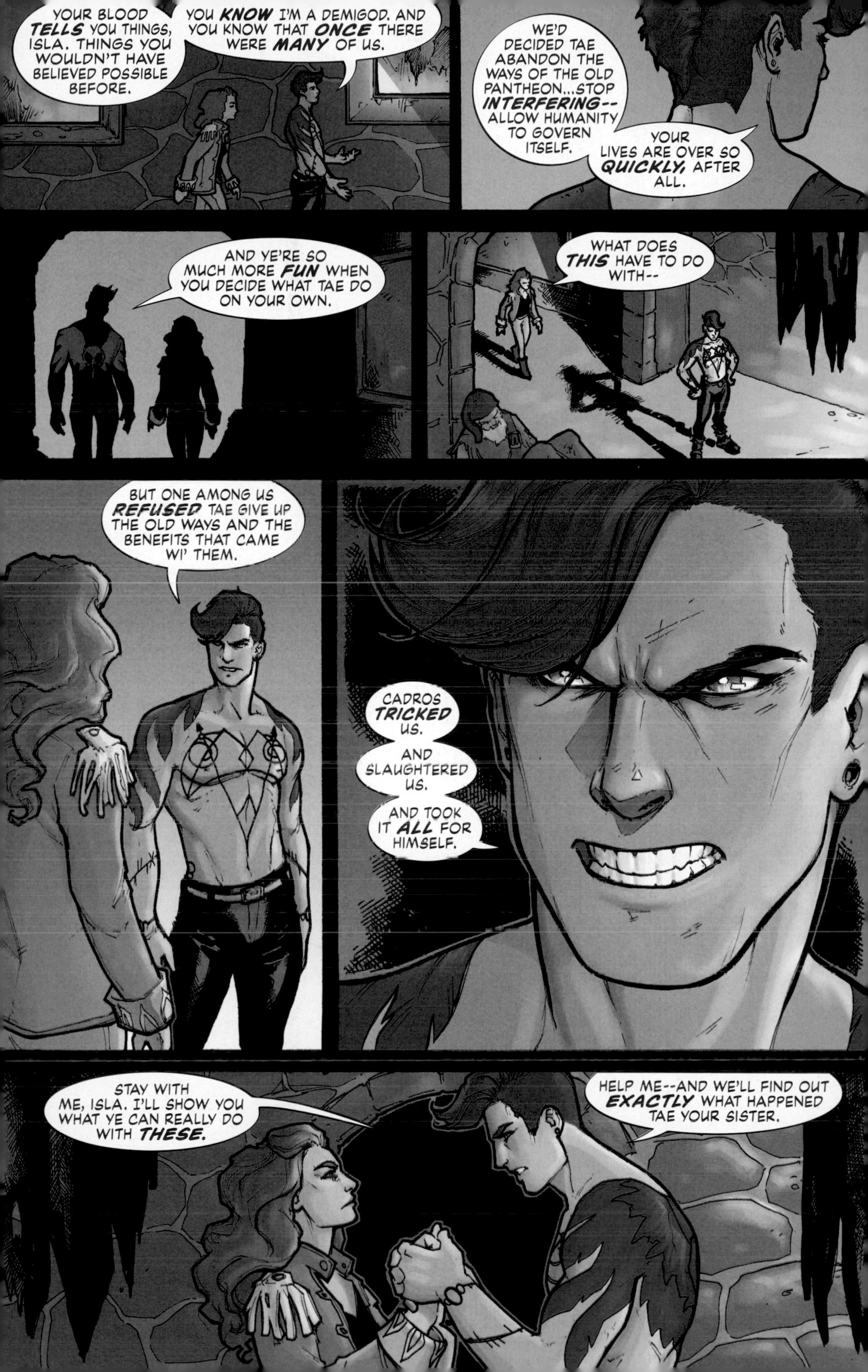

YOUR BLOOD TELLS YOU THINGS, ISLA. THINGS YOU WOULDN'T HAVE BELIEVED POSSIBLE BEFORE.
YOU KNOW I'M A DEMIGOD. AND YOU KNOW THAT ONCE THERE WERE MANY OF US.
WE'D DECIDED TAE ABANDON THE WAYS OF THE OLD PANTHEON...STOP INTERFERING-- ALLOW HUMANITY TO GOVERN ITSELF.
YOUR LIVES ARE OVER SO QUICKLY, AFTER ALL.
AND YE'RE SO MUCH MORE FUN WHEN YOU DECIDE WHAT TAE DO ON YOUR OWN.
WHAT DOES THIS HAVE TO DO WITH--
BUT ONE AMONG US REFUSED TAE GIVE UP THE OLD WAYS AND THE BENEFITS THAT CAME WI' THEM.
CADROS TRICKED US.
AND SLAUGHTERED US.
AND TOOK IT ALL FOR HIMSELF.
STAY WITH ME, ISLA. I'LL SHOW YOU WHAT YE CAN REALLY DO WITH THESE.
HELP ME--AND WE'LL FIND OUT EXACTLY WHAT HAPPENED TAE YOUR SISTER.

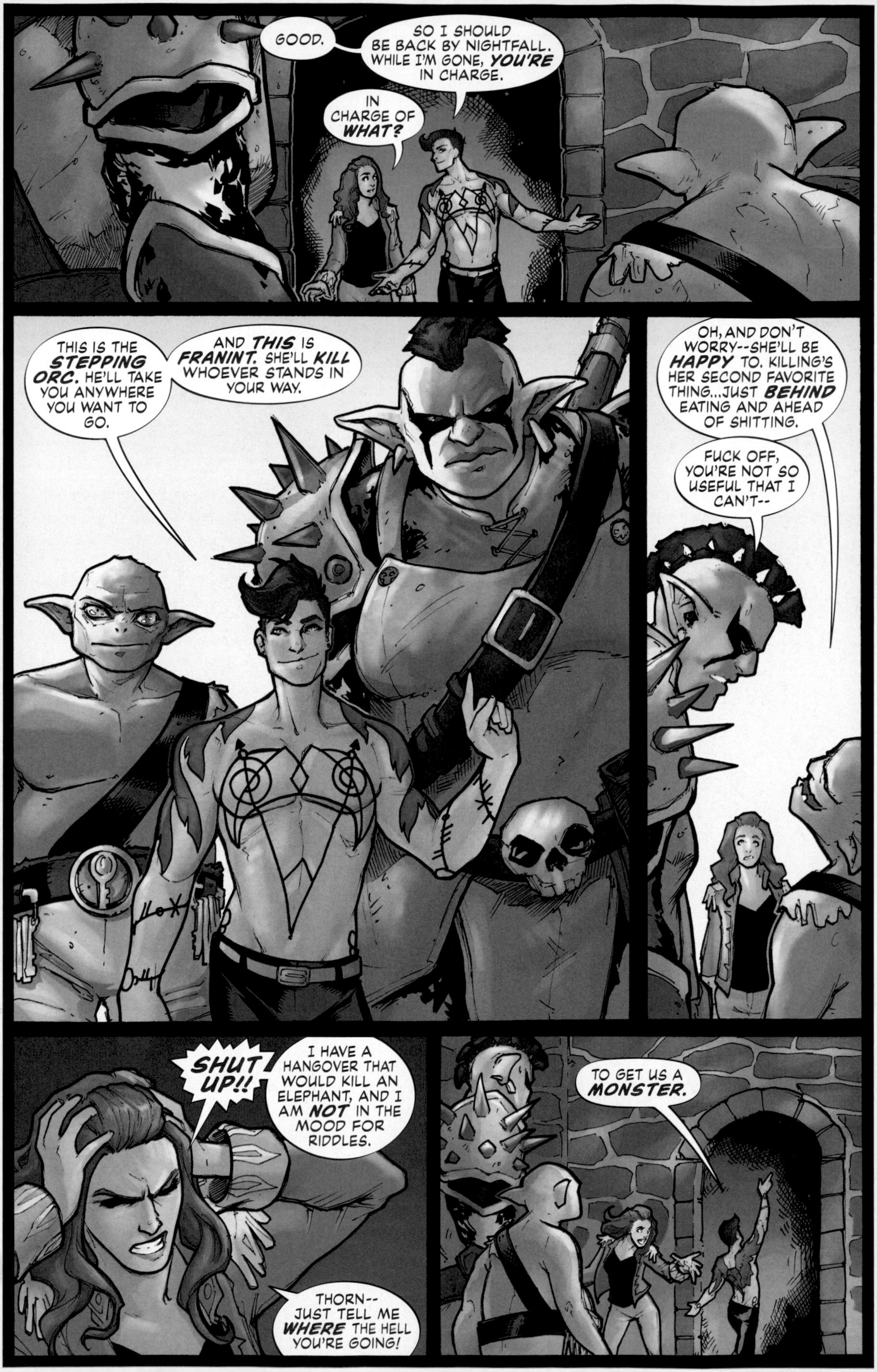
SO I SHOULD BE BACK BY NIGHTFALL. WHILE I'M GONE, *YOU'RE* IN CHARGE.
GOOD.
IN CHARGE OF *WHAT?*
THIS IS THE *STEPPING ORC.* HE'LL TAKE YOU ANYWHERE YOU WANT TO GO.
AND *THIS* IS *FRANINT.* SHE'LL *KILL* WHOEVER STANDS IN YOUR WAY.
OH, AND DON'T WORRY--SHE'LL BE *HAPPY* TO. KILLING'S HER SECOND FAVORITE THING...JUST *BEHIND* EATING AND AHEAD OF SHITTING.
FUCK OFF, YOU'RE NOT SO USEFUL THAT I CAN'T--
SHUT UP!!
I HAVE A HANGOVER THAT WOULD KILL AN ELEPHANT, AND I AM *NOT* IN THE MOOD FOR RIDDLES.
THORN-- JUST TELL ME *WHERE* THE HELL YOU'RE GOING!
TO GET US A *MONSTER.*

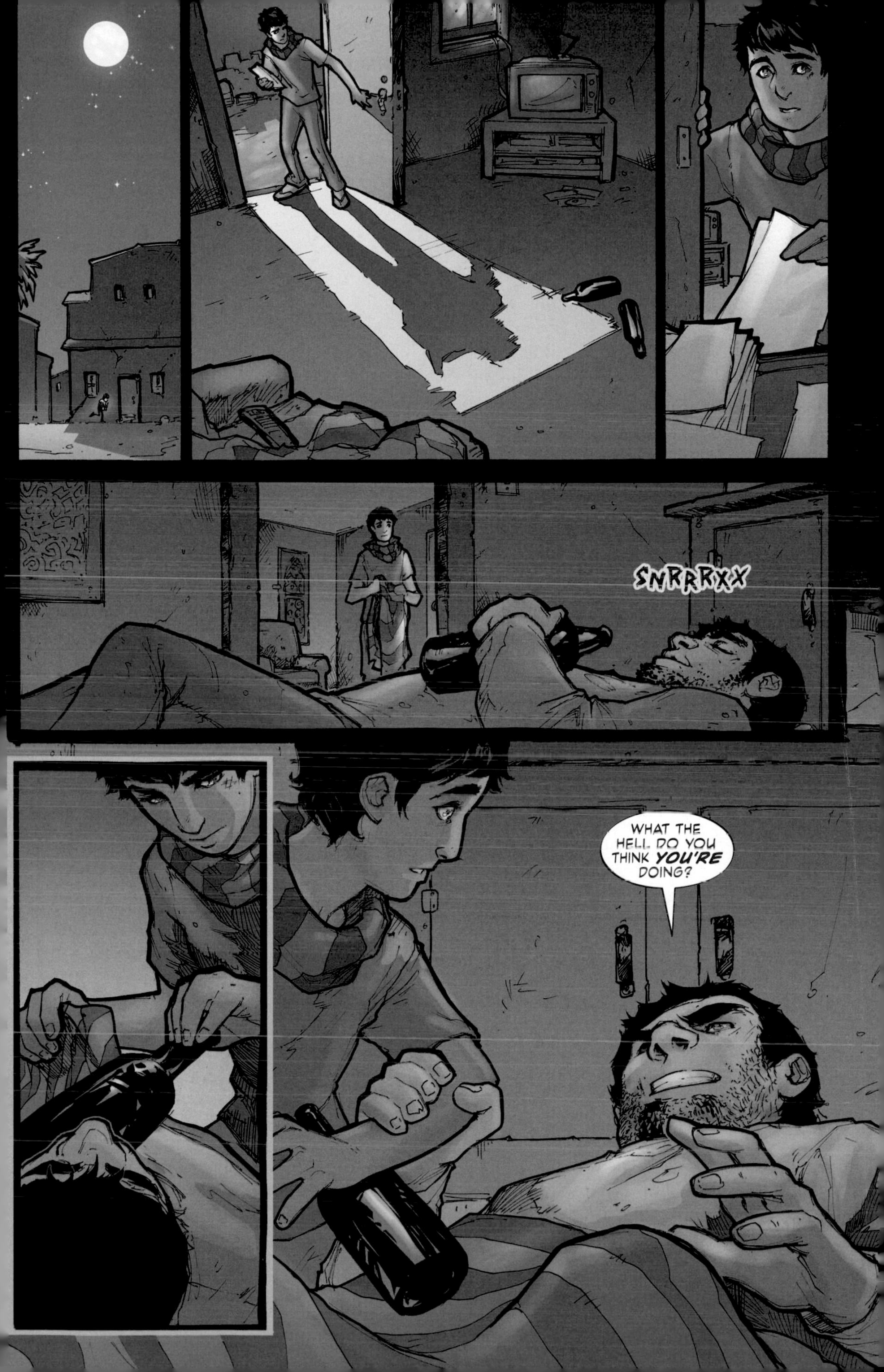
SNRRRXX
WHAT THE HELL DO YOU THINK *YOU'RE* DOING?

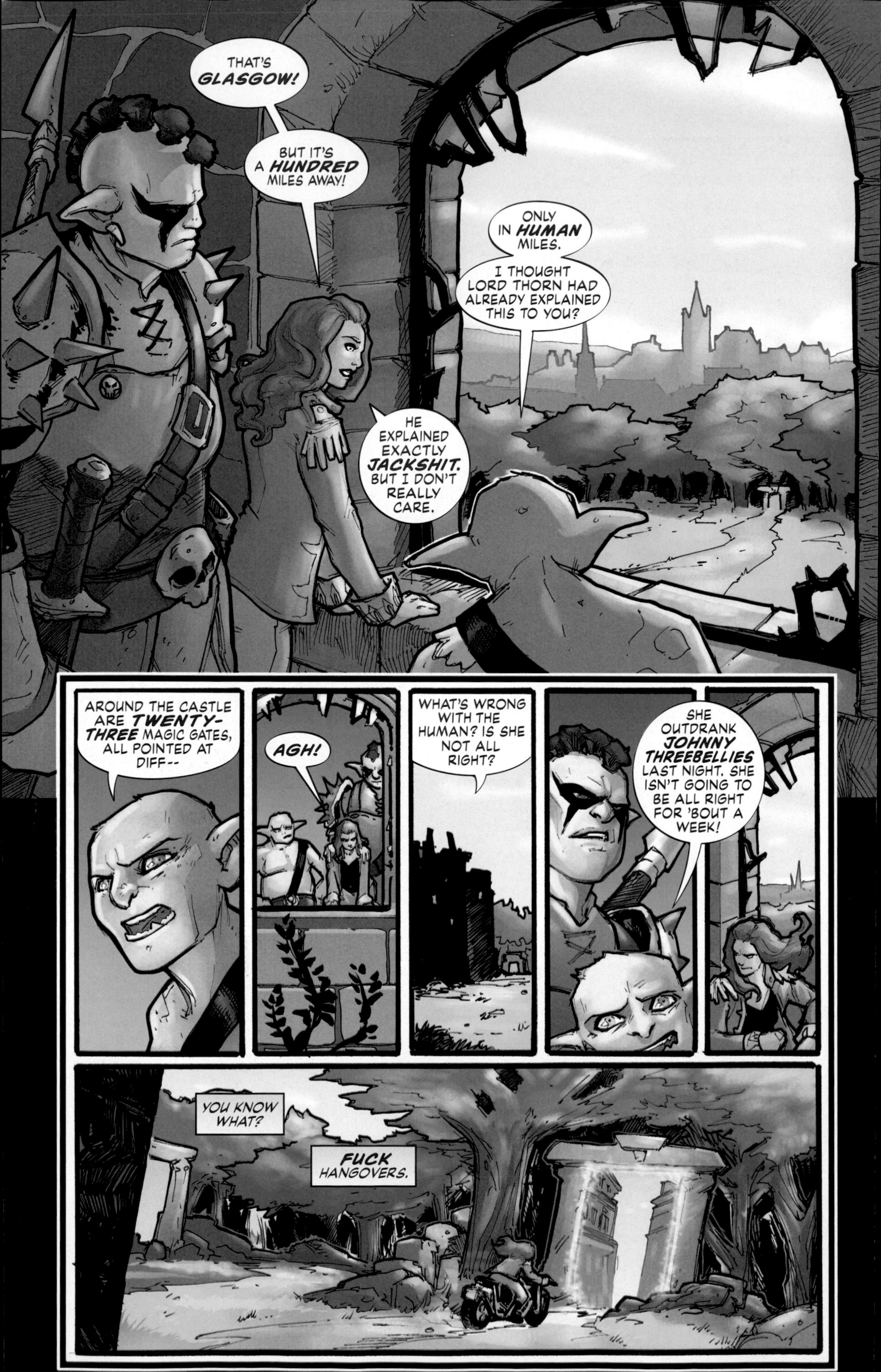
THAT'S GLASGOW!
BUT IT'S A HUNDRED MILES AWAY!
ONLY IN HUMAN MILES.
I THOUGHT LORD THORN HAD ALREADY EXPLAINED THIS TO YOU?
HE EXPLAINED EXACTLY JACKSHIT. BUT I DON'T REALLY CARE.
AROUND THE CASTLE ARE TWENTY-THREE MAGIC GATES, ALL POINTED AT DIFF--
AGH!
WHAT'S WRONG WITH THE HUMAN? IS SHE NOT ALL RIGHT?
SHE OUTDRANK JOHNNY THREEBELLIES LAST NIGHT. SHE ISN'T GOING TO BE ALL RIGHT FOR 'BOUT A WEEK!
YOU KNOW WHAT?
FUCK HANGOVERS.

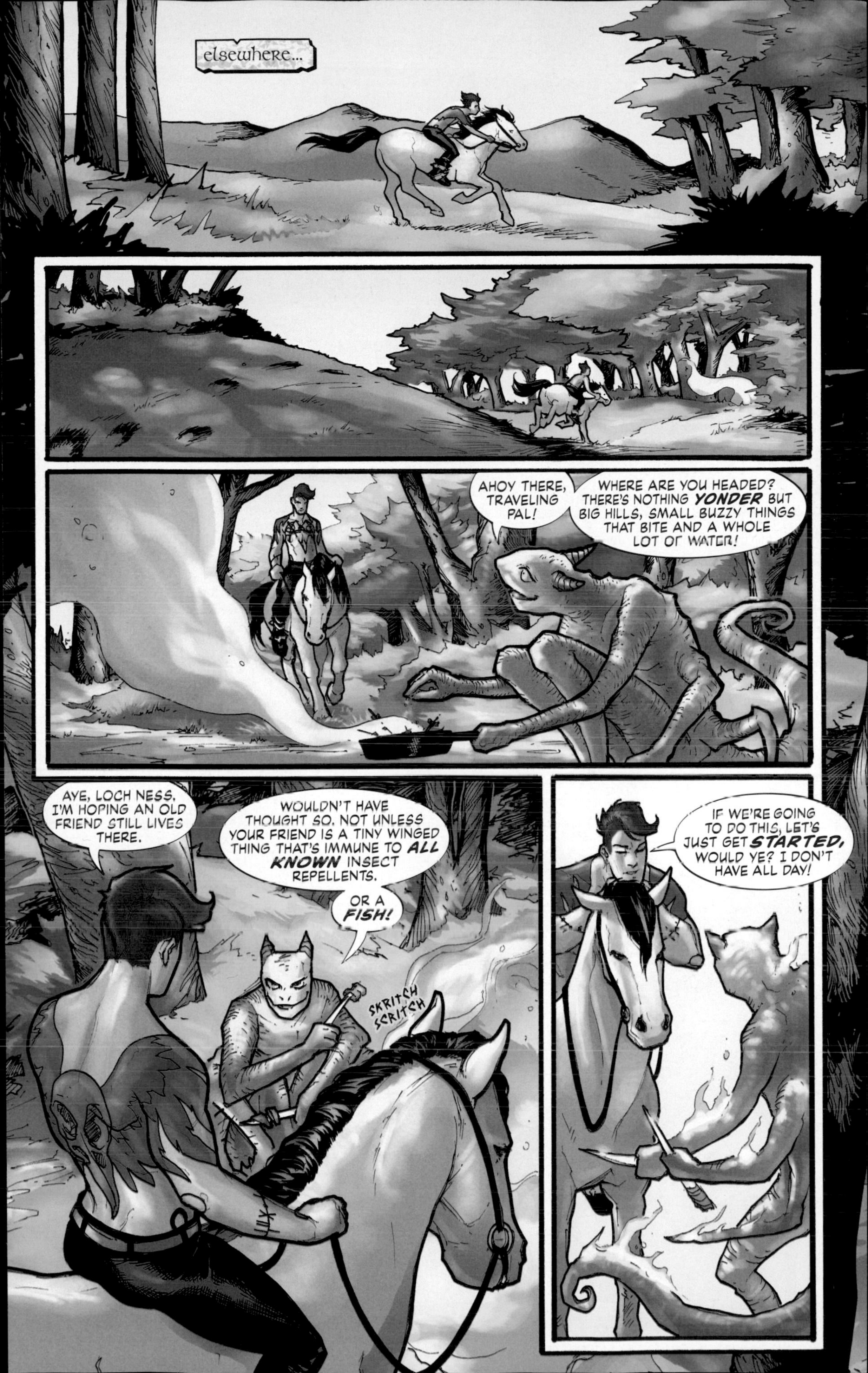
elsewhere...
AHOY THERE, TRAVELING PAL!
WHERE ARE YOU HEADED? THERE'S NOTHING YONDER BUT BIG HILLS, SMALL BUZZY THINGS THAT BITE AND A WHOLE LOT OF WATER!
AYE, LOCH NESS. I'M HOPING AN OLD FRIEND STILL LIVES THERE.
WOULDN'T HAVE THOUGHT SO. NOT UNLESS YOUR FRIEND IS A TINY WINGED THING THAT'S IMMUNE TO ALL KNOWN INSECT REPELLENTS.
OR A FISH!
SKRITCH SCRITCH
IF WE'RE GOING TO DO THIS, LET'S JUST GET STARTED, WOULD YE? I DON'T HAVE ALL DAY!

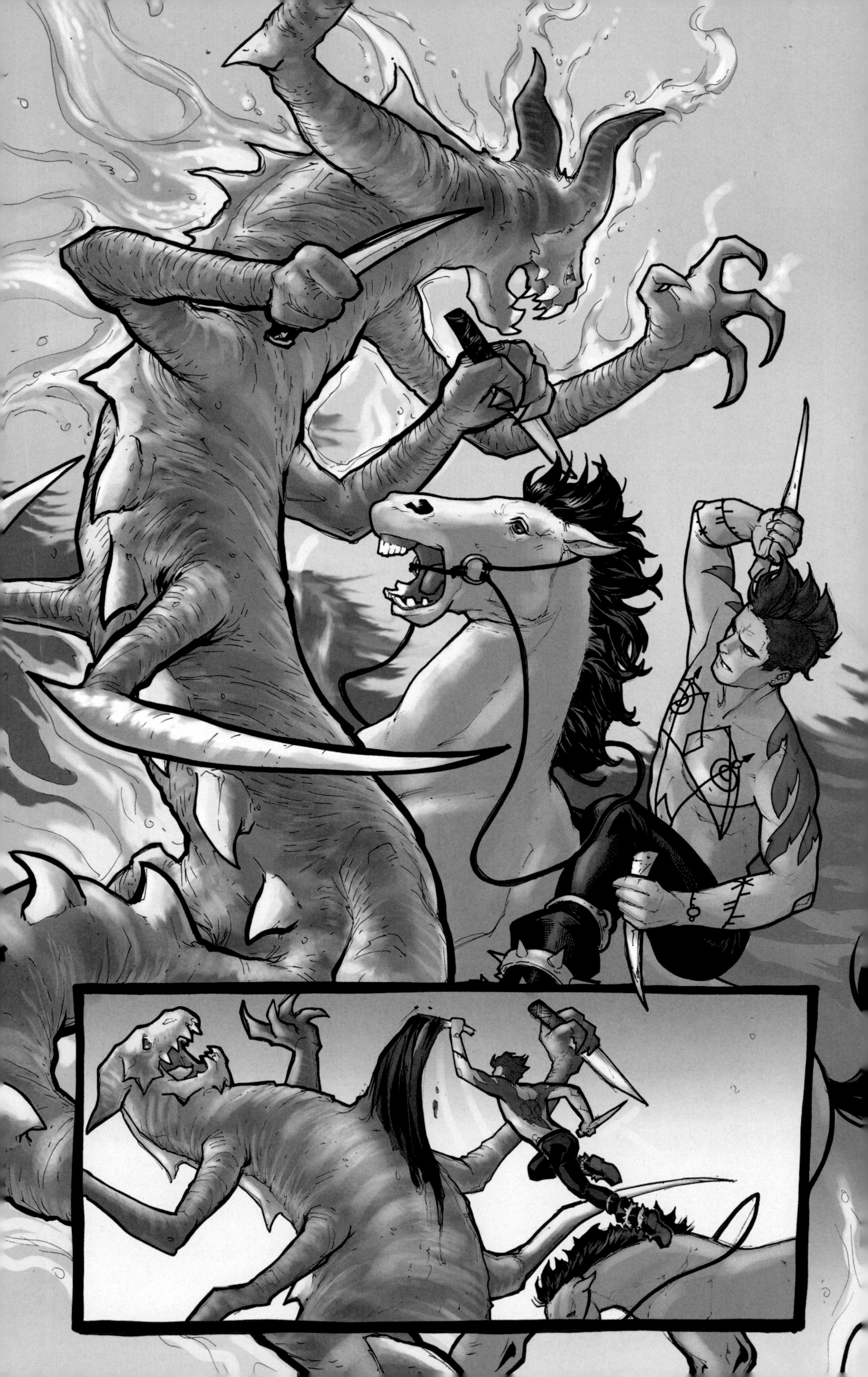

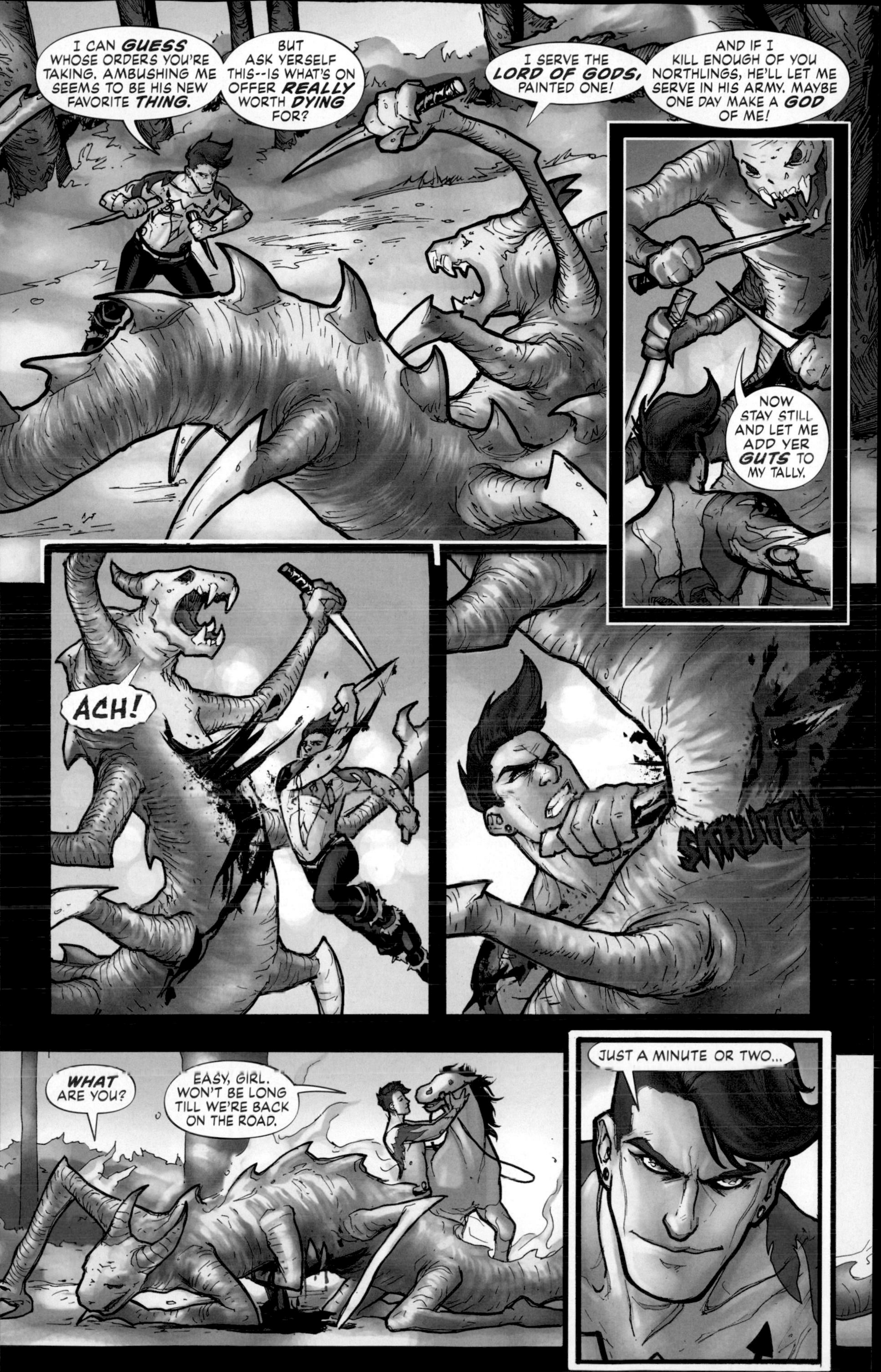

I CAN GUESS WHOSE ORDERS YOU'RE TAKING. AMBUSHING ME SEEMS TO BE HIS NEW FAVORITE THING.
BUT ASK YERSELF THIS--IS WHAT'S ON OFFER REALLY WORTH DYING FOR?
I SERVE THE LORD OF GODS, PAINTED ONE!
AND IF I KILL ENOUGH OF YOU NORTHLINGS, HE'LL LET ME SERVE IN HIS ARMY. MAYBE ONE DAY MAKE A GOD OF ME!
NOW STAY STILL AND LET ME ADD YER GUTS TO MY TALLY.
ACH!
SKRUTCH
WHAT ARE YOU?
EASY, GIRL. WON'T BE LONG TILL WE'RE BACK ON THE ROAD.
JUST A MINUTE OR TWO...

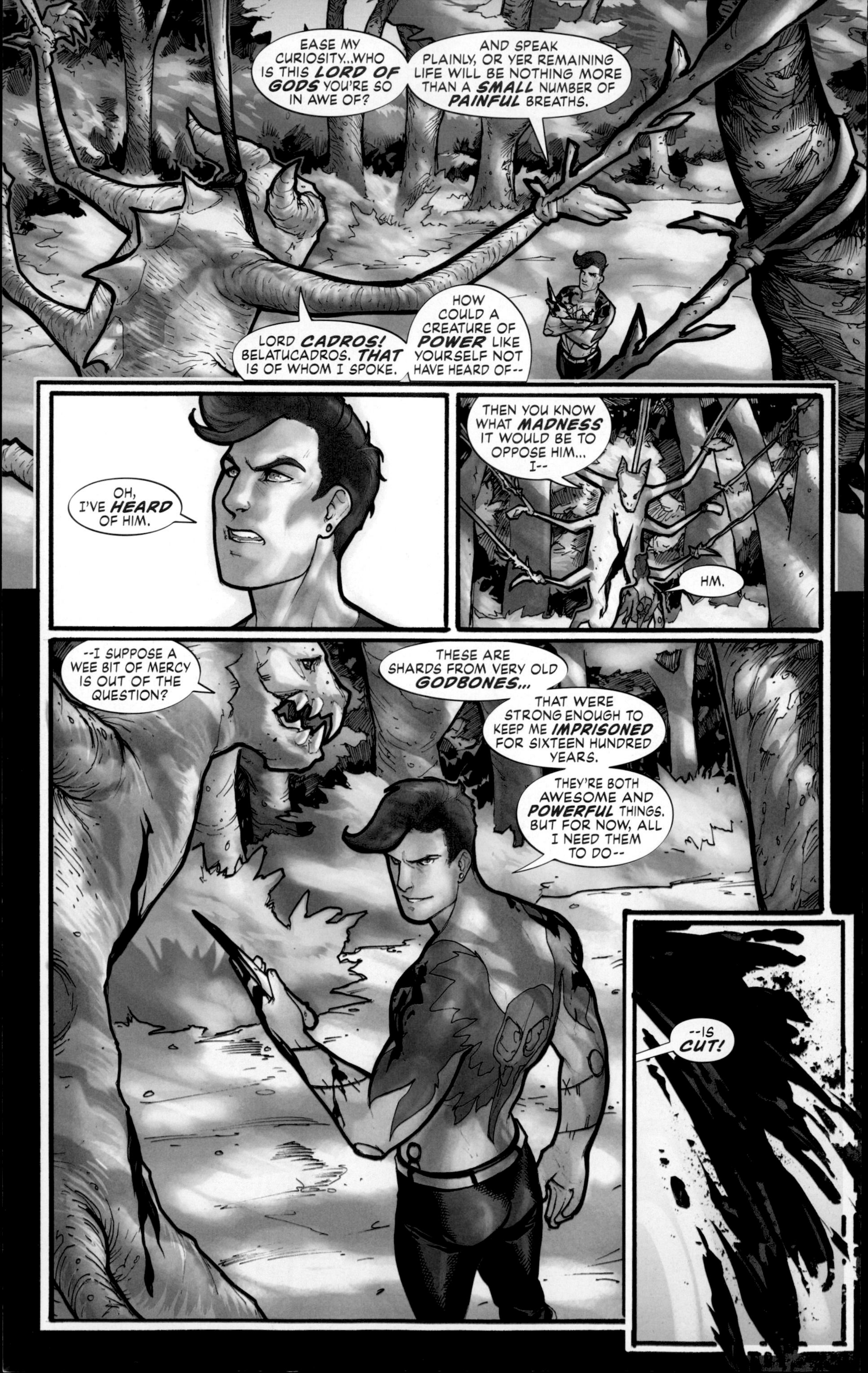

EASE MY CURIOSITY...WHO IS THIS LORD OF GODS YOU'RE SO IN AWE OF?
AND SPEAK PLAINLY, OR YER REMAINING LIFE WILL BE NOTHING MORE THAN A SMALL NUMBER OF PAINFUL BREATHS.
LORD CADROS! BELATUCADROS. THAT IS OF WHOM I SPOKE.
HOW COULD A CREATURE OF POWER LIKE YOURSELF NOT HAVE HEARD OF--
OH, I'VE HEARD OF HIM.
THEN YOU KNOW WHAT MADNESS IT WOULD BE TO OPPOSE HIM... I--
HM.
--I SUPPOSE A WEE BIT OF MERCY IS OUT OF THE QUESTION?
THESE ARE SHARDS FROM VERY OLD GODBONES...
THAT WERE STRONG ENOUGH TO KEEP ME IMPRISONED FOR SIXTEEN HUNDRED YEARS.
THEY'RE BOTH AWESOME AND POWERFUL THINGS. BUT FOR NOW, ALL I NEED THEM TO DO--
--IS CUT!

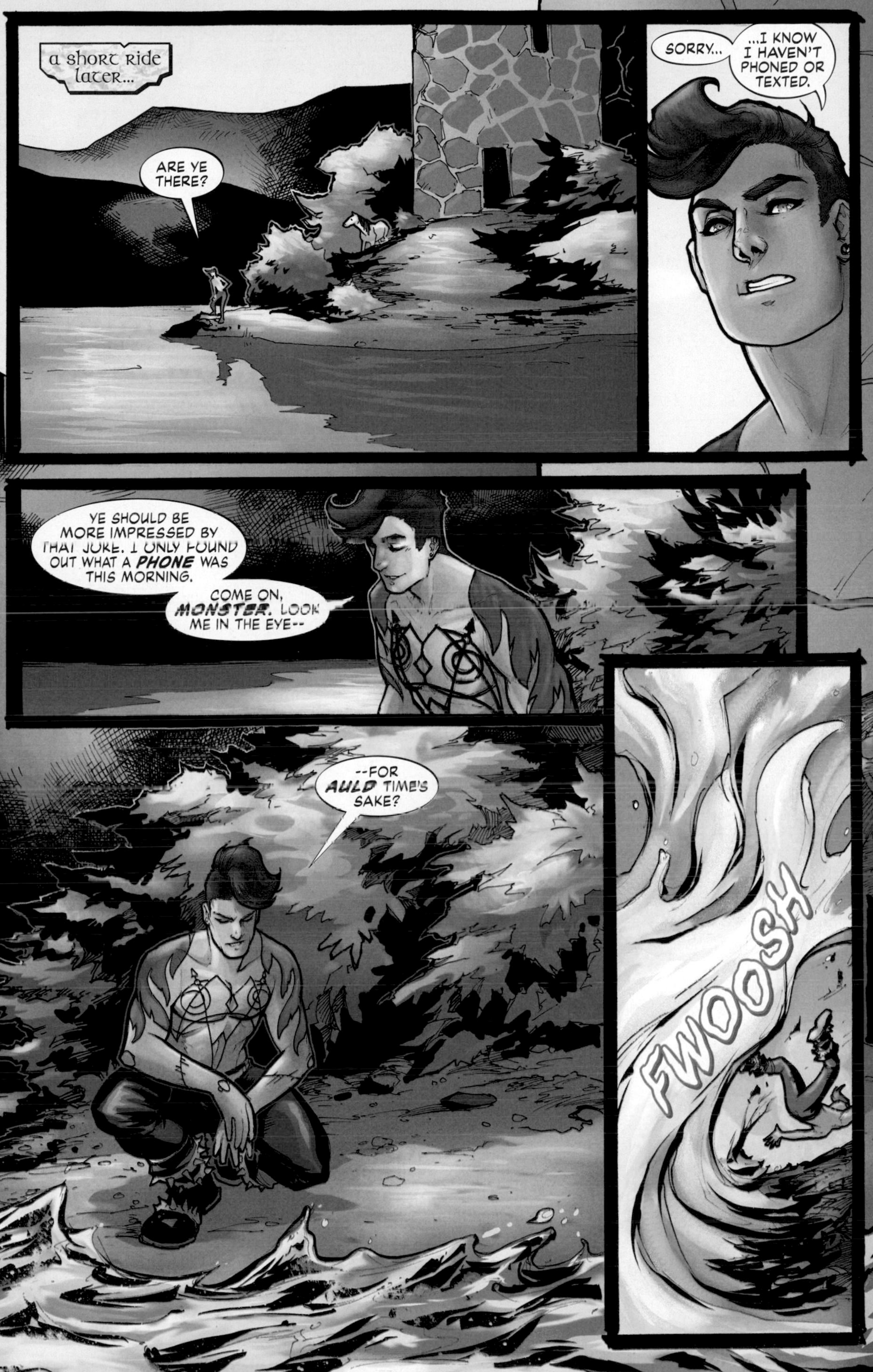
a short ride later...
ARE YE THERE?
SORRY...
...I KNOW I HAVEN'T PHONED OR TEXTED.
YE SHOULD BE MORE IMPRESSED BY THAT JOKE. I ONLY FOUND OUT WHAT A PHONE WAS THIS MORNING.
COME ON, MONSTER. LOOK ME IN THE EYE--
--FOR AULD TIME'S SAKE?
FWOOSH

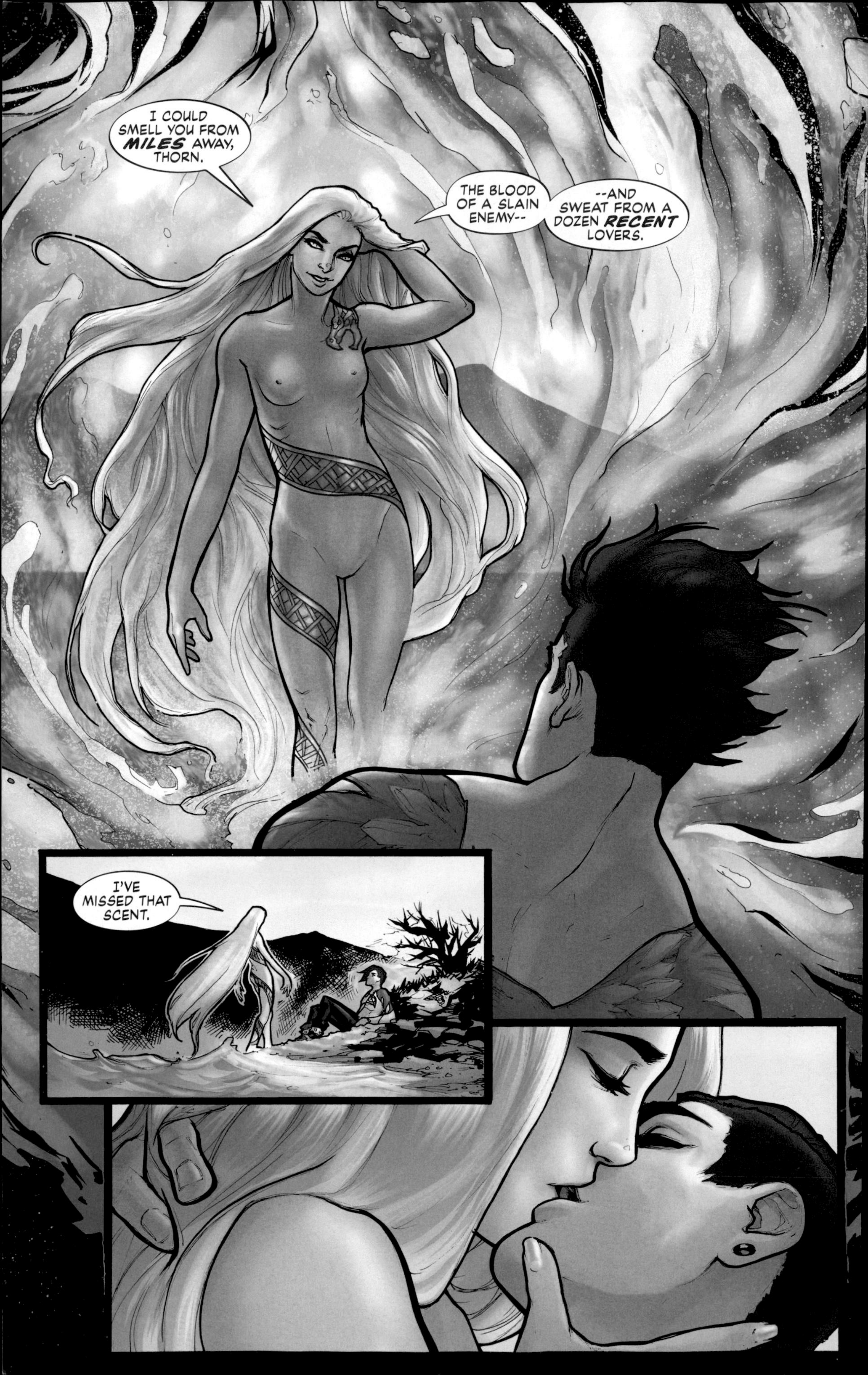
I COULD SMELL YOU FROM MILES AWAY, THORN.
THE BLOOD OF A SLAIN ENEMY--
--AND SWEAT FROM A DOZEN RECENT LOVERS.
I'VE MISSED THAT SCENT.

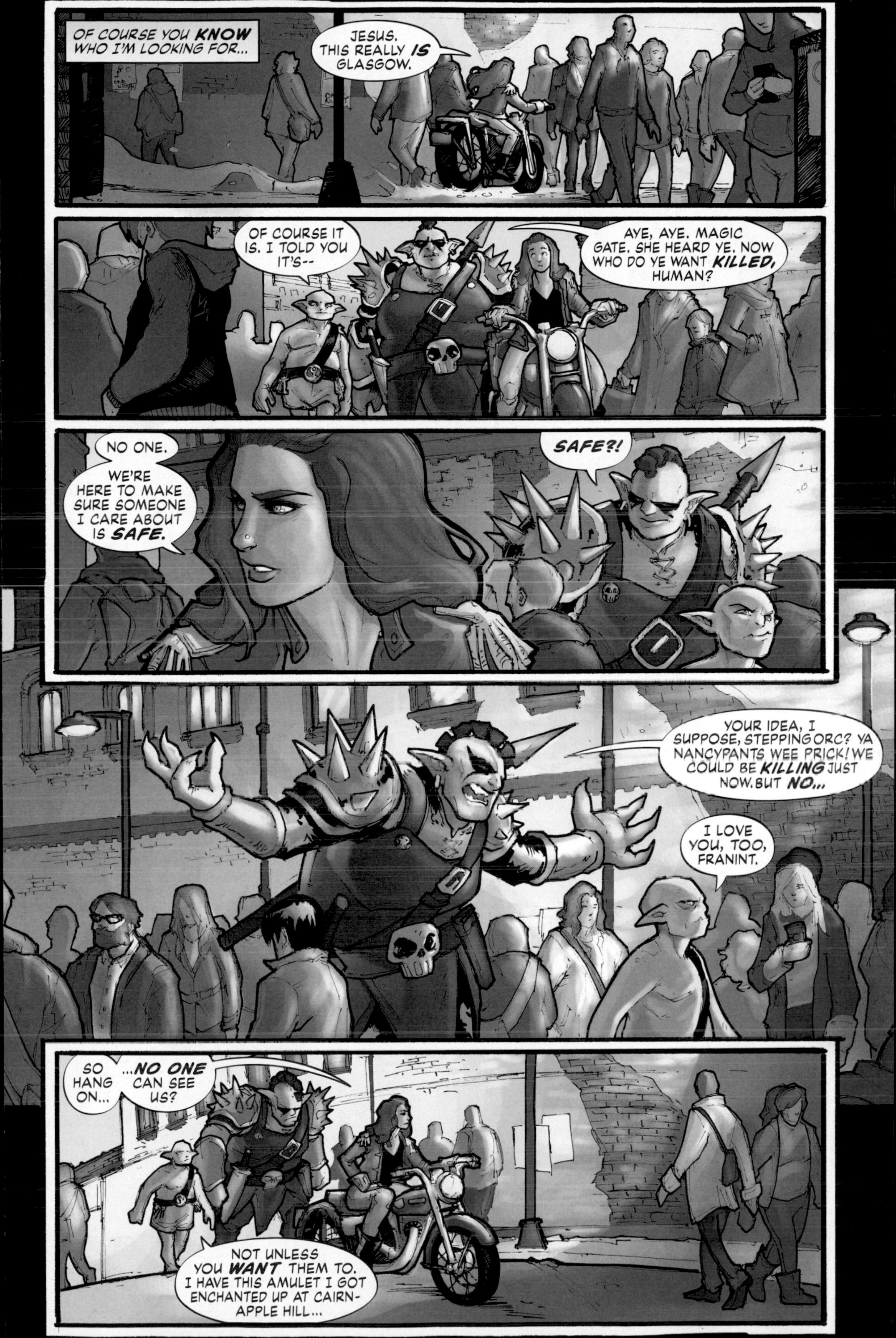

OF COURSE YOU KNOW WHO I'M LOOKING FOR...
JESUS. THIS REALLY IS GLASGOW.
OF COURSE IT IS. I TOLD YOU IT'S--
AYE, AYE. MAGIC GATE. SHE HEARD YE. NOW WHO DO YE WANT KILLED, HUMAN?
NO ONE.
WE'RE HERE TO MAKE SURE SOMEONE I CARE ABOUT IS SAFE.
SAFE?!
YOUR IDEA, I SUPPOSE, STEPPING ORC? YA NANCYPANTS WEE PRICK! WE COULD BE KILLING JUST NOW. BUT NO...
I LOVE YOU, TOO, FRANINT.
SO HANG ON...
...NO ONE CAN SEE US?
NOT UNLESS YOU WANT THEM TO. I HAVE THIS AMULET I GOT ENCHANTED UP AT CAIRN-APPLE HILL...

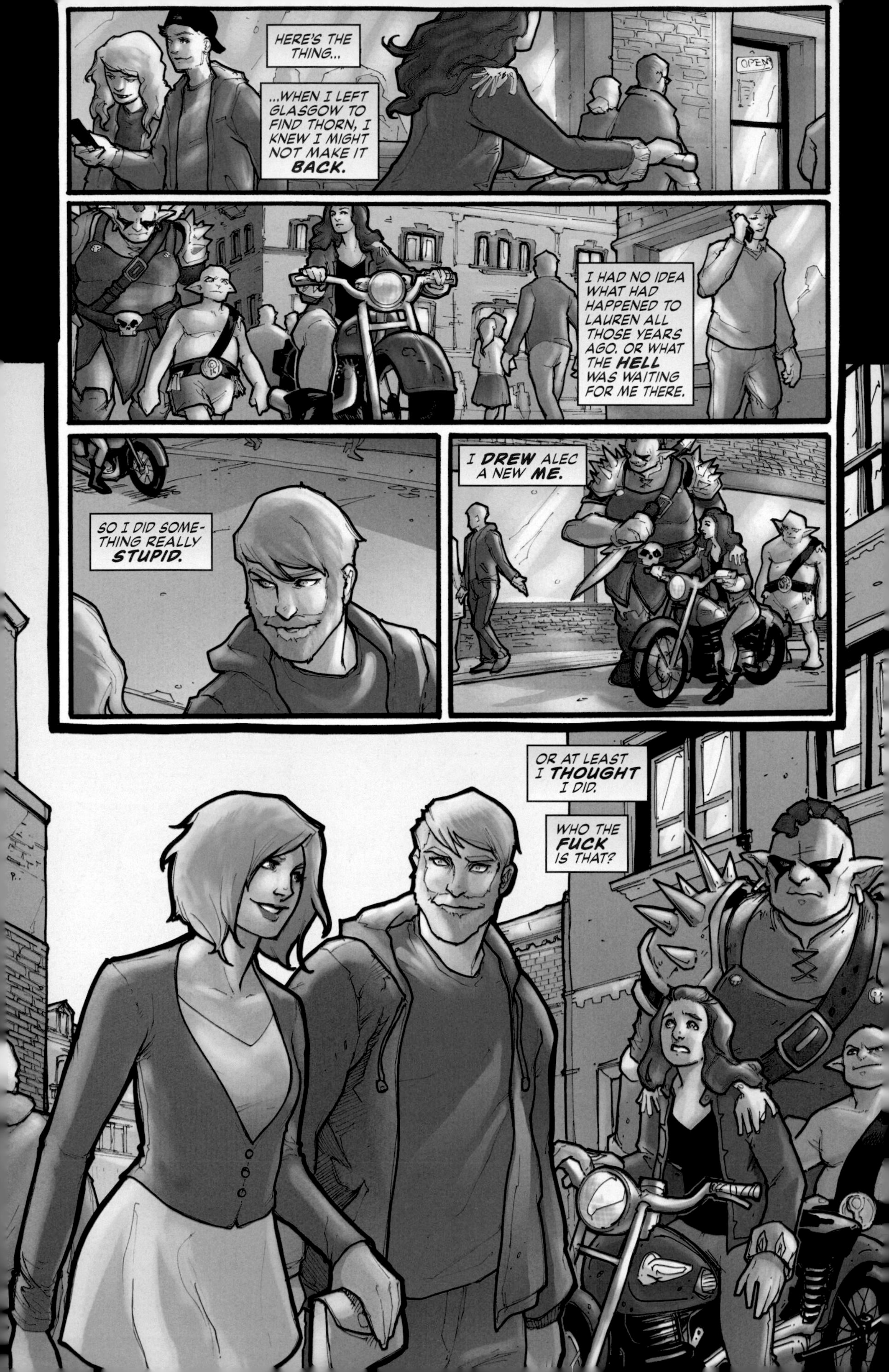
HERE'S THE THING...
...WHEN I LEFT GLASGOW TO FIND THORN, I KNEW I MIGHT NOT MAKE IT **BACK.**
OPEN
I HAD NO IDEA WHAT HAD HAPPENED TO LAUREN ALL THOSE YEARS AGO. OR WHAT THE **HELL** WAS WAITING FOR ME THERE.
SO I DID SOME-THING REALLY **STUPID.**
I **DREW** ALEC A NEW **ME.**
OR AT LEAST I **THOUGHT** I DID.
WHO THE **FUCK** IS THAT?

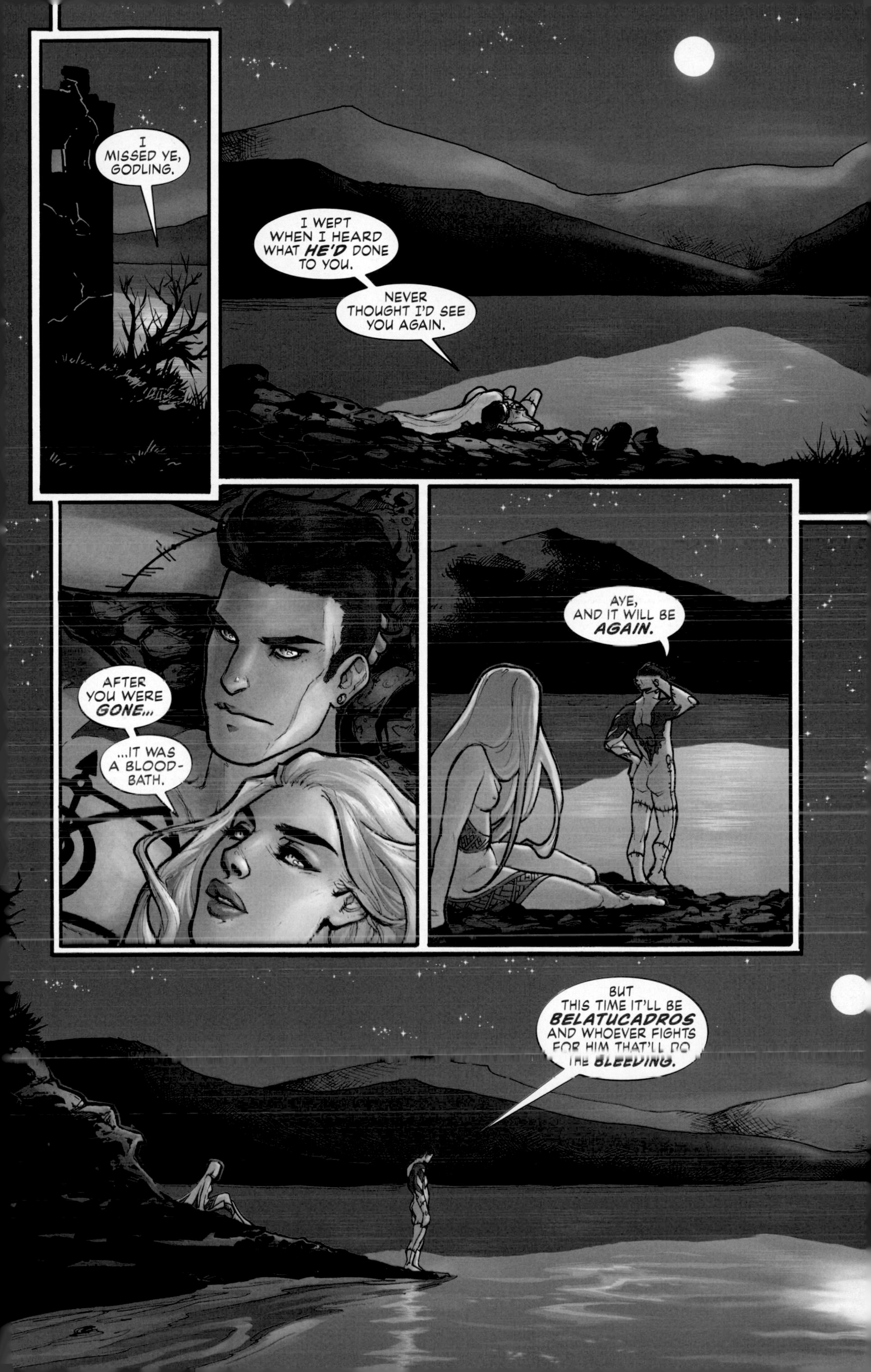
I MISSED YE, GODLING.
I WEPT WHEN I HEARD WHAT HE'D DONE TO YOU.
NEVER THOUGHT I'D SEE YOU AGAIN.
AFTER YOU WERE GONE...
...IT WAS A BLOOD-BATH.
AYE, AND IT WILL BE AGAIN.
BUT THIS TIME IT'LL BE BELATUCADROS AND WHOEVER FIGHTS FOR HIM THAT'LL DO THE BLEEDING.

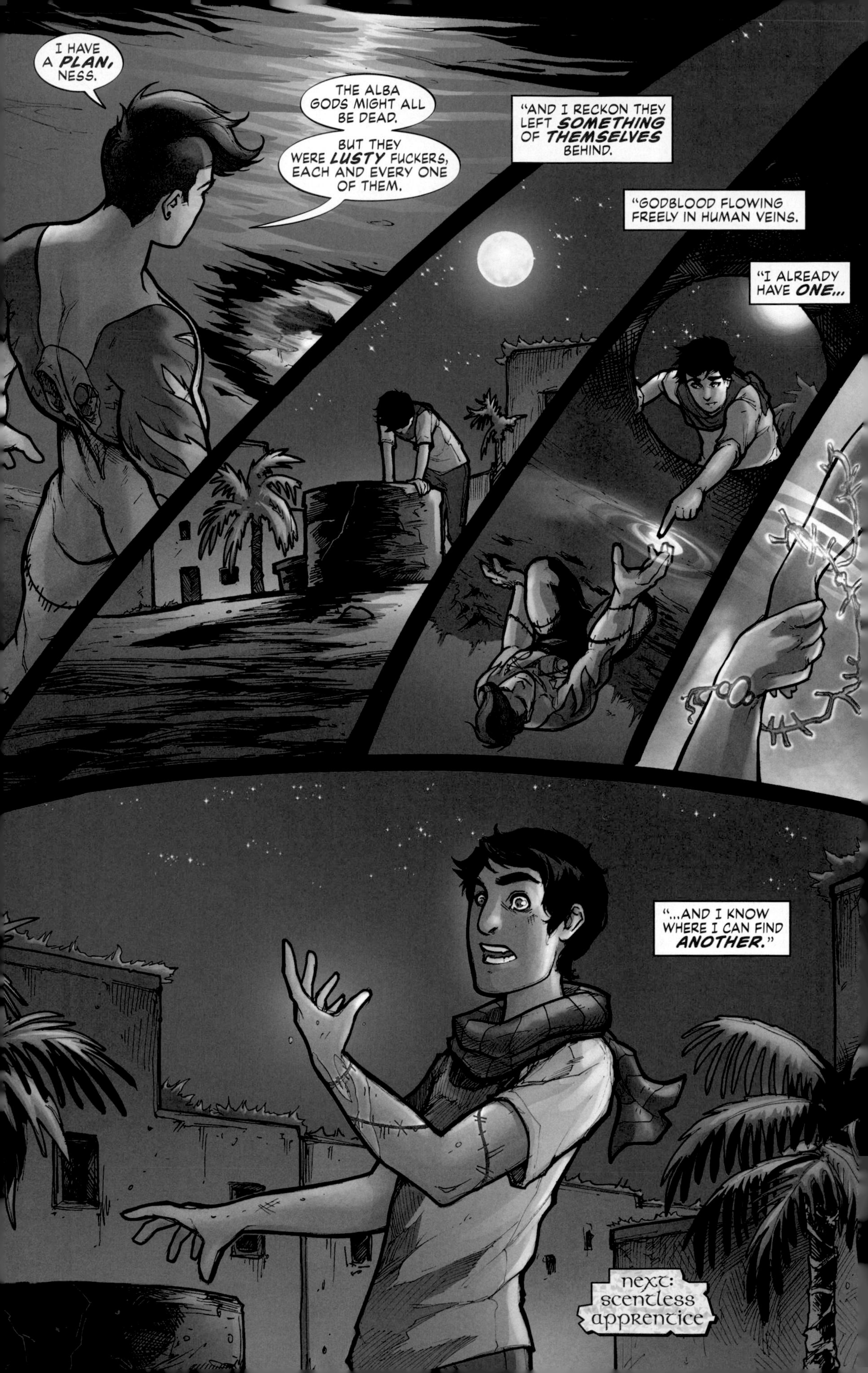
I HAVE A PLAN, NESS.
THE ALBA GODS MIGHT ALL BE DEAD.
BUT THEY WERE LUSTY FUCKERS, EACH AND EVERY ONE OF THEM.
"AND I RECKON THEY LEFT SOMETHING OF THEMSELVES BEHIND.
"GODBLOOD FLOWING FREELY IN HUMAN VEINS.
"I ALREADY HAVE ONE...
"...AND I KNOW WHERE I CAN FIND ANOTHER."
next: scentless apprentice

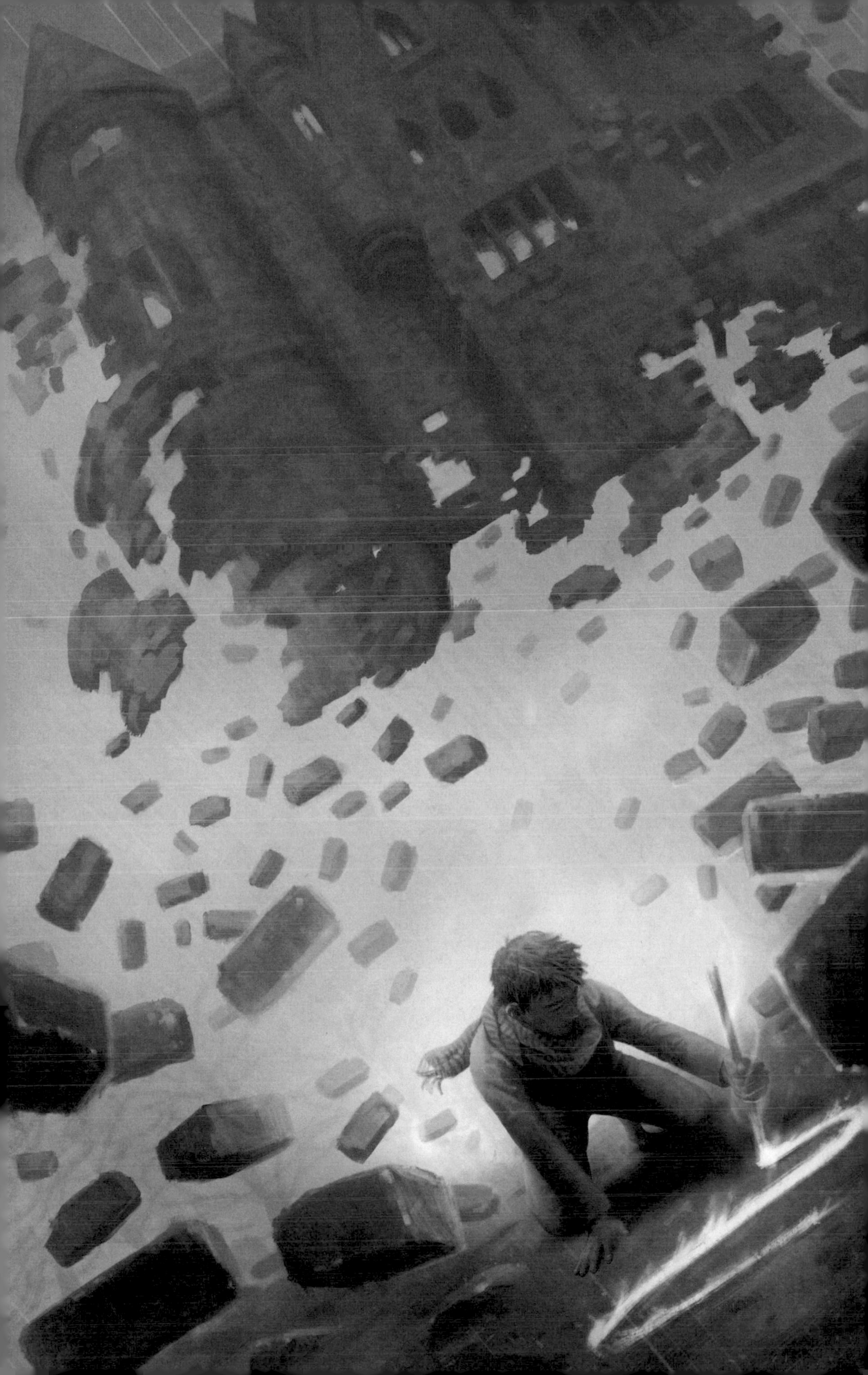

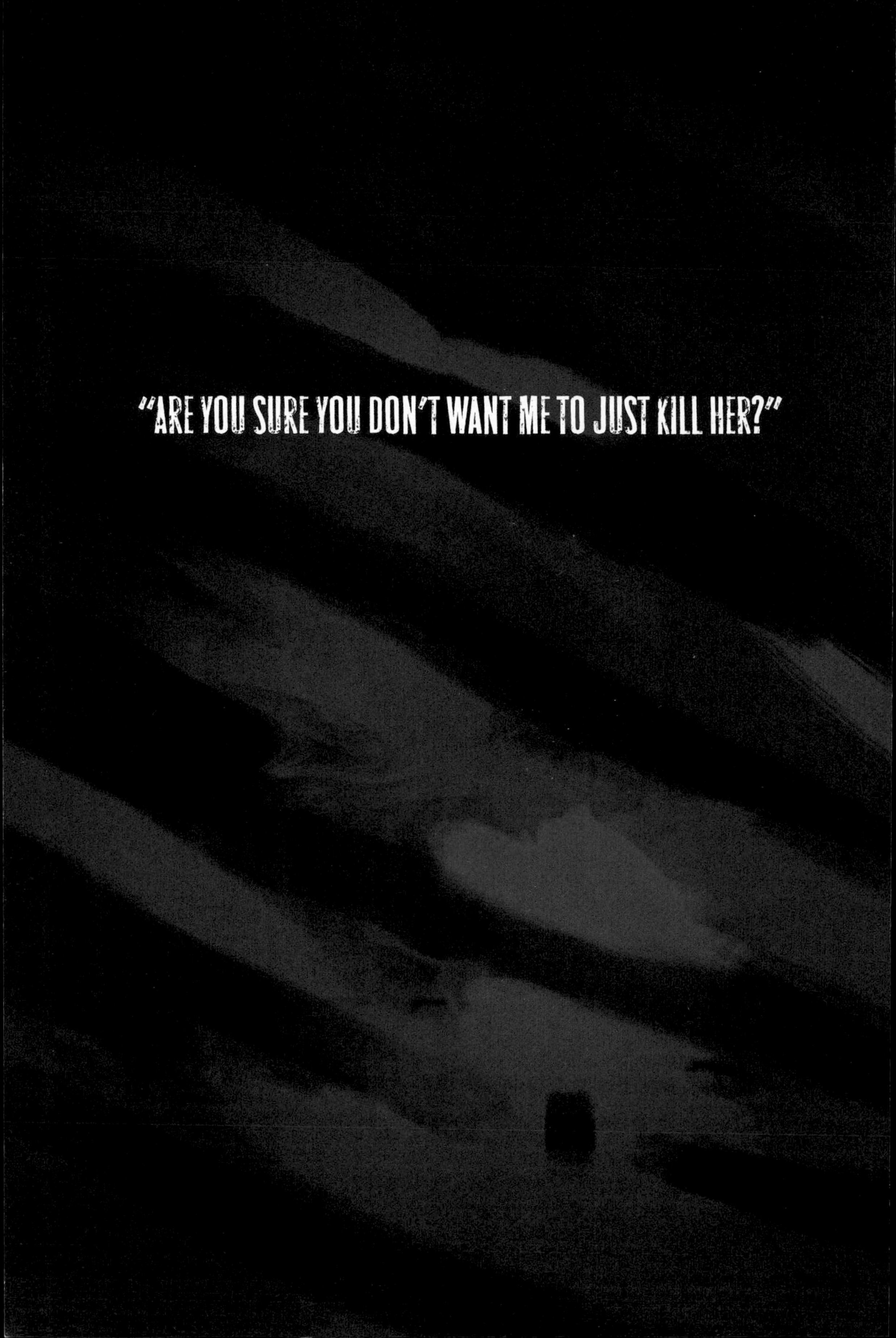
"ARE YOU SURE YOU DON'T WANT ME TO JUST KILL HER?"

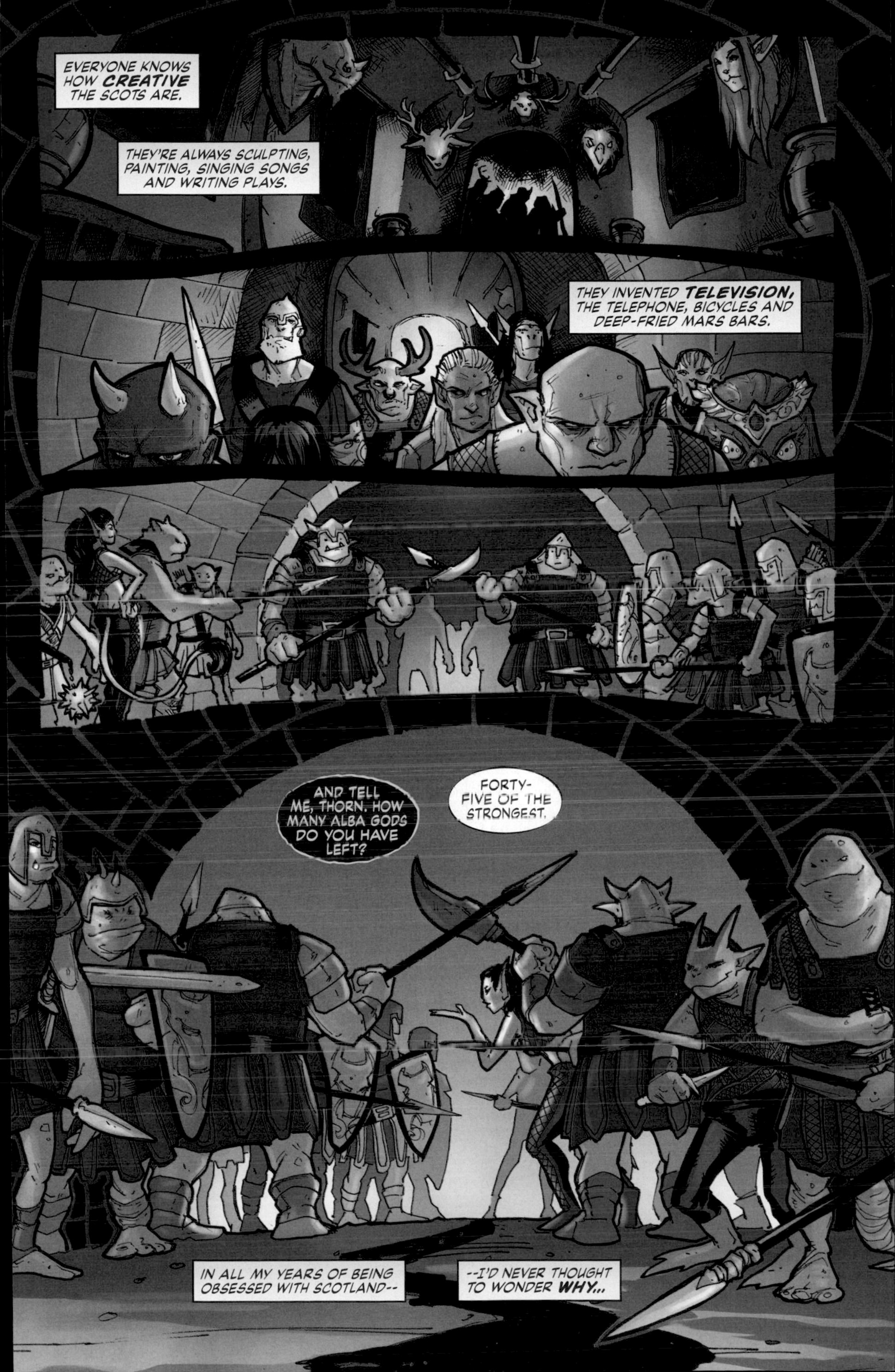
EVERYONE KNOWS HOW CREATIVE THE SCOTS ARE.
THEY'RE ALWAYS SCULPTING, PAINTING, SINGING SONGS AND WRITING PLAYS.
THEY INVENTED TELEVISION, THE TELEPHONE, BICYCLES AND DEEP-FRIED MARS BARS.
AND TELL ME, THORN. HOW MANY ALBA GODS DO YOU HAVE LEFT?
FORTY-FIVE OF THE STRONGEST.
IN ALL MY YEARS OF BEING OBSESSED WITH SCOTLAND--
--I'D NEVER THOUGHT TO WONDER WHY...

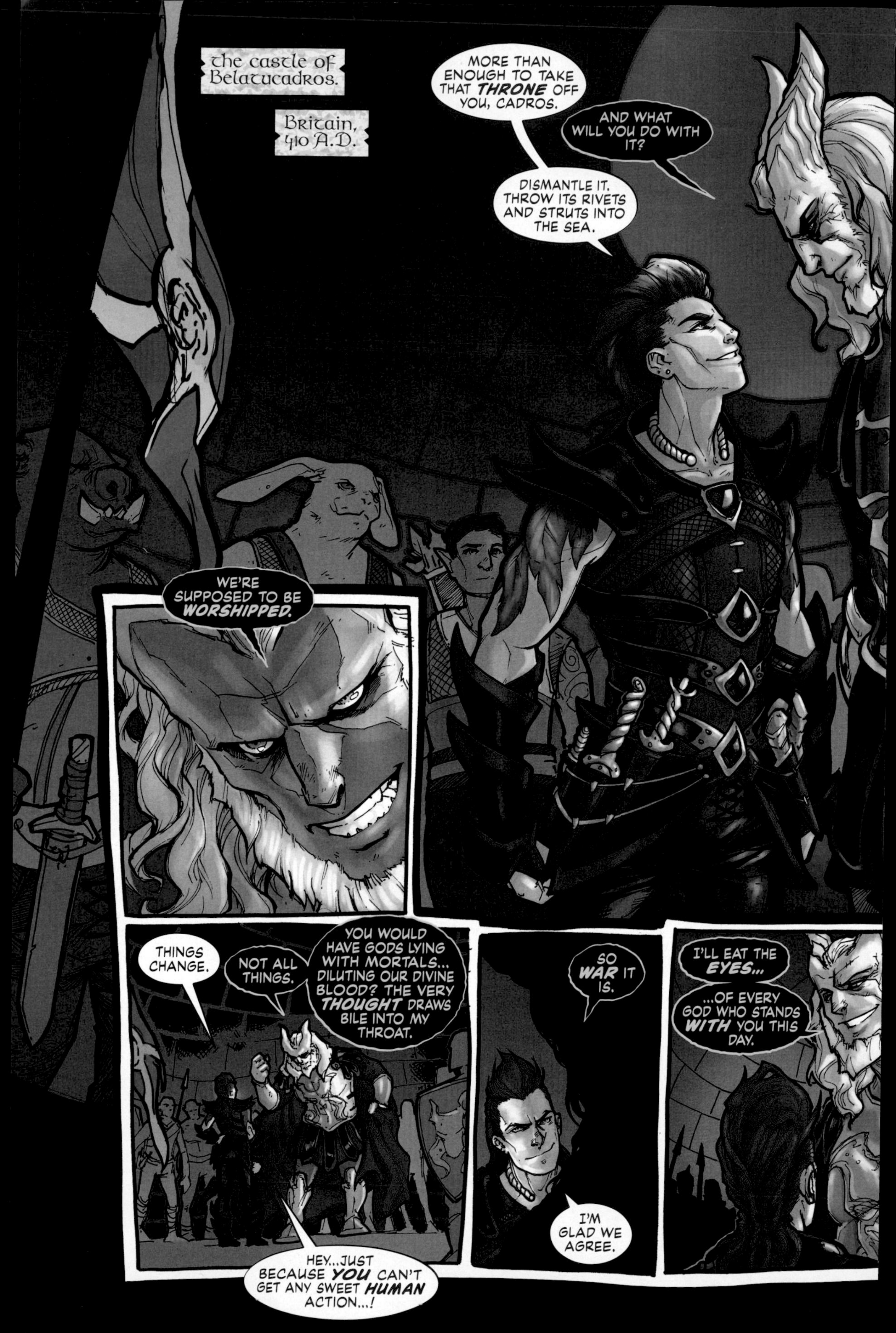
the castle of Belatucadros.
Britain, 410 A.D.
MORE THAN ENOUGH TO TAKE THAT THRONE OFF YOU, CADROS.
AND WHAT WILL YOU DO WITH IT?
DISMANTLE IT. THROW ITS RIVETS AND STRUTS INTO THE SEA.
WE'RE SUPPOSED TO BE WORSHIPPED.
THINGS CHANGE.
NOT ALL THINGS.
YOU WOULD HAVE GODS LYING WITH MORTALS... DILUTING OUR DIVINE BLOOD? THE VERY THOUGHT DRAWS BILE INTO MY THROAT.
HEY...JUST BECAUSE YOU CAN'T GET ANY SWEET HUMAN ACTION...!
SO WAR IT IS.
I'M GLAD WE AGREE.
I'LL EAT THE EYES...
...OF EVERY GOD WHO STANDS WITH YOU THIS DAY.

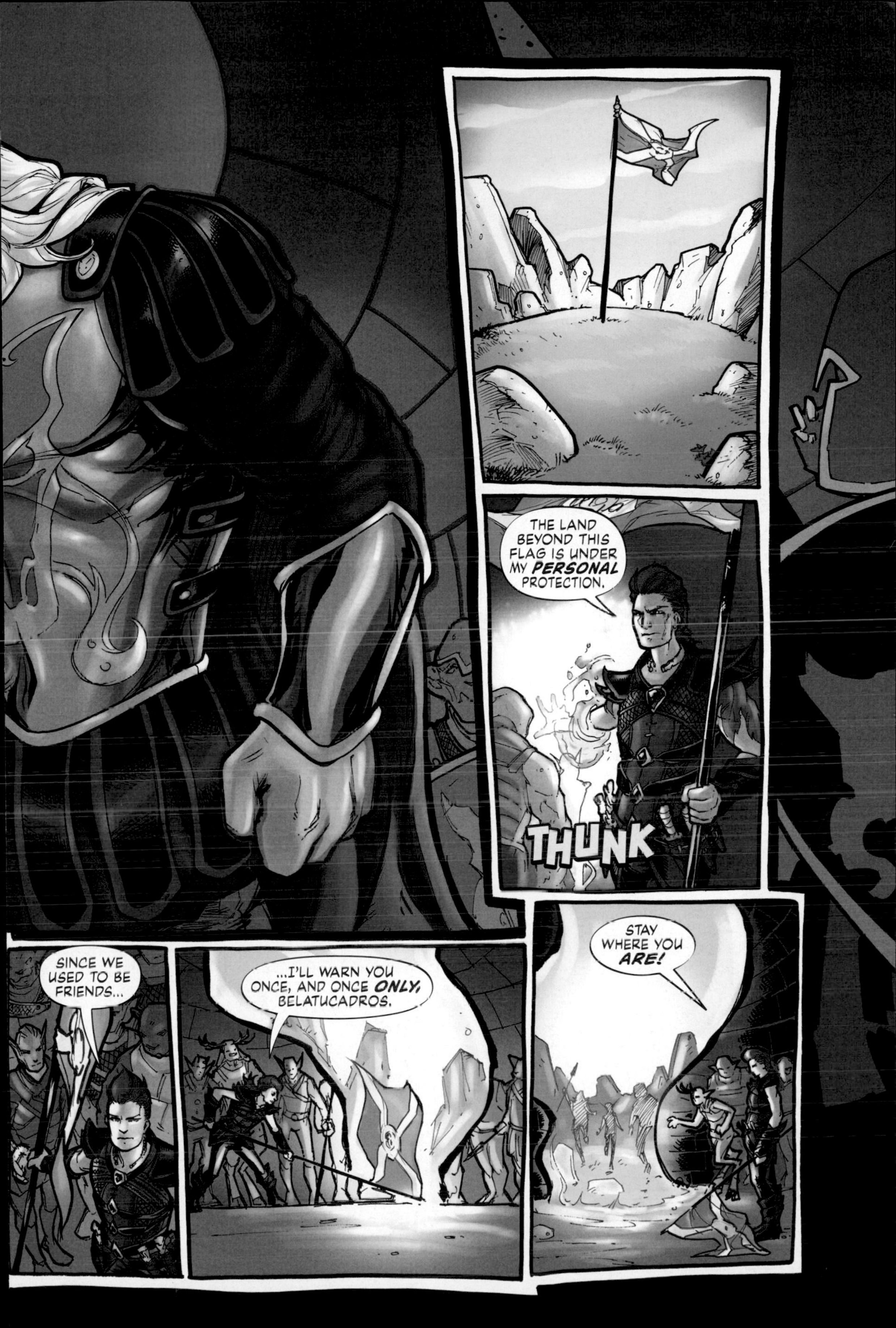
THE LAND BEYOND THIS FLAG IS UNDER MY **PERSONAL** PROTECTION.
THUNK
STAY WHERE YOU **ARE!**
SINCE WE USED TO BE FRIENDS...
...I'LL WARN YOU ONCE, AND ONCE **ONLY,** BELATUCADROS.

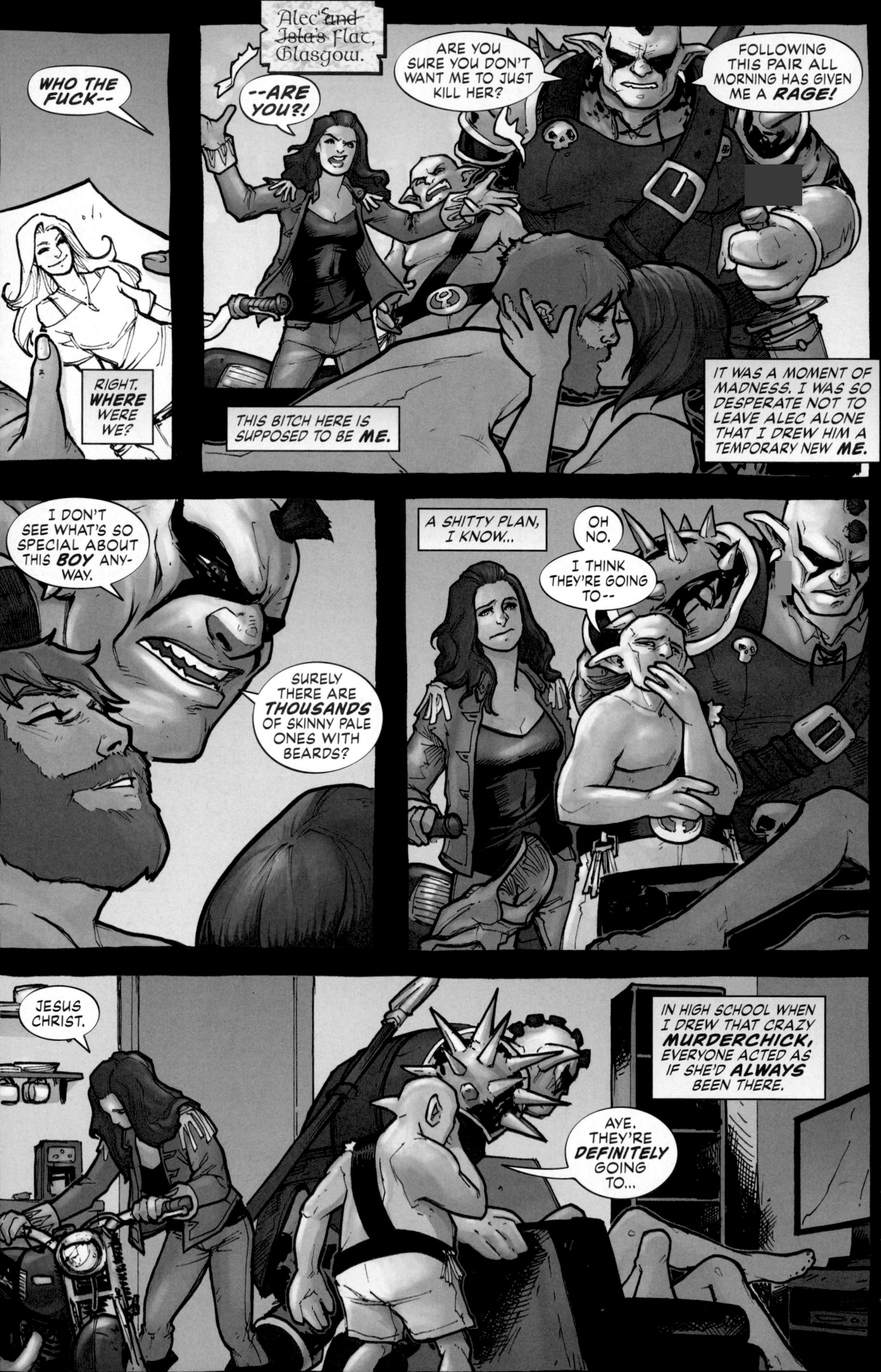
WHO THE FUCK--
RIGHT. WHERE WERE WE?
Alec' ~~and Isla~~'s Flat, Glasgow.
--ARE YOU?!
ARE YOU SURE YOU DON'T WANT ME TO JUST KILL HER?
FOLLOWING THIS PAIR ALL MORNING HAS GIVEN ME A RAGE!
THIS BITCH HERE IS SUPPOSED TO BE ME.
IT WAS A MOMENT OF MADNESS. I WAS SO DESPERATE NOT TO LEAVE ALEC ALONE THAT I DREW HIM A TEMPORARY NEW ME.
I DON'T SEE WHAT'S SO SPECIAL ABOUT THIS BOY ANY-WAY.
SURELY THERE ARE THOUSANDS OF SKINNY PALE ONES WITH BEARDS?
A SHITTY PLAN, I KNOW...
OH NO.
I THINK THEY'RE GOING TO--
JESUS CHRIST.
IN HIGH SCHOOL WHEN I DREW THAT CRAZY MURDERCHICK, EVERYONE ACTED AS IF SHE'D ALWAYS BEEN THERE.
AYE. THEY'RE DEFINITELY GOING TO...

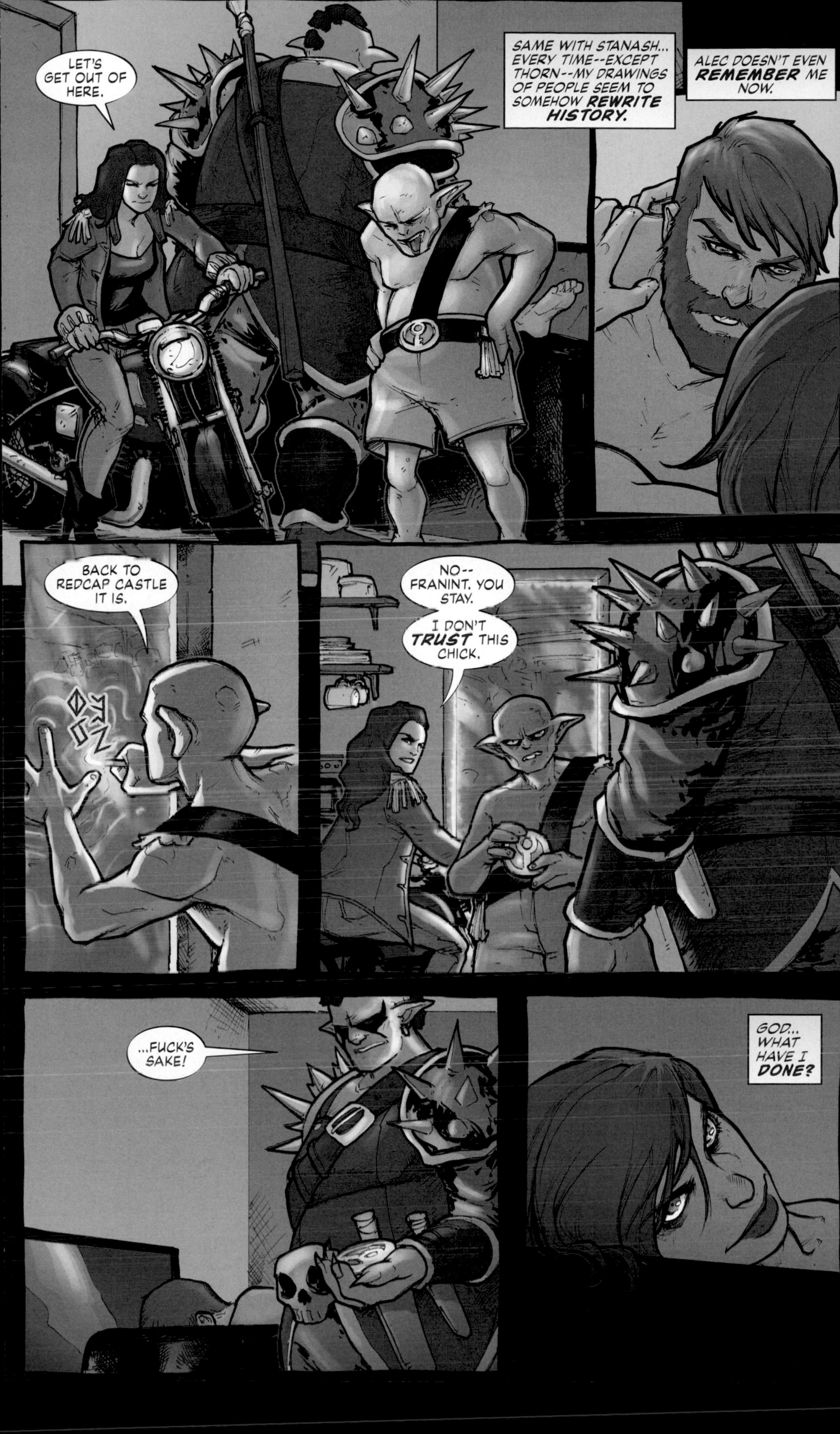
LET'S GET OUT OF HERE.
SAME WITH STANASH... EVERY TIME--EXCEPT THORN--MY DRAWINGS OF PEOPLE SEEM TO SOMEHOW **REWRITE HISTORY.**
ALEC DOESN'T EVEN **REMEMBER** ME NOW.
BACK TO REDCAP CASTLE IT IS.
NO-- FRANINT. YOU STAY.
I DON'T **TRUST** THIS CHICK.
...FUCK'S SAKE!
GOD... WHAT HAVE I **DONE?**

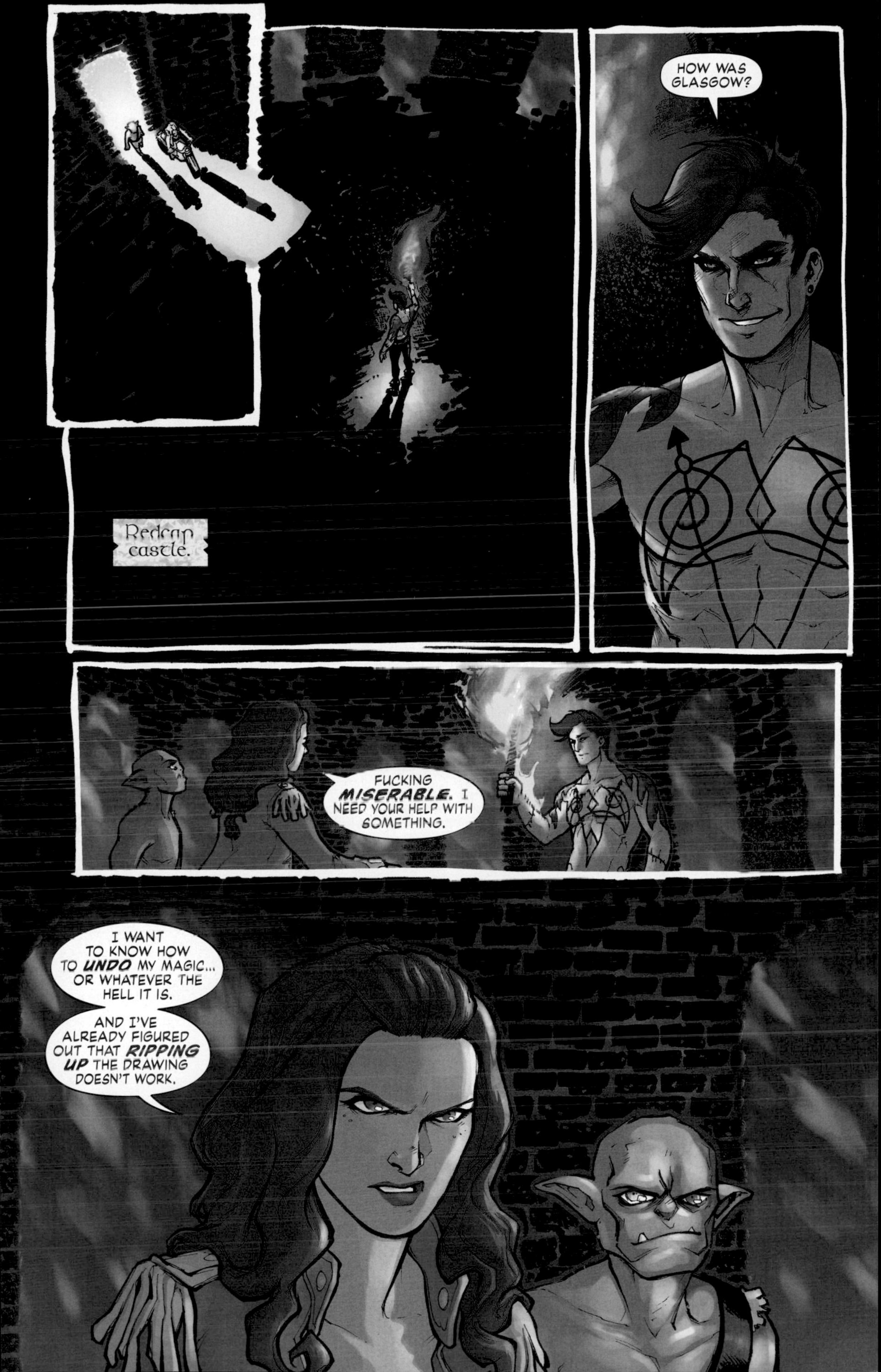
Redcap castle.
HOW WAS GLASGOW?
FUCKING MISERABLE. I NEED YOUR HELP WITH SOMETHING.
I WANT TO KNOW HOW TO UNDO MY MAGIC... OR WHATEVER THE HELL IT IS.
AND I'VE ALREADY FIGURED OUT THAT RIPPING UP THE DRAWING DOESN'T WORK.

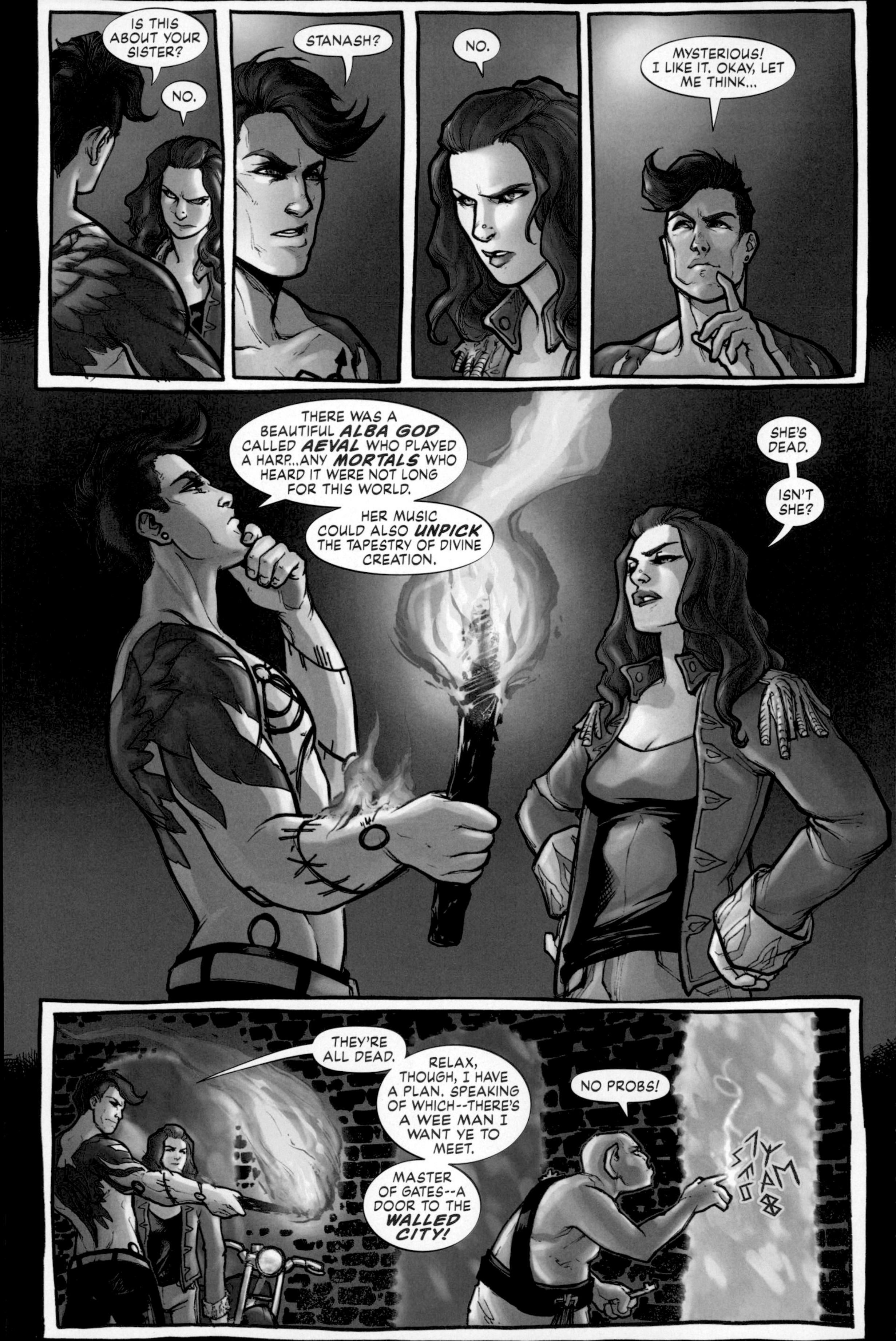

IS THIS ABOUT YOUR SISTER?
NO.
STANASH?
NO.
MYSTERIOUS! I LIKE IT. OKAY, LET ME THINK...
THERE WAS A BEAUTIFUL ALBA GOD CALLED AEVAL WHO PLAYED A HARP...ANY MORTALS WHO HEARD IT WERE NOT LONG FOR THIS WORLD.
HER MUSIC COULD ALSO UNPICK THE TAPESTRY OF DIVINE CREATION.
SHE'S DEAD.
ISN'T SHE?
THEY'RE ALL DEAD.
RELAX, THOUGH, I HAVE A PLAN. SPEAKING OF WHICH--THERE'S A WEE MAN I WANT YE TO MEET.
MASTER OF GATES--A DOOR TO THE WALLED CITY!
NO PROBS!

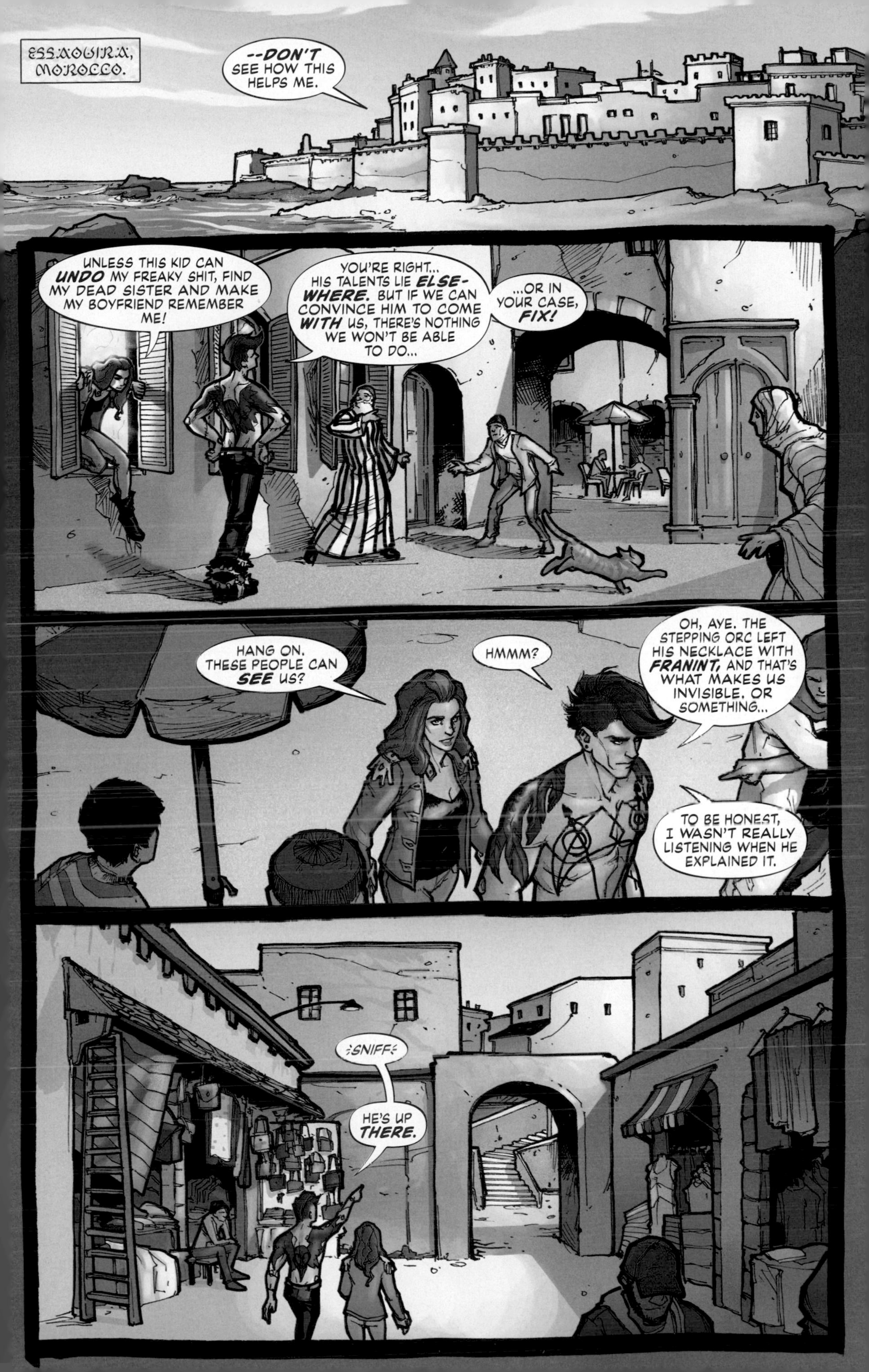
ESSAOUIRA, MOROCCO.
--DON'T SEE HOW THIS HELPS ME.
UNLESS THIS KID CAN UNDO MY FREAKY SHIT, FIND MY DEAD SISTER AND MAKE MY BOYFRIEND REMEMBER ME!
YOU'RE RIGHT... HIS TALENTS LIE ELSE-WHERE. BUT IF WE CAN CONVINCE HIM TO COME WITH US, THERE'S NOTHING WE WON'T BE ABLE TO DO...
...OR IN YOUR CASE, FIX!
HANG ON. THESE PEOPLE CAN SEE US?
HMMM?
OH, AYE. THE STEPPING ORC LEFT HIS NECKLACE WITH FRANINT, AND THAT'S WHAT MAKES US INVISIBLE. OR SOMETHING...
TO BE HONEST, I WASN'T REALLY LISTENING WHEN HE EXPLAINED IT.
SNIFF
HE'S UP THERE.

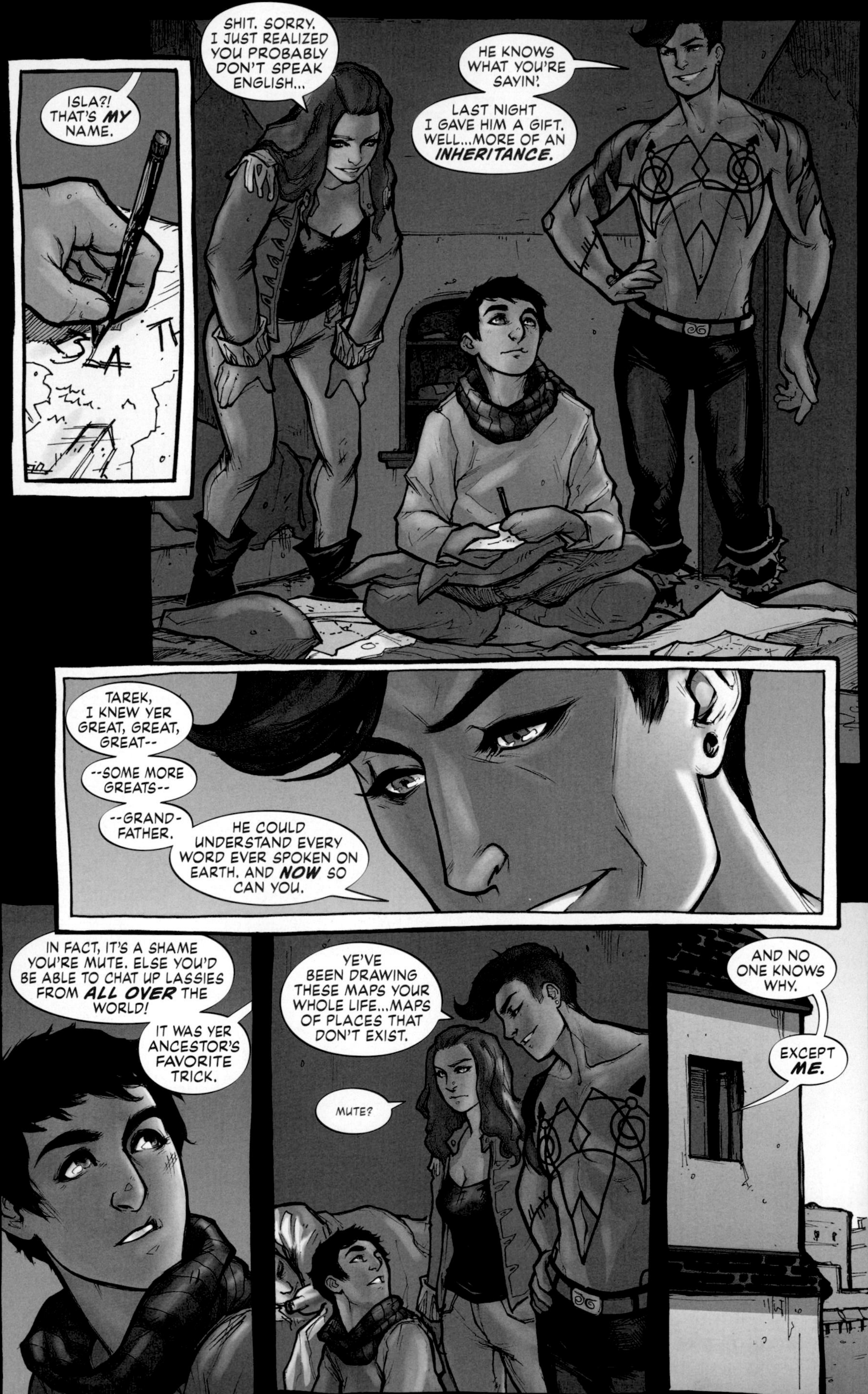
ISLA?! THAT'S MY NAME.
SHIT. SORRY. I JUST REALIZED YOU PROBABLY DON'T SPEAK ENGLISH...
HE KNOWS WHAT YOU'RE SAYIN'.
LAST NIGHT I GAVE HIM A GIFT. WELL...MORE OF AN INHERITANCE.
TAREK, I KNEW YER GREAT, GREAT, GREAT--
--SOME MORE GREATS--
--GRAND-FATHER.
HE COULD UNDERSTAND EVERY WORD EVER SPOKEN ON EARTH. AND NOW SO CAN YOU.
IN FACT, IT'S A SHAME YOU'RE MUTE. ELSE YOU'D BE ABLE TO CHAT UP LASSIES FROM ALL OVER THE WORLD!
IT WAS YER ANCESTOR'S FAVORITE TRICK.
YE'VE BEEN DRAWING THESE MAPS YOUR WHOLE LIFE...MAPS OF PLACES THAT DON'T EXIST.
MUTE?
AND NO ONE KNOWS WHY.
EXCEPT ME.

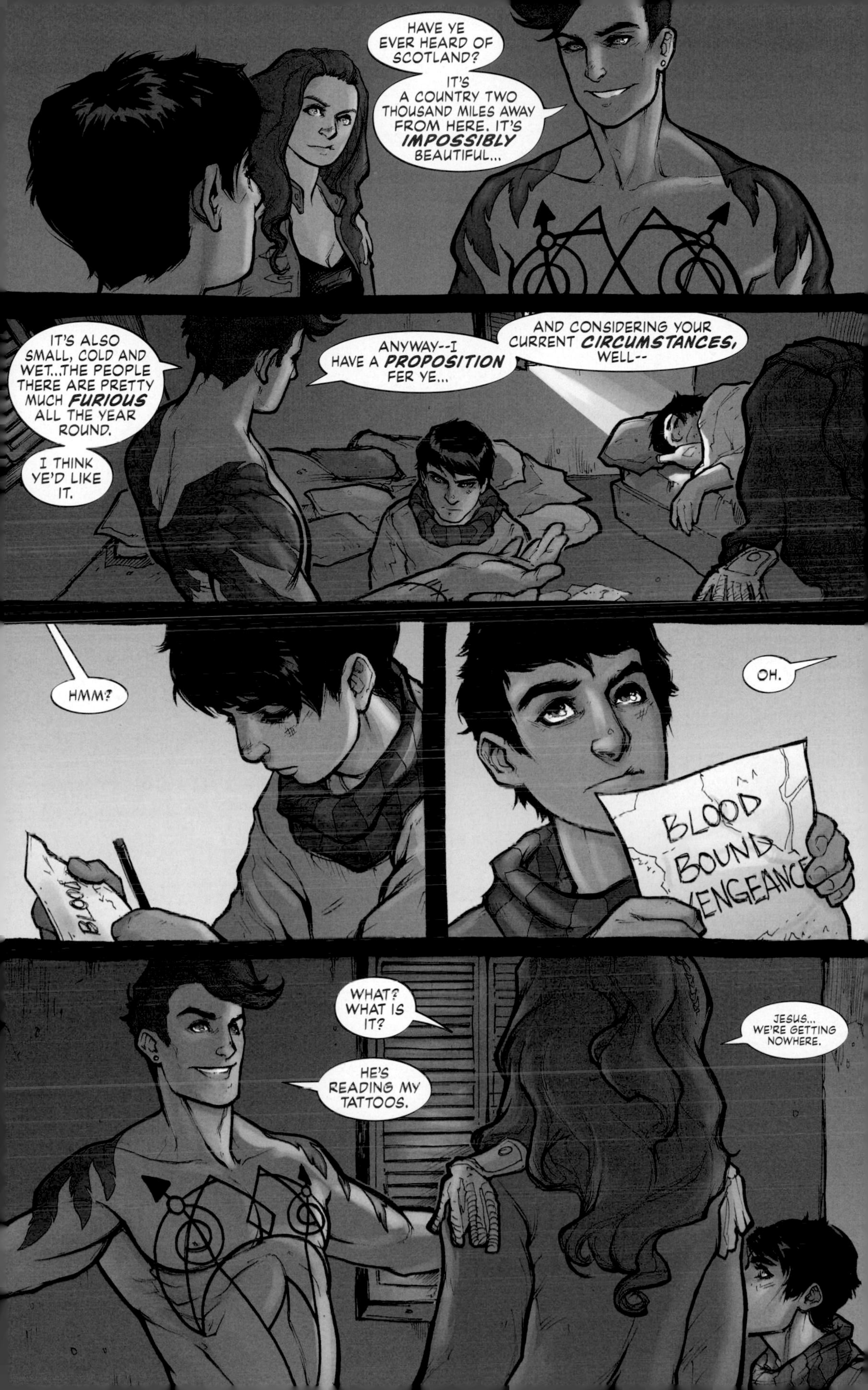
HAVE YE EVER HEARD OF SCOTLAND?
IT'S A COUNTRY TWO THOUSAND MILES AWAY FROM HERE. IT'S IMPOSSIBLY BEAUTIFUL...
IT'S ALSO SMALL, COLD AND WET...THE PEOPLE THERE ARE PRETTY MUCH FURIOUS ALL THE YEAR ROUND.
I THINK YE'D LIKE IT.
ANYWAY--I HAVE A PROPOSITION FER YE...
AND CONSIDERING YOUR CURRENT CIRCUMSTANCES, WELL--
HMM?
OH.
BLOOD BOUND VENGEANCE
WHAT? WHAT IS IT?
HE'S READING MY TATTOOS.
JESUS... WE'RE GETTING NOWHERE.

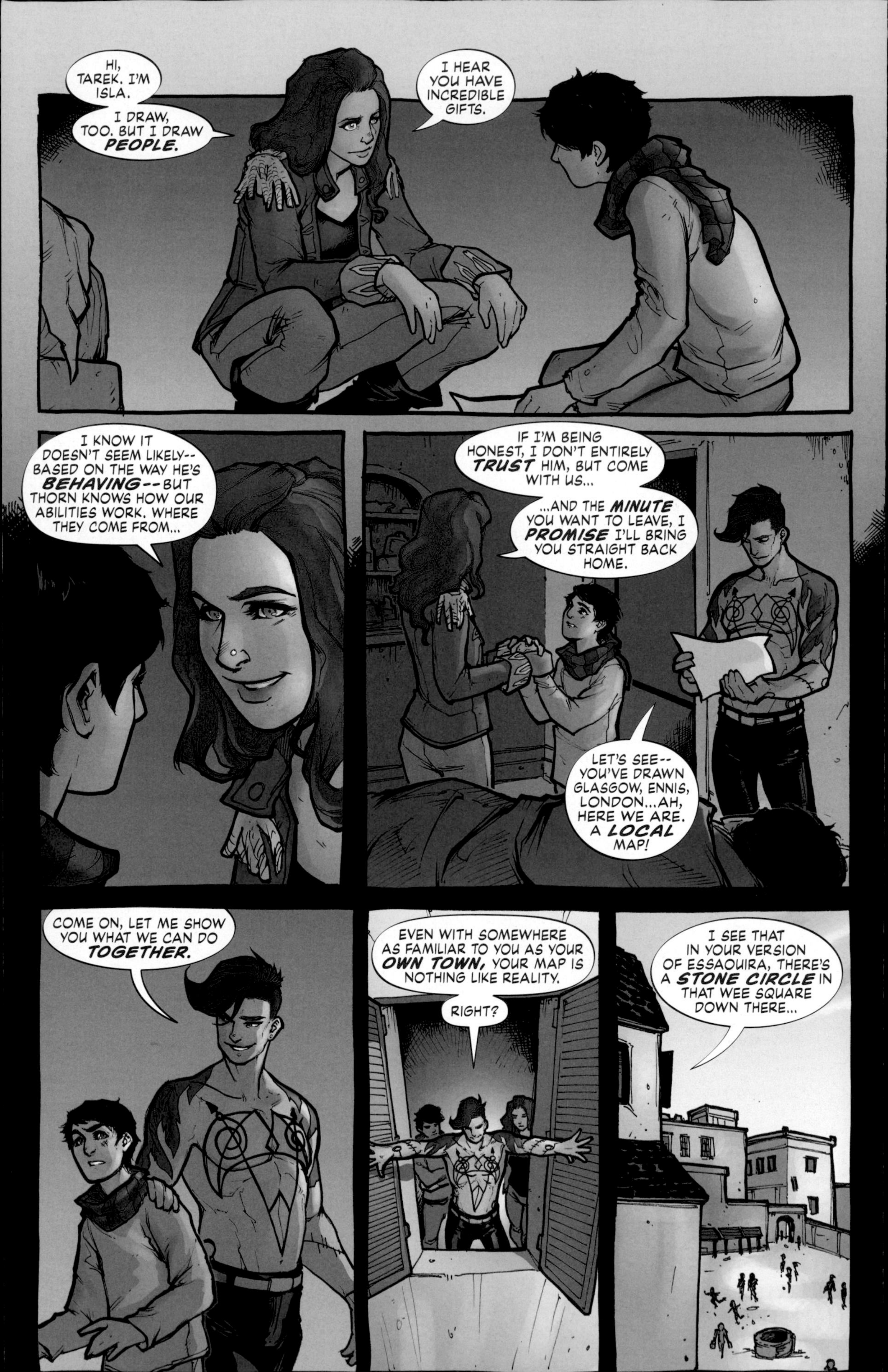
HI, TAREK. I'M ISLA.
I DRAW, TOO. BUT I DRAW PEOPLE.
I HEAR YOU HAVE INCREDIBLE GIFTS.
I KNOW IT DOESN'T SEEM LIKELY-- BASED ON THE WAY HE'S BEHAVING--BUT THORN KNOWS HOW OUR ABILITIES WORK. WHERE THEY COME FROM...
IF I'M BEING HONEST, I DON'T ENTIRELY TRUST HIM, BUT COME WITH US...
...AND THE MINUTE YOU WANT TO LEAVE, I PROMISE I'LL BRING YOU STRAIGHT BACK HOME.
LET'S SEE-- YOU'VE DRAWN GLASGOW, ENNIS, LONDON...AH, HERE WE ARE. A LOCAL MAP!
COME ON, LET ME SHOW YOU WHAT WE CAN DO TOGETHER.
EVEN WITH SOMEWHERE AS FAMILIAR TO YOU AS YOUR OWN TOWN, YOUR MAP IS NOTHING LIKE REALITY.
RIGHT?
I SEE THAT IN YOUR VERSION OF ESSAOUIRA, THERE'S A STONE CIRCLE IN THAT WEE SQUARE DOWN THERE...

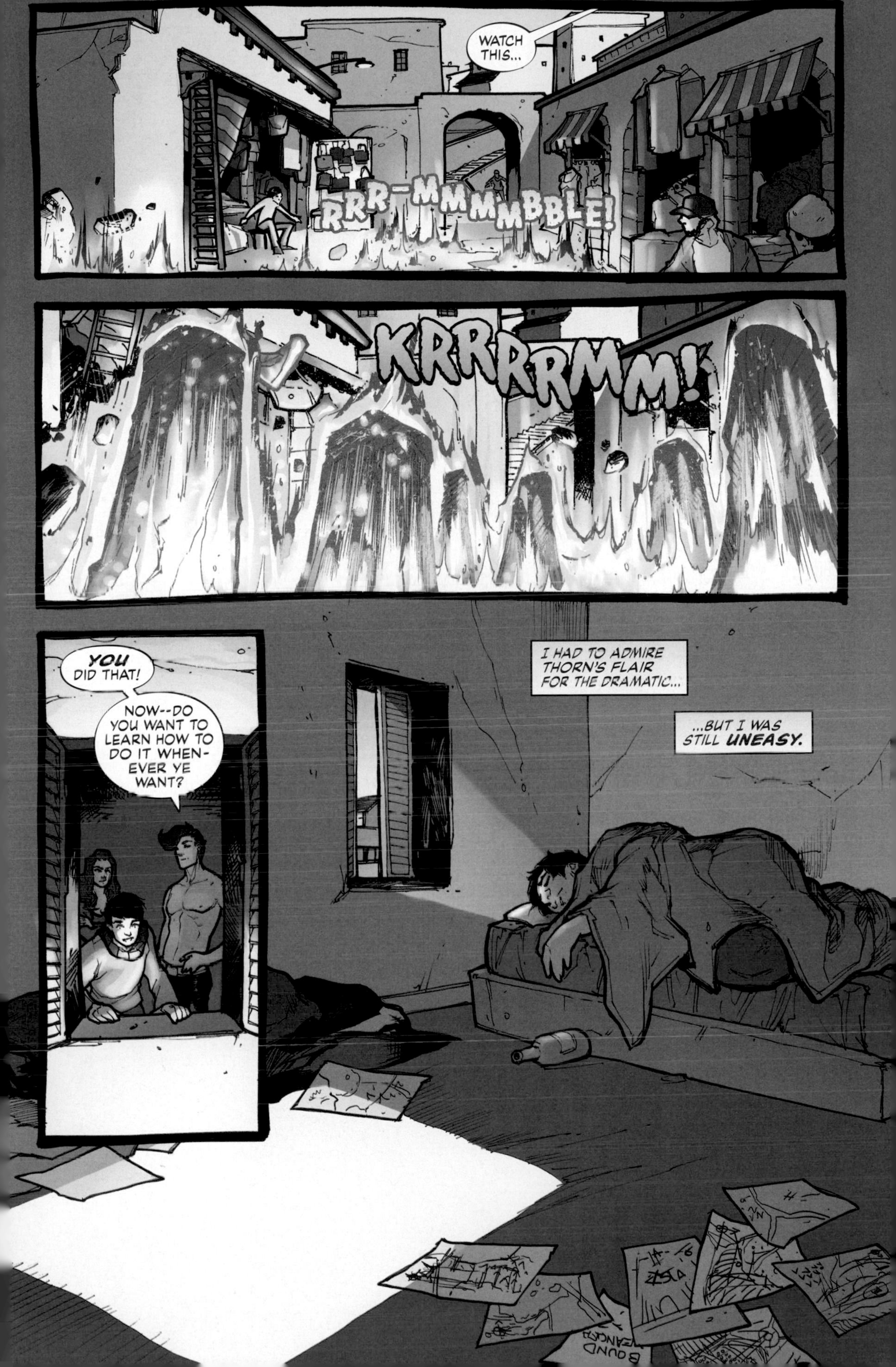
WATCH THIS...
RRR-MMMMMBBLE!
KRRRRRMMM!
YOU DID THAT!
NOW--DO YOU WANT TO LEARN HOW TO DO IT WHEN-EVER YE WANT?
I HAD TO ADMIRE THORN'S FLAIR FOR THE DRAMATIC...
...BUT I WAS STILL UNEASY.

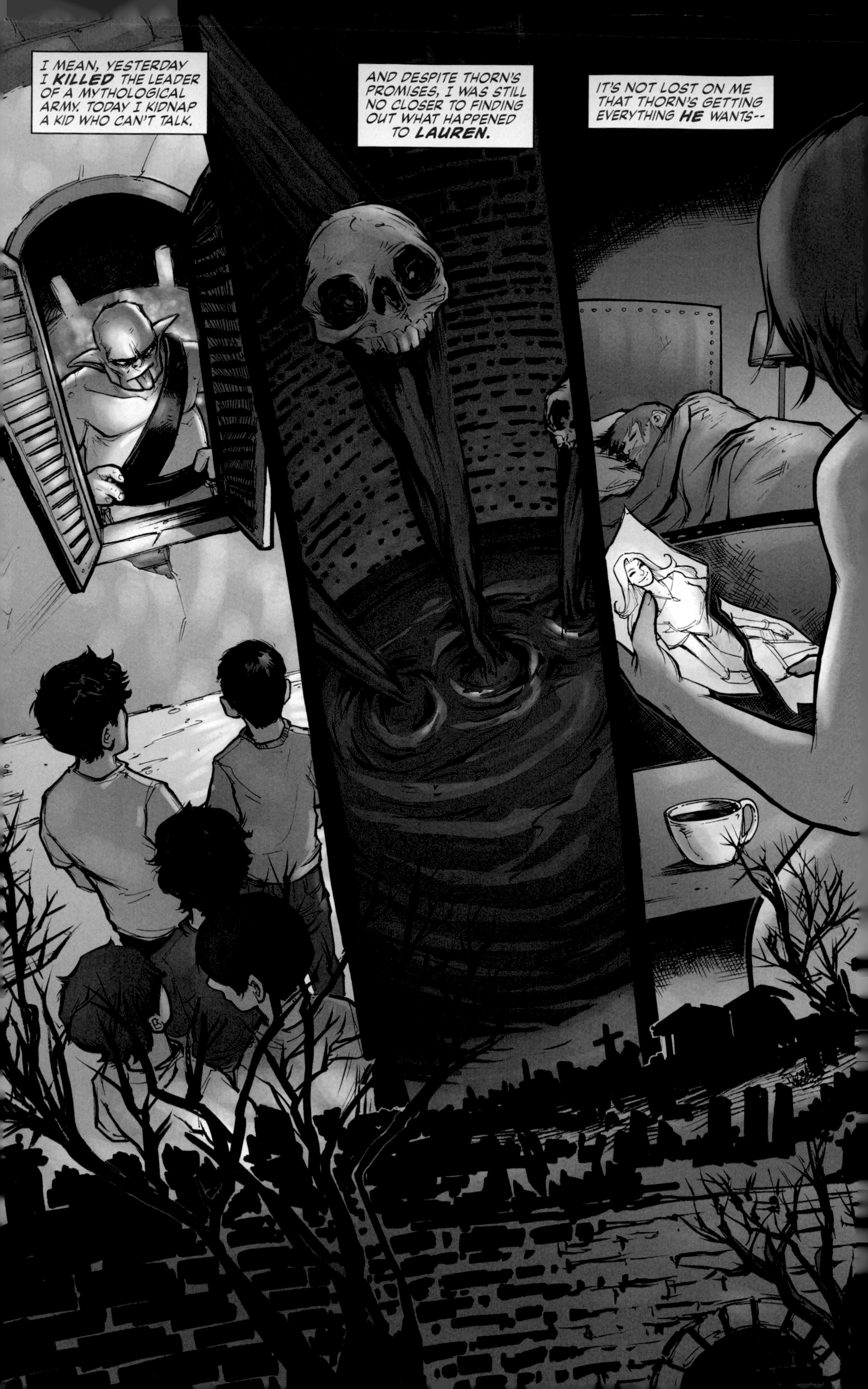
I MEAN, YESTERDAY I **KILLED** THE LEADER OF A MYTHOLOGICAL ARMY. TODAY I KIDNAP A KID WHO CAN'T TALK.
AND DESPITE THORN'S PROMISES, I WAS STILL NO CLOSER TO FINDING OUT WHAT HAPPENED TO **LAUREN.**
IT'S NOT LOST ON ME THAT THORN'S GETTING EVERYTHING **HE** WANTS--

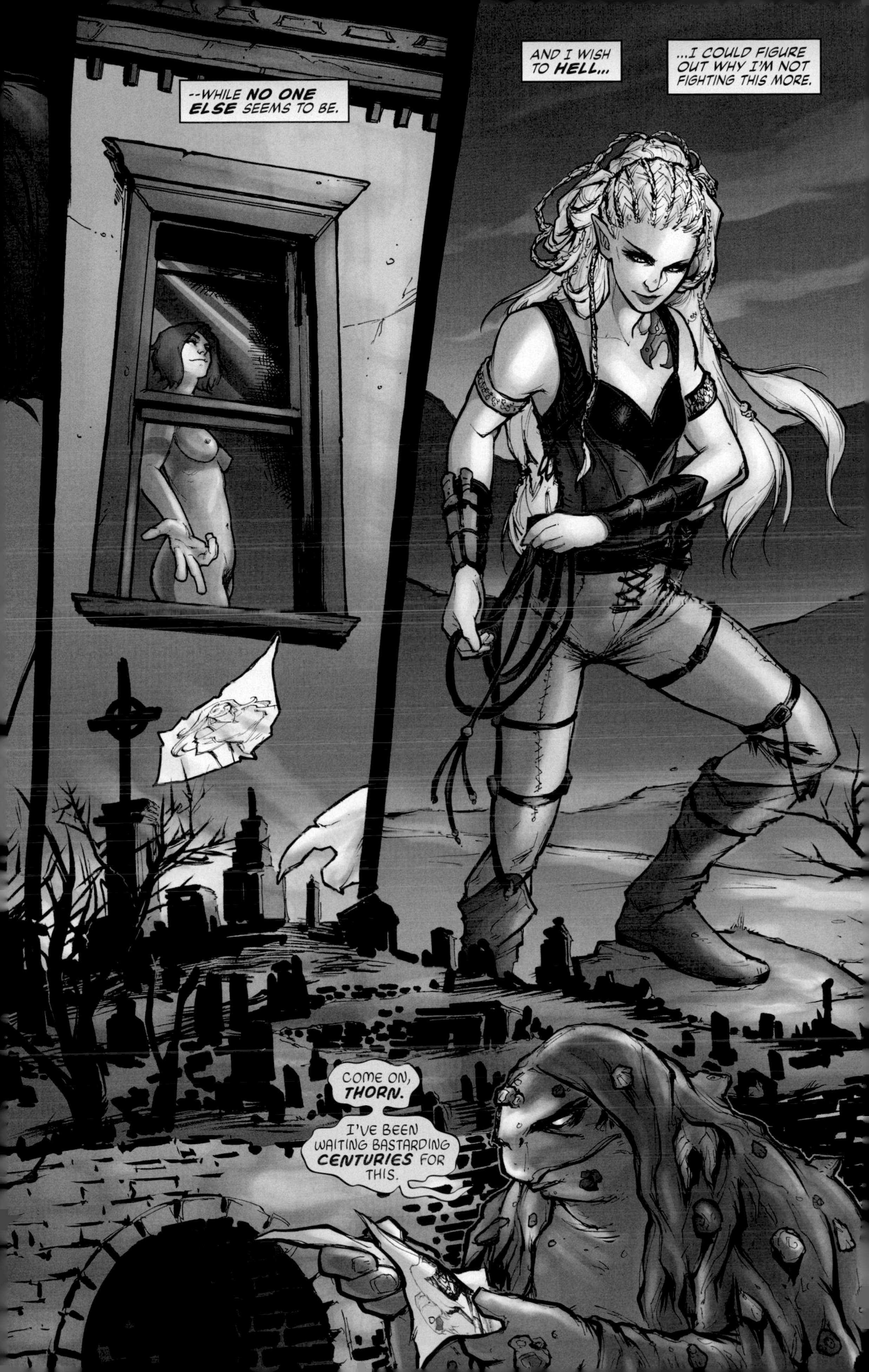
--WHILE NO ONE ELSE SEEMS TO BE.
AND I WISH TO HELL...
...I COULD FIGURE OUT WHY I'M NOT FIGHTING THIS MORE.
COME ON, THORN.
I'VE BEEN WAITING BASTARDING CENTURIES FOR THIS.

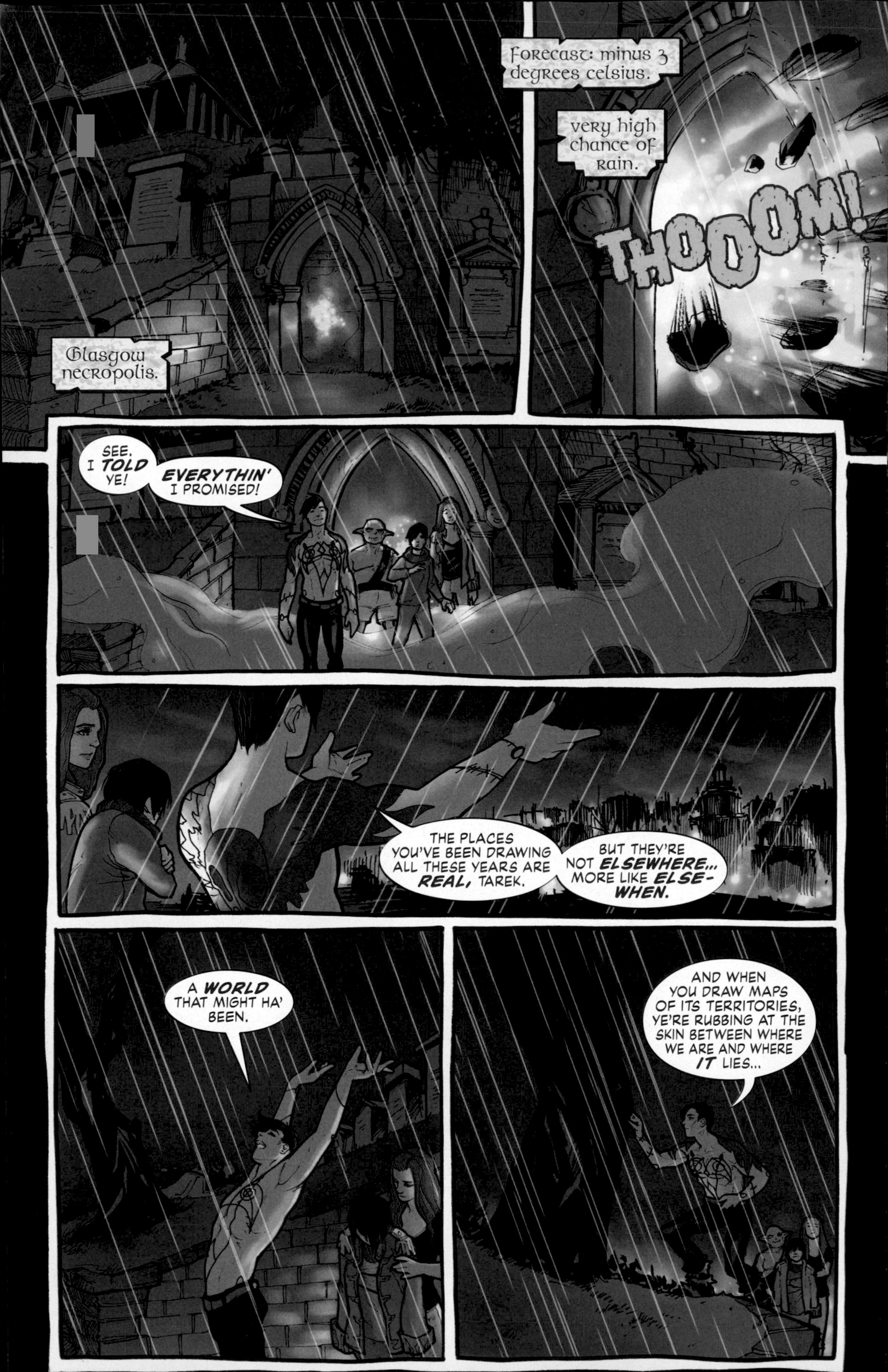
Glasgow necropolis.
Forecast: minus 3 degrees celsius.
very high chance of rain.
THOOOM!
SEE. I TOLD YE!
EVERYTHIN' I PROMISED!
THE PLACES YOU'VE BEEN DRAWING ALL THESE YEARS ARE REAL, TAREK.
BUT THEY'RE NOT ELSEWHERE... MORE LIKE ELSE-WHEN.
A WORLD THAT MIGHT HA' BEEN.
AND WHEN YOU DRAW MAPS OF ITS TERRITORIES, YE'RE RUBBING AT THE SKIN BETWEEN WHERE WE ARE AND WHERE IT LIES...

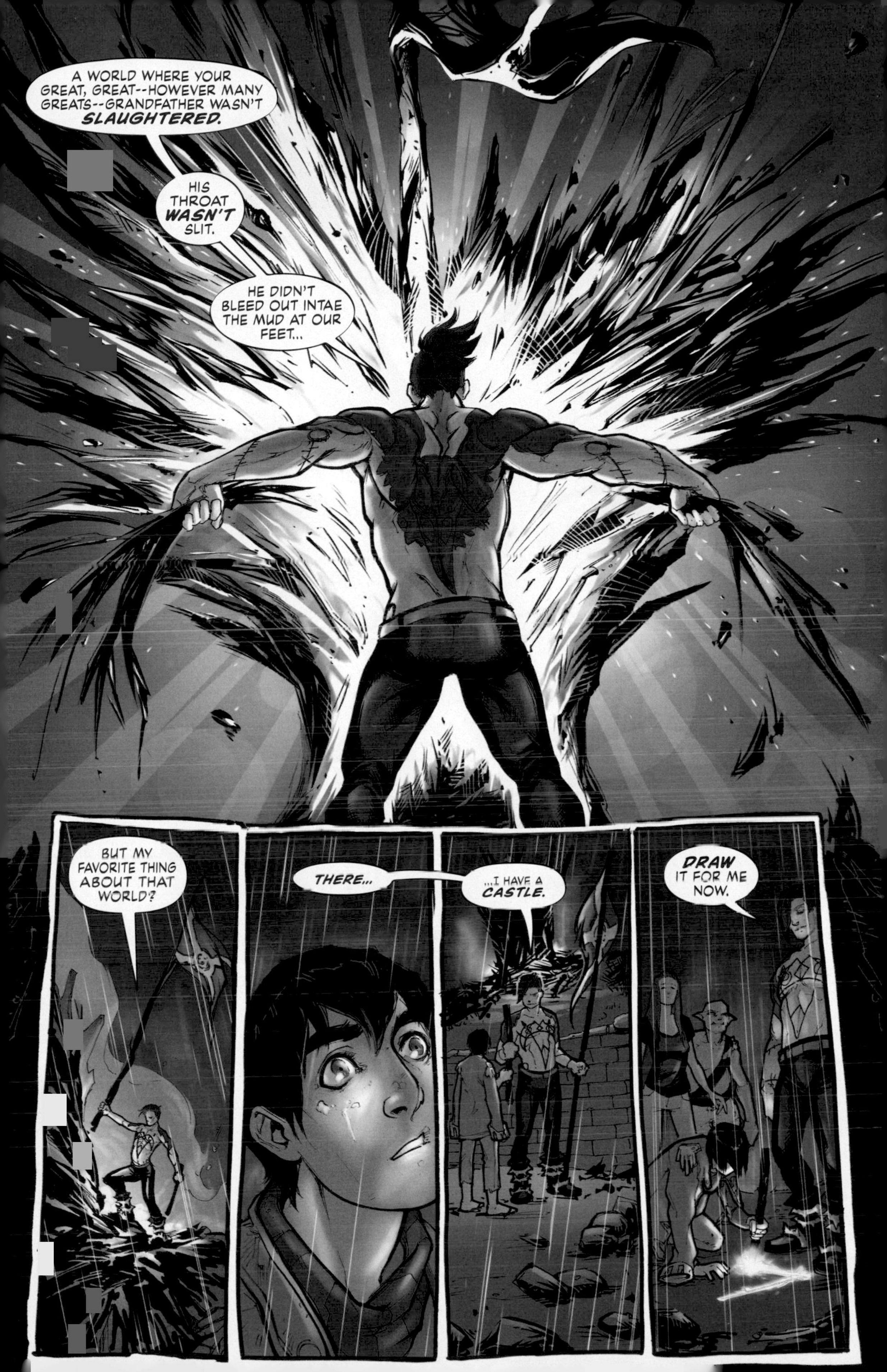
A WORLD WHERE YOUR GREAT, GREAT--HOWEVER MANY GREATS--GRANDFATHER WASN'T *SLAUGHTERED.*
HIS THROAT *WASN'T* SLIT.
HE DIDN'T BLEED OUT INTAE THE MUD AT OUR FEET...
BUT MY FAVORITE THING ABOUT THAT WORLD?
THERE...
...I HAVE A *CASTLE.*
DRAW IT FOR ME NOW.

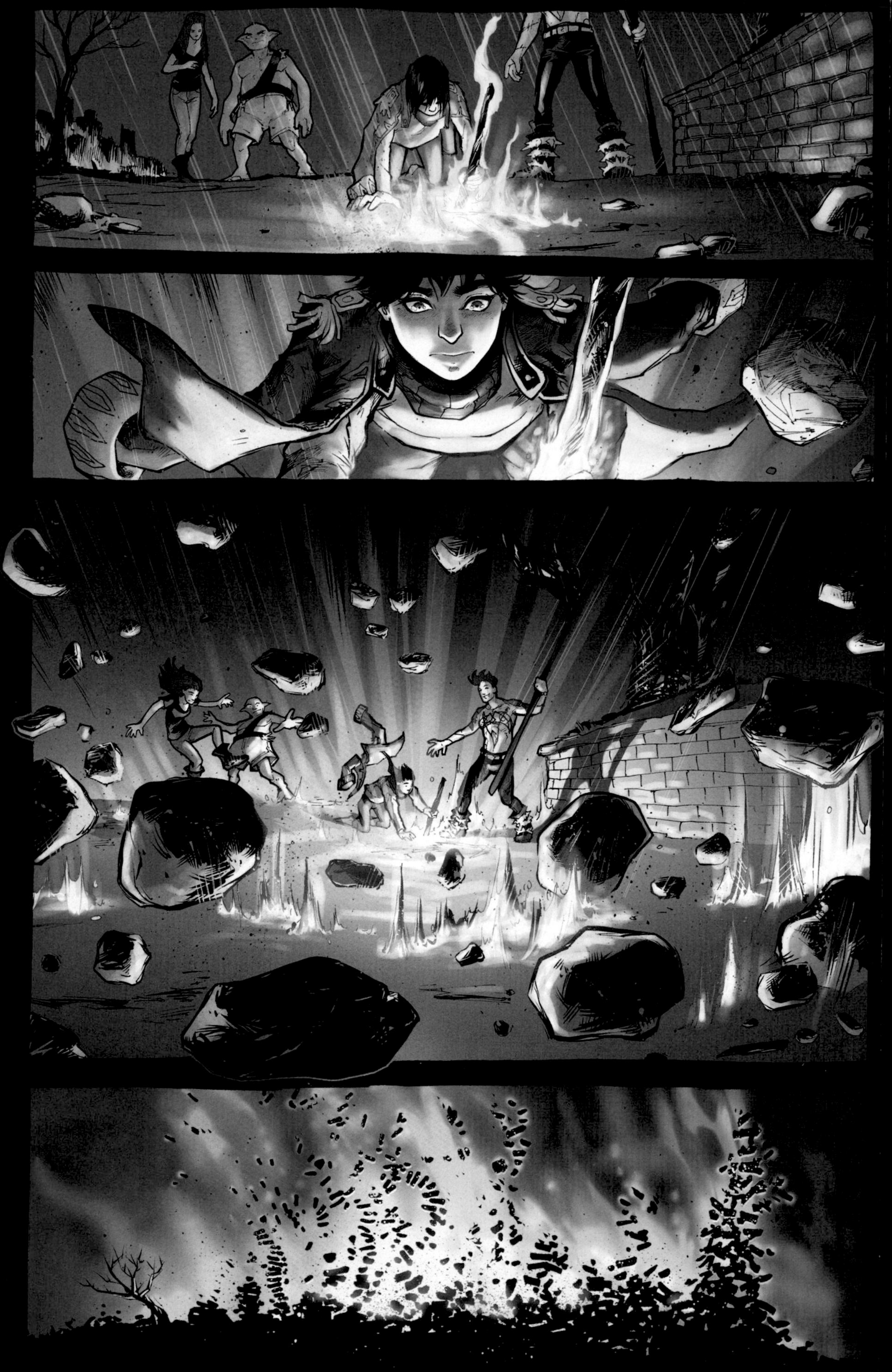

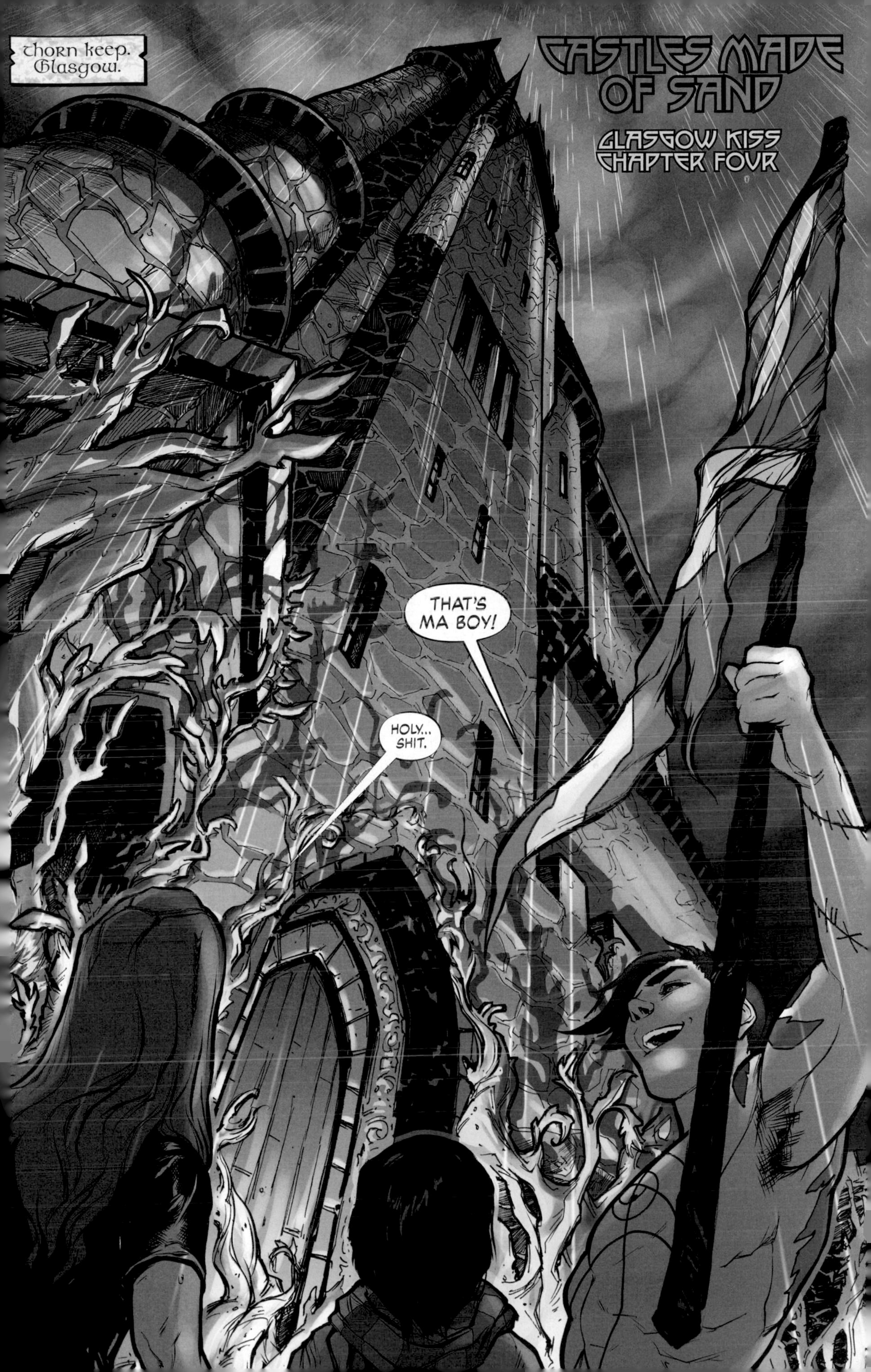

Thorn Keep.
Glasgow.
CASTLES MADE OF SAND
GLASGOW KISS
CHAPTER FOUR
THAT'S MA BOY!
HOLY... SHIT.

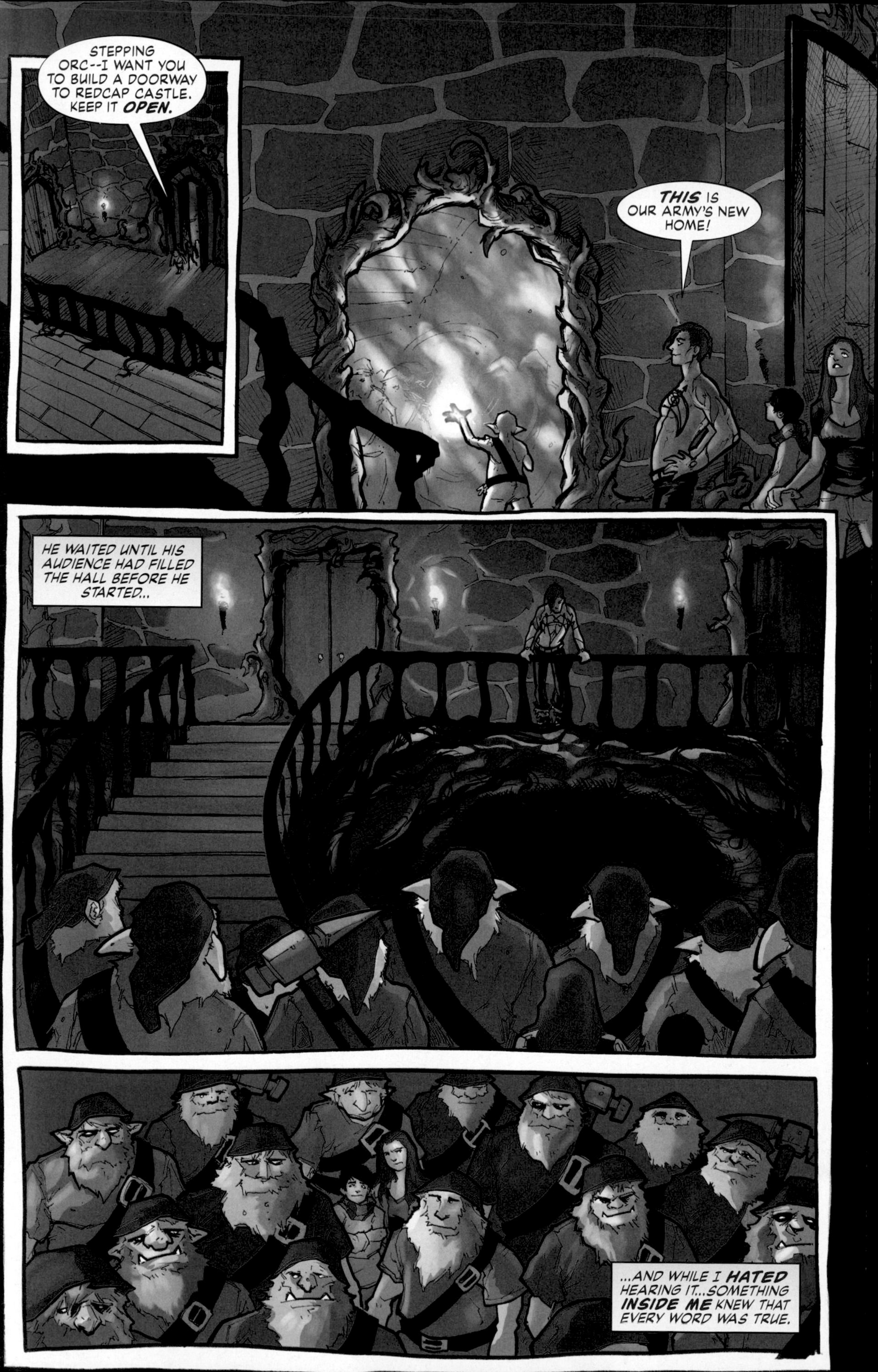
STEPPING ORC--I WANT YOU TO BUILD A DOORWAY TO REDCAP CASTLE. KEEP IT **OPEN.**
THIS IS OUR ARMY'S NEW HOME!
HE WAITED UNTIL HIS AUDIENCE HAD FILLED THE HALL BEFORE HE STARTED...
*...AND WHILE I **HATED** HEARING IT...SOMETHING **INSIDE ME** KNEW THAT EVERY WORD WAS TRUE.*

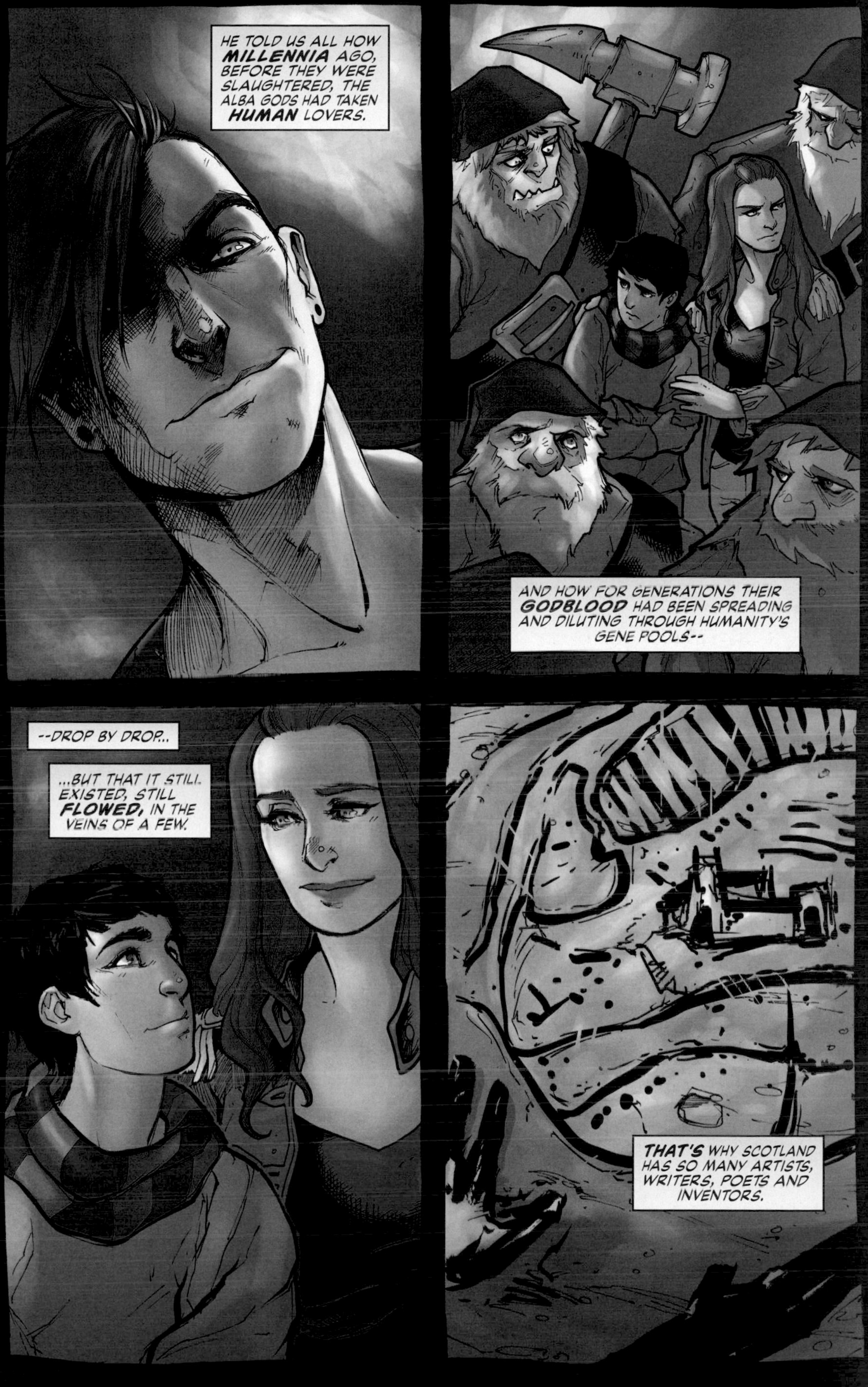
HE TOLD US ALL HOW MILLENNIA AGO, BEFORE THEY WERE SLAUGHTERED, THE ALBA GODS HAD TAKEN HUMAN LOVERS.
AND HOW FOR GENERATIONS THEIR GODBLOOD HAD BEEN SPREADING AND DILUTING THROUGH HUMANITY'S GENE POOLS--
--DROP BY DROP...
...BUT THAT IT STILL EXISTED, STILL FLOWED, IN THE VEINS OF A FEW.
THAT'S WHY SCOTLAND HAS SO MANY ARTISTS, WRITERS, POETS AND INVENTORS.

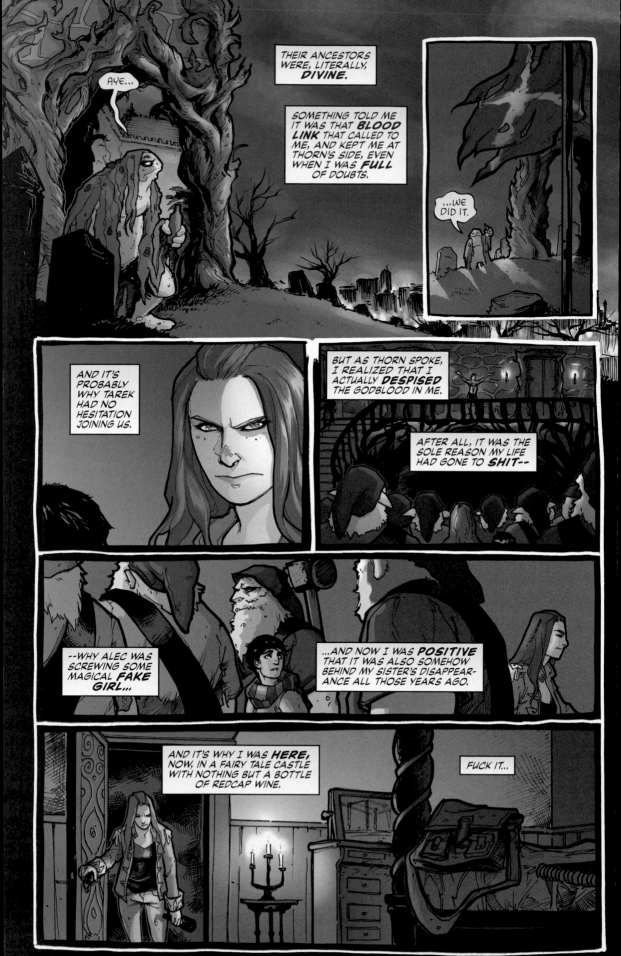

THEIR ANCESTORS WERE, LITERALLY, **DIVINE**.

SOMETHING TOLD ME IT WAS THAT **BLOOD LINK** THAT CALLED TO ME, AND KEPT ME AT THORN'S SIDE, EVEN WHEN I WAS **FULL** OF DOUBTS.

AYE...

....WE DID IT.

AND IT'S PROBABLY WHY TAREK HAD NO HESITATION JOINING US.

BUT AS THORN SPOKE, I REALIZED THAT I ACTUALLY **DESPISED** THE GODBLOOD IN ME.

AFTER ALL, IT WAS THE SOLE REASON MY LIFE HAD GONE TO **SHIT**--

--WHY ALEC WAS SCREWING SOME MAGICAL **FAKE GIRL**...

...AND NOW I WAS **POSITIVE** THAT IT WAS ALSO SOMEHOW BEHIND MY SISTER'S DISAPPEARANCE ALL THOSE YEARS AGO.

AND IT'S WHY I WAS **HERE**, NOW, IN A FAIRY TALE CASTLE WITH NOTHING BUT A BOTTLE OF REDCAP WINE.

FUCK IT...

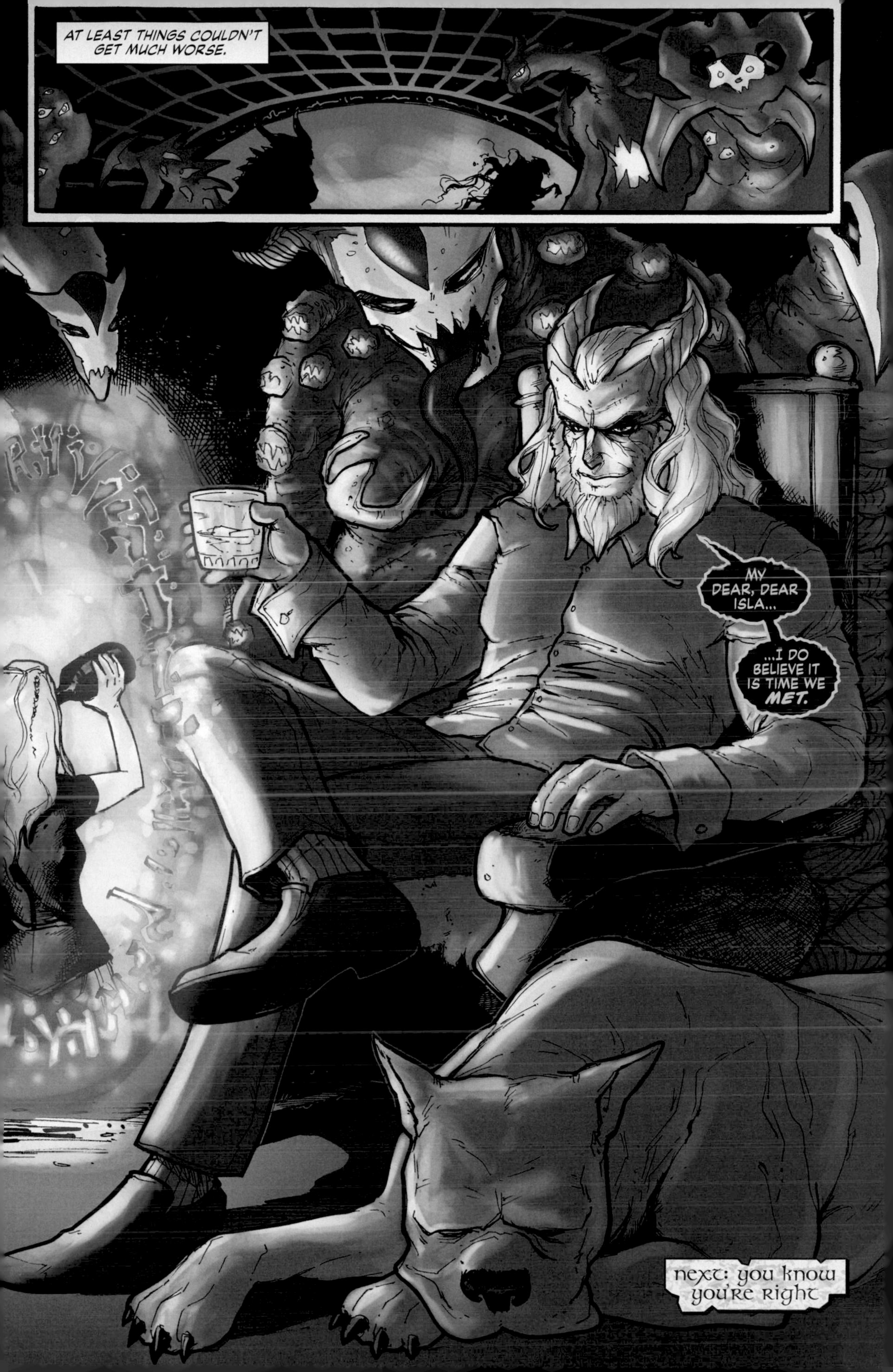
AT LEAST THINGS COULDN'T GET MUCH WORSE.
MY DEAR, DEAR ISLA...
...I DO BELIEVE IT IS TIME WE MET.
next: you know you're right

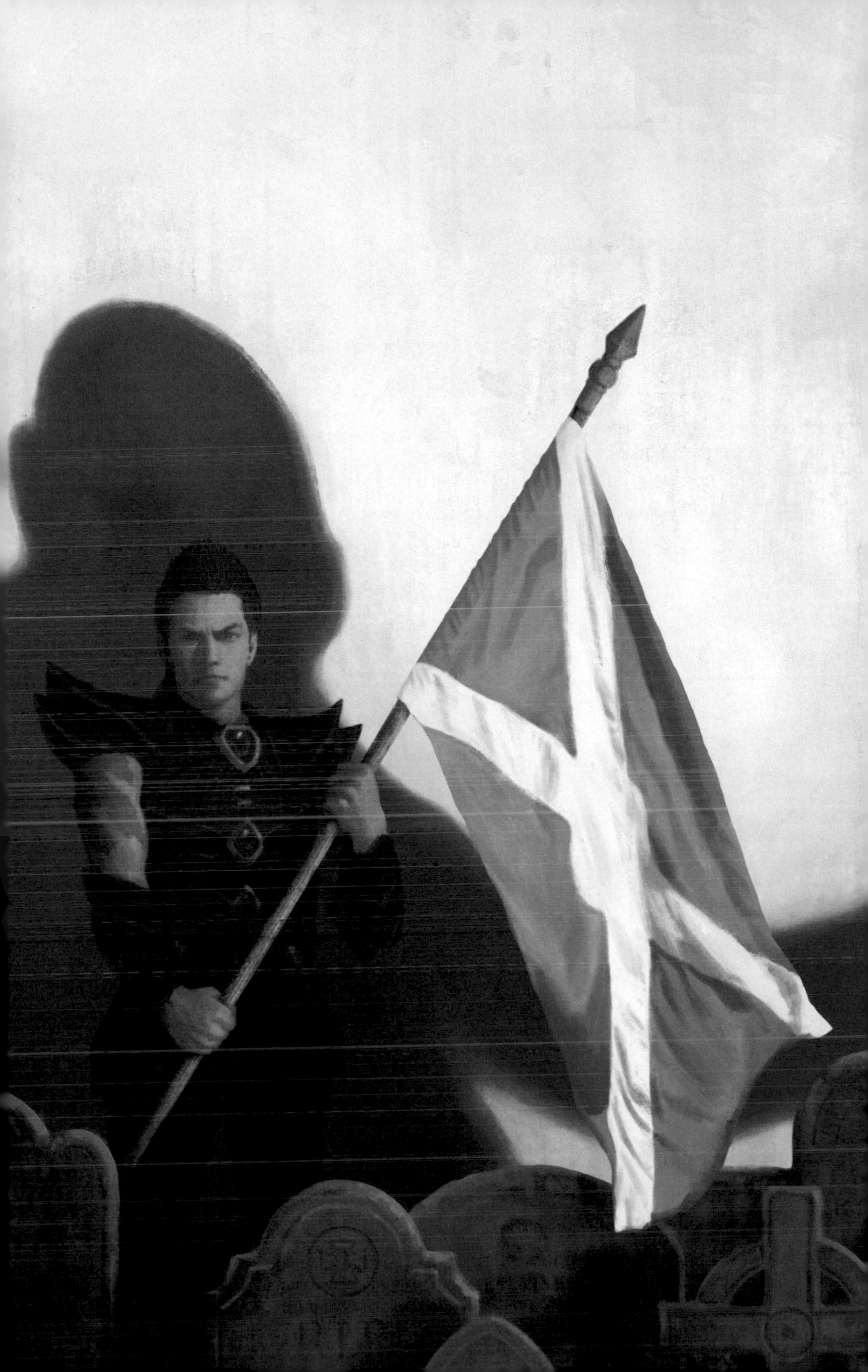

"THAT'S THE LAST INVISIBLE WOMAN I FALL IN LOVE WITH."

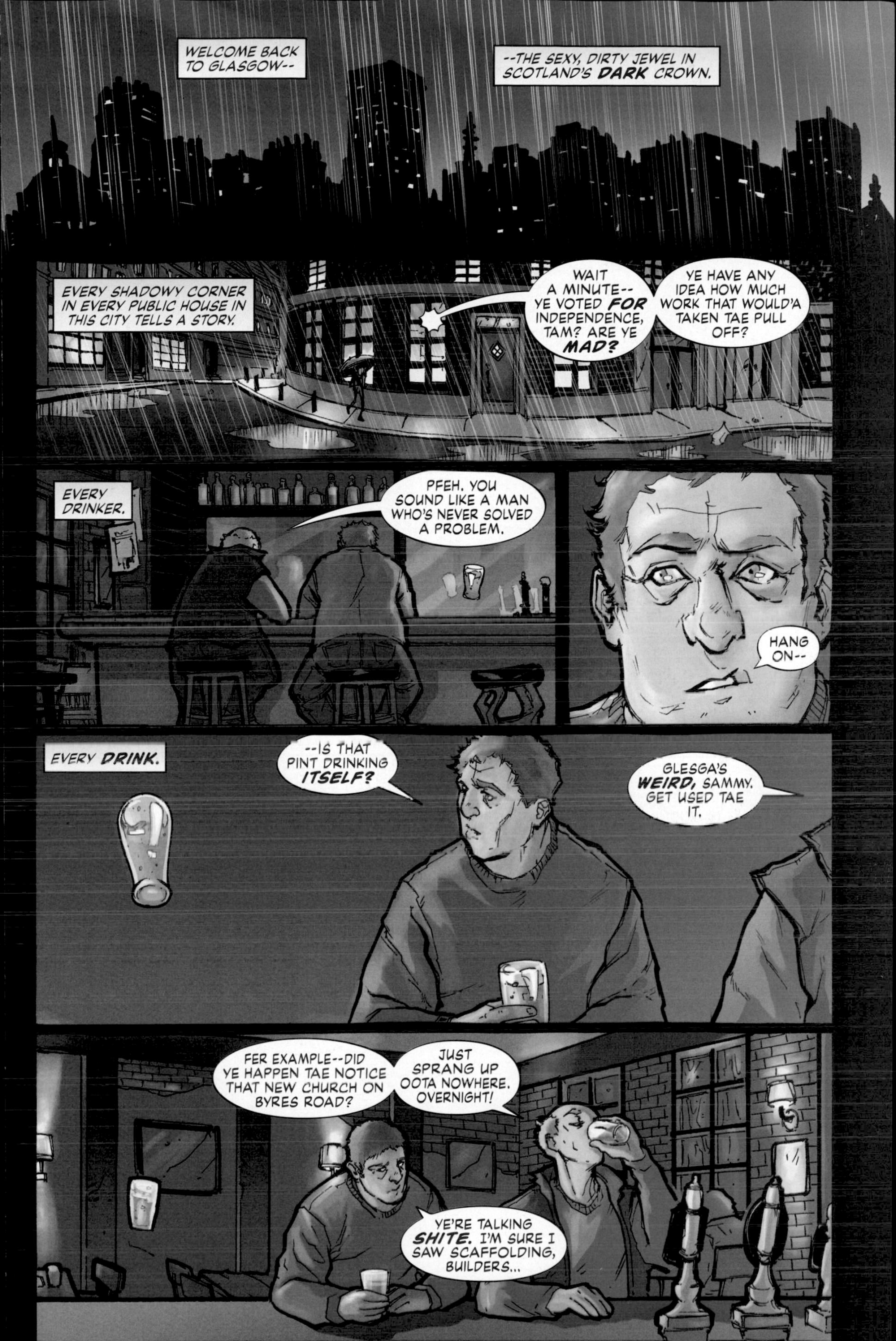
WELCOME BACK TO GLASGOW--
--THE SEXY, DIRTY JEWEL IN SCOTLAND'S DARK CROWN.
EVERY SHADOWY CORNER IN EVERY PUBLIC HOUSE IN THIS CITY TELLS A STORY.
WAIT A MINUTE--YE VOTED FOR INDEPENDENCE, TAM? ARE YE MAD?
YE HAVE ANY IDEA HOW MUCH WORK THAT WOULD'A TAKEN TAE PULL OFF?
EVERY DRINKER.
PFEH. YOU SOUND LIKE A MAN WHO'S NEVER SOLVED A PROBLEM.
HANG ON--
EVERY DRINK.
--IS THAT PINT DRINKING ITSELF?
GLESGA'S WEIRD, SAMMY. GET USED TAE IT.
FER EXAMPLE--DID YE HAPPEN TAE NOTICE THAT NEW CHURCH ON BYRES ROAD?
JUST SPRANG UP OOTA NOWHERE. OVERNIGHT!
YE'RE TALKING SHITE. I'M SURE I SAW SCAFFOLDING, BUILDERS...

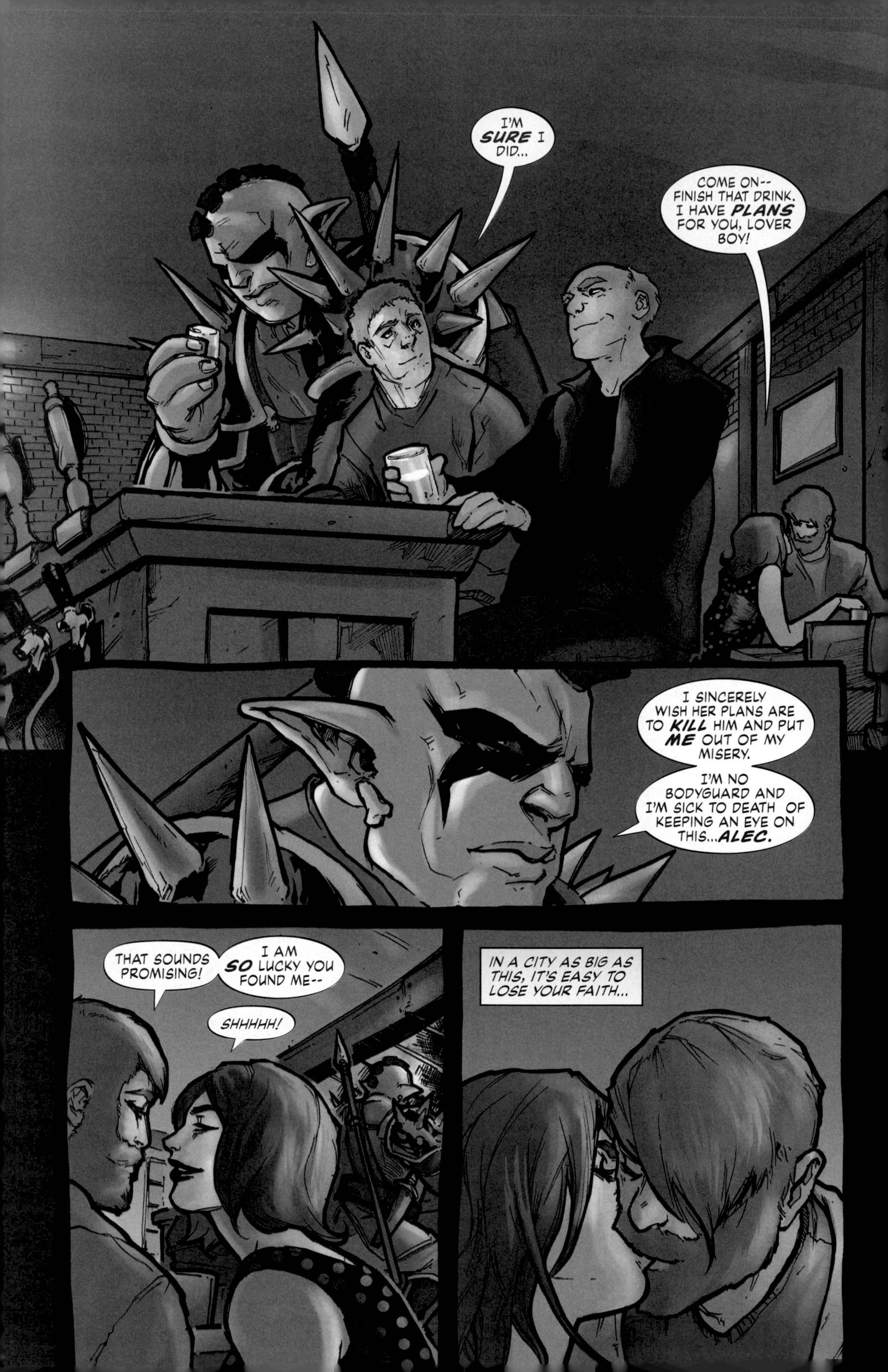
I'M SURE I DID...
COME ON-- FINISH THAT DRINK. I HAVE PLANS FOR YOU, LOVER BOY!
I SINCERELY WISH HER PLANS ARE TO KILL HIM AND PUT ME OUT OF MY MISERY.
I'M NO BODYGUARD AND I'M SICK TO DEATH OF KEEPING AN EYE ON THIS...ALEC.
THAT SOUNDS PROMISING!
I AM SO LUCKY YOU FOUND ME--
SHHHHH!
IN A CITY AS BIG AS THIS, IT'S EASY TO LOSE YOUR FAITH...

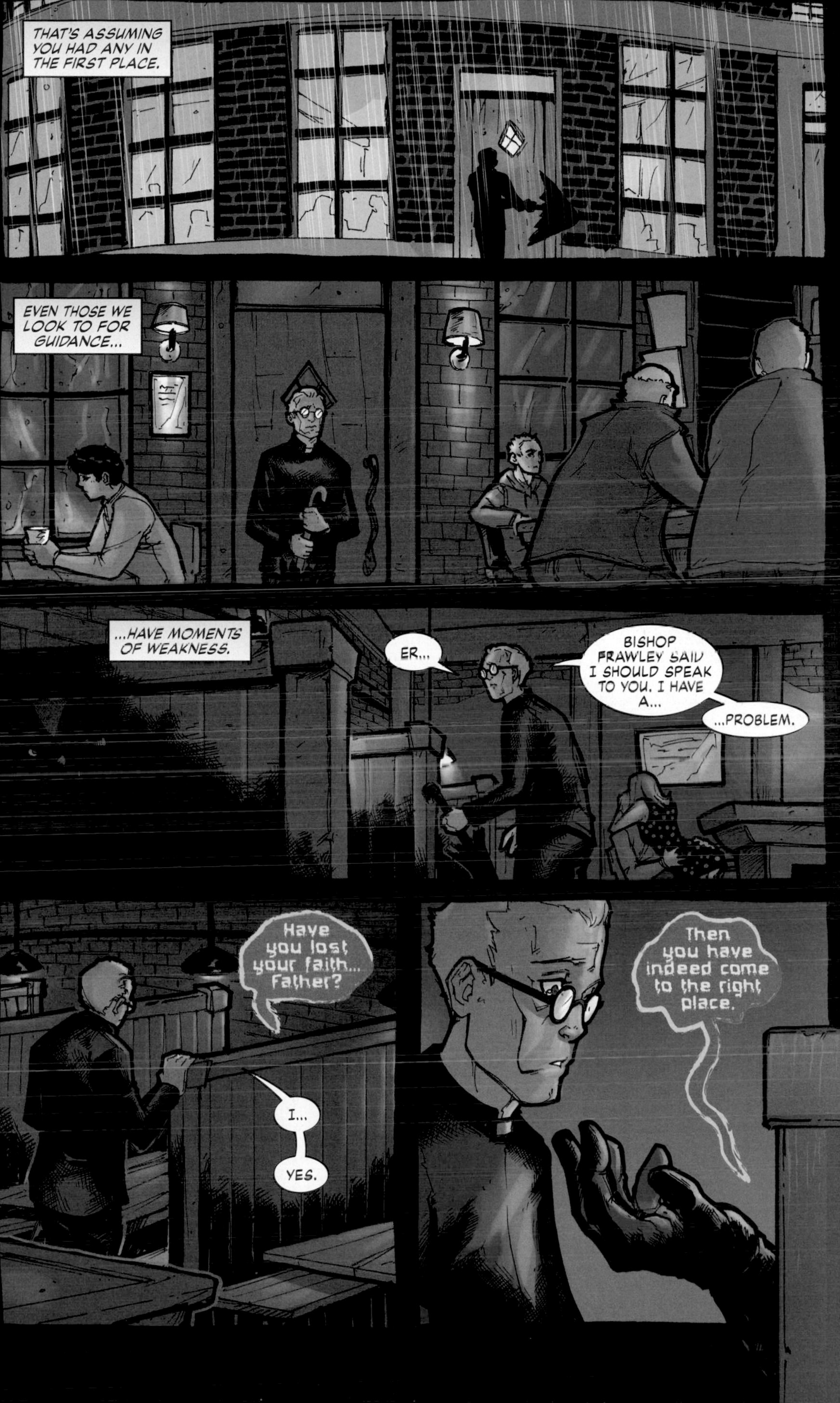
THAT'S ASSUMING YOU HAD ANY IN THE FIRST PLACE.
EVEN THOSE WE LOOK TO FOR GUIDANCE...
...HAVE MOMENTS OF WEAKNESS.
ER...
BISHOP FRAWLEY SAID I SHOULD SPEAK TO YOU. I HAVE A...
...PROBLEM.
Have you lost your faith... Father?
I...
YES.
Then you have indeed come to the right place.

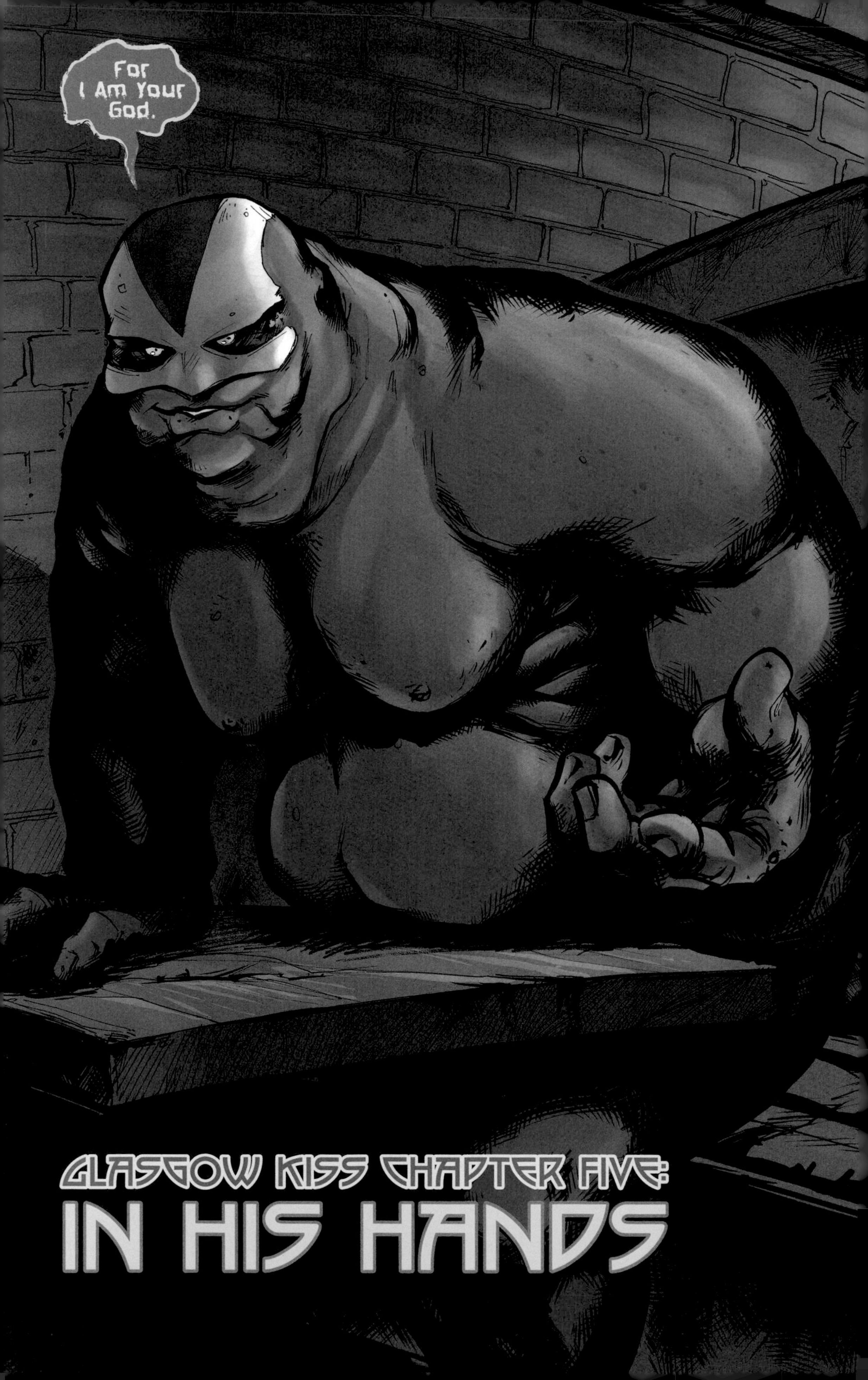
For I Am Your God.
GLASGOW KISS CHAPTER FIVE:
IN HIS HANDS

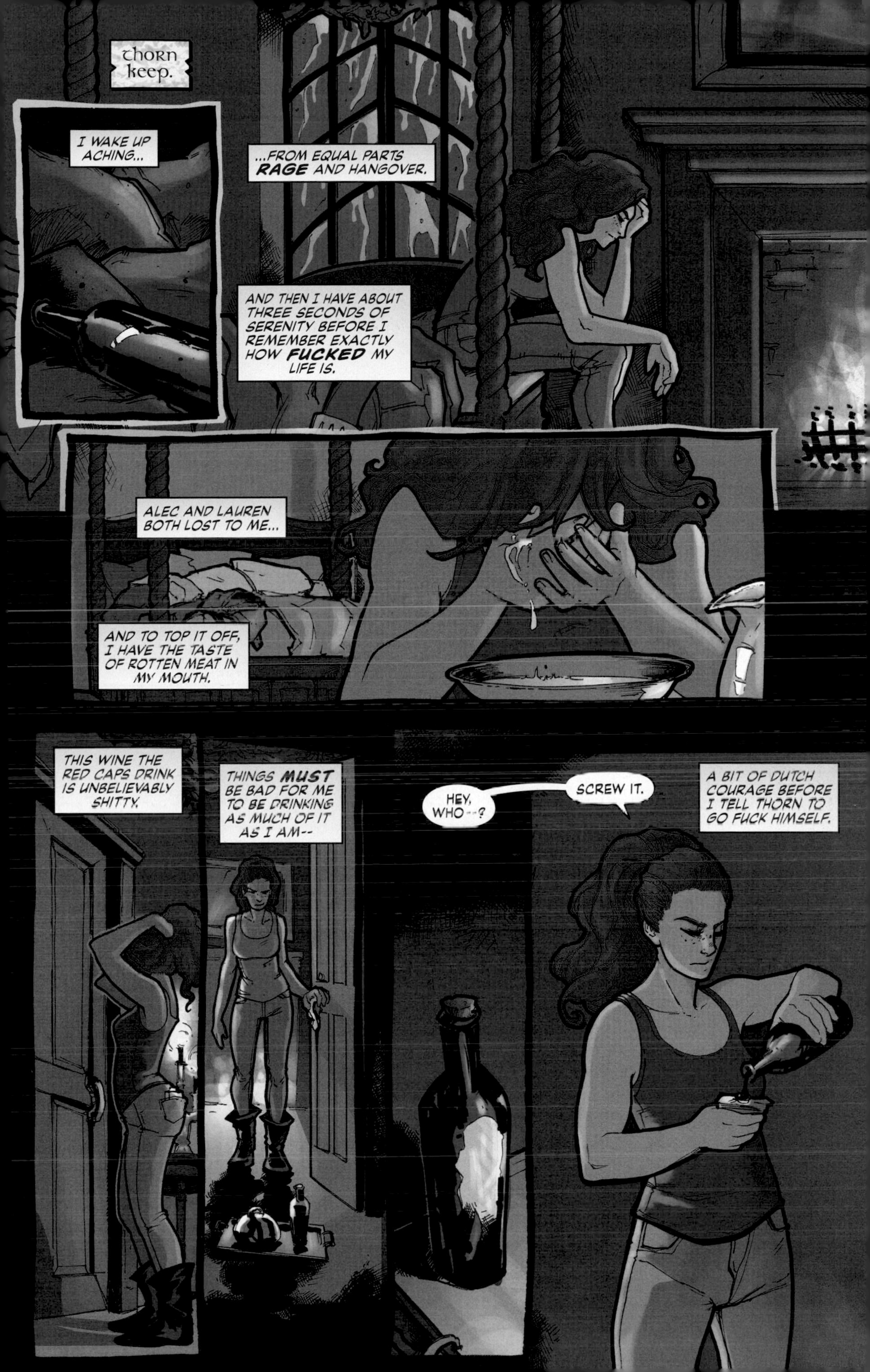
thorn keep.
I WAKE UP ACHING...
...FROM EQUAL PARTS RAGE AND HANGOVER.
AND THEN I HAVE ABOUT THREE SECONDS OF SERENITY BEFORE I REMEMBER EXACTLY HOW FUCKED MY LIFE IS.
ALEC AND LAUREN BOTH LOST TO ME...
AND TO TOP IT OFF, I HAVE THE TASTE OF ROTTEN MEAT IN MY MOUTH.
THIS WINE THE RED CAPS DRINK IS UNBELIEVABLY SHITTY.
THINGS MUST BE BAD FOR ME TO BE DRINKING AS MUCH OF IT AS I AM--
HEY, WHO--?
SCREW IT.
A BIT OF DUTCH COURAGE BEFORE I TELL THORN TO GO FUCK HIMSELF.

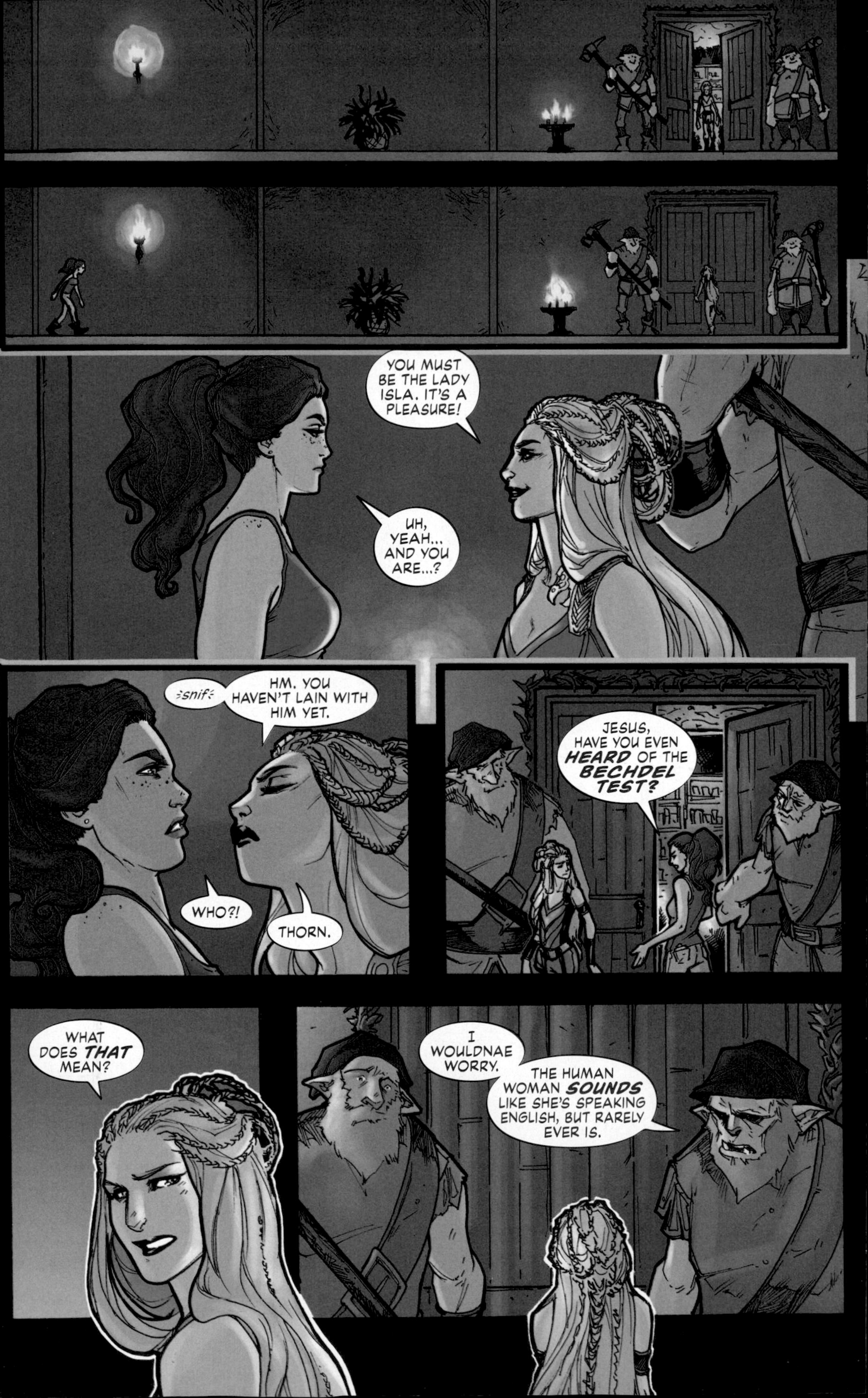
YOU MUST BE THE LADY ISLA. IT'S A PLEASURE!
UH, YEAH... AND YOU ARE...?
:snif:
HM. YOU HAVEN'T LAIN WITH HIM YET.
WHO?!
THORN.
JESUS, HAVE YOU EVEN HEARD OF THE BECHDEL TEST?
WHAT DOES THAT MEAN?
I WOULDNAE WORRY.
THE HUMAN WOMAN SOUNDS LIKE SHE'S SPEAKING ENGLISH, BUT RARELY EVER IS.

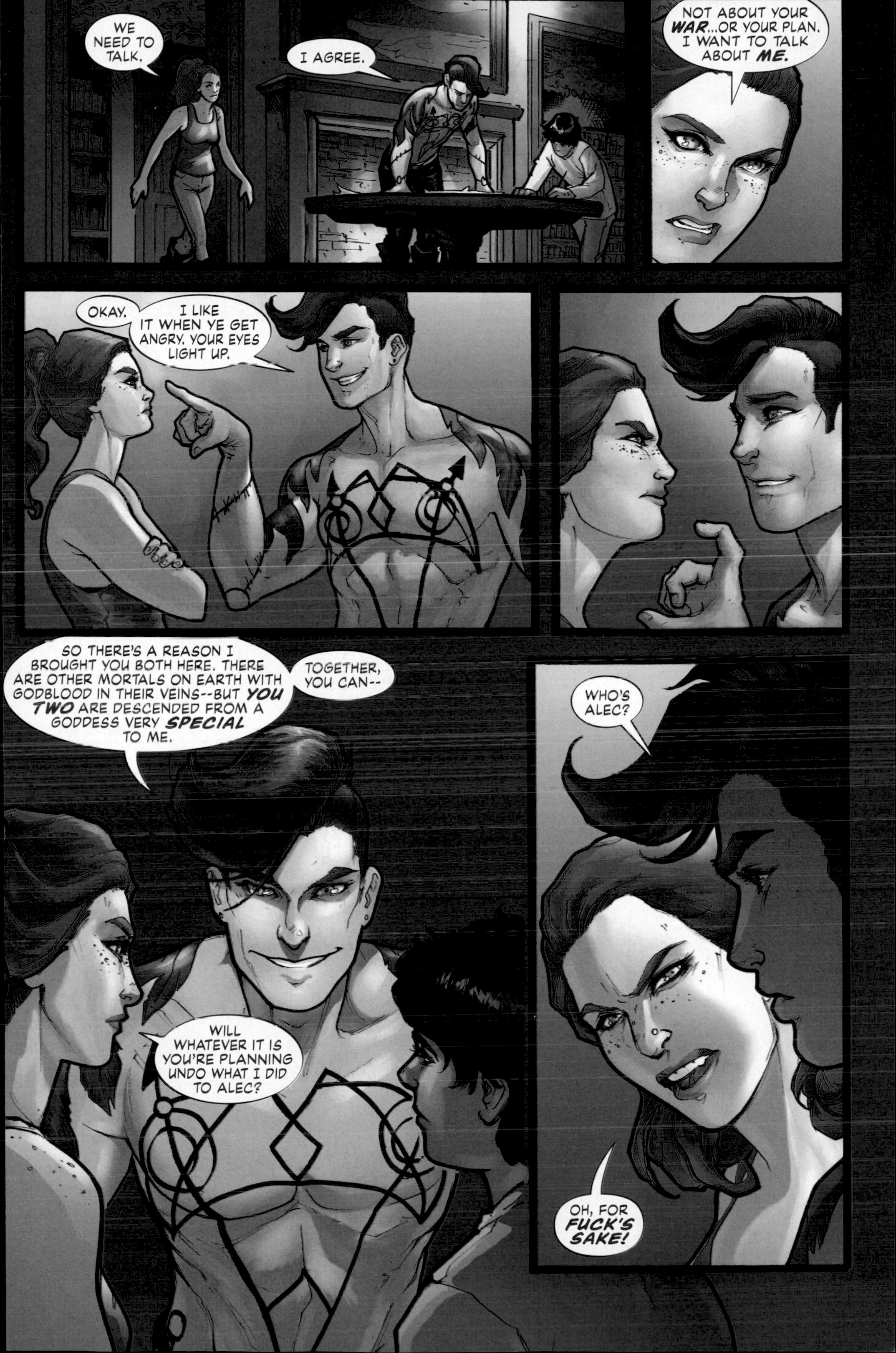

WE NEED TO TALK.
I AGREE.
NOT ABOUT YOUR WAR...OR YOUR PLAN. I WANT TO TALK ABOUT ME.
OKAY.
I LIKE IT WHEN YE GET ANGRY. YOUR EYES LIGHT UP.
SO THERE'S A REASON I BROUGHT YOU BOTH HERE. THERE ARE OTHER MORTALS ON EARTH WITH GODBLOOD IN THEIR VEINS--BUT YOU TWO ARE DESCENDED FROM A GODDESS VERY SPECIAL TO ME.
TOGETHER, YOU CAN--
WILL WHATEVER IT IS YOU'RE PLANNING UNDO WHAT I DID TO ALEC?
WHO'S ALEC?
OH, FOR FUCK'S SAKE!

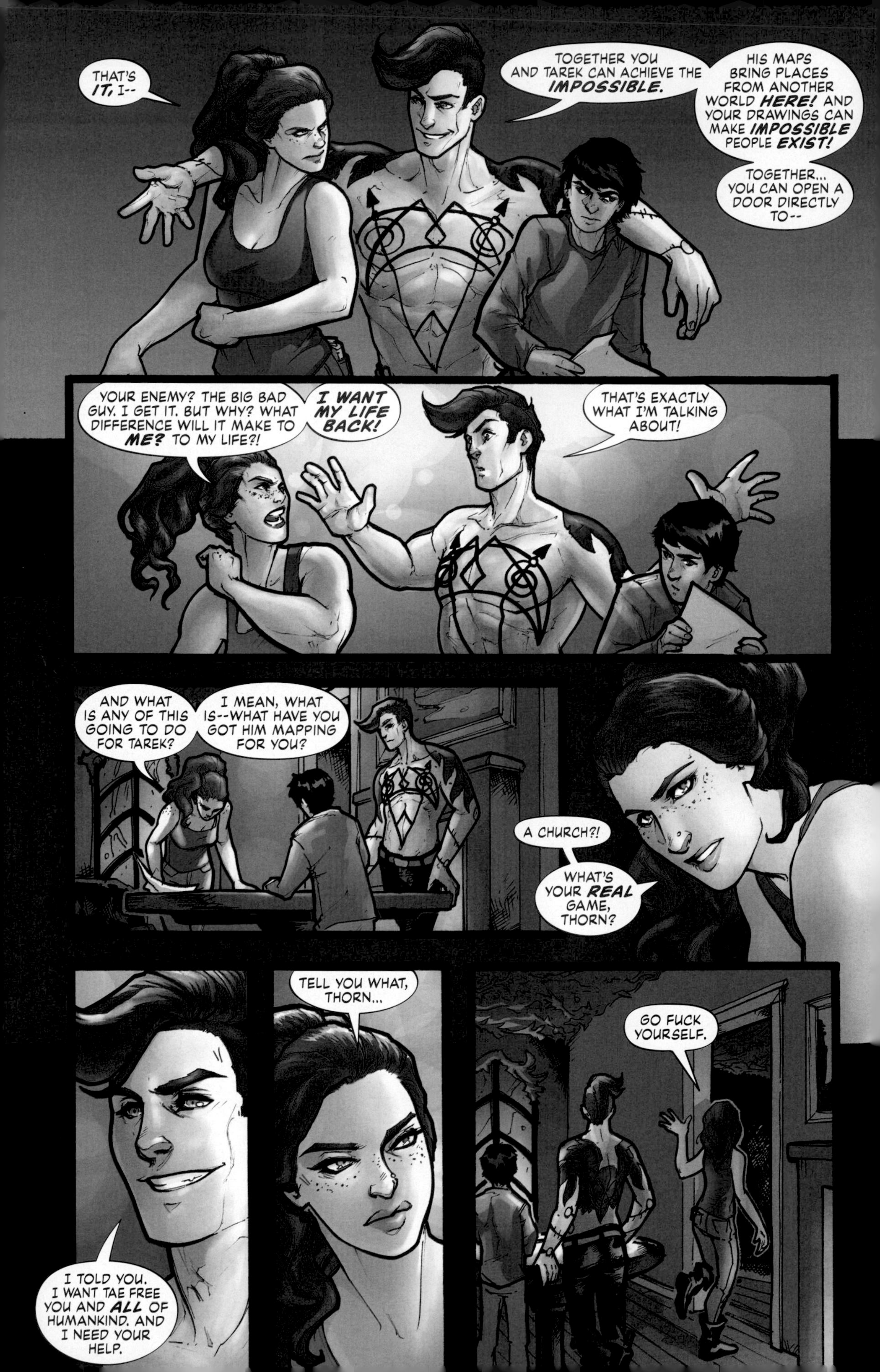
THAT'S IT, I--
TOGETHER YOU AND TAREK CAN ACHIEVE THE IMPOSSIBLE.
HIS MAPS BRING PLACES FROM ANOTHER WORLD HERE! AND YOUR DRAWINGS CAN MAKE IMPOSSIBLE PEOPLE EXIST!
TOGETHER... YOU CAN OPEN A DOOR DIRECTLY TO--
YOUR ENEMY? THE BIG BAD GUY. I GET IT. BUT WHY? WHAT DIFFERENCE WILL IT MAKE TO ME? TO MY LIFE?!
I WANT MY LIFE BACK!
THAT'S EXACTLY WHAT I'M TALKING ABOUT!
AND WHAT IS ANY OF THIS GOING TO DO FOR TAREK?
I MEAN, WHAT IS--WHAT HAVE YOU GOT HIM MAPPING FOR YOU?
A CHURCH?!
WHAT'S YOUR REAL GAME, THORN?
I TOLD YOU. I WANT TAE FREE YOU AND ALL OF HUMANKIND. AND I NEED YOUR HELP.
TELL YOU WHAT, THORN...
GO FUCK YOURSELF.

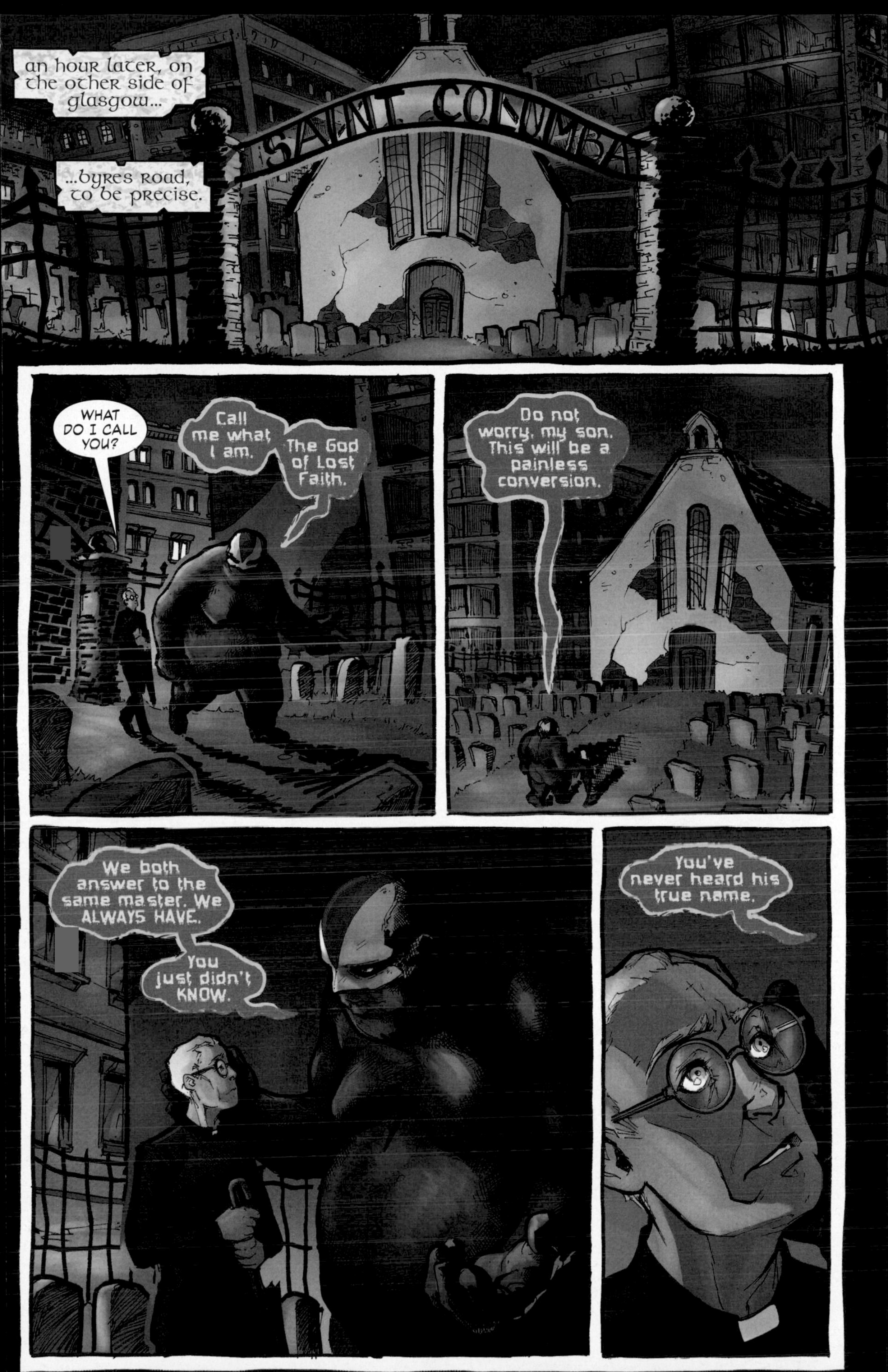

an hour later, on the other side of glasgow...
SAINT COLUMBA
...byres road, to be precise.
WHAT DO I CALL YOU?
Call me what I am.
The God of Lost Faith.
Do not worry, my son. This will be a painless conversion.
We both answer to the same master. We ALWAYS HAVE.
You just didn't KNOW.
You've never heard his true name.

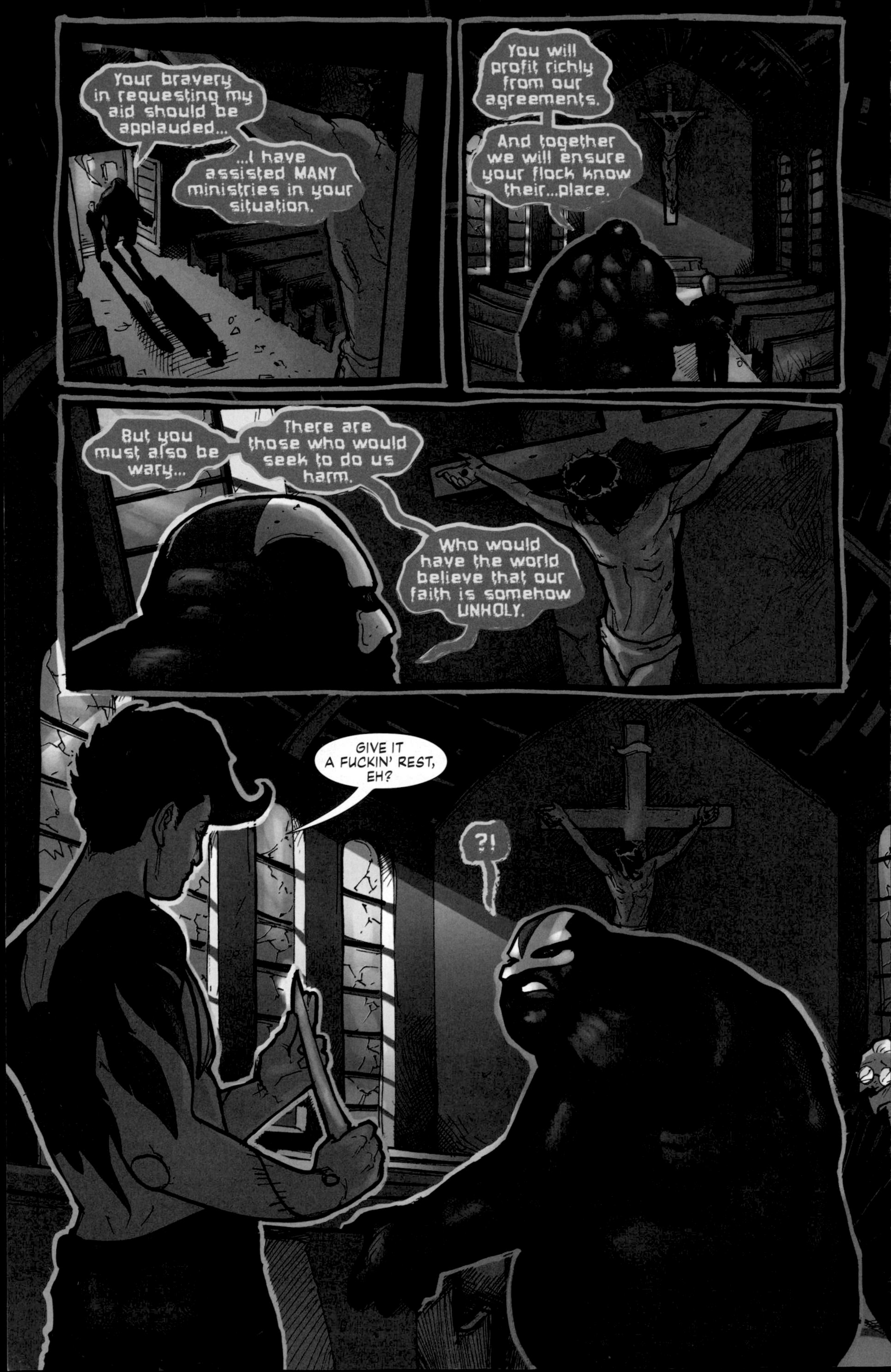
Your bravery in requesting my aid should be applauded...
...I have assisted MANY ministries in your situation.
You will profit richly from our agreements.
And together we will ensure your flock know their...place.
But you must also be wary...
There are those who would seek to do us harm.
Who would have the world believe that our faith is somehow UNHOLY.
GIVE IT A FUCKIN' REST, EH?
?!

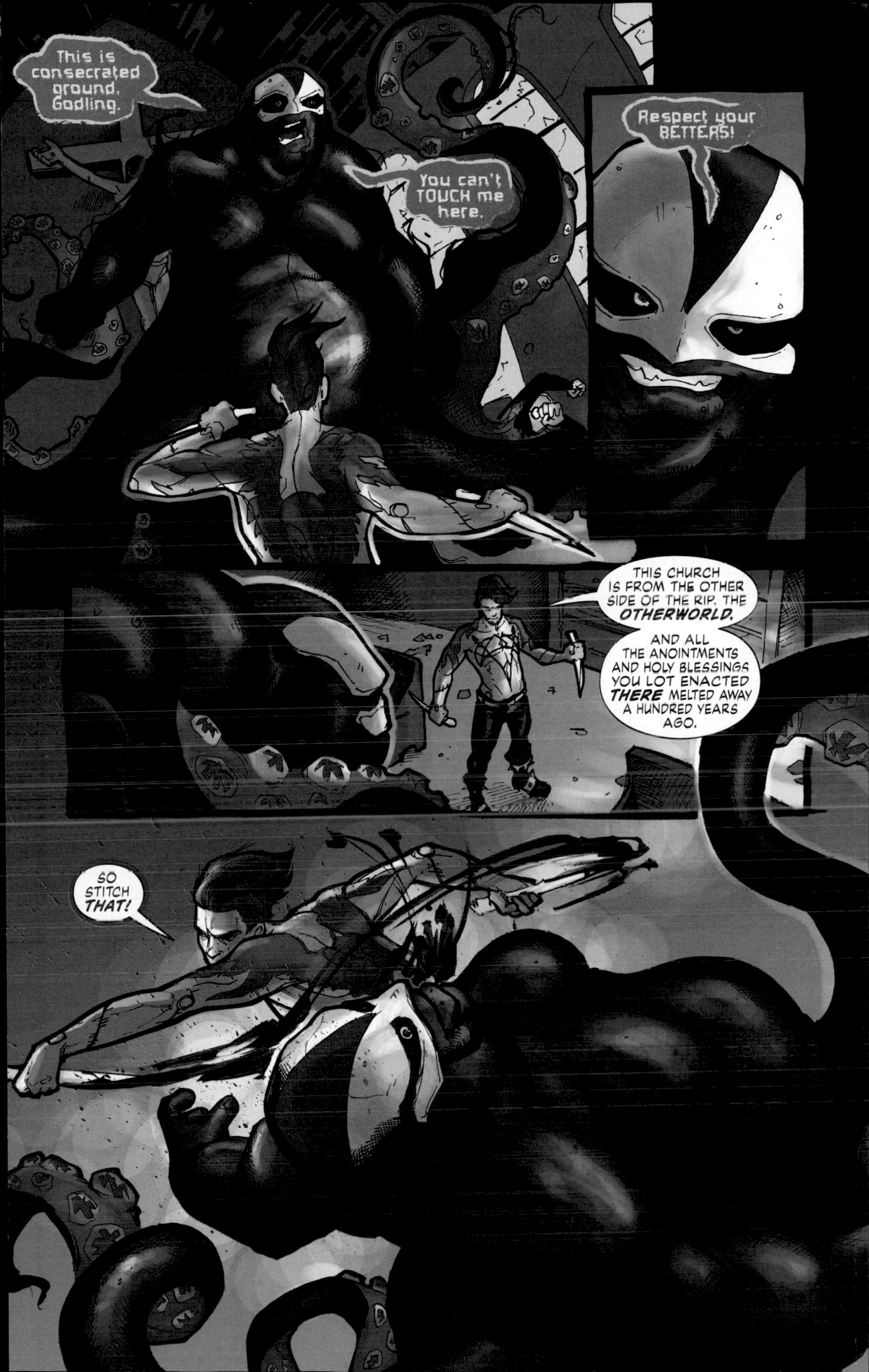
This is consecrated ground, Godling.
You can't TOUCH me here.
Respect your BETTERS!
THIS CHURCH IS FROM THE OTHER SIDE OF THE RIP. THE OTHERWORLD.
AND ALL THE ANOINTMENTS AND HOLY BLESSINGS YOU LOT ENACTED THERE MELTED AWAY A HUNDRED YEARS AGO.
SO STITCH THAT!

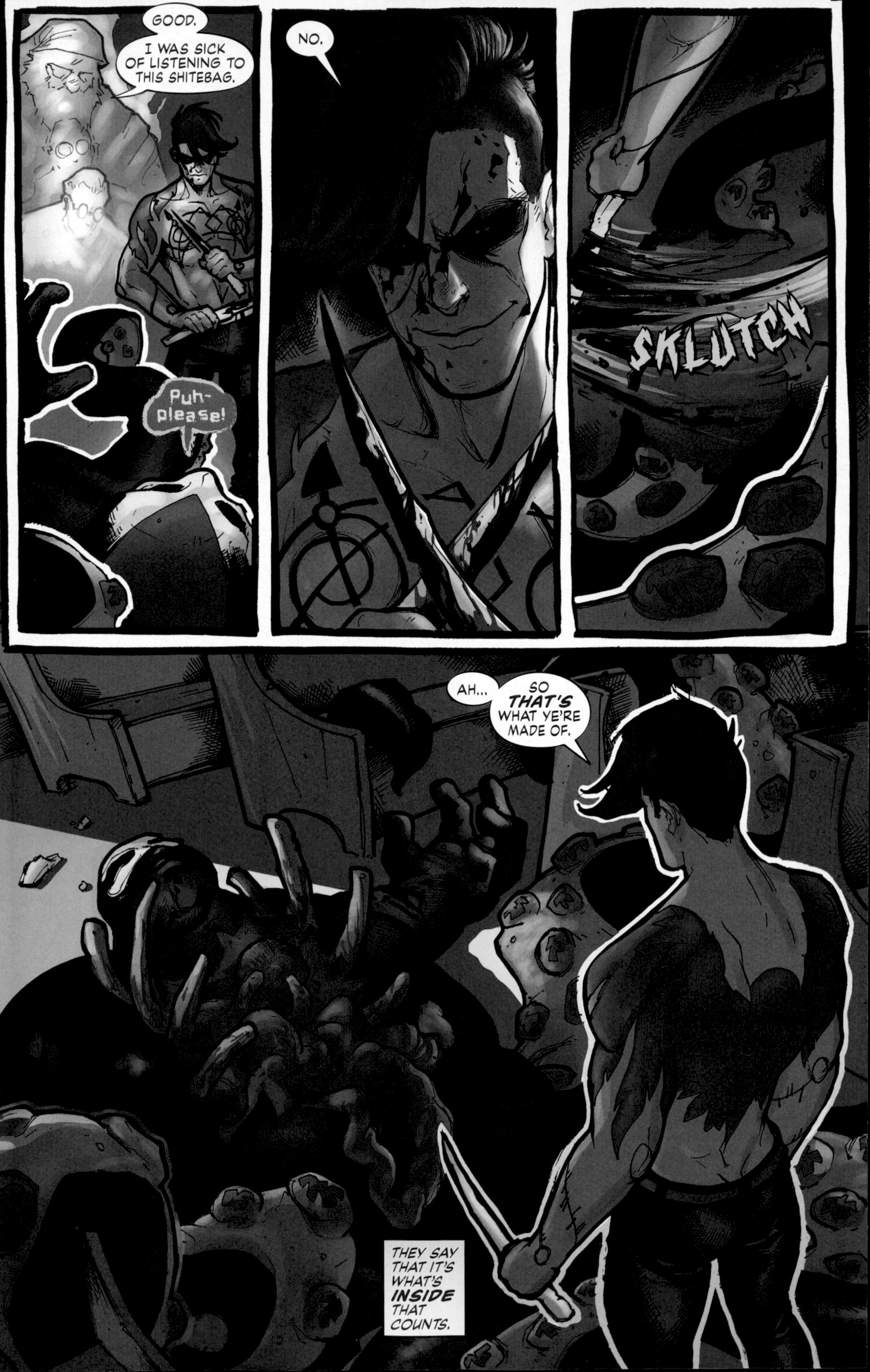
GOOD.
I WAS SICK OF LISTENING TO THIS SHITEBAG.
Puh-please!
NO.
SKLUTCH
AH...
SO THAT'S WHAT YE'RE MADE OF.
THEY SAY THAT IT'S WHAT'S INSIDE THAT COUNTS.

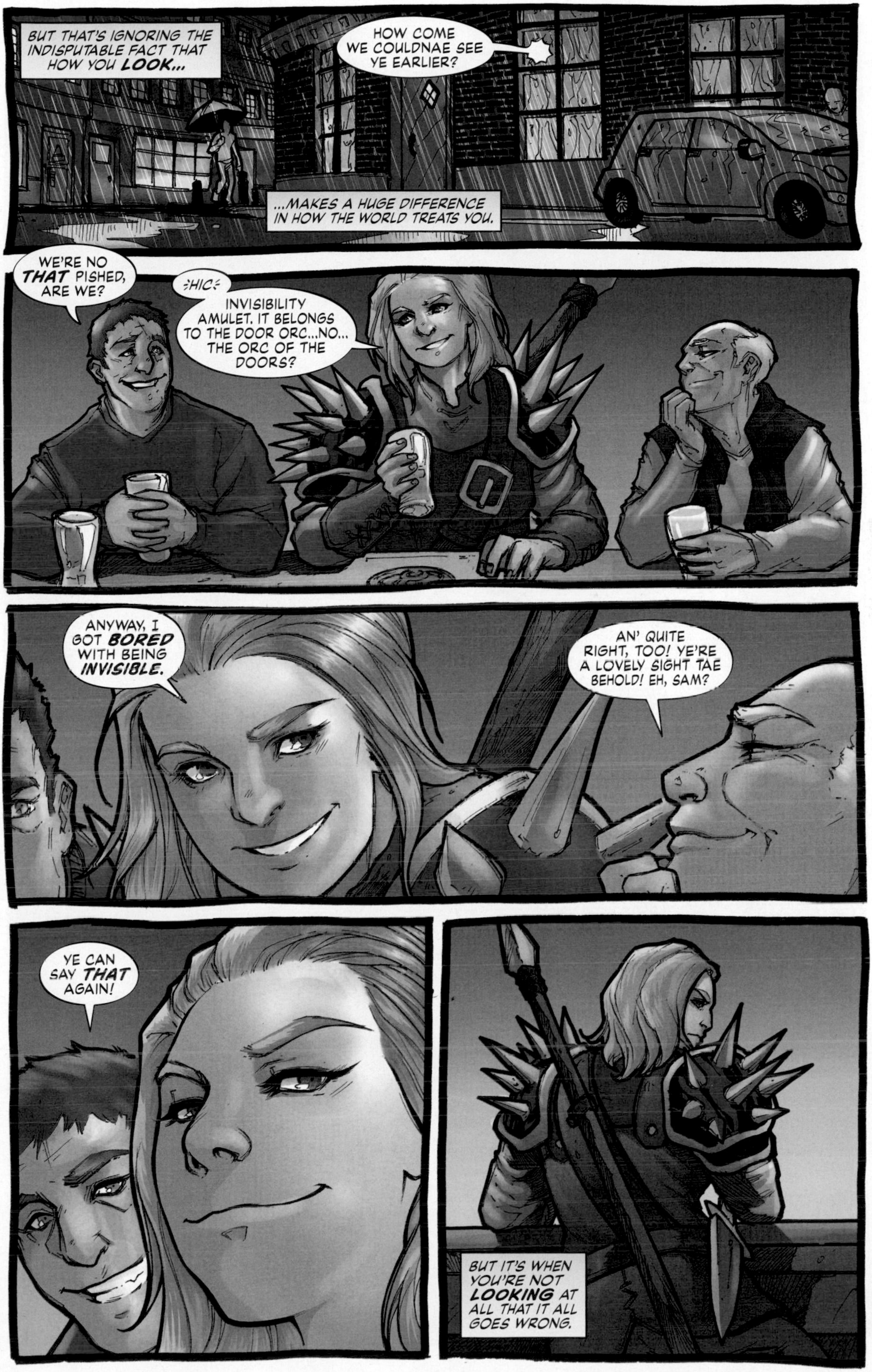
BUT THAT'S IGNORING THE INDISPUTABLE FACT THAT HOW YOU LOOK...
HOW COME WE COULDNAE SEE YE EARLIER?
...MAKES A HUGE DIFFERENCE IN HOW THE WORLD TREATS YOU.
WE'RE NO THAT PISHED, ARE WE?
HIC
INVISIBILITY AMULET. IT BELONGS TO THE DOOR ORC...NO... THE ORC OF THE DOORS?
ANYWAY, I GOT BORED WITH BEING INVISIBLE.
AN' QUITE RIGHT, TOO! YE'RE A LOVELY SIGHT TAE BEHOLD! EH, SAM?
YE CAN SAY THAT AGAIN!
BUT IT'S WHEN YOU'RE NOT LOOKING AT ALL THAT IT ALL GOES WRONG.

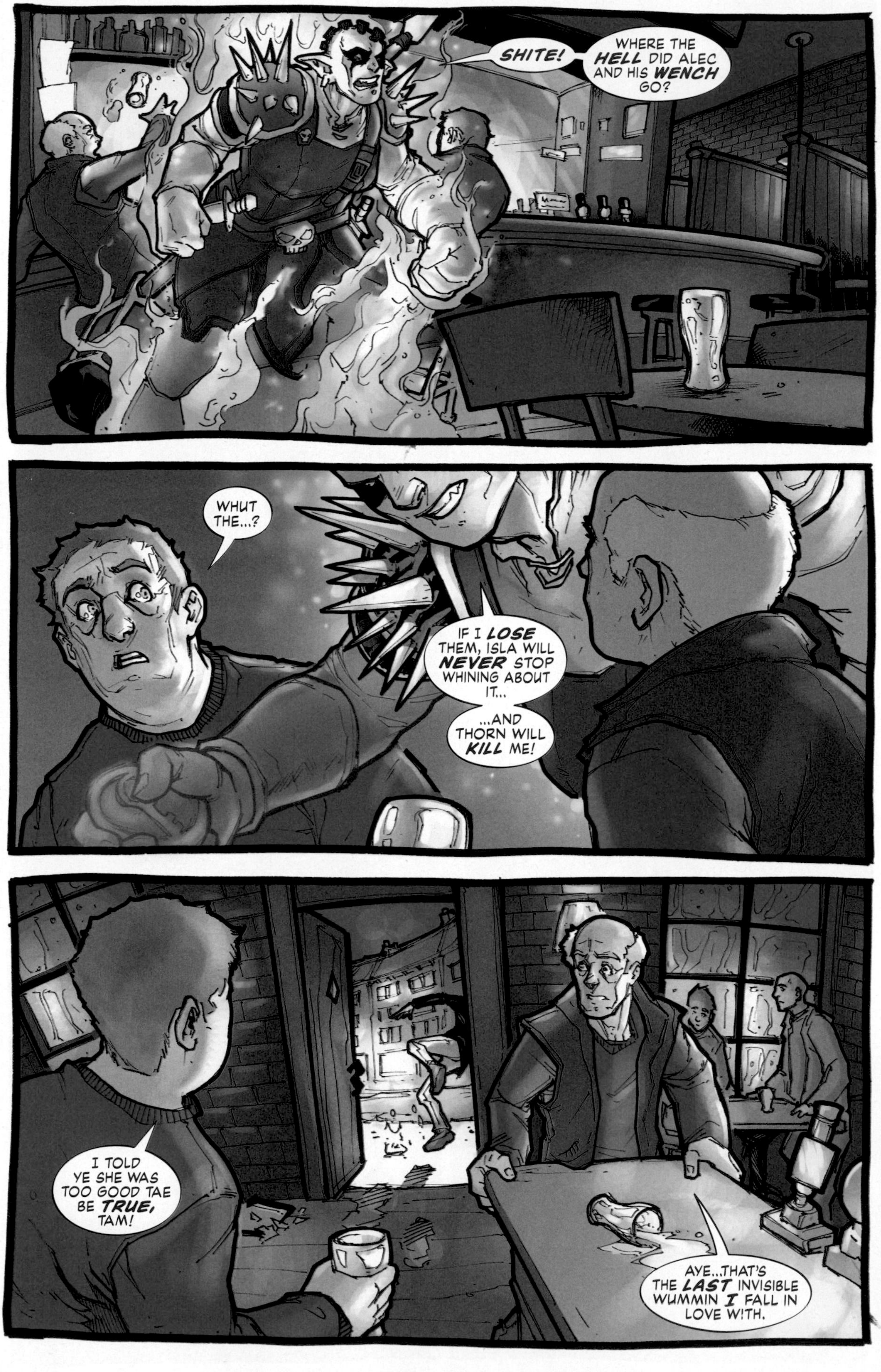
SHITE!
WHERE THE HELL DID ALEC AND HIS WENCH GO?
WHUT THE...?
IF I LOSE THEM, ISLA WILL NEVER STOP WHINING ABOUT IT...
...AND THORN WILL KILL ME!
I TOLD YE SHE WAS TOO GOOD TAE BE TRUE, TAM!
AYE...THAT'S THE LAST INVISIBLE WUMMIN I FALL IN LOVE WITH.

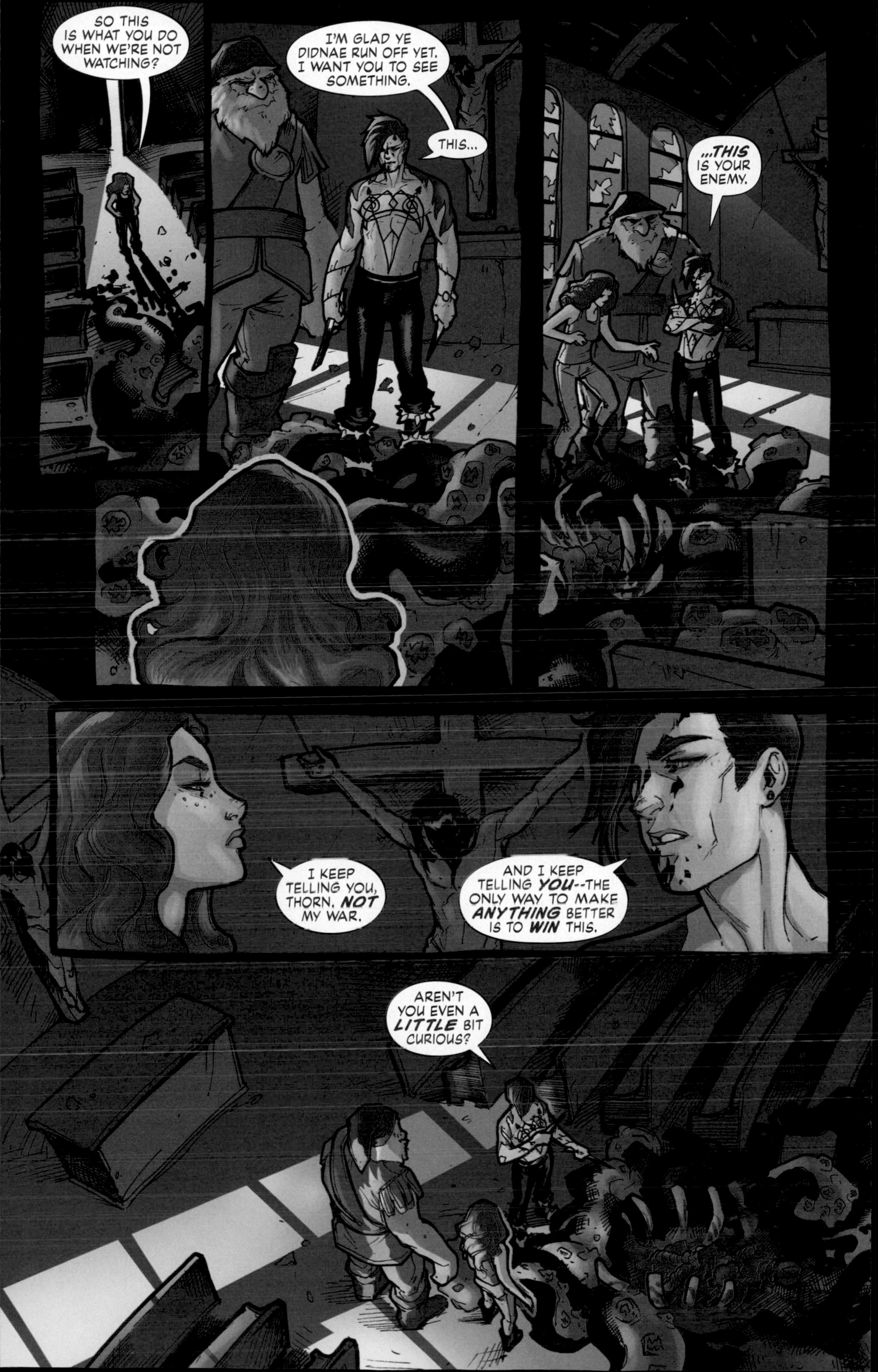
SO THIS IS WHAT YOU DO WHEN WE'RE NOT WATCHING?
I'M GLAD YE DIDNAE RUN OFF YET. I WANT YOU TO SEE SOMETHING.
THIS...
...THIS IS YOUR ENEMY.
I KEEP TELLING YOU, THORN. NOT MY WAR.
AND I KEEP TELLING YOU--THE ONLY WAY TO MAKE ANYTHING BETTER IS TO WIN THIS.
AREN'T YOU EVEN A LITTLE BIT CURIOUS?

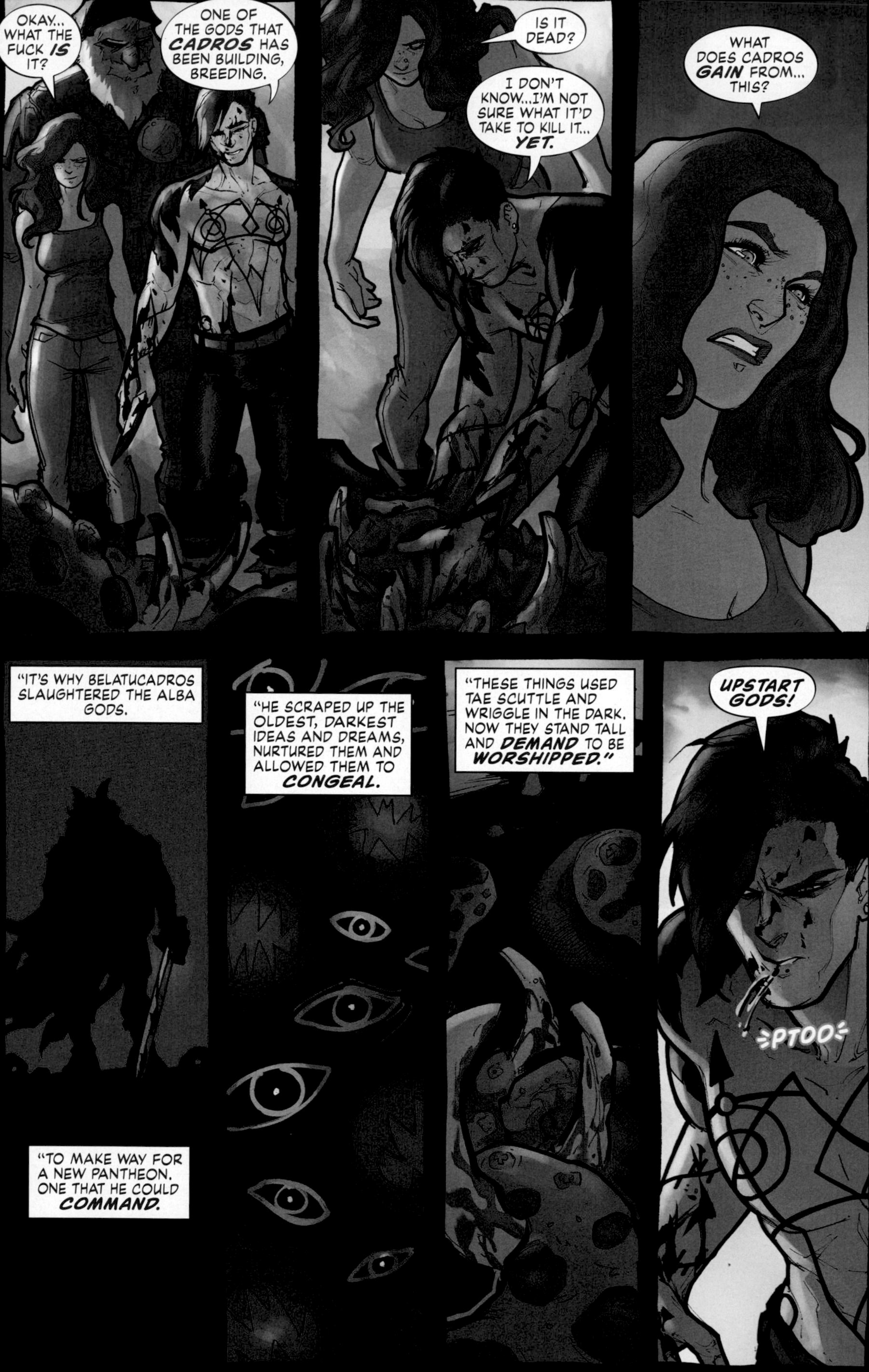
OKAY... WHAT THE FUCK IS IT?
ONE OF THE GODS THAT CADROS HAS BEEN BUILDING, BREEDING.
IS IT DEAD?
I DON'T KNOW...I'M NOT SURE WHAT IT'D TAKE TO KILL IT... YET.
WHAT DOES CADROS GAIN FROM... THIS?
"IT'S WHY BELATUCADROS SLAUGHTERED THE ALBA GODS.
"TO MAKE WAY FOR A NEW PANTHEON. ONE THAT HE COULD COMMAND.
"HE SCRAPED UP THE OLDEST, DARKEST IDEAS AND DREAMS, NURTURED THEM AND ALLOWED THEM TO CONGEAL.
"THESE THINGS USED TAE SCUTTLE AND WRIGGLE IN THE DARK. NOW THEY STAND TALL AND DEMAND TO BE WORSHIPPED."
UPSTART GODS!
PTOO

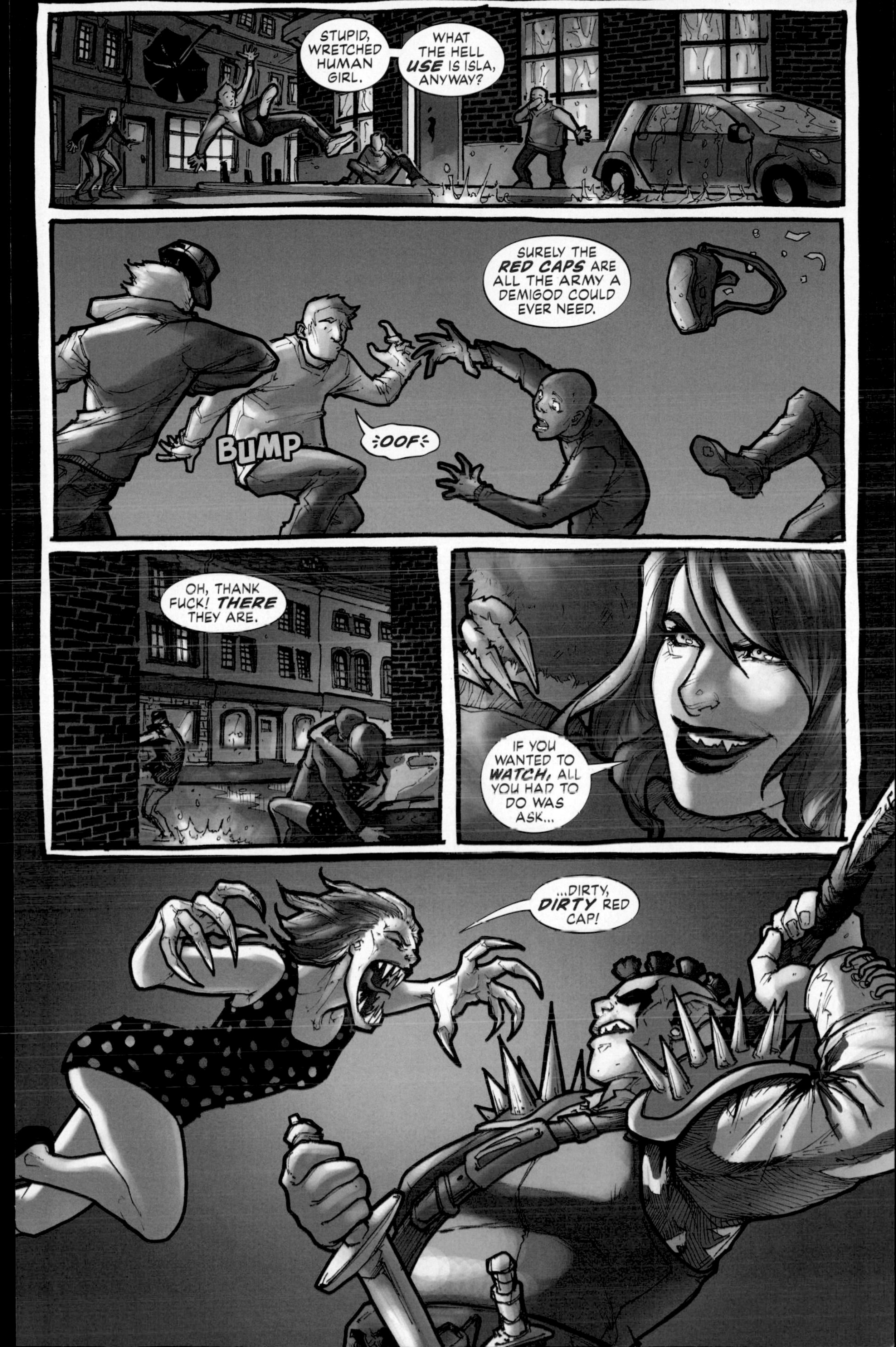
STUPID, WRETCHED HUMAN GIRL.
WHAT THE HELL USE IS ISLA, ANYWAY?
SURELY THE RED CAPS ARE ALL THE ARMY A DEMIGOD COULD EVER NEED.
BUMP
OOF
OH, THANK FUCK! THERE THEY ARE.
IF YOU WANTED TO WATCH, ALL YOU HAD TO DO WAS ASK...
...DIRTY, DIRTY RED CAP!

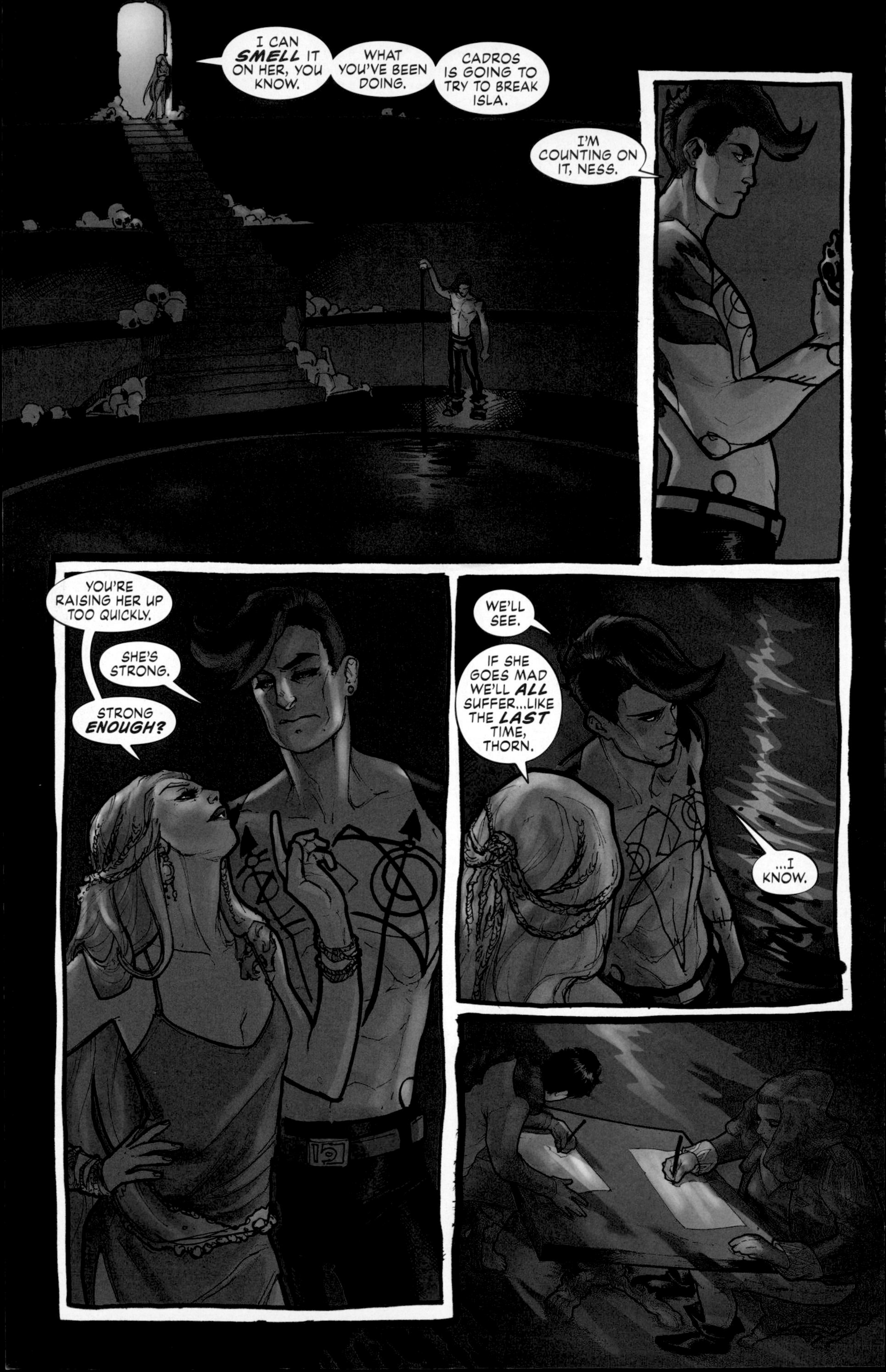
I CAN SMELL IT ON HER, YOU KNOW.
WHAT YOU'VE BEEN DOING.
CADROS IS GOING TO TRY TO BREAK ISLA.
I'M COUNTING ON IT, NESS.
YOU'RE RAISING HER UP TOO QUICKLY.
SHE'S STRONG.
STRONG ENOUGH?
WE'LL SEE.
IF SHE GOES MAD WE'LL ALL SUFFER...LIKE THE LAST TIME, THORN.
...I KNOW.

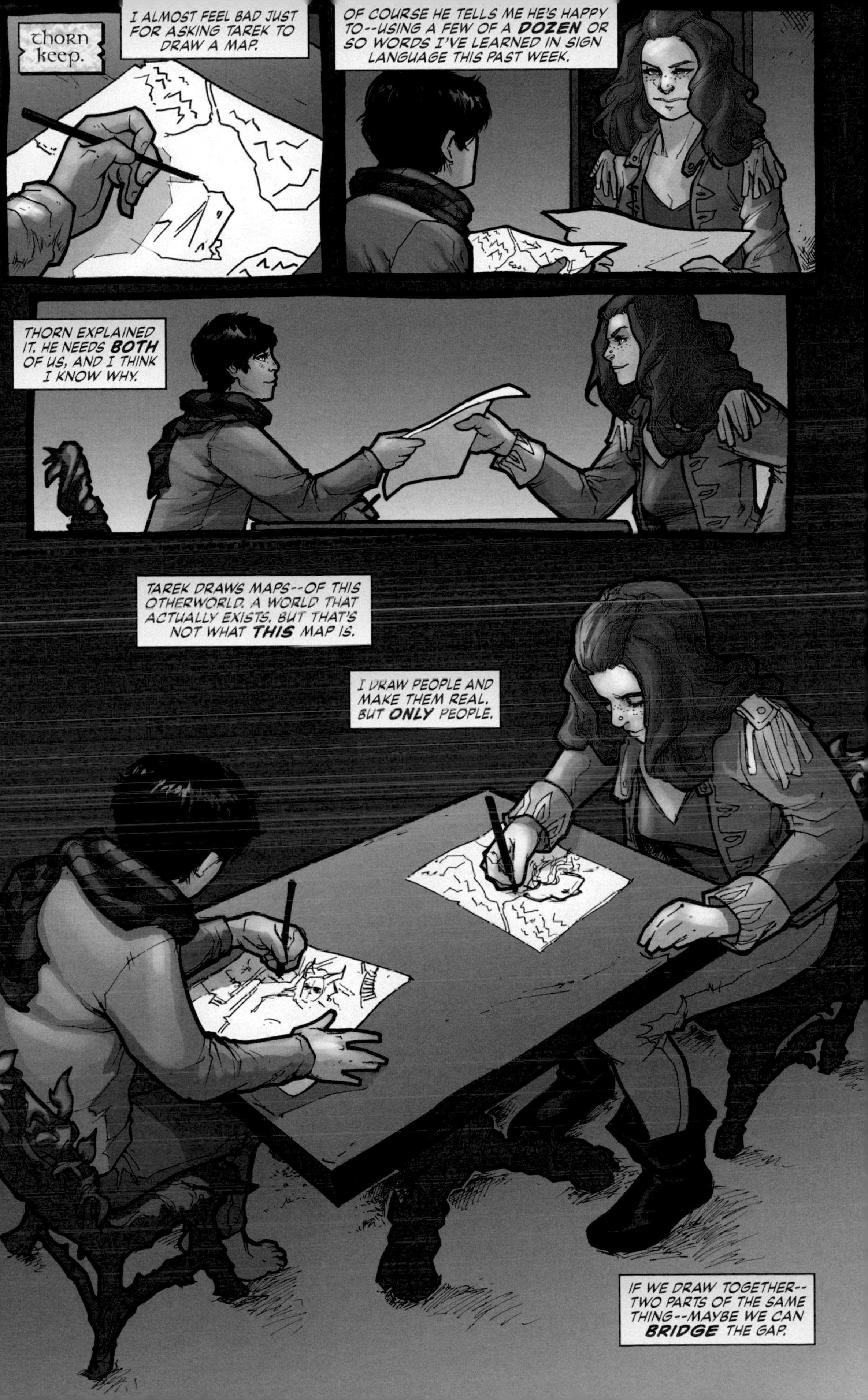
Thorn keep.
I ALMOST FEEL BAD JUST FOR ASKING TAREK TO DRAW A MAP.
OF COURSE HE TELLS ME HE'S HAPPY TO--USING A FEW OF A DOZEN OR SO WORDS I'VE LEARNED IN SIGN LANGUAGE THIS PAST WEEK.
THORN EXPLAINED IT. HE NEEDS BOTH OF US, AND I THINK I KNOW WHY.
TAREK DRAWS MAPS--OF THIS OTHERWORLD, A WORLD THAT ACTUALLY EXISTS. BUT THAT'S NOT WHAT THIS MAP IS.
I DRAW PEOPLE AND MAKE THEM REAL. BUT ONLY PEOPLE.
IF WE DRAW TOGETHER--TWO PARTS OF THE SAME THING--MAYBE WE CAN BRIDGE THE GAP.

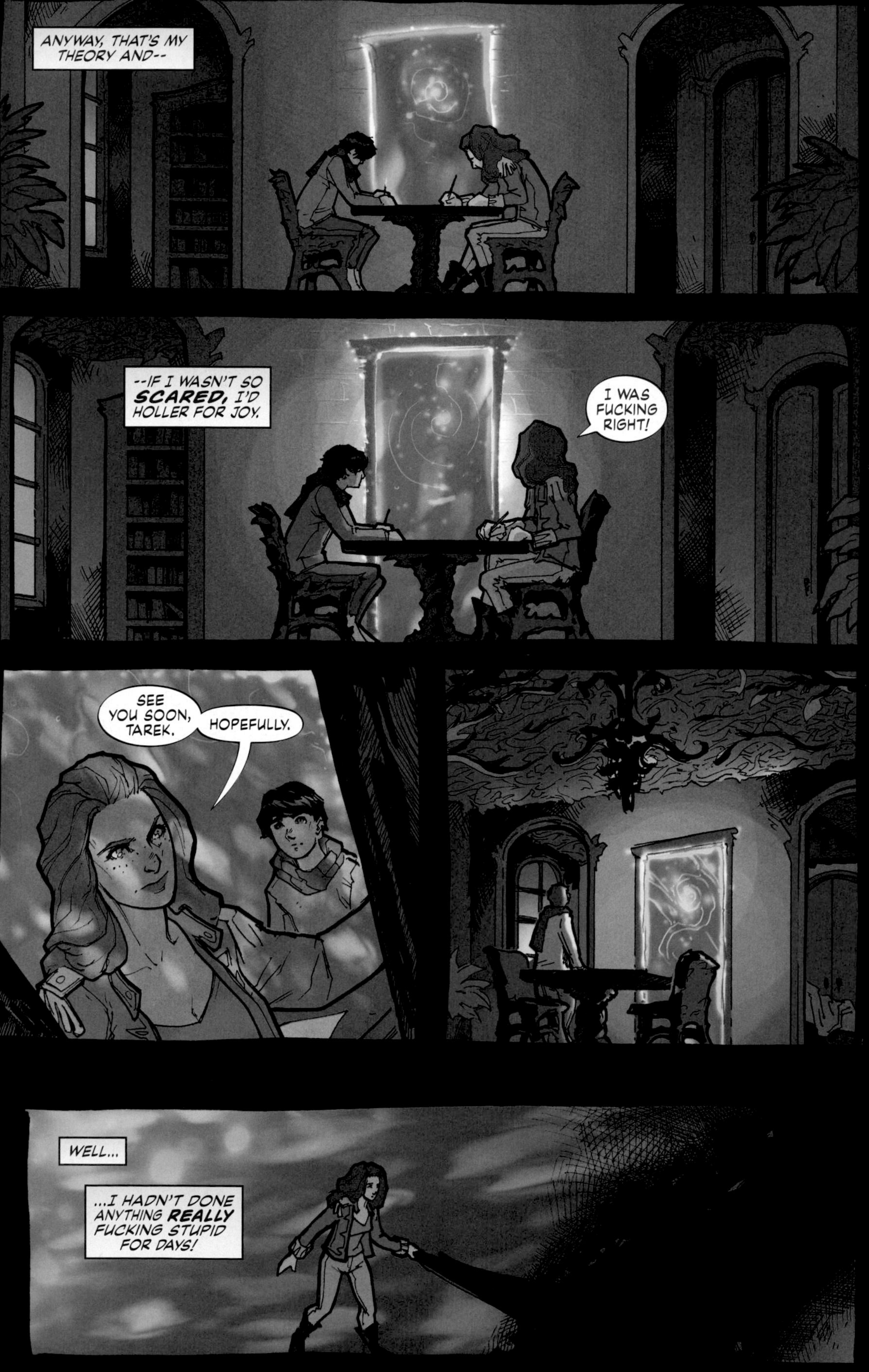
ANYWAY, THAT'S MY THEORY AND--
--IF I WASN'T SO **SCARED,** I'D HOLLER FOR JOY.
I WAS FUCKING RIGHT!
SEE YOU SOON, TAREK.
HOPEFULLY.
WELL...
...I HADN'T DONE ANYTHING **REALLY** FUCKING STUPID FOR DAYS!

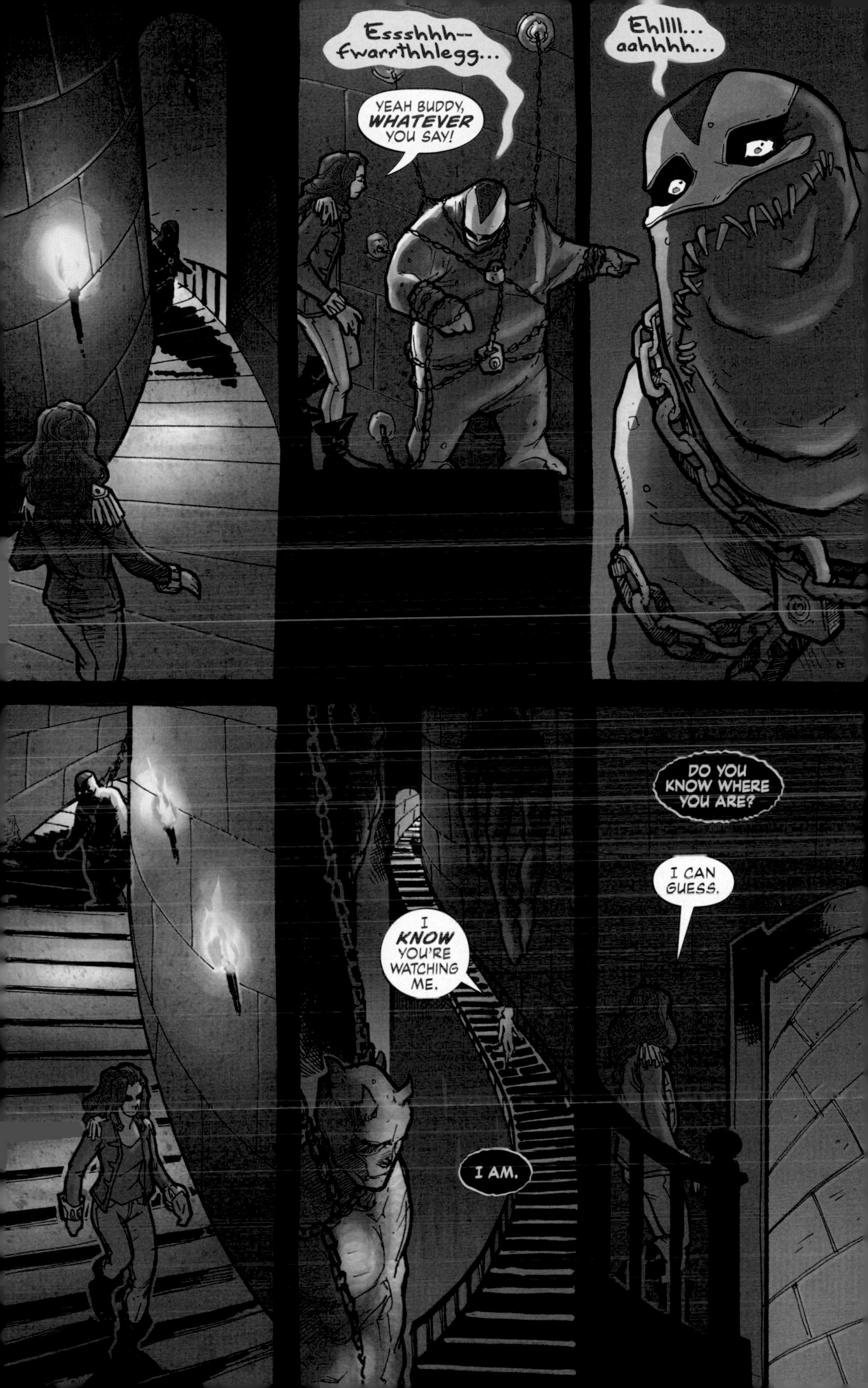
Essshhh-- fwarrthhlegg...
YEAH BUDDY, WHATEVER YOU SAY!
Ehllll... aahhhh...
I KNOW YOU'RE WATCHING ME.
I AM.
DO YOU KNOW WHERE YOU ARE?
I CAN GUESS.

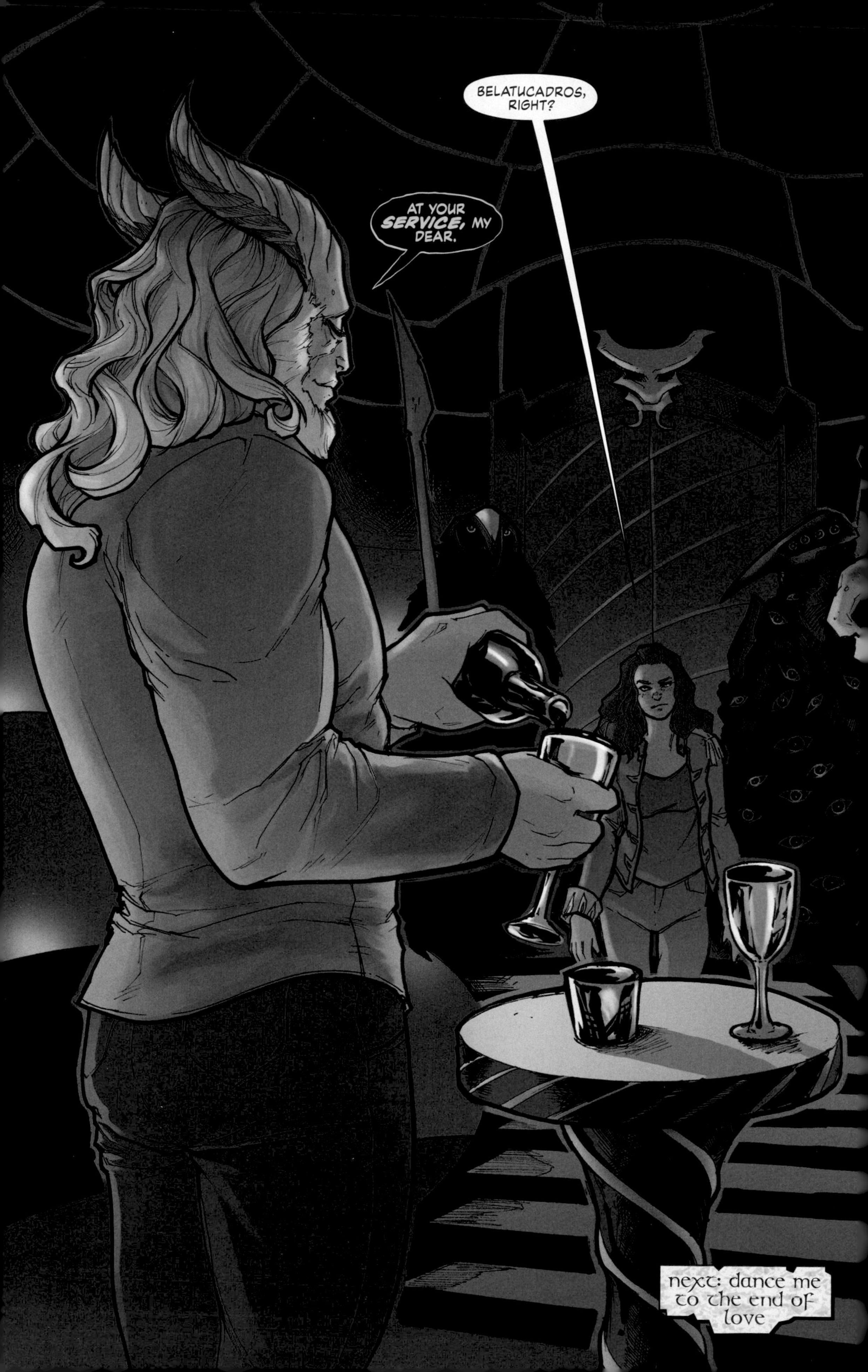
BELATUCADROS, RIGHT?
AT YOUR SERVICE, MY DEAR.
next: dance me to the end of love

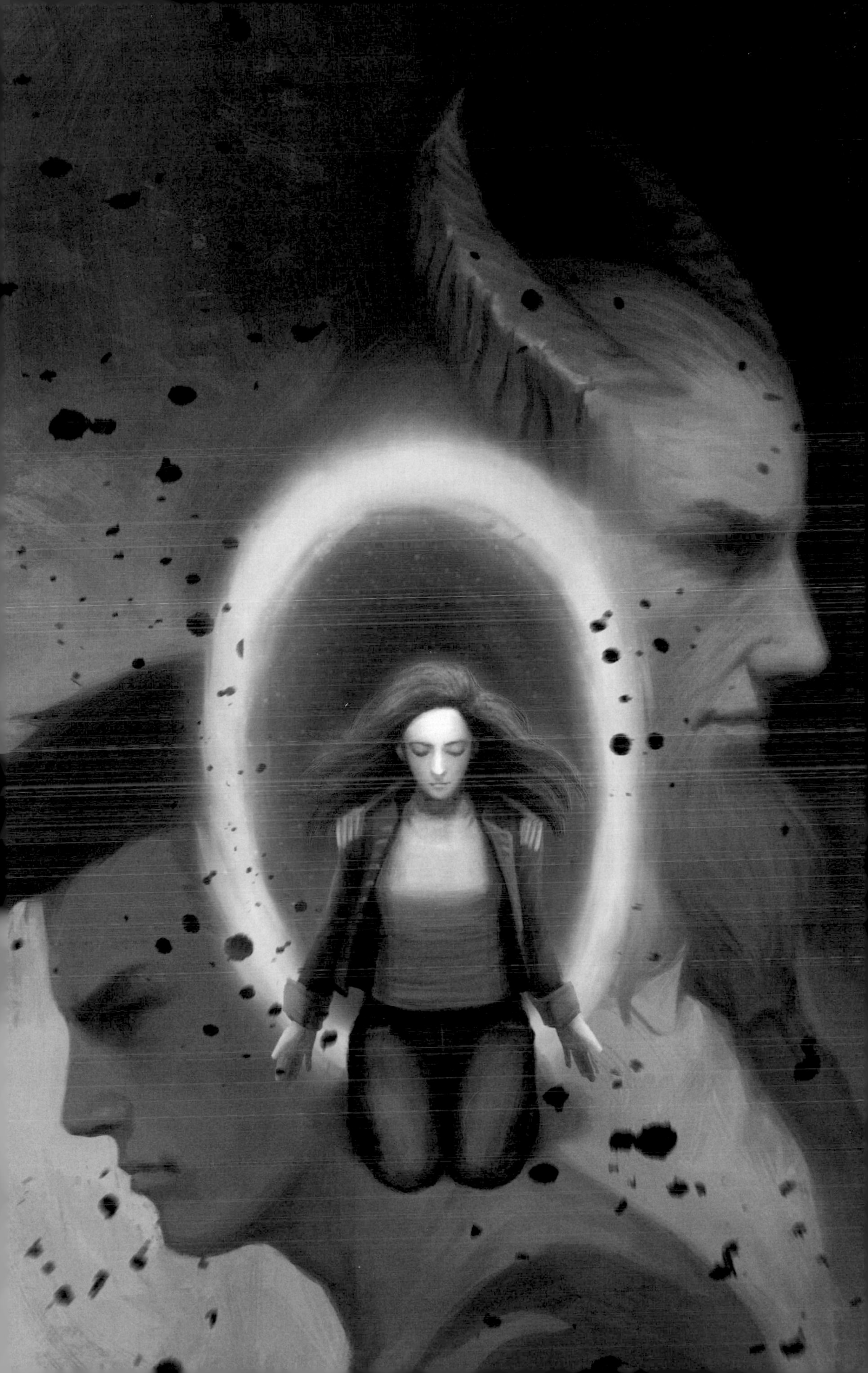

"IF YOU'RE TRYING TO SHOCK ME, IT WON'T WORK."

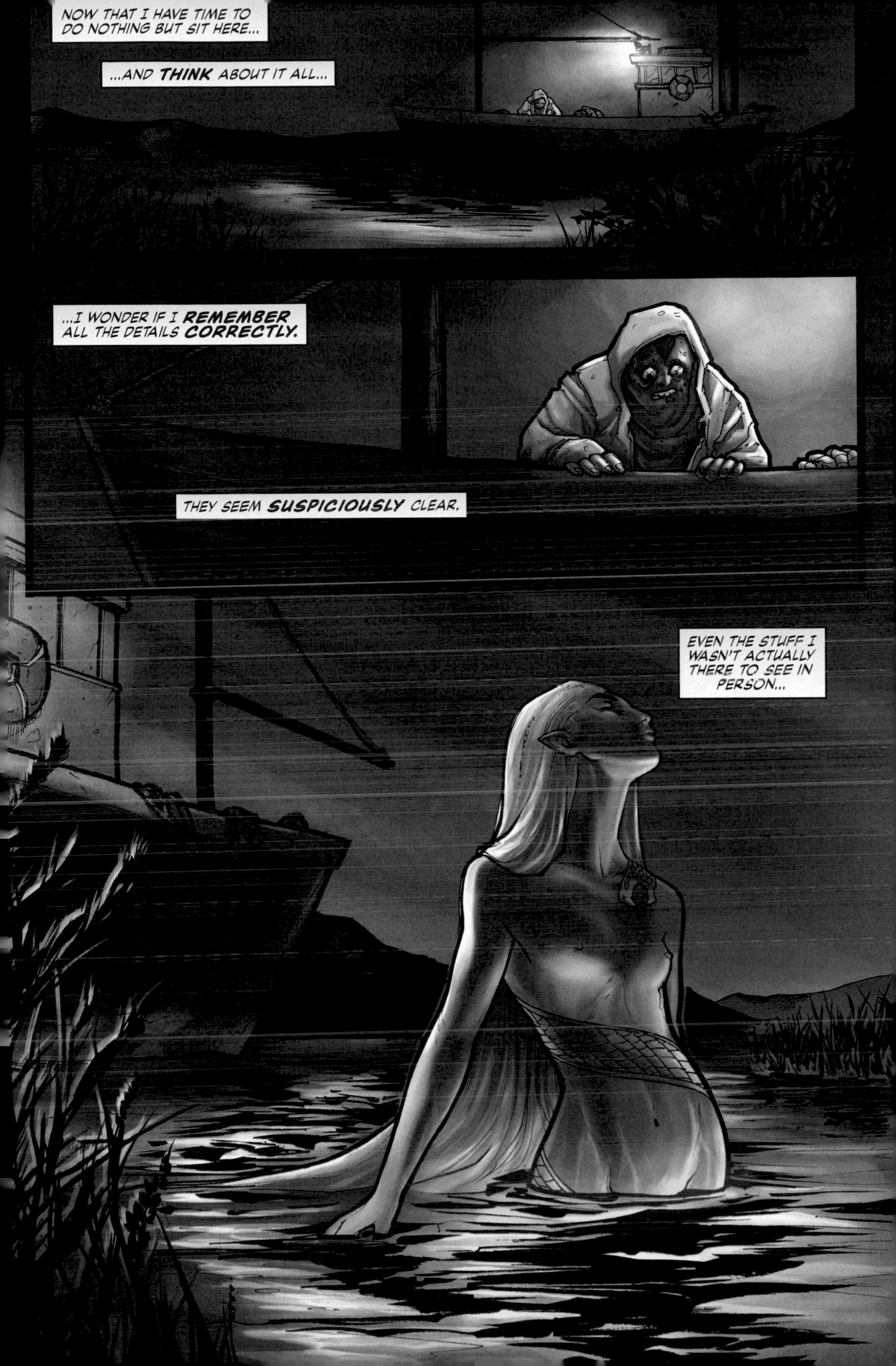
NOW THAT I HAVE TIME TO DO NOTHING BUT SIT HERE...
...AND **THINK** ABOUT IT ALL...
...I WONDER IF I **REMEMBER** ALL THE DETAILS **CORRECTLY.**
THEY SEEM **SUSPICIOUSLY** CLEAR.
EVEN THE STUFF I WASN'T ACTUALLY THERE TO SEE IN PERSON...

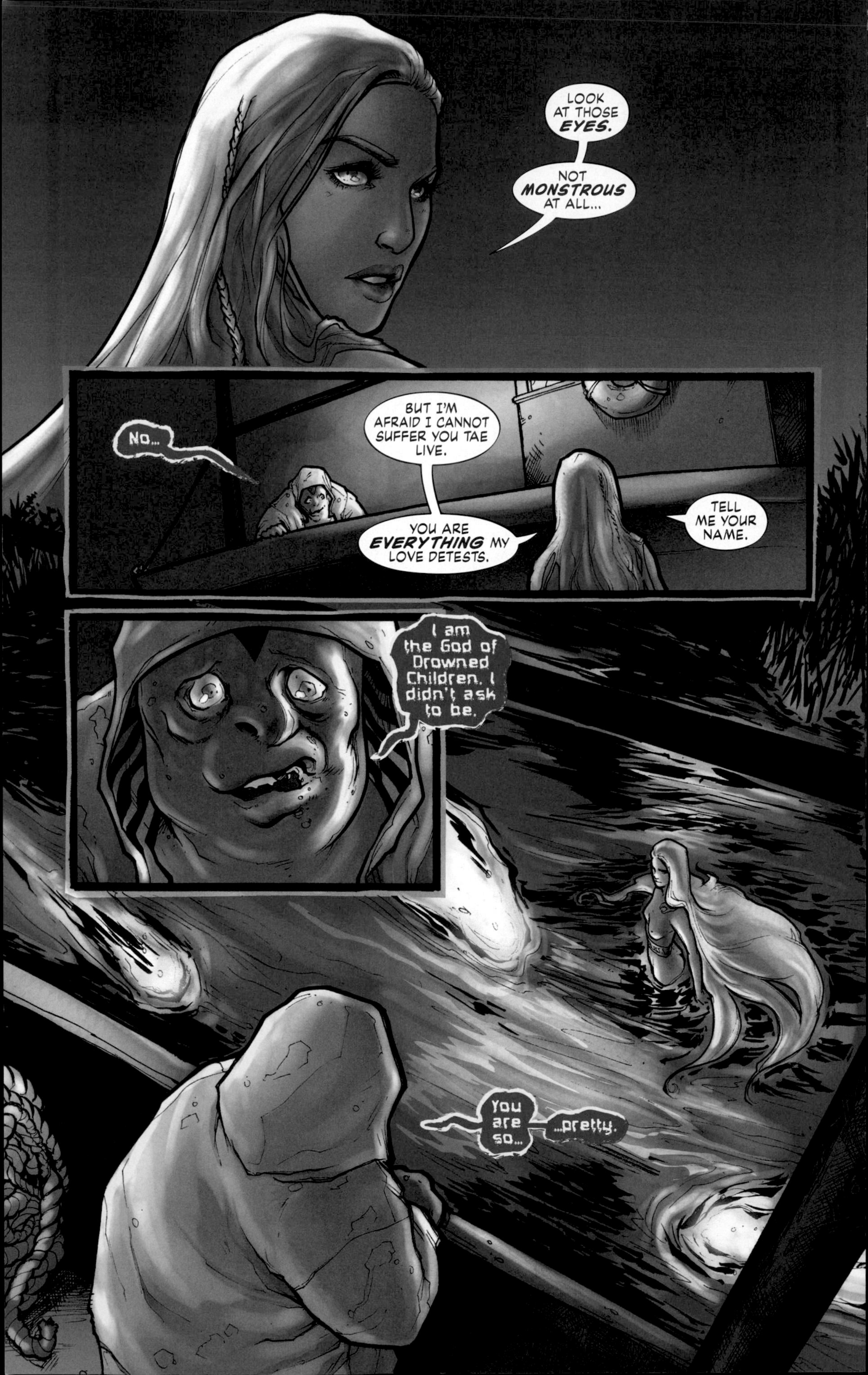
LOOK AT THOSE EYES.
NOT MONSTROUS AT ALL...
BUT I'M AFRAID I CANNOT SUFFER YOU TAE LIVE.
YOU ARE EVERYTHING MY LOVE DETESTS.
No...
TELL ME YOUR NAME.
I am the God of Drowned Children. I didn't ask to be.
You are so...
...pretty.

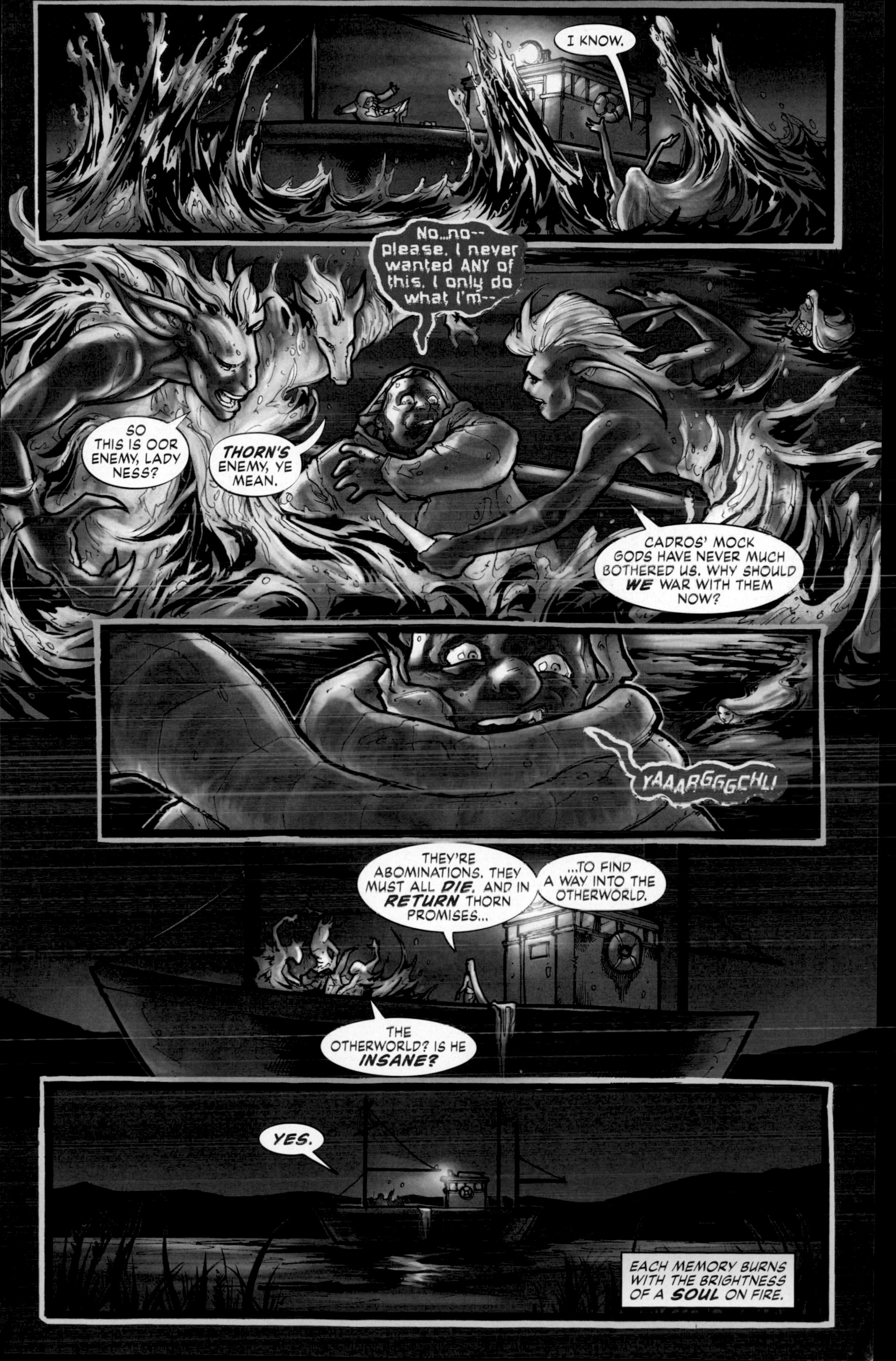
I KNOW.
No...no-- please. I never wanted ANY of this. I only do what I'm--
SO THIS IS OOR ENEMY, LADY NESS?
THORN'S ENEMY, YE MEAN.
CADROS' MOCK GODS HAVE NEVER MUCH BOTHERED US. WHY SHOULD WE WAR WITH THEM NOW?
YAAARGGGCHL!
THEY'RE ABOMINATIONS. THEY MUST ALL DIE. AND IN RETURN THORN PROMISES...
...TO FIND A WAY INTO THE OTHERWORLD.
THE OTHERWORLD? IS HE INSANE?
YES.
EACH MEMORY BURNS WITH THE BRIGHTNESS OF A SOUL ON FIRE.

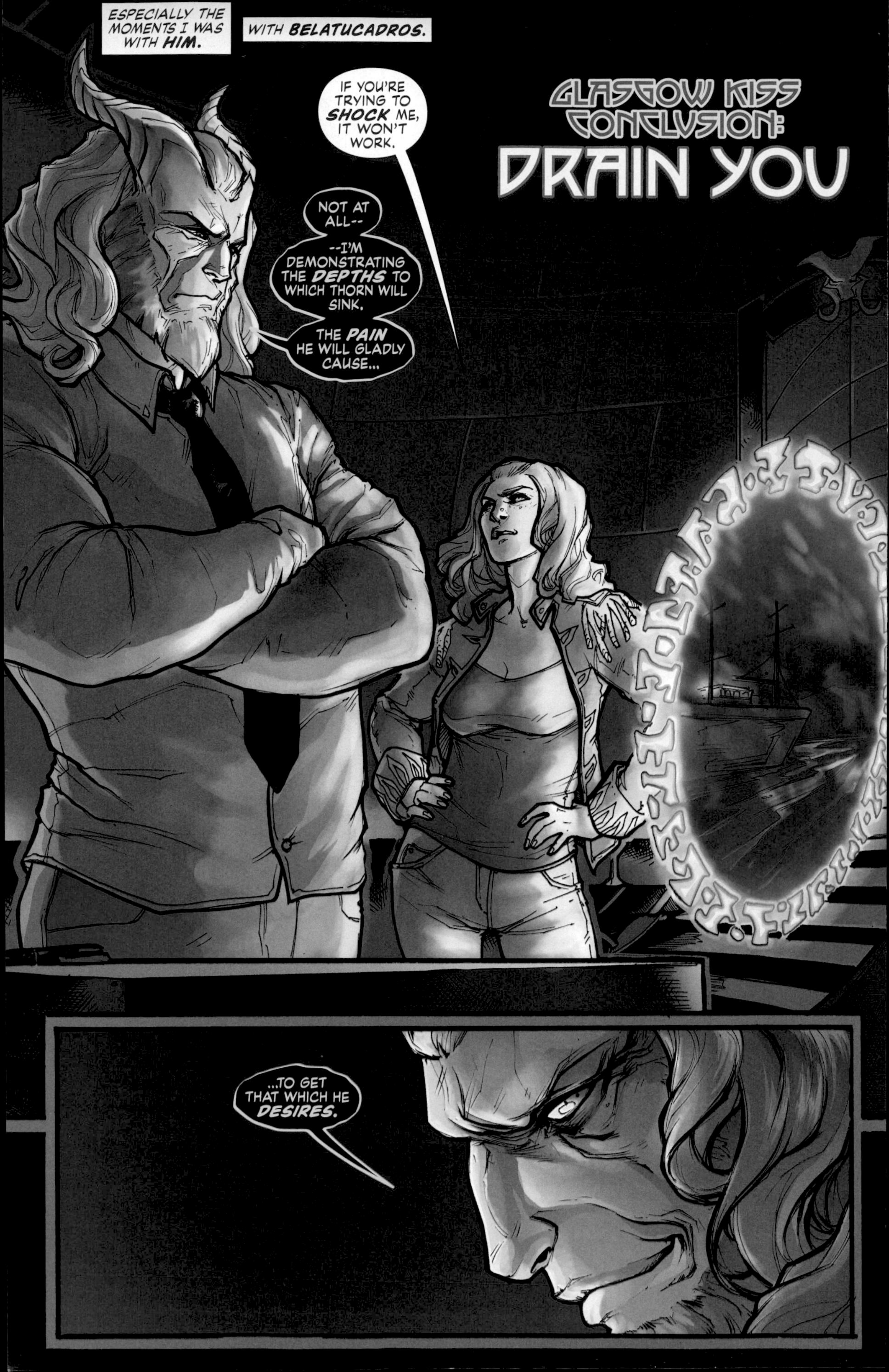
ESPECIALLY THE MOMENTS I WAS WITH HIM.
WITH BELATUCADROS.
GLASGOW KISS CONCLUSION:
DRAIN YOU
IF YOU'RE TRYING TO SHOCK ME, IT WON'T WORK.
NOT AT ALL--
--I'M DEMONSTRATING THE DEPTHS TO WHICH THORN WILL SINK.
THE PAIN HE WILL GLADLY CAUSE...
...TO GET THAT WHICH HE DESIRES.

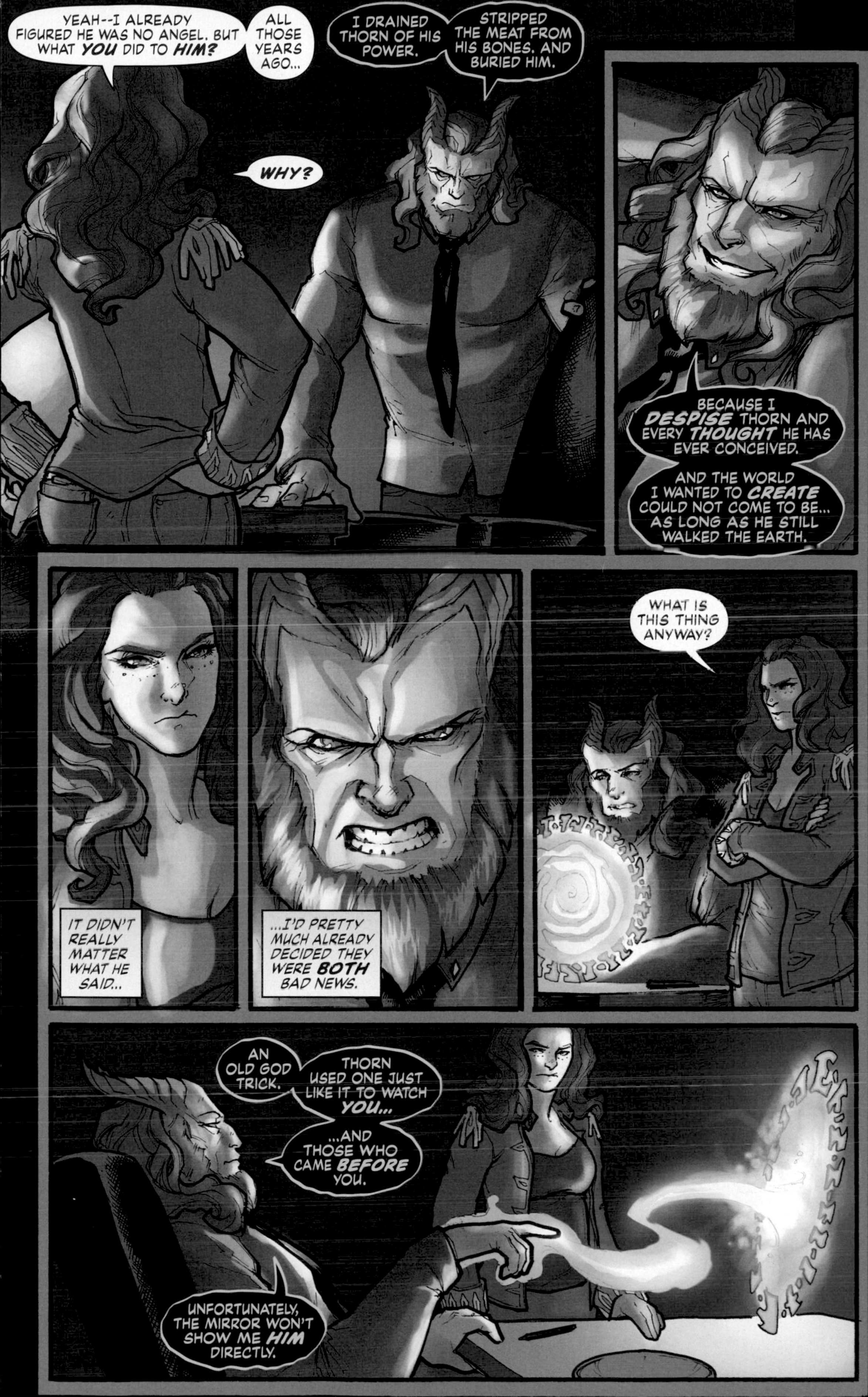
YEAH--I ALREADY FIGURED HE WAS NO ANGEL. BUT WHAT *YOU* DID TO *HIM?*
ALL THOSE YEARS AGO...
I DRAINED THORN OF HIS POWER.
STRIPPED THE MEAT FROM HIS BONES. AND BURIED HIM.
WHY?
BECAUSE I *DESPISE* THORN AND EVERY *THOUGHT* HE HAS EVER CONCEIVED.
AND THE WORLD I WANTED TO *CREATE* COULD NOT COME TO BE... AS LONG AS HE STILL WALKED THE EARTH.
IT DIDN'T REALLY MATTER WHAT HE SAID...
...I'D PRETTY MUCH ALREADY DECIDED THEY WERE *BOTH* BAD NEWS.
WHAT IS THIS THING ANYWAY?
AN OLD GOD TRICK.
THORN USED ONE JUST LIKE IT TO WATCH *YOU...*
...AND THOSE WHO CAME *BEFORE* YOU.
UNFORTUNATELY, THE MIRROR WON'T SHOW ME *HIM* DIRECTLY.

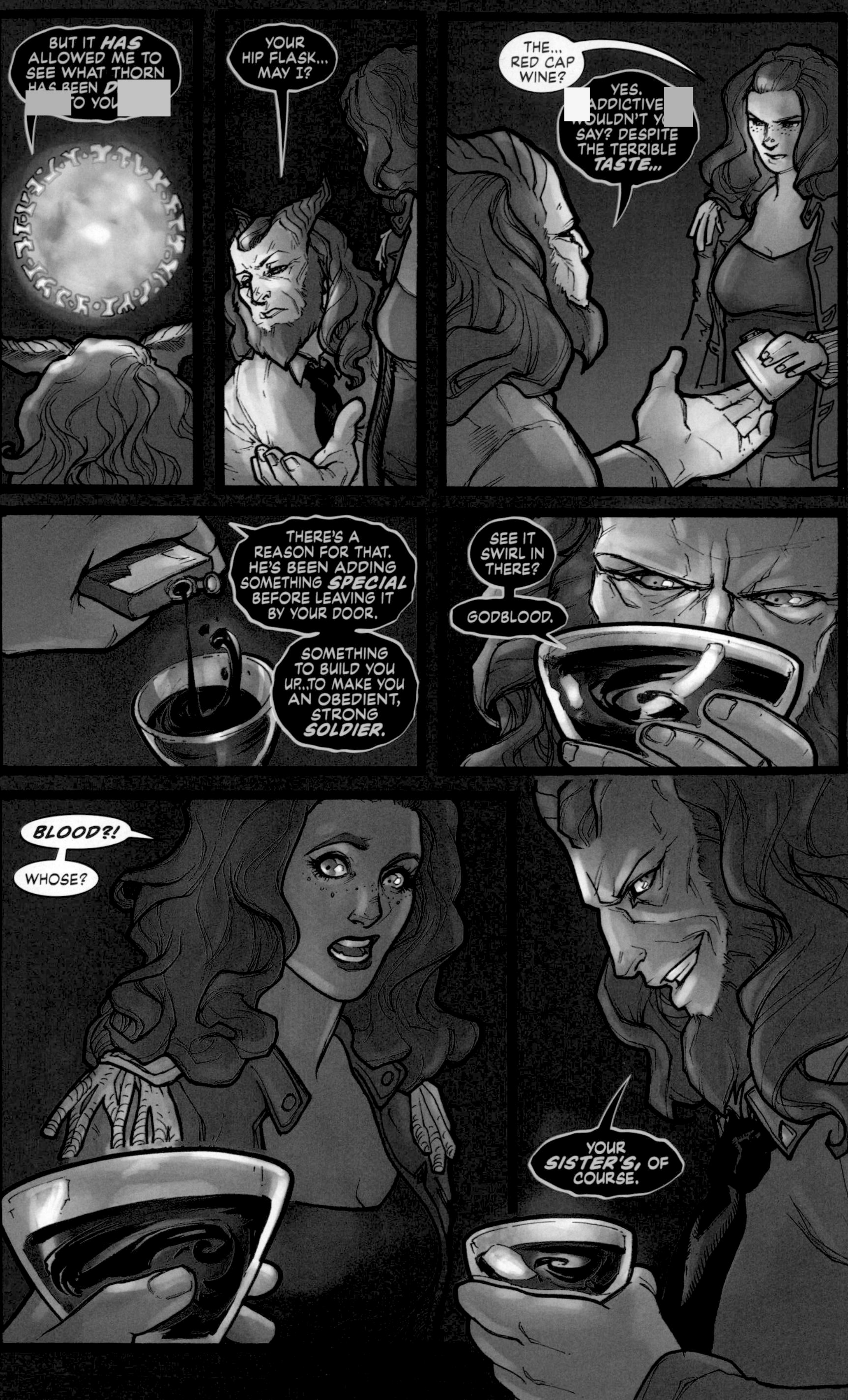
BUT IT HAS ALLOWED ME TO SEE WHAT THORN HAS BEEN
YOUR HIP FLASK... MAY I?
THE... RED CAP WINE?
YES. ADDICTIVE SAY? DESPITE THE TERRIBLE TASTE...
THERE'S A REASON FOR THAT. HE'S BEEN ADDING SOMETHING SPECIAL BEFORE LEAVING IT BY YOUR DOOR.
SOMETHING TO BUILD YOU UP...TO MAKE YOU AN OBEDIENT, STRONG SOLDIER.
SEE IT SWIRL IN THERE?
GODBLOOD.
BLOOD?!
WHOSE?
YOUR SISTER'S, OF COURSE.

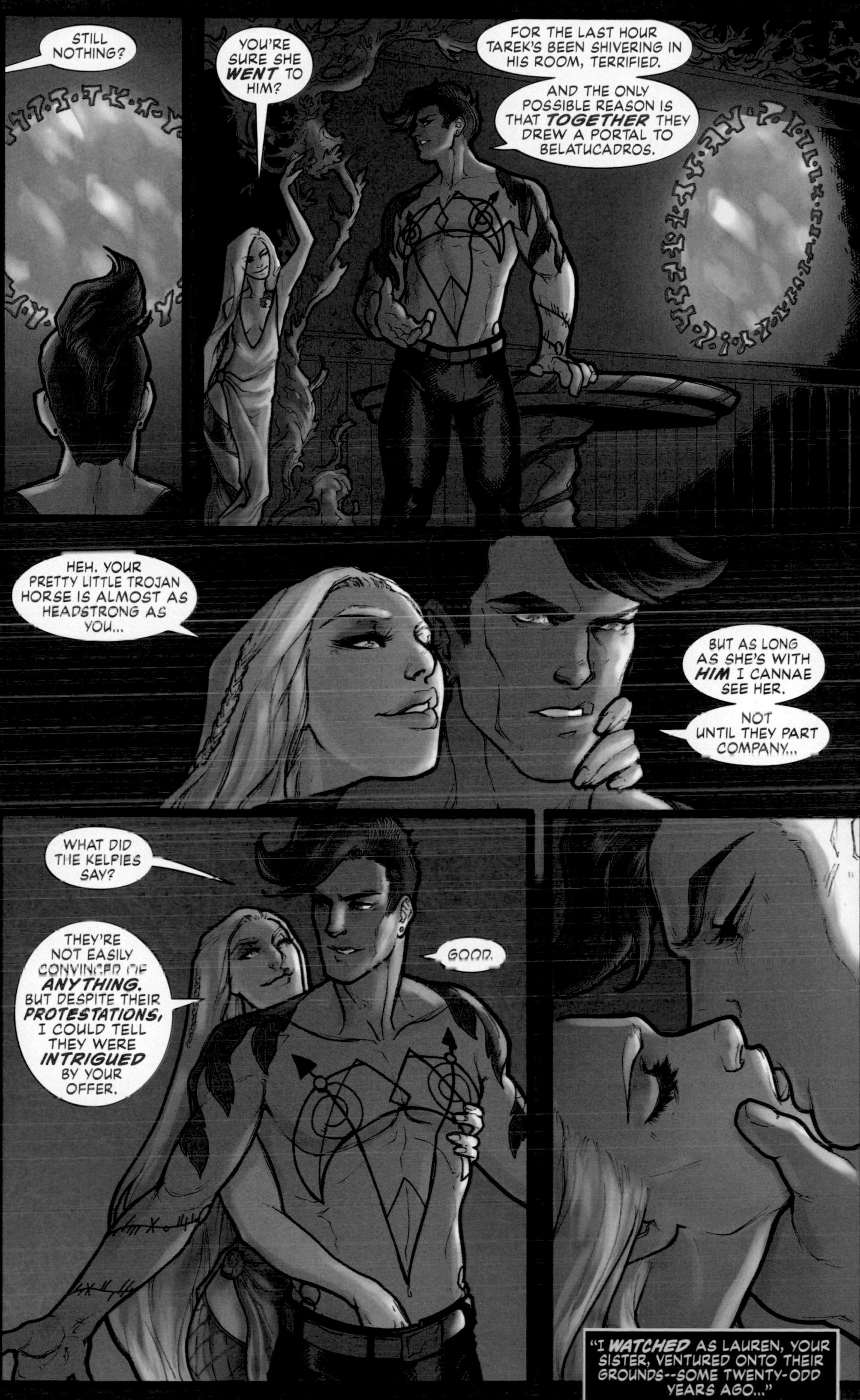
STILL NOTHING?
YOU'RE SURE SHE WENT TO HIM?
FOR THE LAST HOUR TAREK'S BEEN SHIVERING IN HIS ROOM, TERRIFIED.
AND THE ONLY POSSIBLE REASON IS THAT TOGETHER THEY DREW A PORTAL TO BELATUCADROS.
HEH. YOUR PRETTY LITTLE TROJAN HORSE IS ALMOST AS HEADSTRONG AS YOU...
BUT AS LONG AS SHE'S WITH HIM I CANNAE SEE HER.
NOT UNTIL THEY PART COMPANY...
WHAT DID THE KELPIES SAY?
THEY'RE NOT EASILY CONVINCED OF ANYTHING. BUT DESPITE THEIR PROTESTATIONS, I COULD TELL THEY WERE INTRIGUED BY YOUR OFFER.
GOOD.
"I WATCHED AS LAUREN, YOUR SISTER, VENTURED ONTO THEIR GROUNDS--SOME TWENTY-ODD YEARS AGO..."

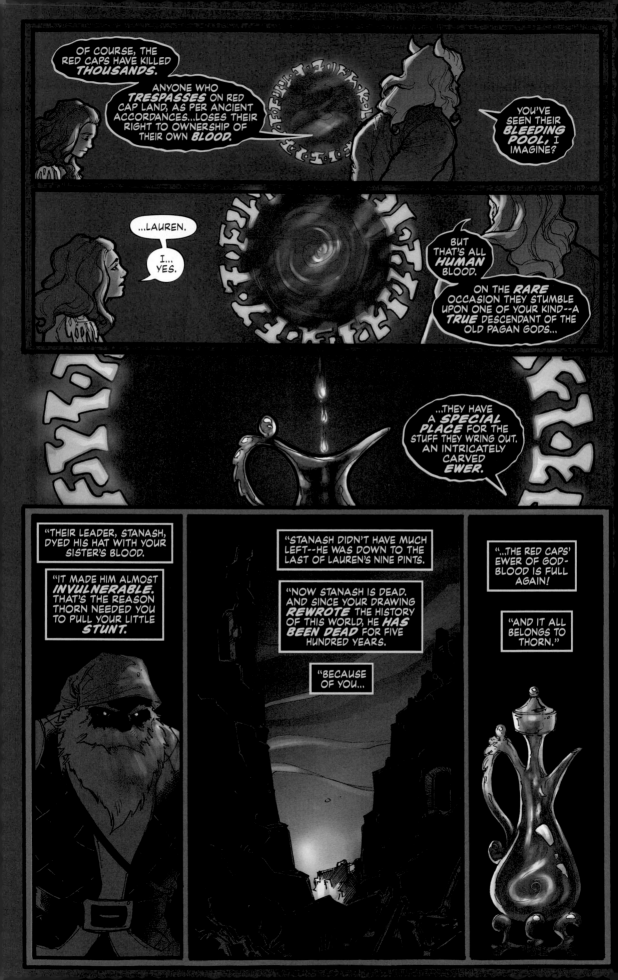

OF COURSE, THE RED CAPS HAVE KILLED *THOUSANDS.*

ANYONE WHO *TRESPASSES* ON RED CAP LAND, AS PER ANCIENT ACCORDANCES...LOSES THEIR RIGHT TO OWNERSHIP OF THEIR OWN *BLOOD.*

YOU'VE SEEN THEIR *BLEEDING POOL,* I IMAGINE?

...LAUREN.

I... YES.

BUT THAT'S ALL *HUMAN* BLOOD.

ON THE *RARE* OCCASION THEY STUMBLE UPON ONE OF YOUR KIND--A *TRUE* DESCENDANT OF THE OLD PAGAN GODS...

...THEY HAVE A *SPECIAL PLACE* FOR THE STUFF THEY WRING OUT. AN INTRICATELY CARVED *EWER.*

"THEIR LEADER, STANASH, DYED HIS HAT WITH YOUR SISTER'S BLOOD.

"IT MADE HIM ALMOST *INVULNERABLE.* THAT'S THE REASON THORN NEEDED YOU TO PULL YOUR LITTLE *STUNT.*

"STANASH DIDN'T HAVE MUCH LEFT--HE WAS DOWN TO THE LAST OF LAUREN'S NINE PINTS.

"NOW STANASH IS DEAD. AND SINCE YOUR DRAWING *REWROTE* THE HISTORY OF THIS WORLD, HE *HAS BEEN DEAD* FOR FIVE HUNDRED YEARS.

"BECAUSE OF YOU...

"...THE RED CAPS' EWER OF GOD-BLOOD IS FULL AGAIN!

"AND IT ALL BELONGS TO THORN."

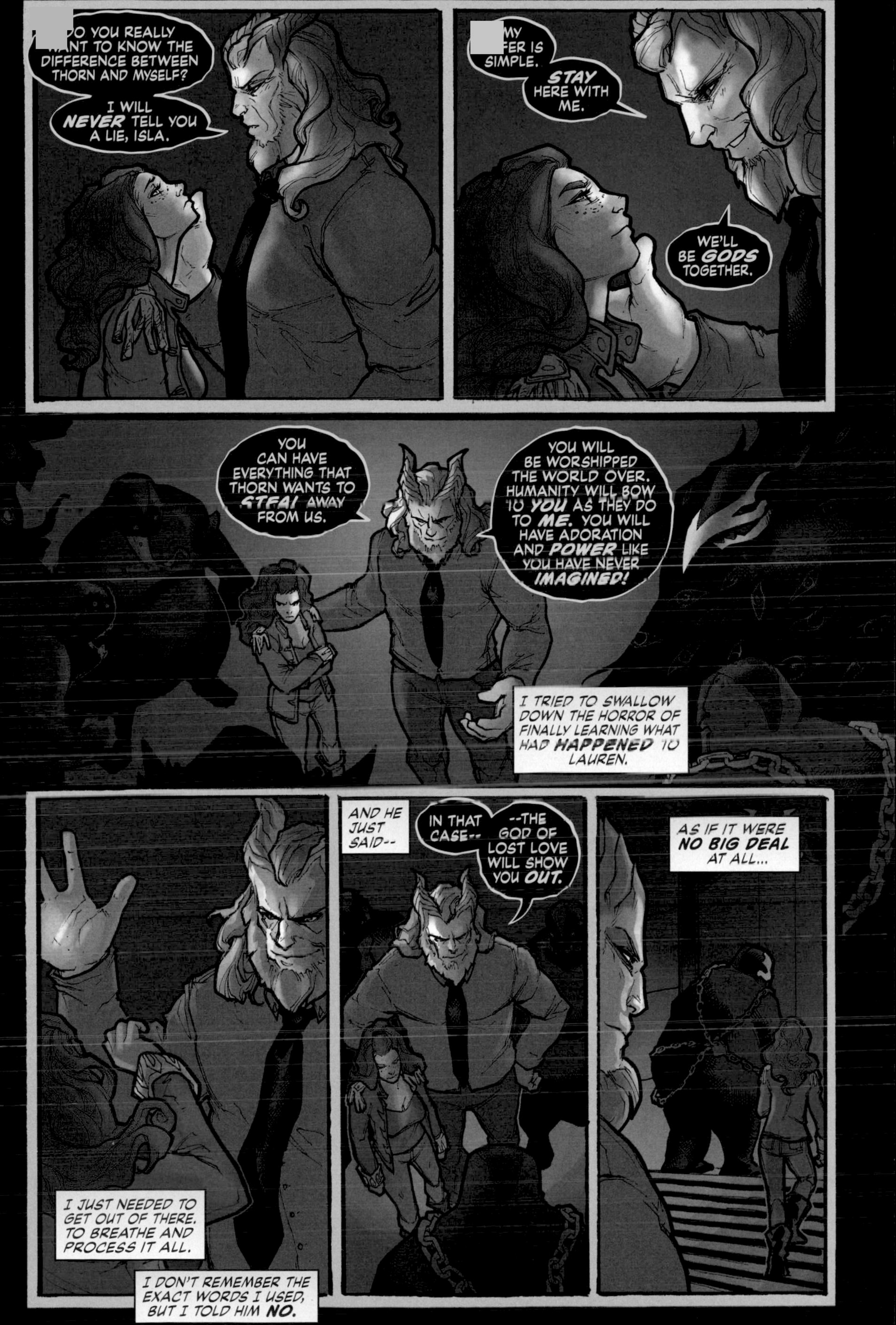
O YOU REALLY
ANT TO KNOW THE DIFFERENCE BETWEEN THORN AND MYSELF?
I WILL NEVER TELL YOU A LIE, ISLA.
MY
FER IS SIMPLE.
STAY HERE WITH ME.
WE'LL BE GODS TOGETHER.
YOU CAN HAVE EVERYTHING THAT THORN WANTS TO STEAL AWAY FROM US.
YOU WILL BE WORSHIPPED THE WORLD OVER. HUMANITY WILL BOW TO YOU AS THEY DO TO ME. YOU WILL HAVE ADORATION AND POWER LIKE YOU HAVE NEVER IMAGINED!
I TRIED TO SWALLOW DOWN THE HORROR OF FINALLY LEARNING WHAT HAD HAPPENED TO LAUREN.
I JUST NEEDED TO GET OUT OF THERE. TO BREATHE AND PROCESS IT ALL.
I DON'T REMEMBER THE EXACT WORDS I USED, BUT I TOLD HIM NO.
AND HE JUST SAID--
IN THAT CASE--
--THE GOD OF LOST LOVE WILL SHOW YOU OUT.
AS IF IT WERE NO BIG DEAL AT ALL...

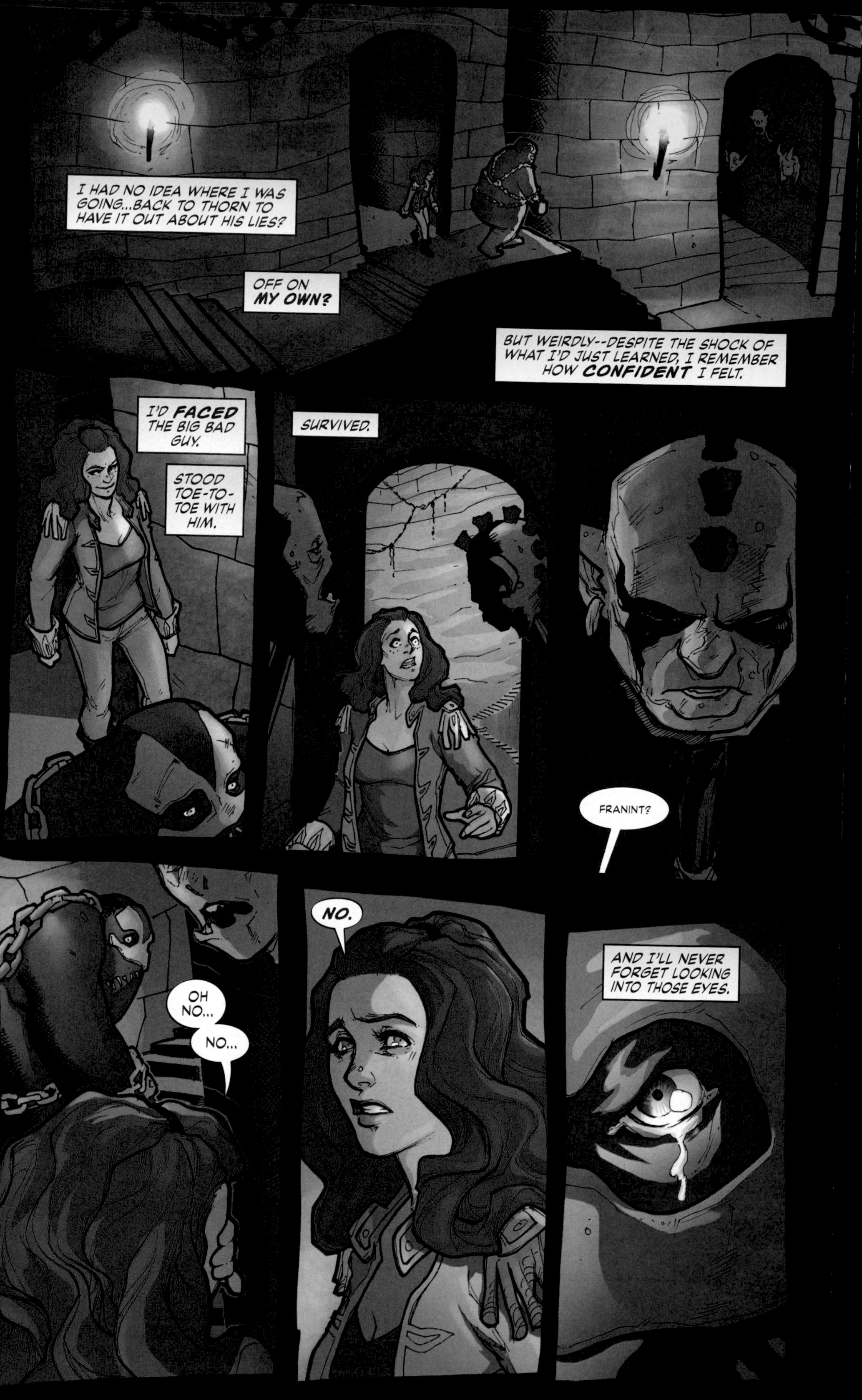
I HAD NO IDEA WHERE I WAS GOING...BACK TO THORN TO HAVE IT OUT ABOUT HIS LIES?
OFF ON MY OWN?
BUT WEIRDLY--DESPITE THE SHOCK OF WHAT I'D JUST LEARNED, I REMEMBER HOW CONFIDENT I FELT.
I'D FACED THE BIG BAD GUY.
STOOD TOE-TO-TOE WITH HIM.
SURVIVED.
FRANINT?
OH NO...
NO...
NO.
AND I'LL NEVER FORGET LOOKING INTO THOSE EYES.

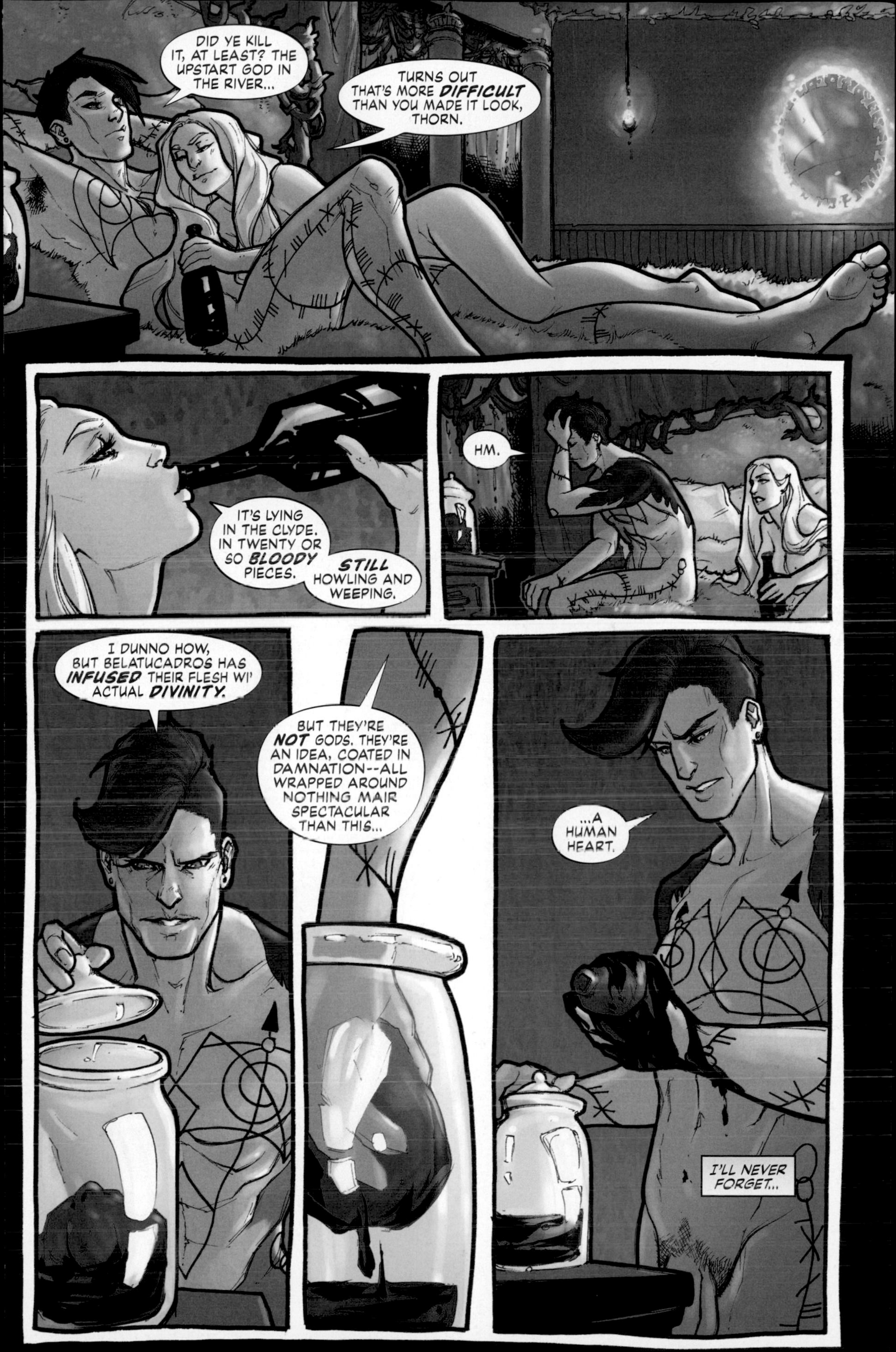
DID YE KILL IT, AT LEAST? THE UPSTART GOD IN THE RIVER...
TURNS OUT THAT'S MORE DIFFICULT THAN YOU MADE IT LOOK, THORN.
IT'S LYING IN THE CLYDE. IN TWENTY OR SO BLOODY PIECES.
STILL HOWLING AND WEEPING.
HM.
I DUNNO HOW, BUT BELATUCADROS HAS INFUSED THEIR FLESH WI' ACTUAL DIVINITY.
BUT THEY'RE NOT GODS. THEY'RE AN IDEA, COATED IN DAMNATION--ALL WRAPPED AROUND NOTHING MAIR SPECTACULAR THAN THIS...
...A HUMAN HEART.
I'LL NEVER FORGET...

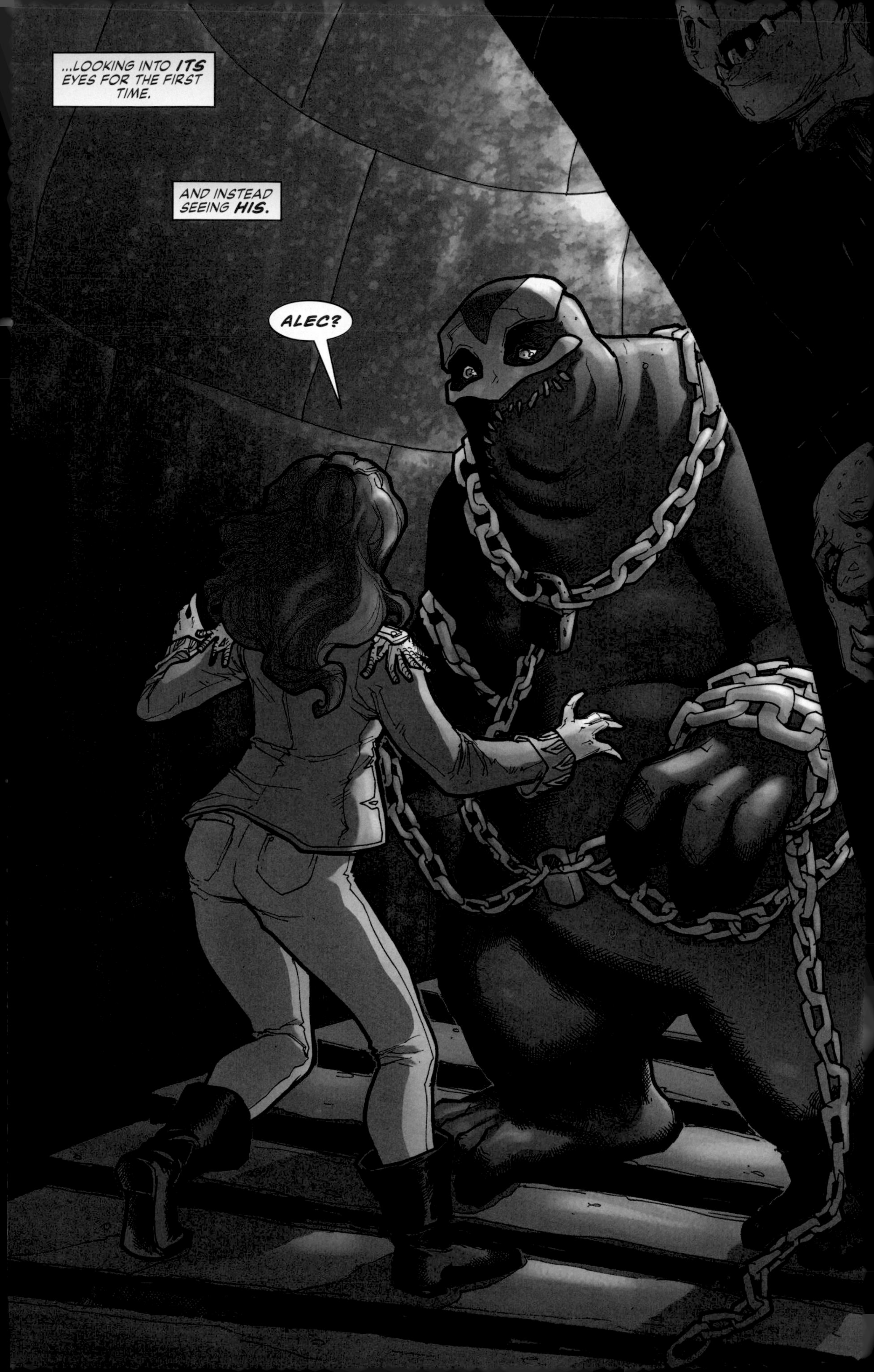
...LOOKING INTO ITS EYES FOR THE FIRST TIME.
AND INSTEAD SEEING HIS.
ALEC?

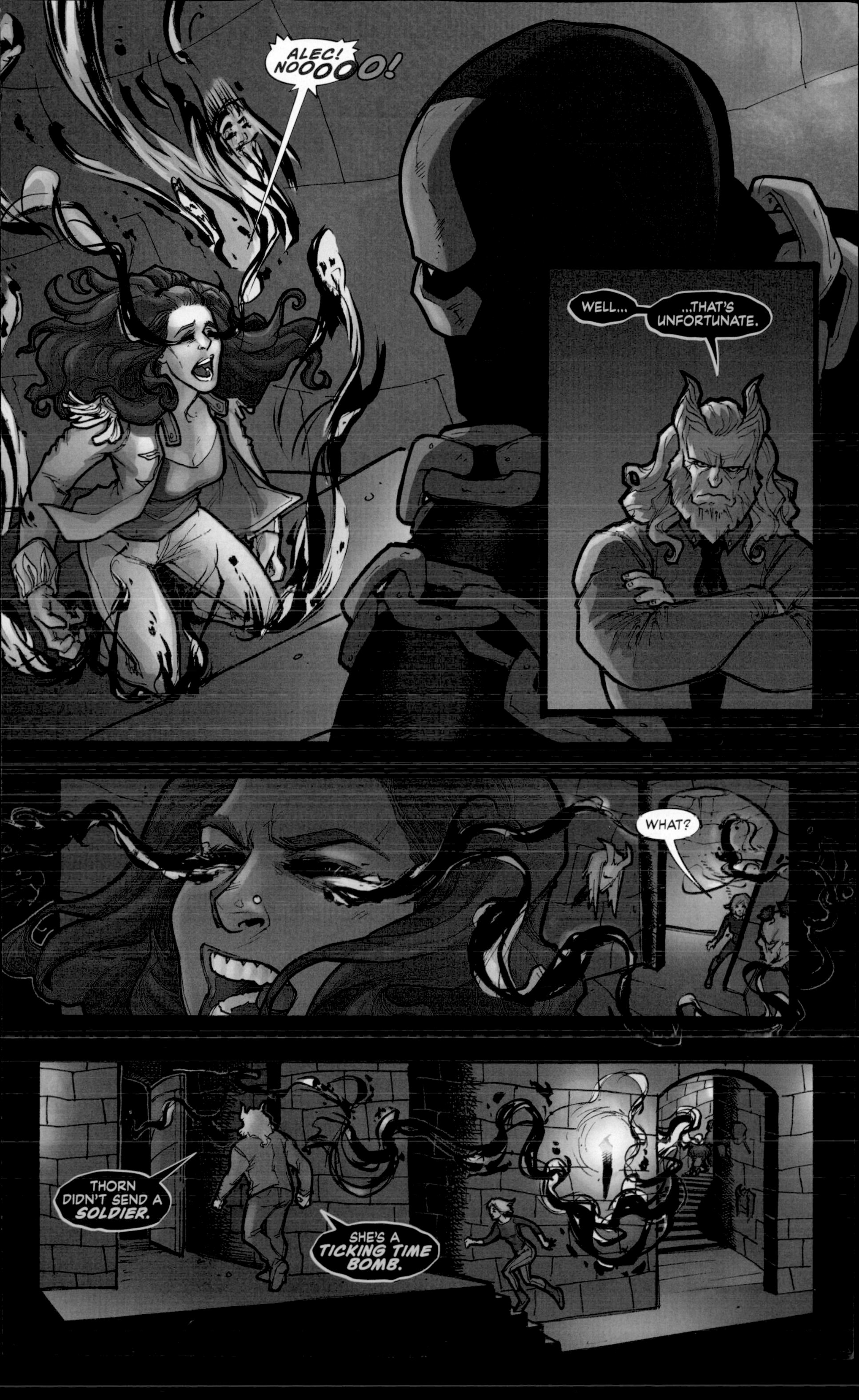
ALEC! NOOOOOO!
WELL...
...THAT'S UNFORTUNATE.
WHAT?
THORN DIDN'T SEND A SOLDIER.
SHE'S A TICKING TIME BOMB.

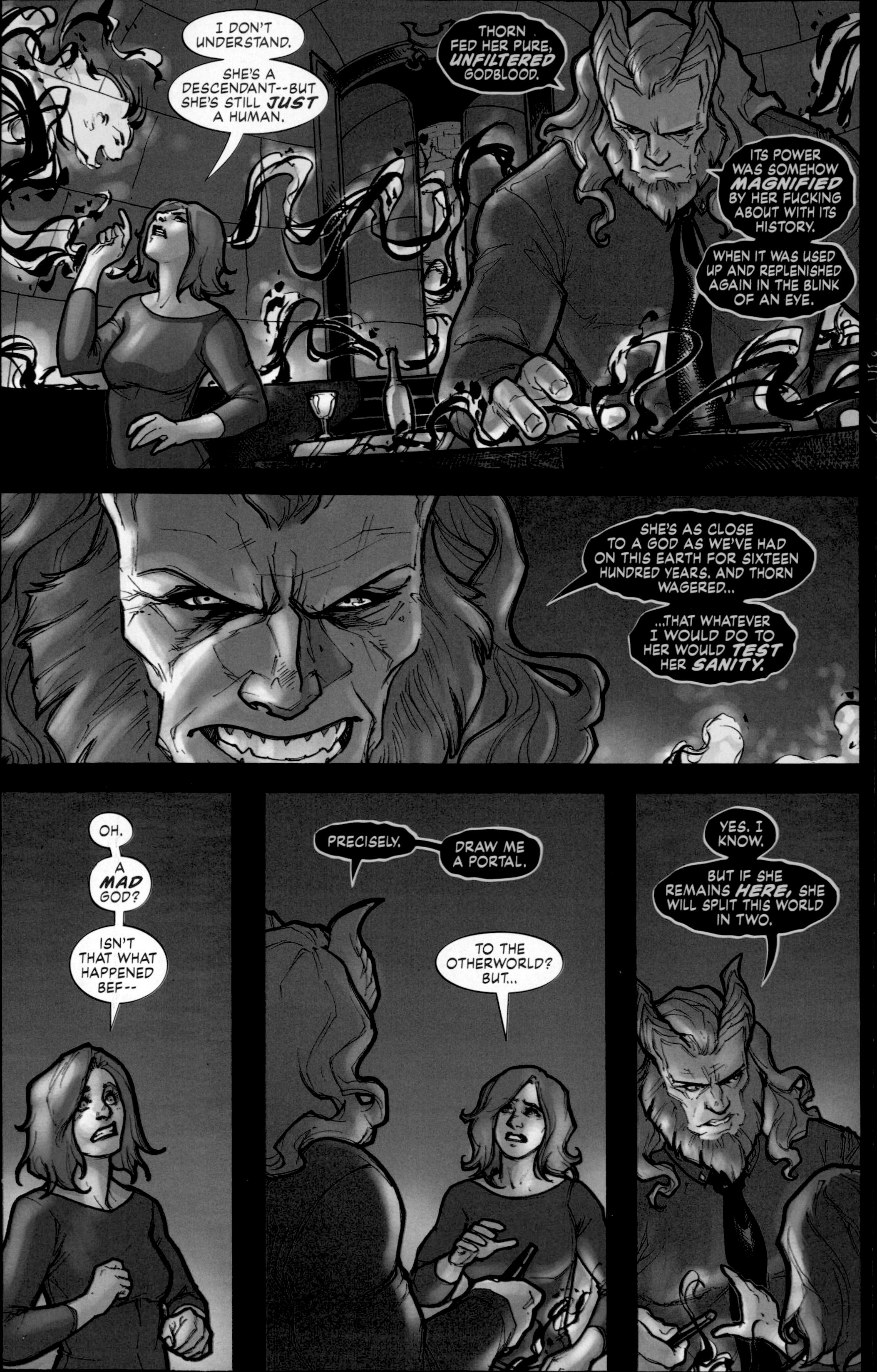
I DON'T UNDERSTAND.
SHE'S A DESCENDANT--BUT SHE'S STILL *JUST* A HUMAN.
THORN FED HER PURE, *UNFILTERED* GODBLOOD.
ITS POWER WAS SOMEHOW *MAGNIFIED* BY HER FUCKING ABOUT WITH ITS HISTORY.
WHEN IT WAS USED UP AND REPLENISHED AGAIN IN THE BLINK OF AN EYE.
SHE'S AS CLOSE TO A GOD AS WE'VE HAD ON THIS EARTH FOR SIXTEEN HUNDRED YEARS. AND THORN WAGERED...
...THAT WHATEVER I WOULD DO TO HER WOULD *TEST* HER *SANITY.*
OH.
A *MAD* GOD?
ISN'T THAT WHAT HAPPENED BEF--
PRECISELY.
DRAW ME A PORTAL.
TO THE OTHERWORLD? BUT...
YES. I KNOW.
BUT IF SHE REMAINS *HERE,* SHE WILL SPLIT THIS WORLD IN TWO.

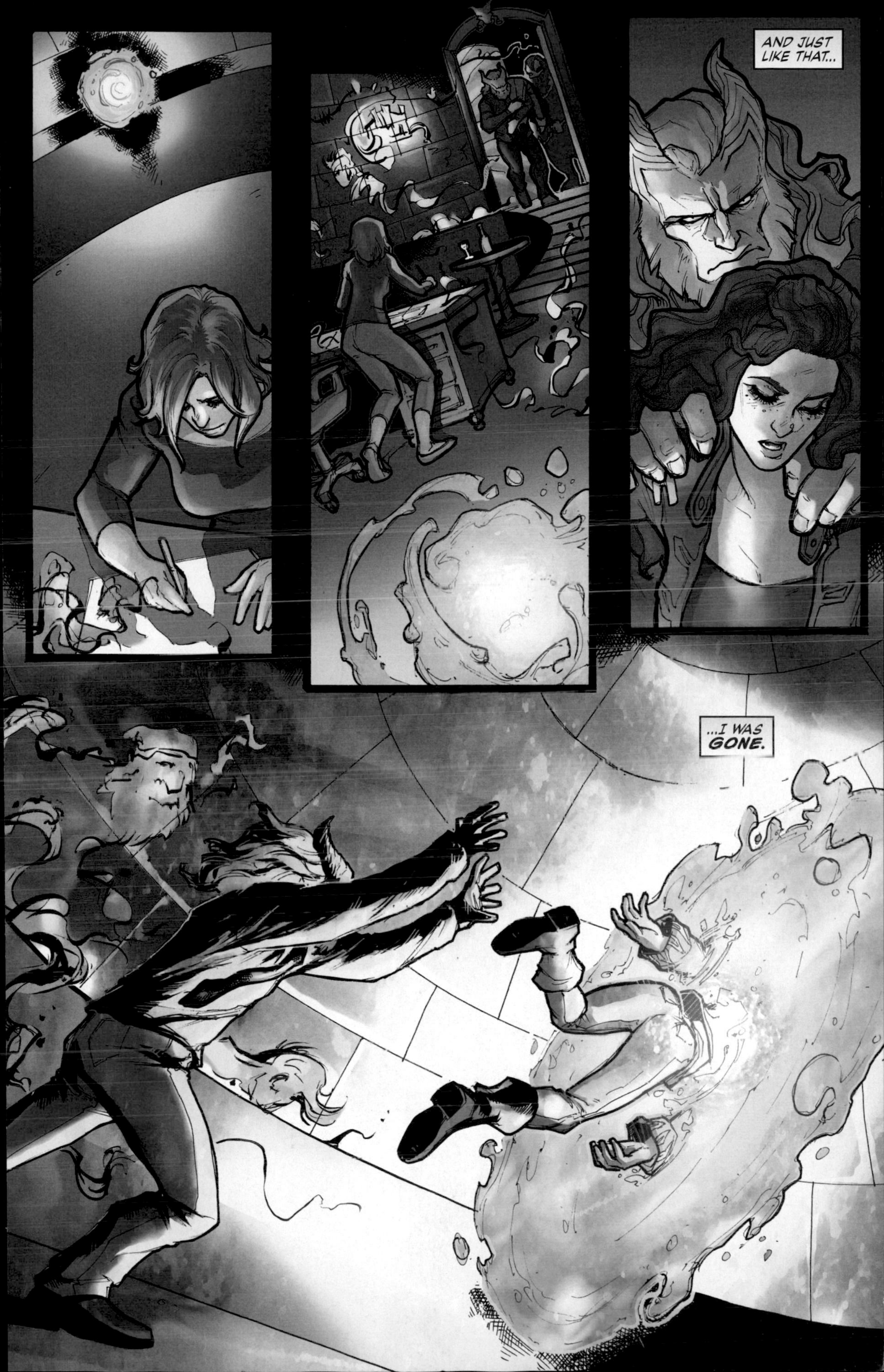
AND JUST LIKE THAT...
...I WAS GONE.

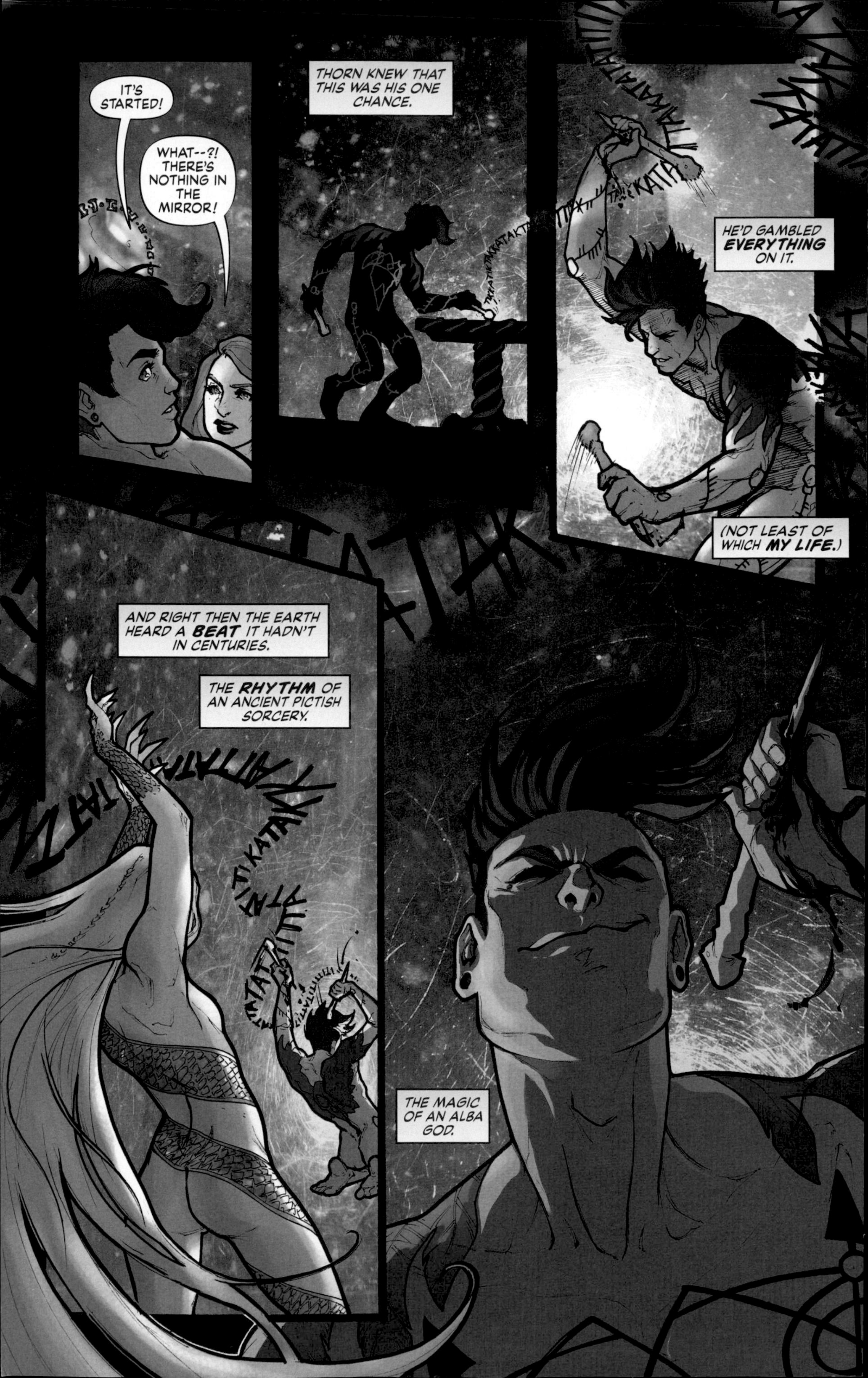
IT'S STARTED!
WHAT--?! THERE'S NOTHING IN THE MIRROR!
THORN KNEW THAT THIS WAS HIS ONE CHANCE.
HE'D GAMBLED EVERYTHING ON IT.
(NOT LEAST OF WHICH MY LIFE.)
AND RIGHT THEN THE EARTH HEARD A BEAT IT HADN'T IN CENTURIES.
THE RHYTHM OF AN ANCIENT PICTISH SORCERY.
THE MAGIC OF AN ALBA GOD.

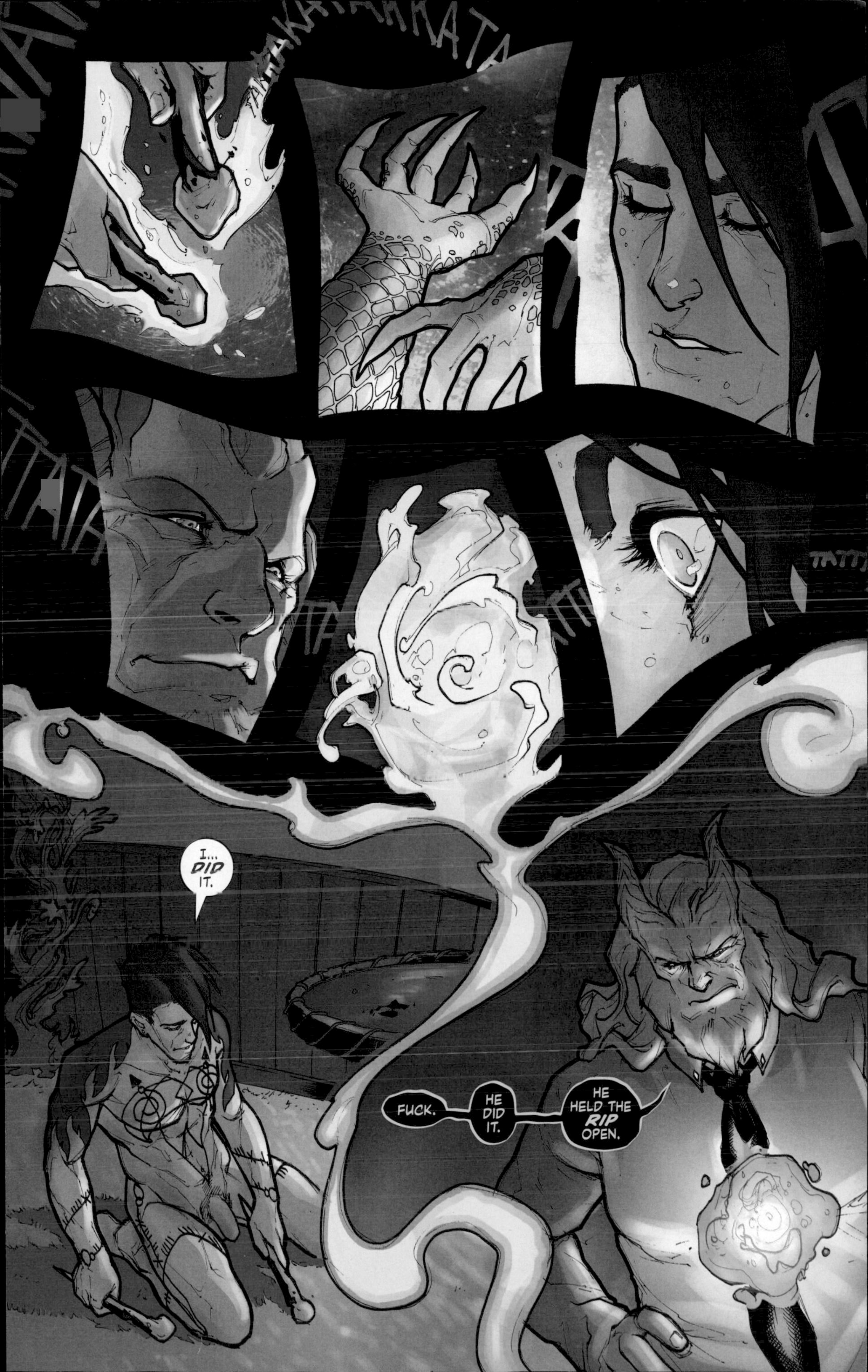
I... DID IT.
FUCK.
HE DID IT.
HE HELD THE RIP OPEN.

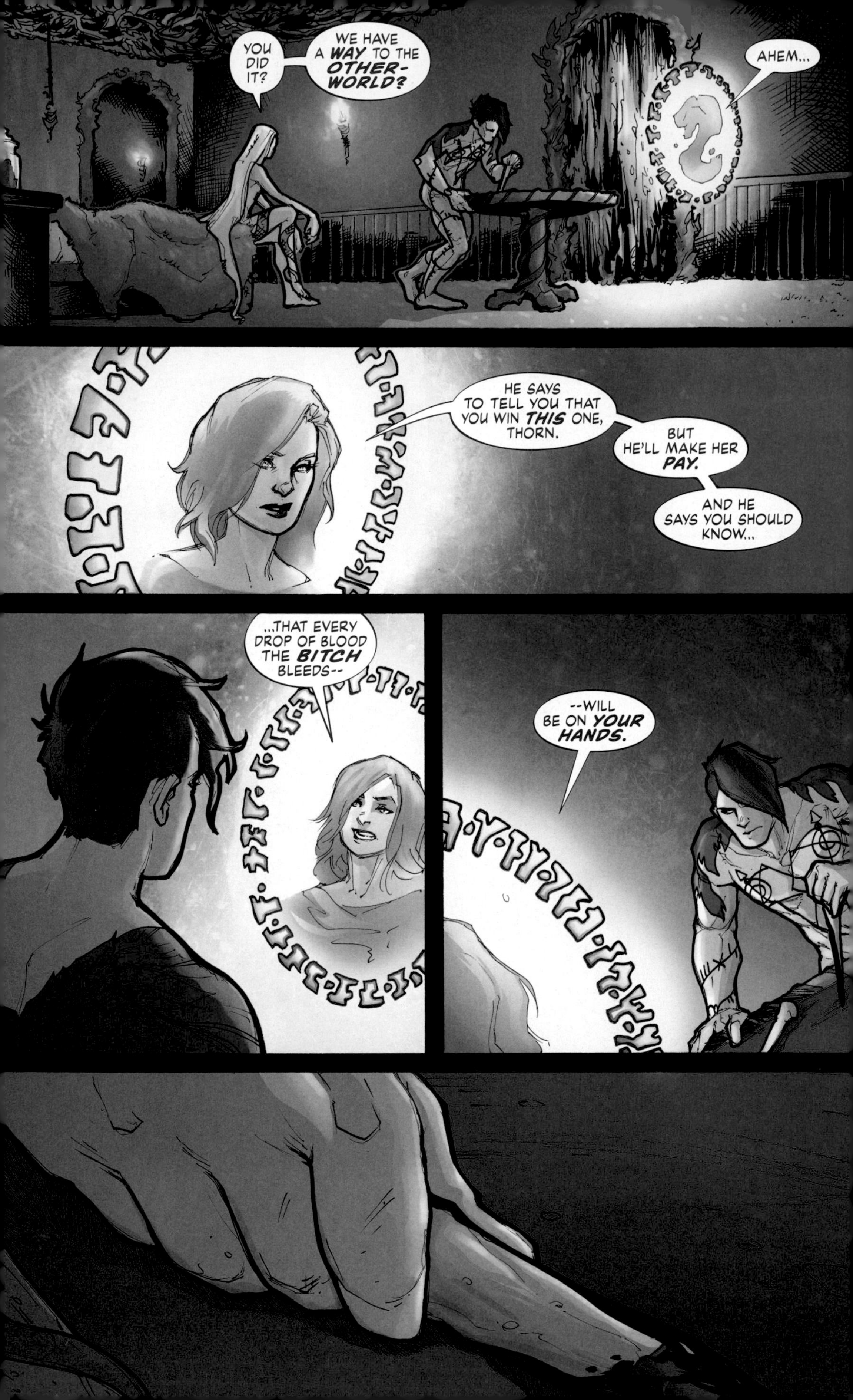
YOU DID IT?
WE HAVE A WAY TO THE OTHER-WORLD?
AHEM...
HE SAYS TO TELL YOU THAT YOU WIN THIS ONE, THORN.
BUT HE'LL MAKE HER PAY.
AND HE SAYS YOU SHOULD KNOW...
...THAT EVERY DROP OF BLOOD THE BITCH BLEEDS--
--WILL BE ON YOUR HANDS.

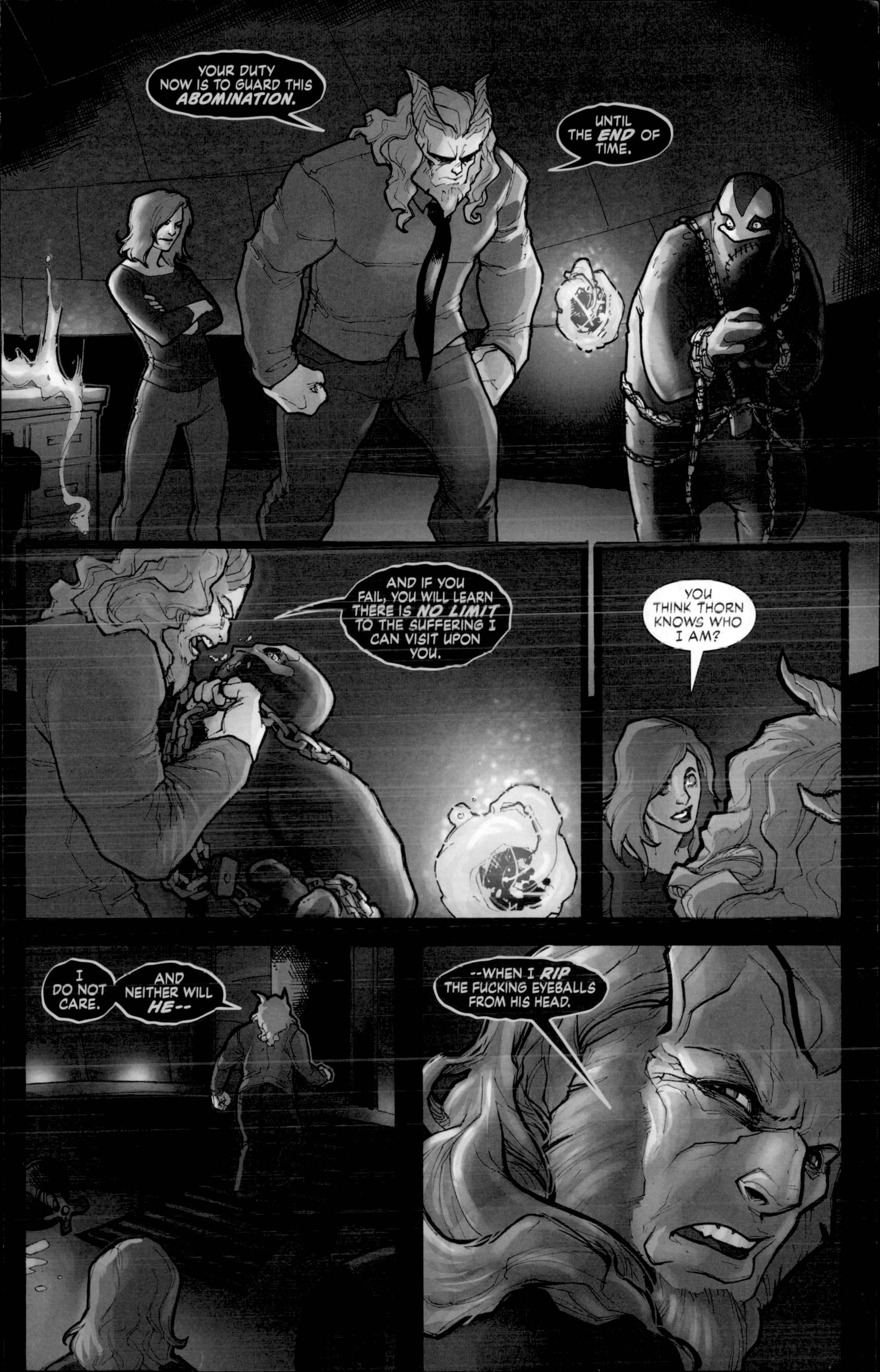
YOUR DUTY NOW IS TO GUARD THIS ABOMINATION.
UNTIL THE END OF TIME.
AND IF YOU FAIL, YOU WILL LEARN THERE IS NO LIMIT TO THE SUFFERING I CAN VISIT UPON YOU.
YOU THINK THORN KNOWS WHO I AM?
I DO NOT CARE.
AND NEITHER WILL HE--
--WHEN I RIP THE FUCKING EYEBALLS FROM HIS HEAD.

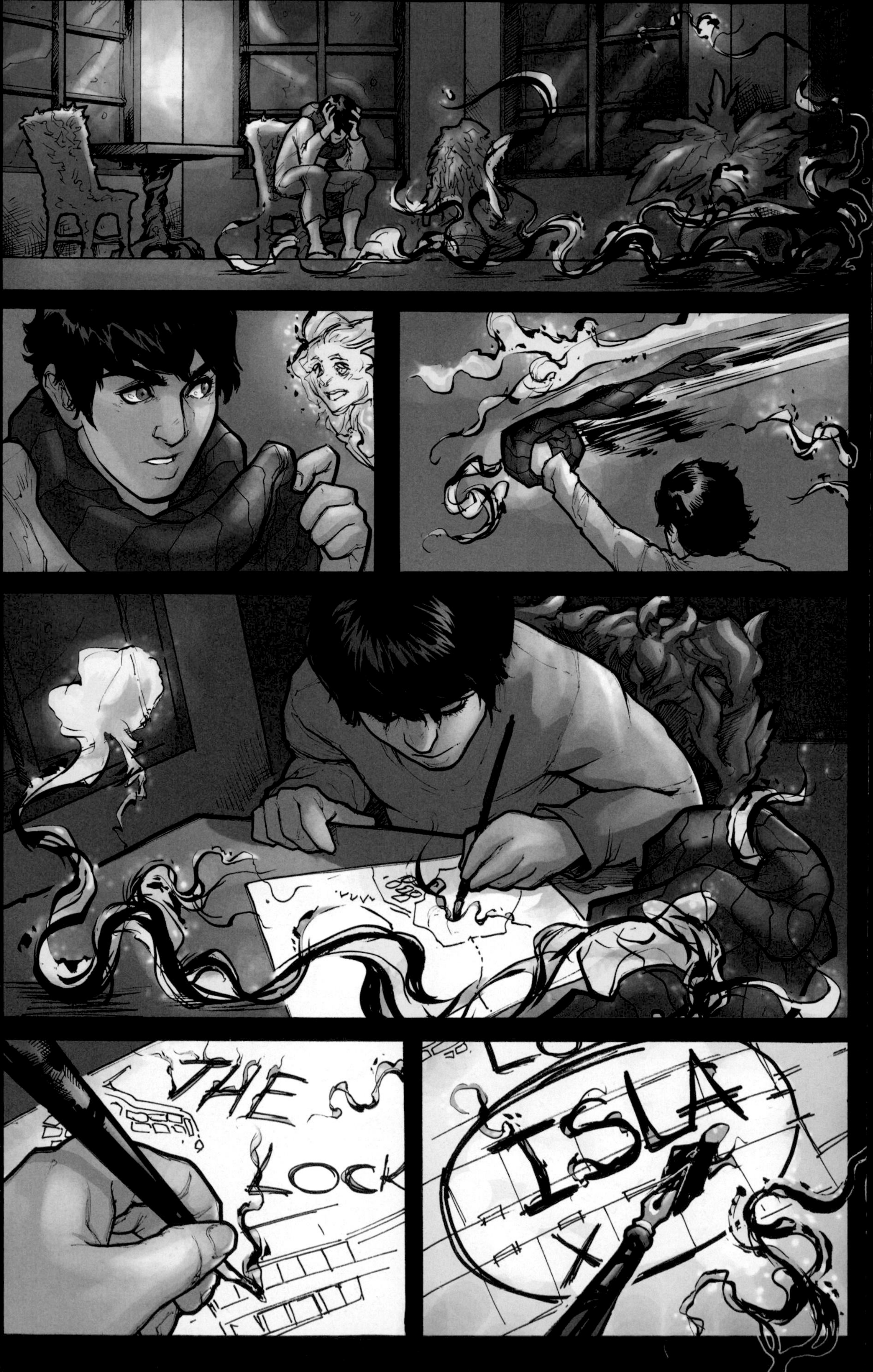
THE
LOCK
ISLA
X

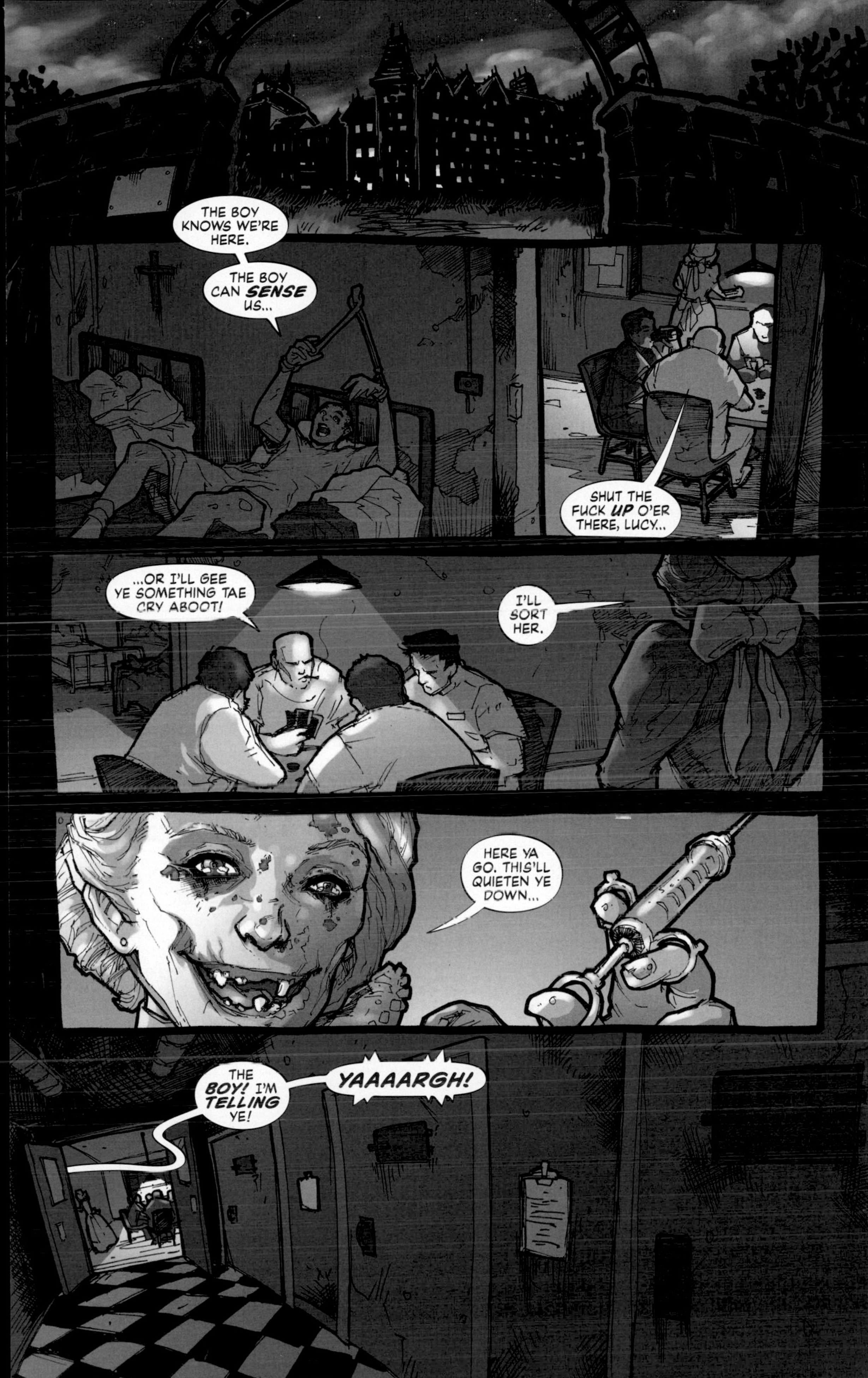
THE BOY KNOWS WE'RE HERE.
THE BOY CAN SENSE US...
SHUT THE FUCK UP O'ER THERE, LUCY...
...OR I'LL GEE YE SOMETHING TAE CRY ABOOT!
I'LL SORT HER.
HERE YA GO. THIS'LL QUIETEN YE DOWN...
THE BOY! I'M TELLING YE!
YAAAARGH!

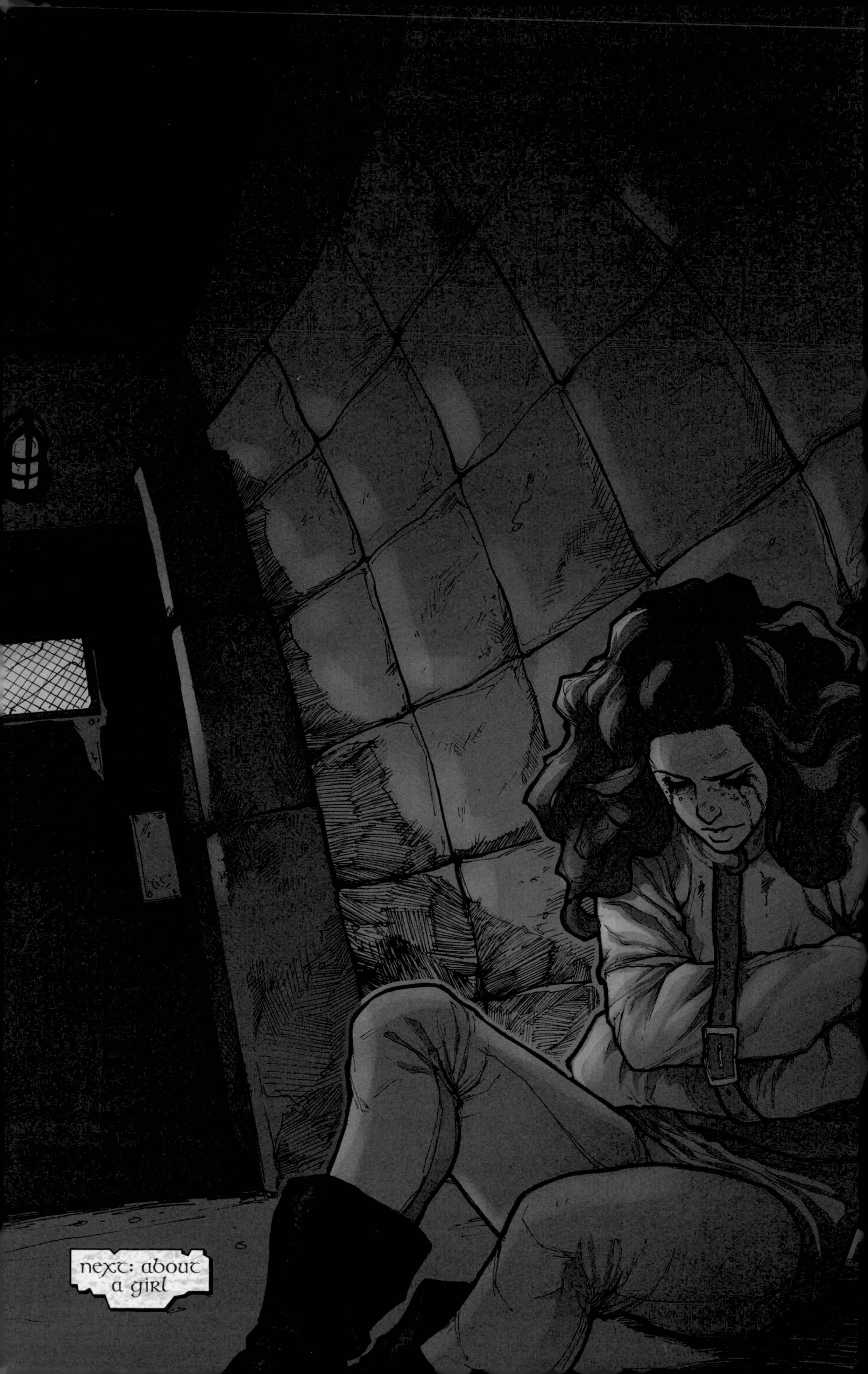
next: about a girl

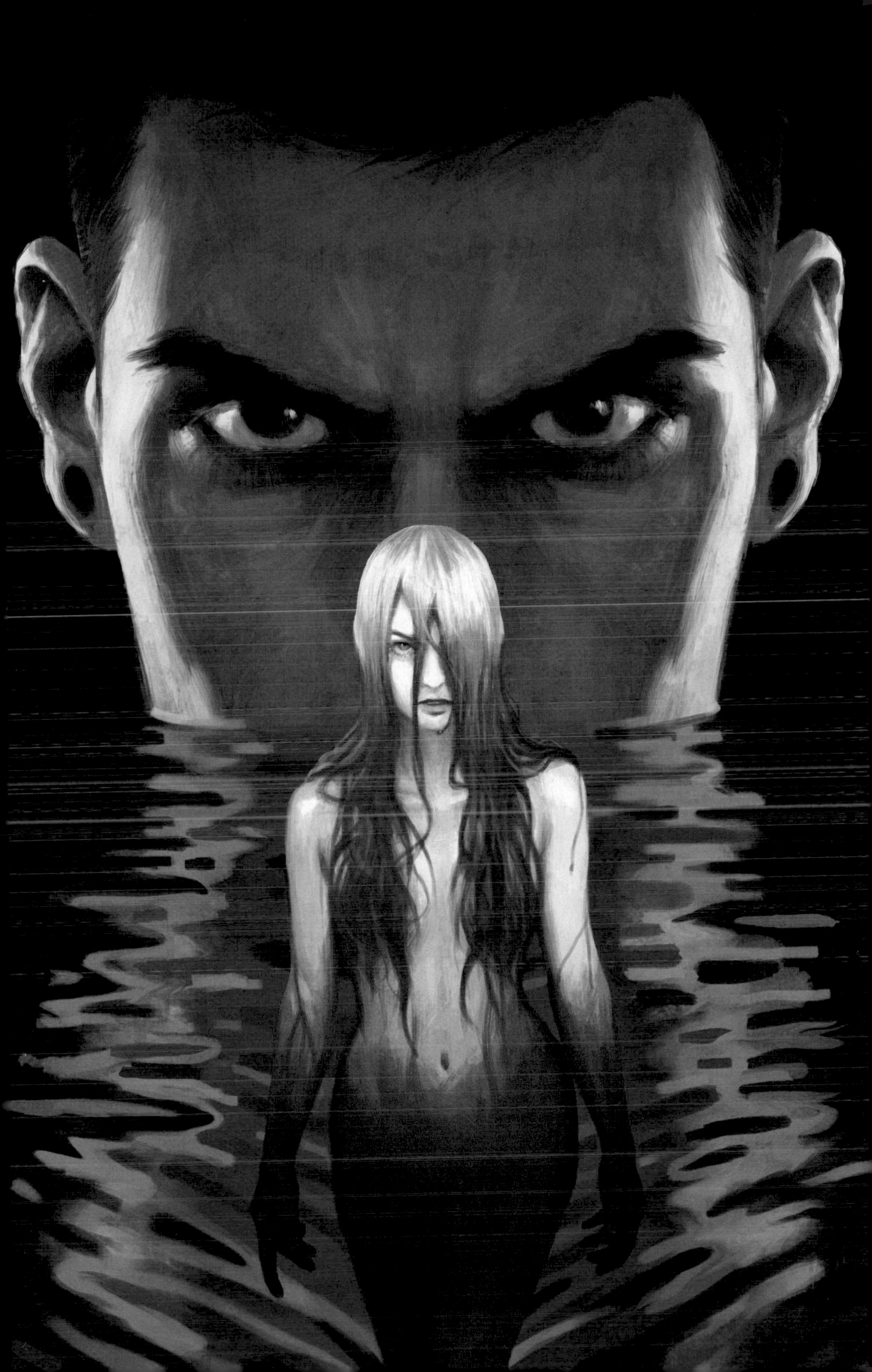

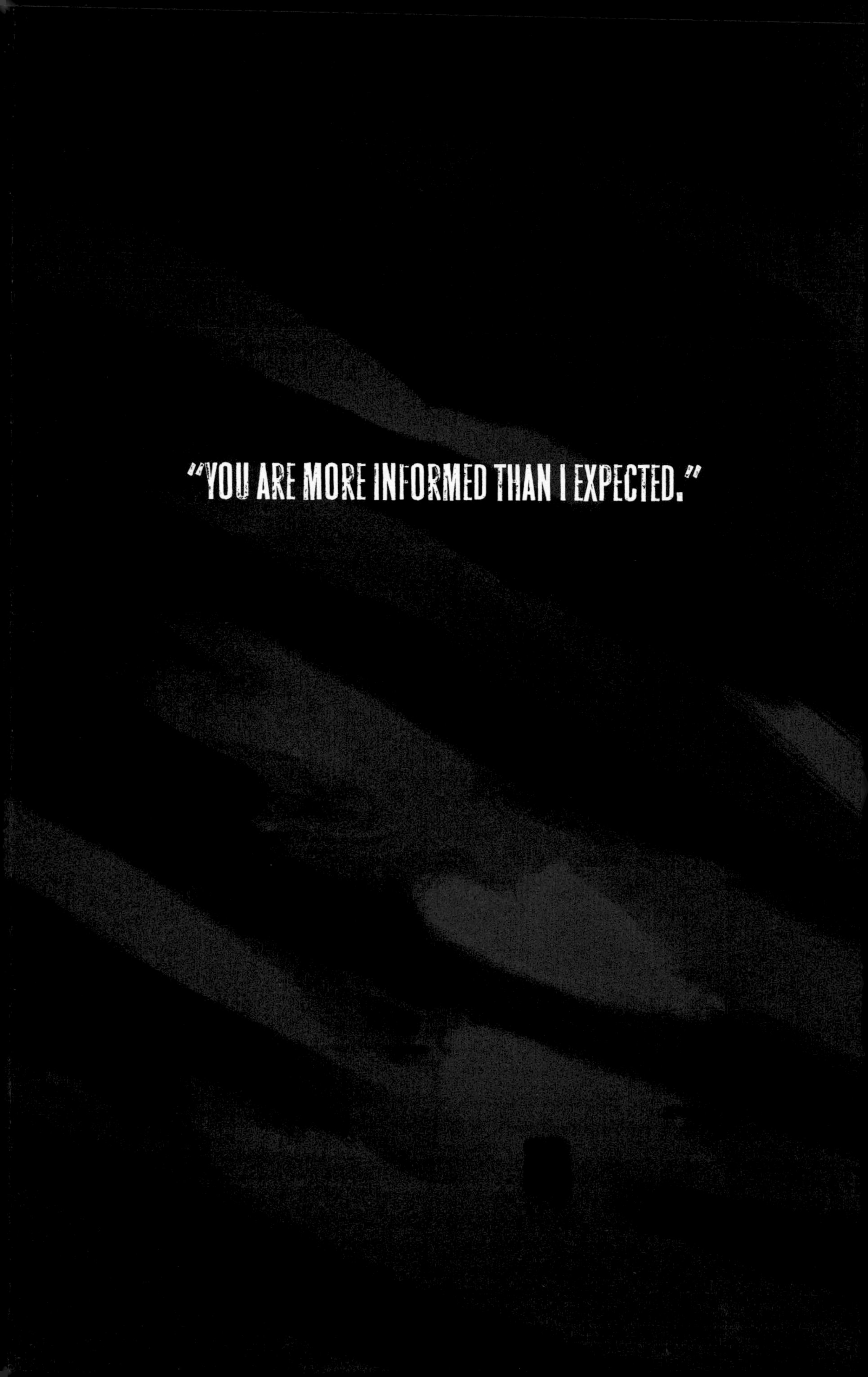
"YOU ARE MORE INFORMED THAN I EXPECTED."

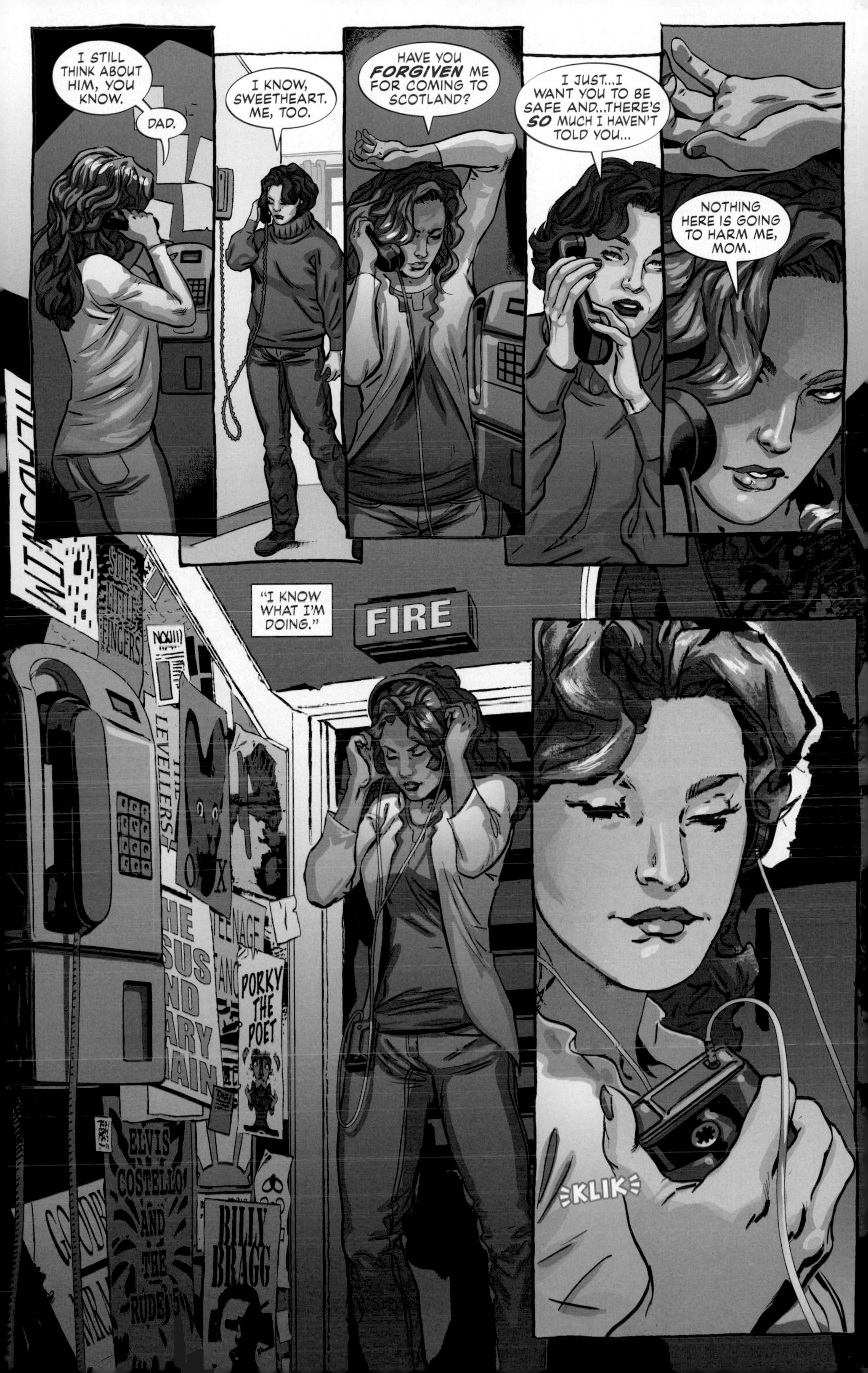
I STILL THINK ABOUT HIM, YOU KNOW.
DAD.
I KNOW, SWEETHEART. ME, TOO.
HAVE YOU *FORGIVEN* ME FOR COMING TO SCOTLAND?
I JUST...I WANT YOU TO BE SAFE AND...THERE'S *SO* MUCH I HAVEN'T TOLD YOU...
NOTHING HERE IS GOING TO HARM ME, MOM.
"I KNOW WHAT I'M DOING."
FIRE
PORKY THE POET
ELVIS COSTELLO AND THE
BILLY BRAGG
KLIK

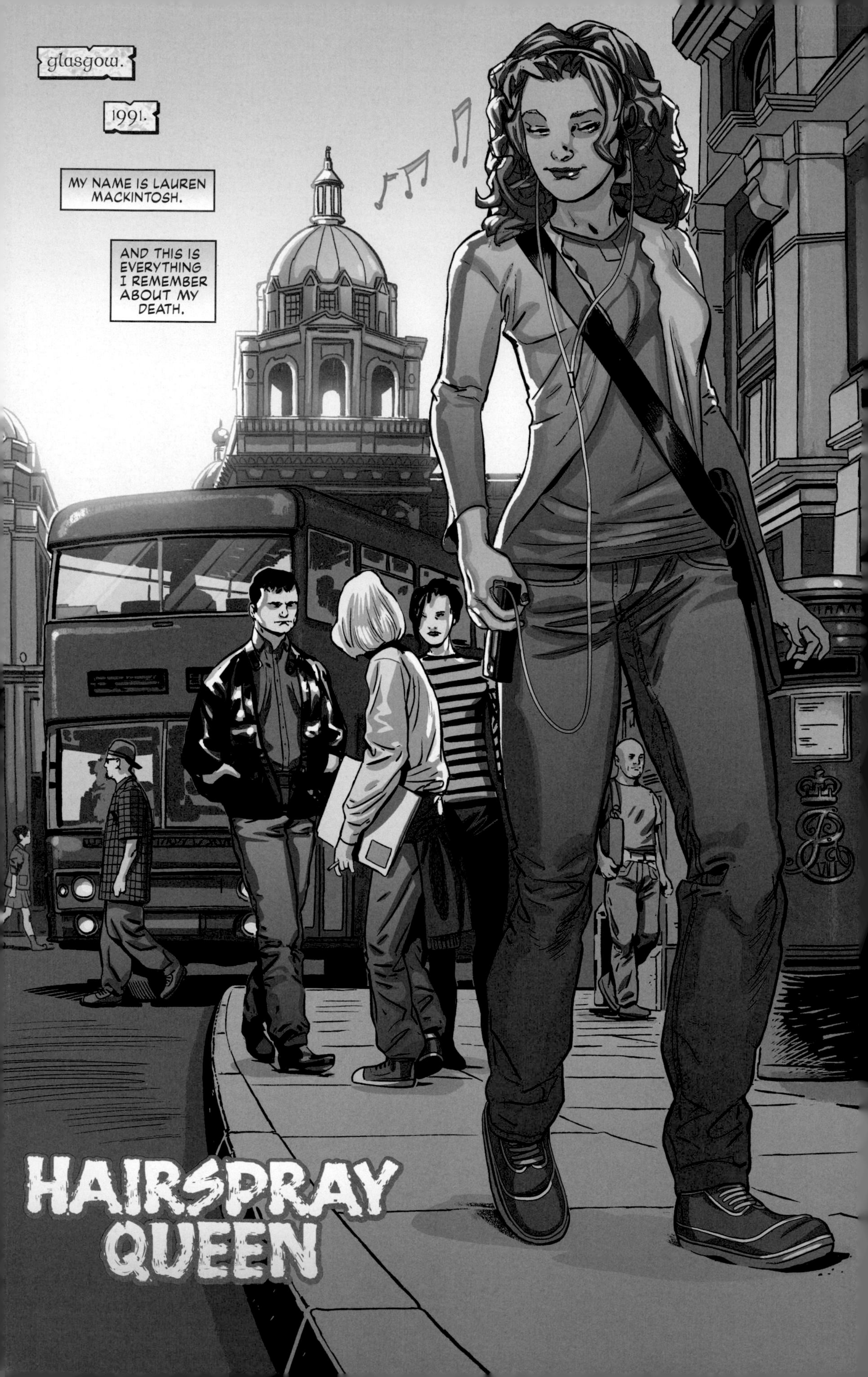
glasgow.
1991.
MY NAME IS LAUREN MACKINTOSH.
AND THIS IS EVERYTHING I REMEMBER ABOUT MY DEATH.
HAIRSPRAY QUEEN

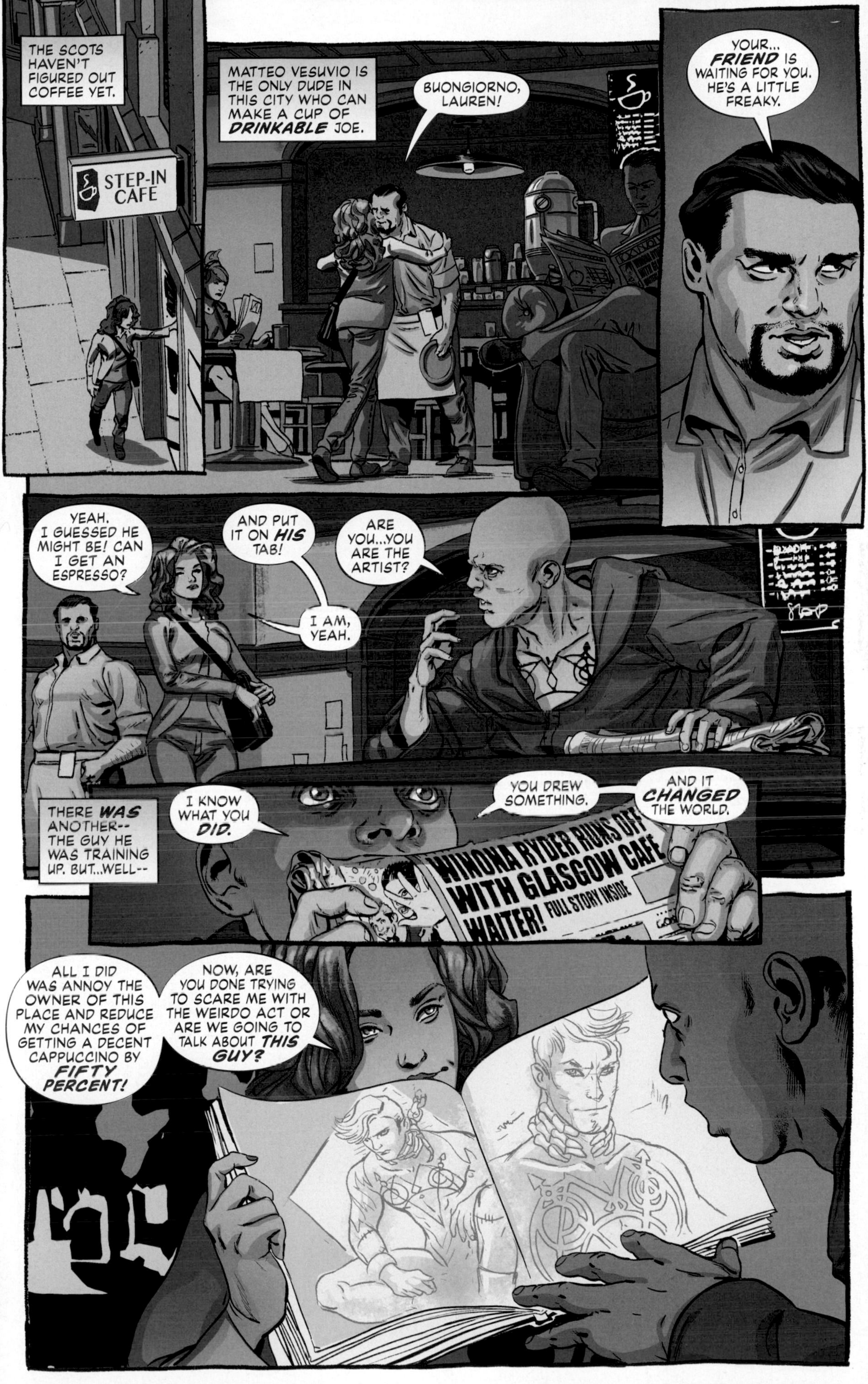
THE SCOTS HAVEN'T FIGURED OUT COFFEE YET.
STEP-IN CAFE
MATTEO VESUVIO IS THE ONLY DUDE IN THIS CITY WHO CAN MAKE A CUP OF DRINKABLE JOE.
BUONGIORNO, LAUREN!
YOUR... FRIEND IS WAITING FOR YOU. HE'S A LITTLE FREAKY.
YEAH. I GUESSED HE MIGHT BE! CAN I GET AN ESPRESSO?
AND PUT IT ON HIS TAB!
ARE YOU...YOU ARE THE ARTIST?
I AM, YEAH.
THERE WAS ANOTHER-- THE GUY HE WAS TRAINING UP. BUT...WELL--
I KNOW WHAT YOU DID.
YOU DREW SOMETHING.
AND IT CHANGED THE WORLD.
WINONA RYDER RUNS OFF WITH GLASGOW CAFE WAITER! FULL STORY INSIDE
ALL I DID WAS ANNOY THE OWNER OF THIS PLACE AND REDUCE MY CHANCES OF GETTING A DECENT CAPPUCCINO BY FIFTY PERCENT!
NOW, ARE YOU DONE TRYING TO SCARE ME WITH THE WEIRDO ACT OR ARE WE GOING TO TALK ABOUT THIS GUY?

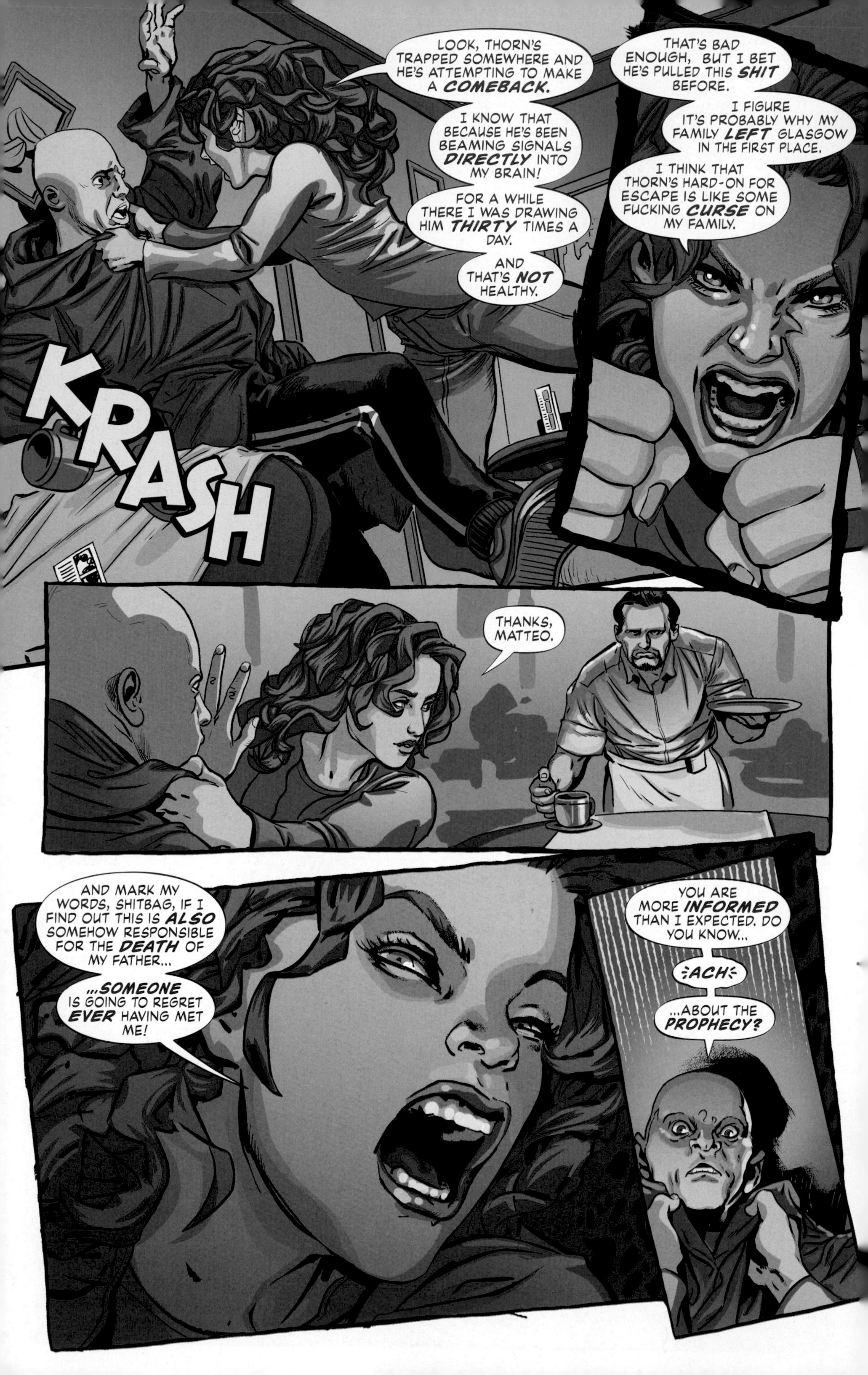
LOOK, THORN'S TRAPPED SOMEWHERE AND HE'S ATTEMPTING TO MAKE A COMEBACK.
I KNOW THAT BECAUSE HE'S BEEN BEAMING SIGNALS DIRECTLY INTO MY BRAIN!
FOR A WHILE THERE I WAS DRAWING HIM THIRTY TIMES A DAY.
AND THAT'S NOT HEALTHY.
KRASH
THAT'S BAD ENOUGH, BUT I BET HE'S PULLED THIS SHIT BEFORE.
I FIGURE IT'S PROBABLY WHY MY FAMILY LEFT GLASGOW IN THE FIRST PLACE.
I THINK THAT THORN'S HARD-ON FOR ESCAPE IS LIKE SOME FUCKING CURSE ON MY FAMILY.
THANKS, MATTEO.
AND MARK MY WORDS, SHITBAG, IF I FIND OUT THIS IS ALSO SOMEHOW RESPONSIBLE FOR THE DEATH OF MY FATHER...
...SOMEONE IS GOING TO REGRET EVER HAVING MET ME!
YOU ARE MORE INFORMED THAN I EXPECTED. DO YOU KNOW...
ACH
...ABOUT THE PROPHECY?

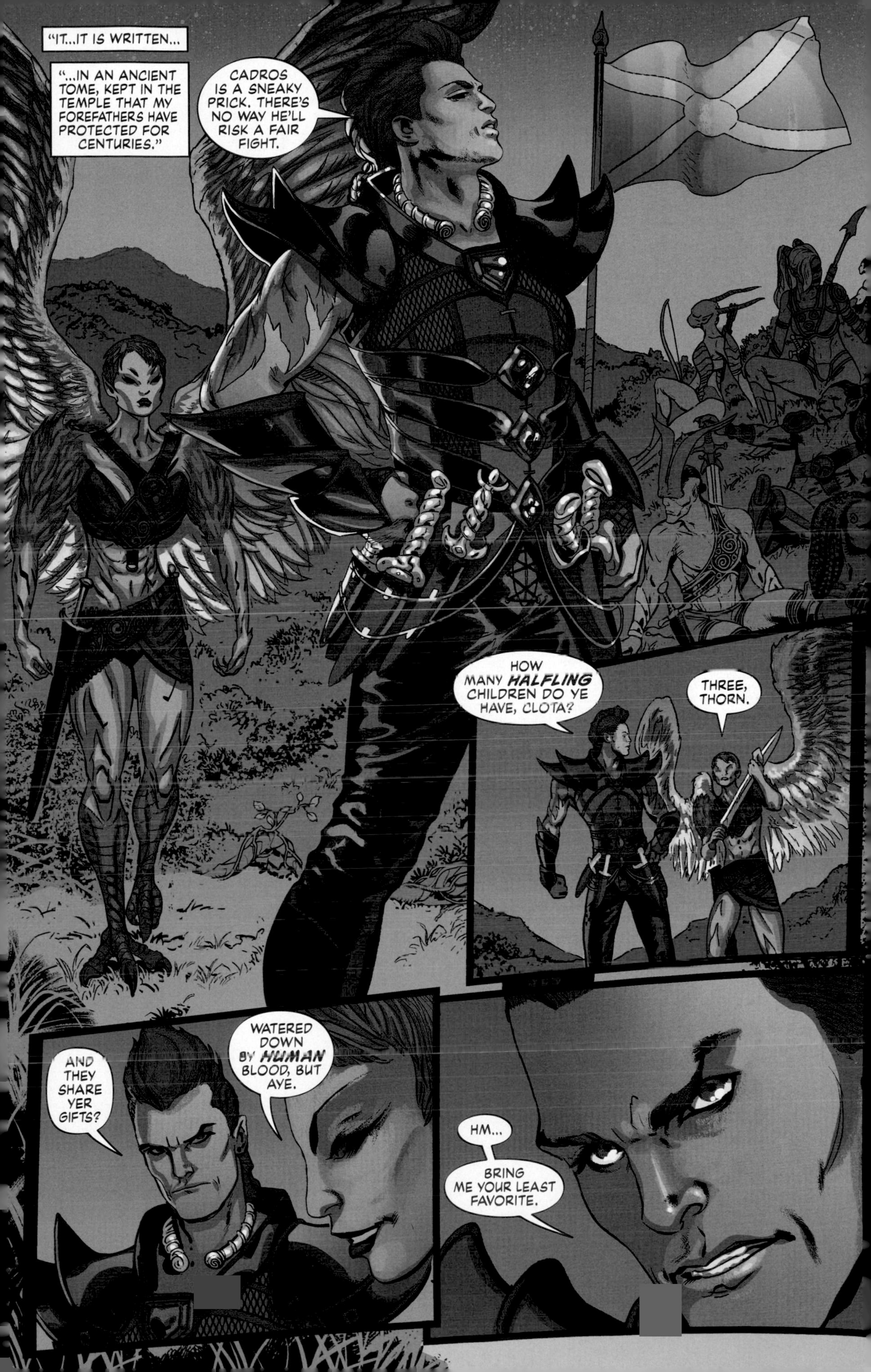
"IT...IT IS WRITTEN...
"...IN AN ANCIENT TOME, KEPT IN THE TEMPLE THAT MY FOREFATHERS HAVE PROTECTED FOR CENTURIES."
CADROS IS A SNEAKY PRICK. THERE'S NO WAY HE'LL RISK A FAIR FIGHT.
HOW MANY HALFLING CHILDREN DO YE HAVE, CLOTA?
THREE, THORN.
AND THEY SHARE YER GIFTS?
WATERED DOWN BY HUMAN BLOOD, BUT AYE.
HM...
BRING ME YOUR LEAST FAVORITE.

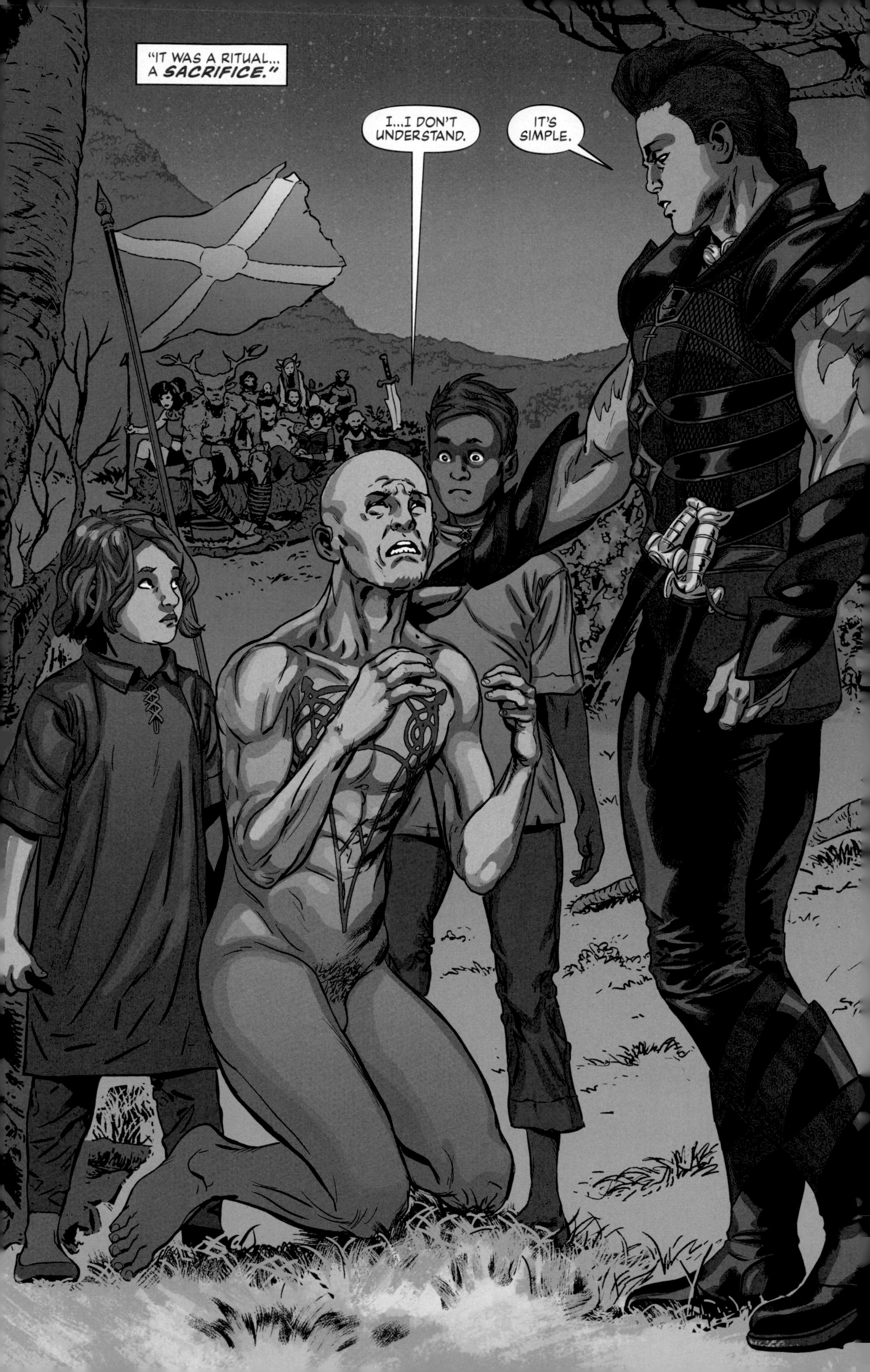
"IT WAS A RITUAL... A SACRIFICE."
I...I DON'T UNDERSTAND.
IT'S SIMPLE.

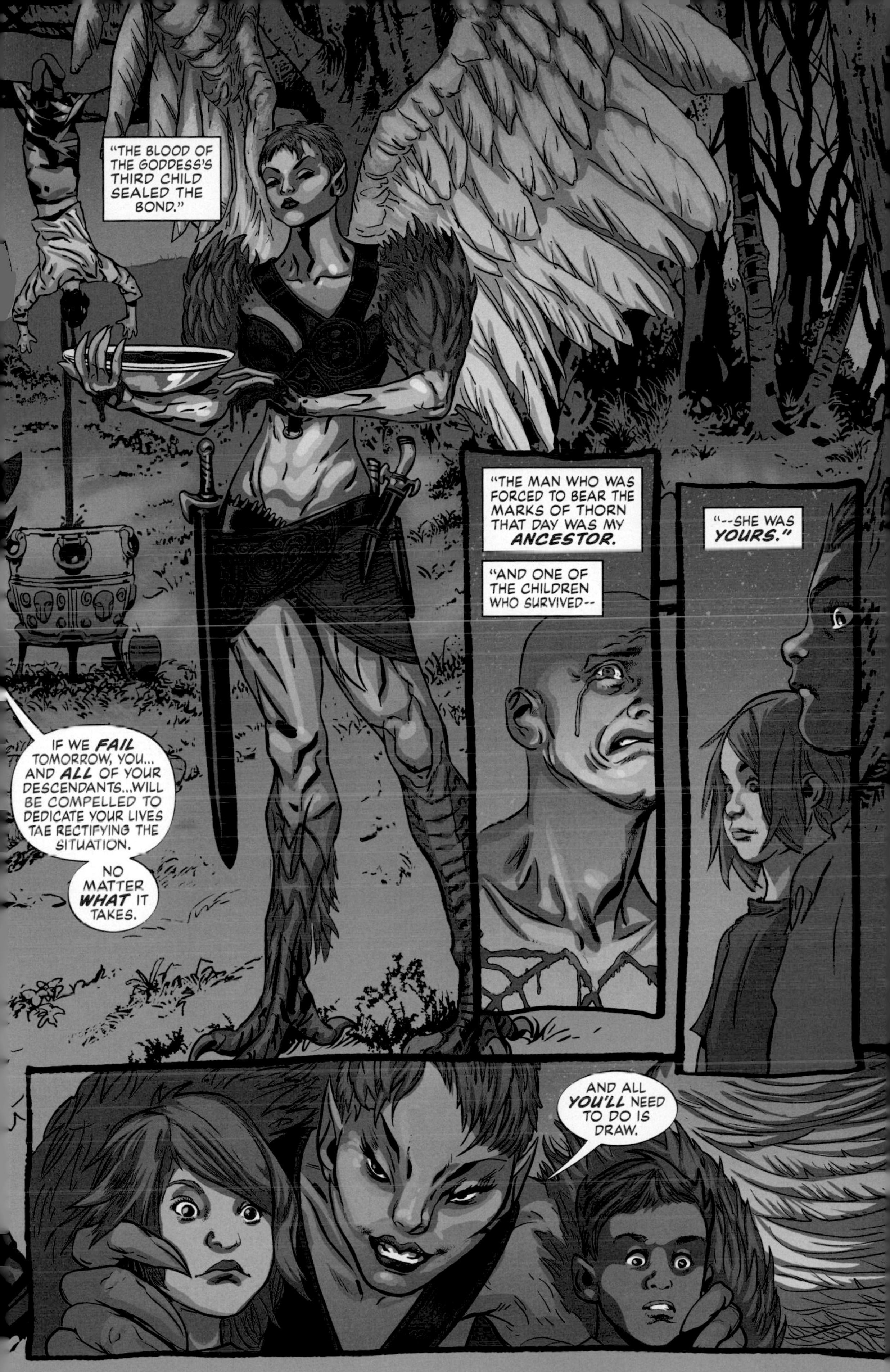
"THE BLOOD OF THE GODDESS'S THIRD CHILD SEALED THE BOND."
IF WE FAIL TOMORROW, YOU... AND ALL OF YOUR DESCENDANTS...WILL BE COMPELLED TO DEDICATE YOUR LIVES TAE RECTIFYING THE SITUATION.
NO MATTER WHAT IT TAKES.
"THE MAN WHO WAS FORCED TO BEAR THE MARKS OF THORN THAT DAY WAS MY ANCESTOR.
"AND ONE OF THE CHILDREN WHO SURVIVED--
"--SHE WAS YOURS."
AND ALL YOU'LL NEED TO DO IS DRAW.

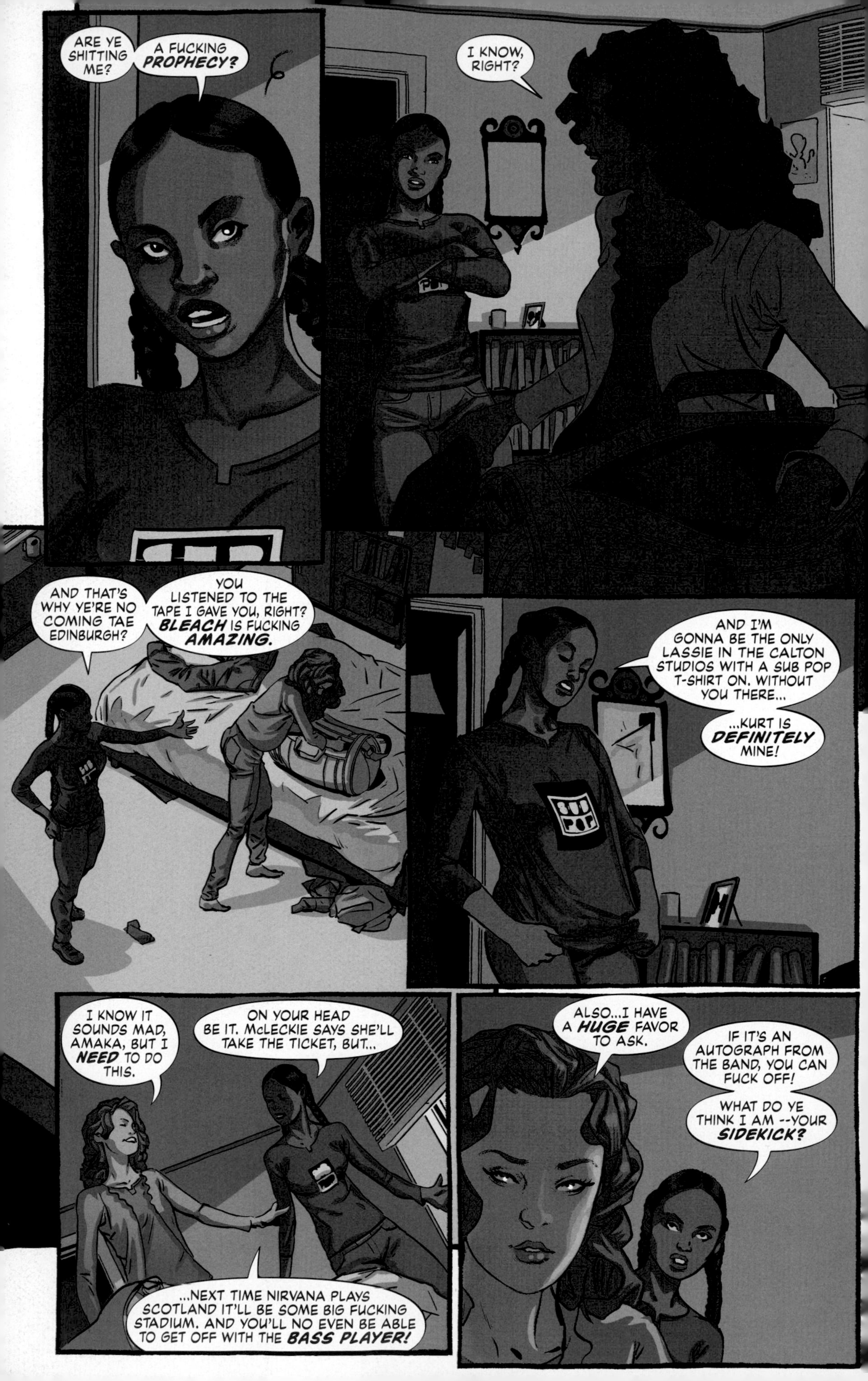

ARE YE SHITTING ME?
A FUCKING PROPHECY?
I KNOW, RIGHT?
AND THAT'S WHY YE'RE NO COMING TAE EDINBURGH?
YOU LISTENED TO THE TAPE I GAVE YOU, RIGHT? BLEACH IS FUCKING AMAZING.
AND I'M GONNA BE THE ONLY LASSIE IN THE CALTON STUDIOS WITH A SUB POP T-SHIRT ON. WITHOUT YOU THERE...
...KURT IS DEFINITELY MINE!
I KNOW IT SOUNDS MAD, AMAKA, BUT I NEED TO DO THIS.
ON YOUR HEAD BE IT. McLECKIE SAYS SHE'LL TAKE THE TICKET, BUT...
...NEXT TIME NIRVANA PLAYS SCOTLAND IT'LL BE SOME BIG FUCKING STADIUM. AND YOU'LL NO EVEN BE ABLE TO GET OFF WITH THE BASS PLAYER!
ALSO...I HAVE A HUGE FAVOR TO ASK.
IF IT'S AN AUTOGRAPH FROM THE BAND, YOU CAN FUCK OFF!
WHAT DO YE THINK I AM --YOUR SIDEKICK?

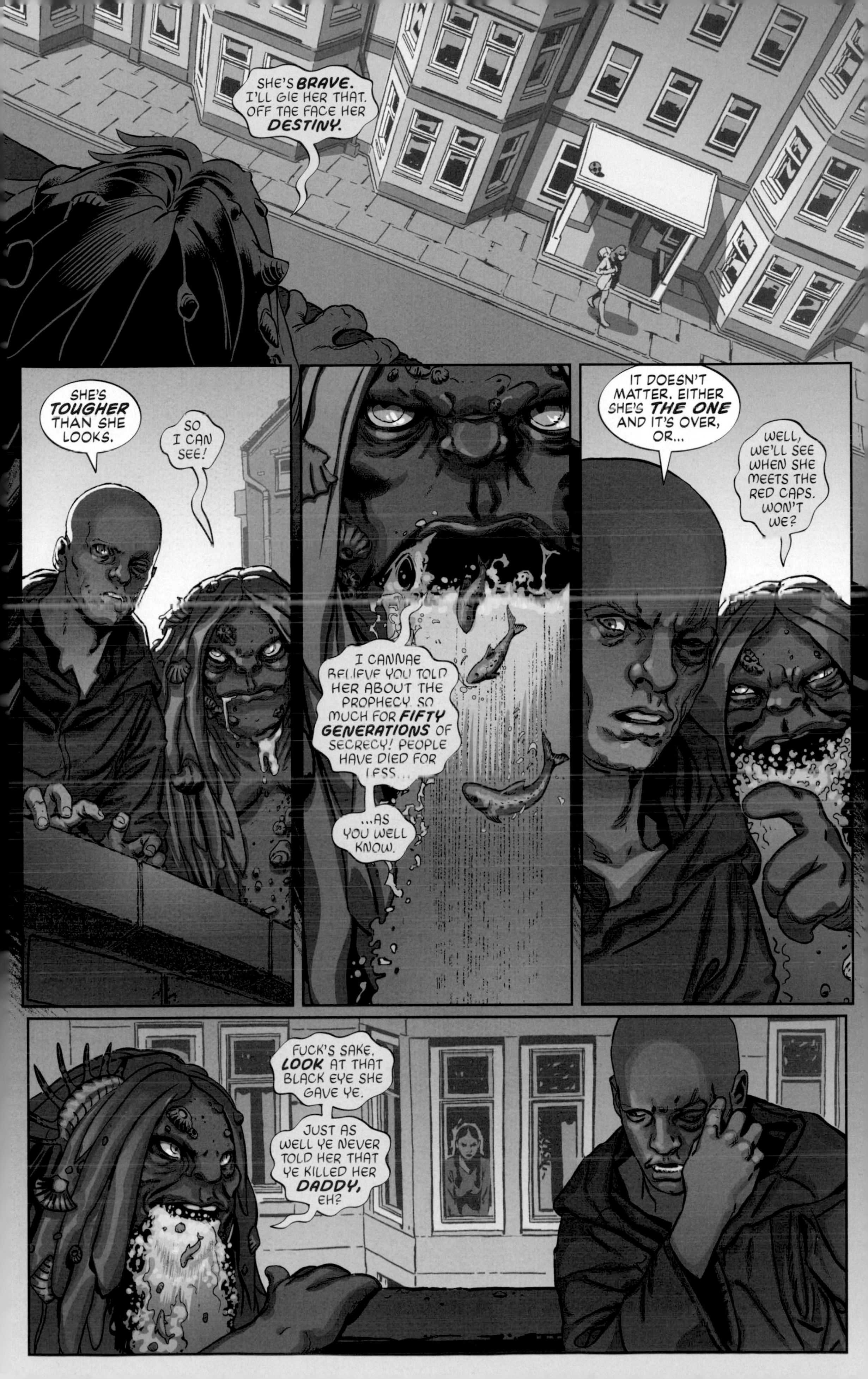
SHE'S BRAVE. I'LL GIE HER THAT. OFF TAE FACE HER DESTINY.
SHE'S TOUGHER THAN SHE LOOKS.
SO I CAN SEE!
I CANNAE BELIEVE YOU TOLD HER ABOUT THE PROPHECY. SO MUCH FOR FIFTY GENERATIONS OF SECRECY! PEOPLE HAVE DIED FOR LESS...
...AS YOU WELL KNOW.
IT DOESN'T MATTER. EITHER SHE'S THE ONE AND IT'S OVER, OR...
WELL, WE'LL SEE WHEN SHE MEETS THE RED CAPS. WON'T WE?
FUCK'S SAKE, LOOK AT THAT BLACK EYE SHE GAVE YE.
JUST AS WELL YE NEVER TOLD HER THAT YE KILLED HER DADDY, EH?

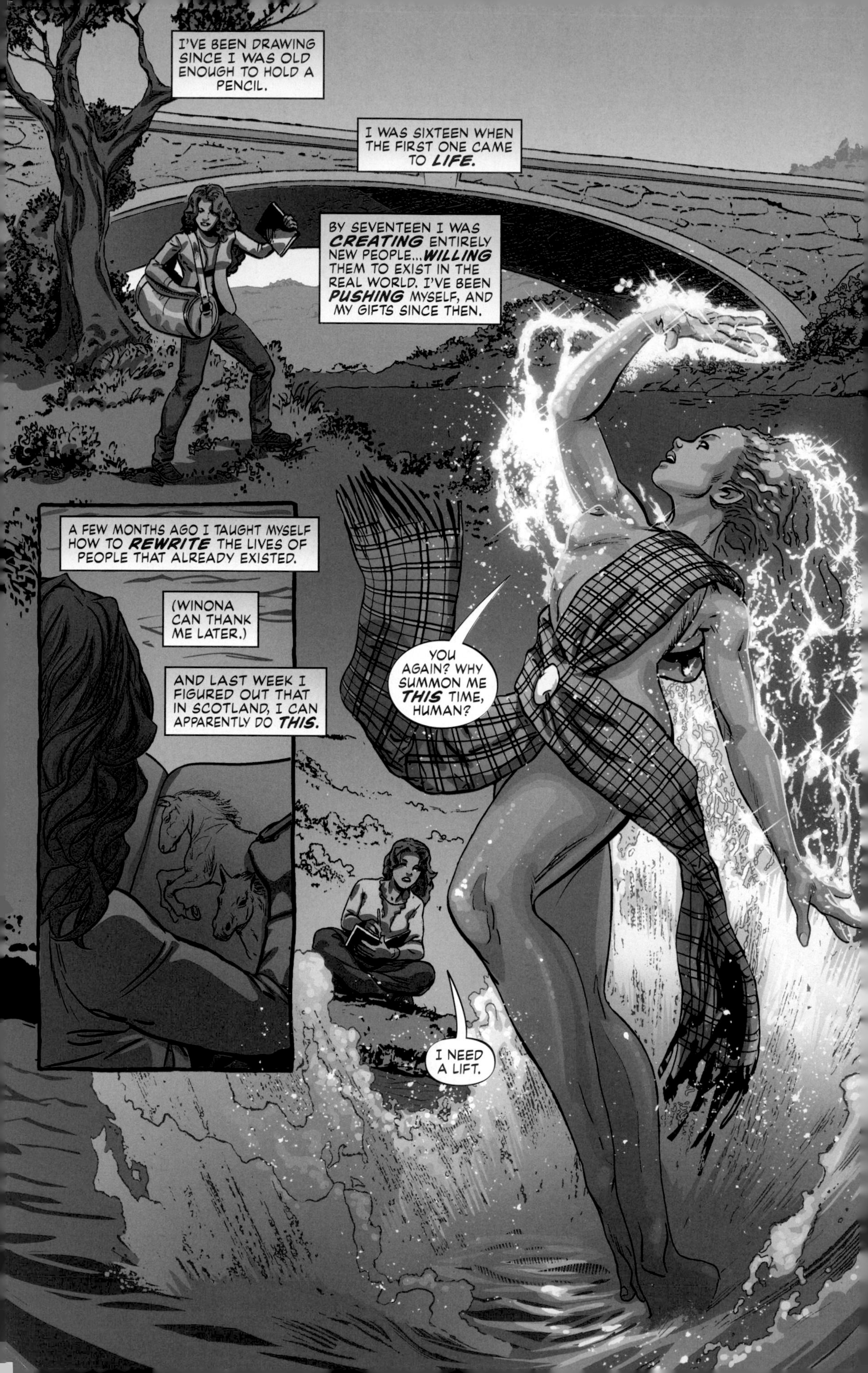
I'VE BEEN DRAWING SINCE I WAS OLD ENOUGH TO HOLD A PENCIL.
I WAS SIXTEEN WHEN THE FIRST ONE CAME TO LIFE.
BY SEVENTEEN I WAS CREATING ENTIRELY NEW PEOPLE...WILLING THEM TO EXIST IN THE REAL WORLD. I'VE BEEN PUSHING MYSELF, AND MY GIFTS SINCE THEN.
A FEW MONTHS AGO I TAUGHT MYSELF HOW TO REWRITE THE LIVES OF PEOPLE THAT ALREADY EXISTED.
(WINONA CAN THANK ME LATER.)
AND LAST WEEK I FIGURED OUT THAT IN SCOTLAND, I CAN APPARENTLY DO THIS.
YOU AGAIN? WHY SUMMON ME THIS TIME, HUMAN?
I NEED A LIFT.

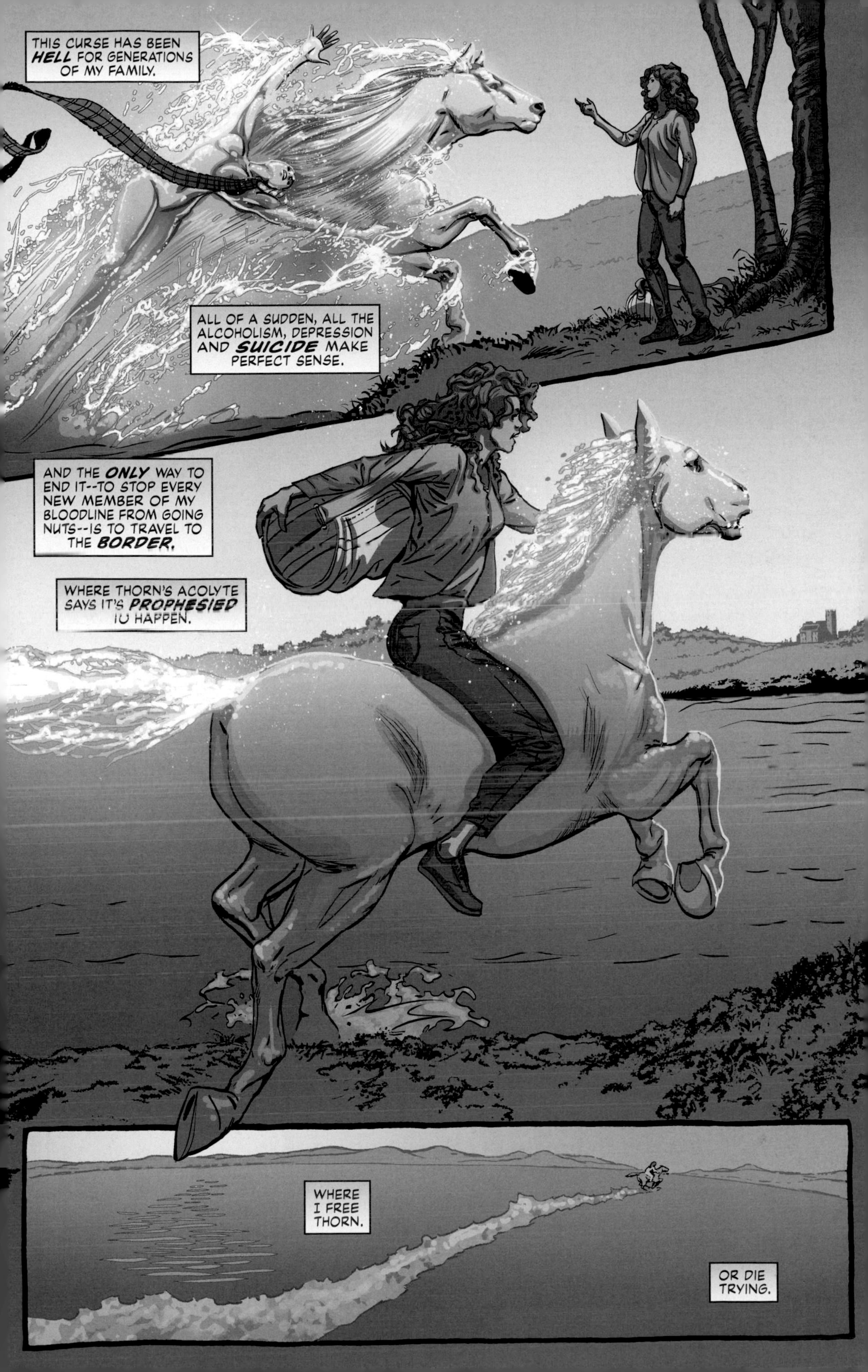
THIS CURSE HAS BEEN HELL FOR GENERATIONS OF MY FAMILY.
ALL OF A SUDDEN, ALL THE ALCOHOLISM, DEPRESSION AND SUICIDE MAKE PERFECT SENSE.
AND THE ONLY WAY TO END IT--TO STOP EVERY NEW MEMBER OF MY BLOODLINE FROM GOING NUTS--IS TO TRAVEL TO THE BORDER.
WHERE THORN'S ACOLYTE SAYS IT'S PROPHESIED TO HAPPEN.
WHERE I FREE THORN.
OR DIE TRYING.

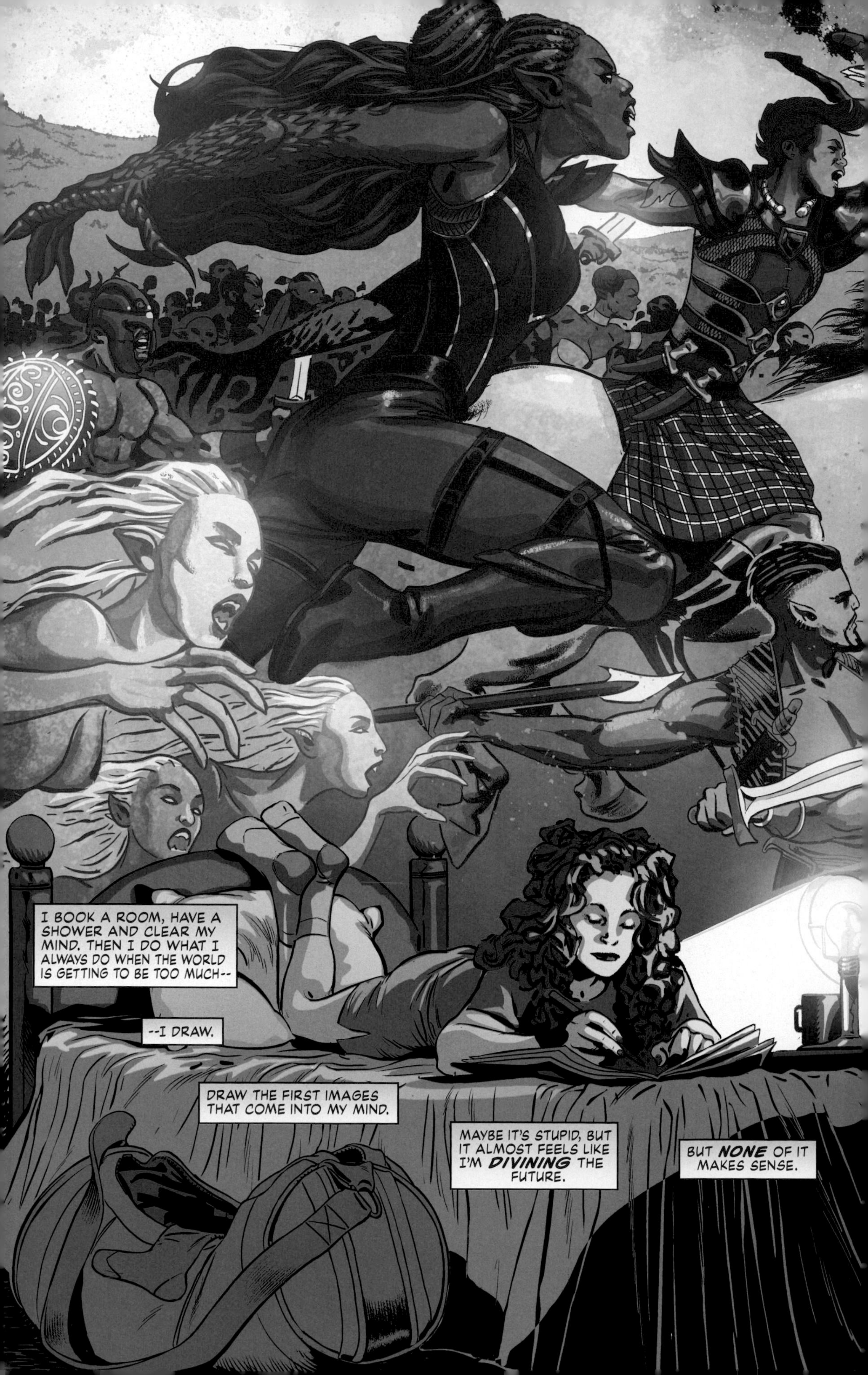
I BOOK A ROOM, HAVE A SHOWER AND CLEAR MY MIND. THEN I DO WHAT I ALWAYS DO WHEN THE WORLD IS GETTING TO BE TOO MUCH--
--I DRAW.
DRAW THE FIRST IMAGES THAT COME INTO MY MIND.
MAYBE IT'S STUPID, BUT IT ALMOST FEELS LIKE I'M ***DIVINING*** THE FUTURE.
BUT ***NONE*** OF IT MAKES SENSE.

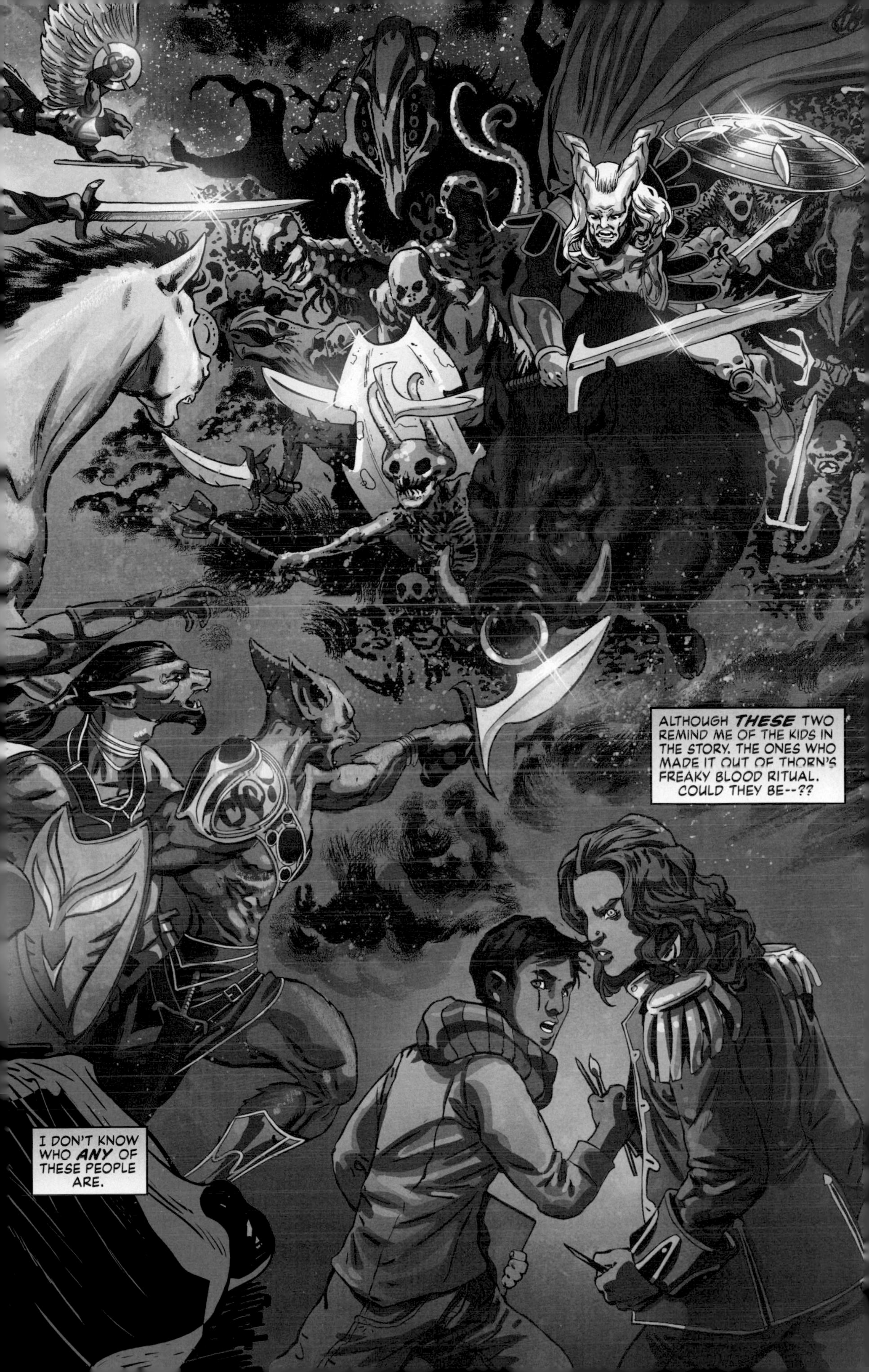
ALTHOUGH THESE TWO REMIND ME OF THE KIDS IN THE STORY. THE ONES WHO MADE IT OUT OF THORN'S FREAKY BLOOD RITUAL. COULD THEY BE--??
I DON'T KNOW WHO ANY OF THESE PEOPLE ARE.

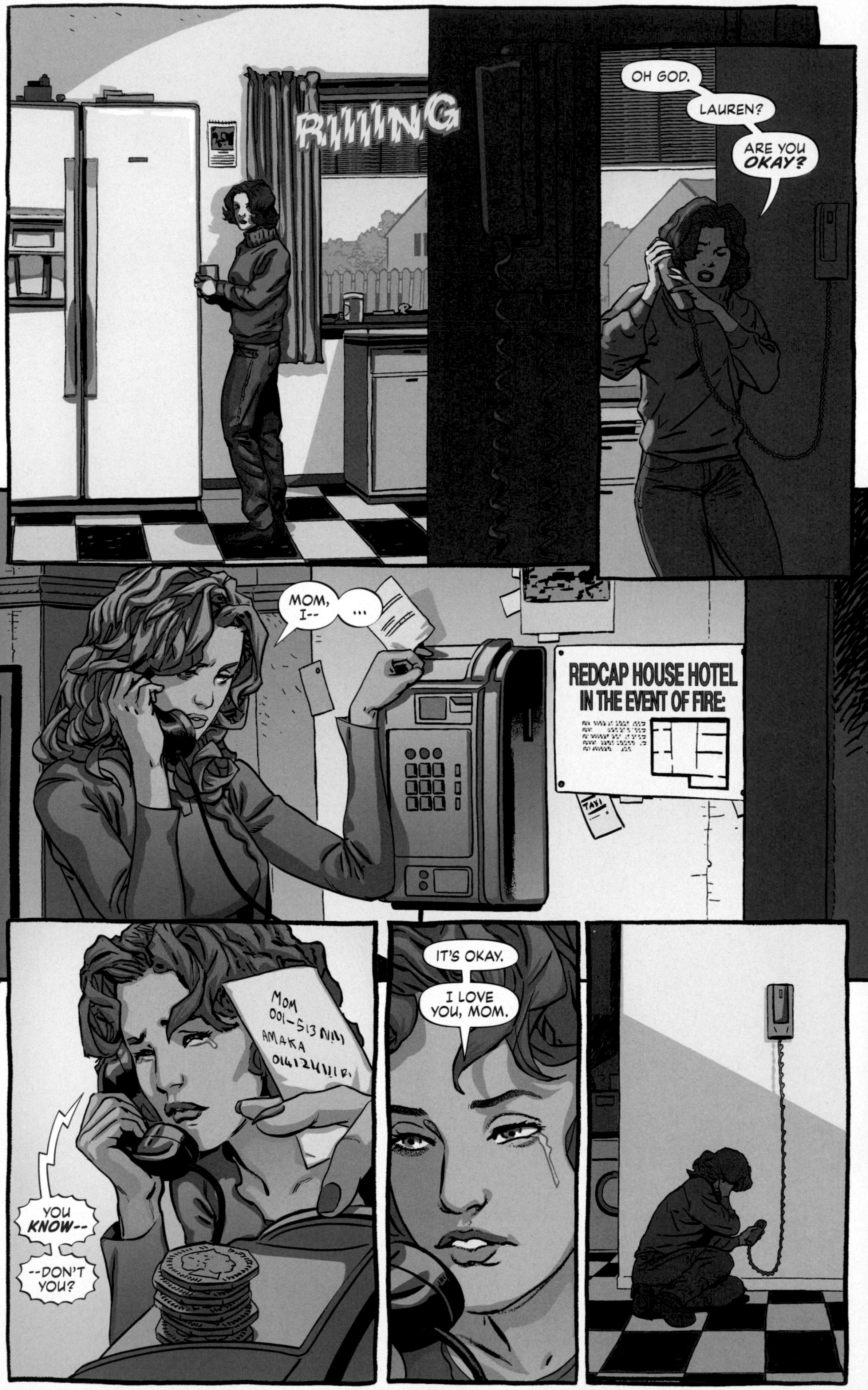
RIIIING
OH GOD.
LAUREN?
ARE YOU OKAY?
MOM, I--
...
REDCAP HOUSE HOTEL
IN THE EVENT OF FIRE:
TAXI
MOM
AMAKA
YOU KNOW--
--DON'T YOU?
IT'S OKAY.
I LOVE YOU, MOM.

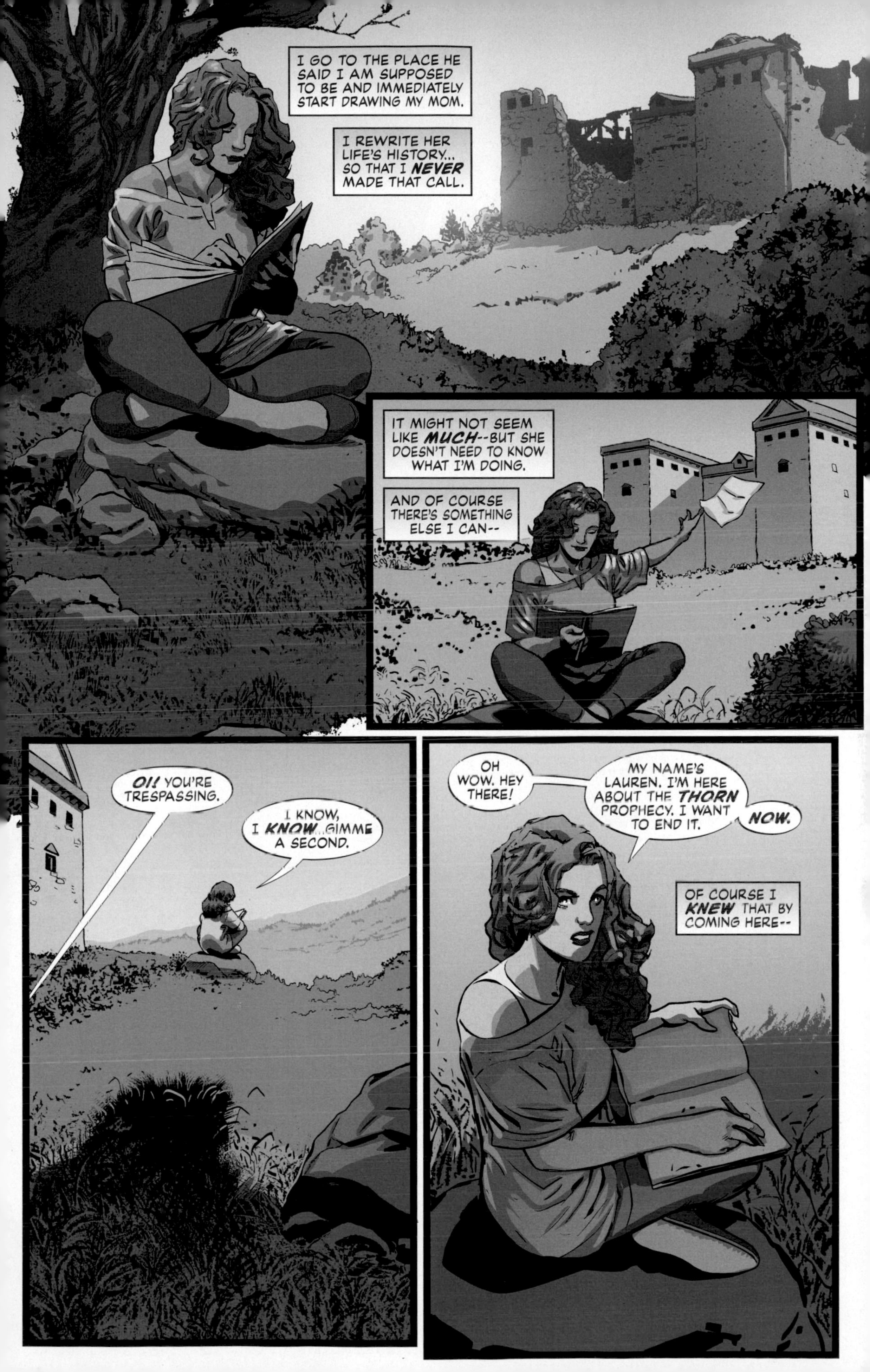
I GO TO THE PLACE HE SAID I AM SUPPOSED TO BE AND IMMEDIATELY START DRAWING MY MOM.
I REWRITE HER LIFE'S HISTORY... SO THAT I NEVER MADE THAT CALL.
IT MIGHT NOT SEEM LIKE MUCH--BUT SHE DOESN'T NEED TO KNOW WHAT I'M DOING.
AND OF COURSE THERE'S SOMETHING ELSE I CAN--
OI! YOU'RE TRESPASSING.
I KNOW, I KNOW...GIMME A SECOND.
OH WOW. HEY THERE!
MY NAME'S LAUREN. I'M HERE ABOUT THE THORN PROPHECY. I WANT TO END IT.
NOW.
OF COURSE I KNEW THAT BY COMING HERE--

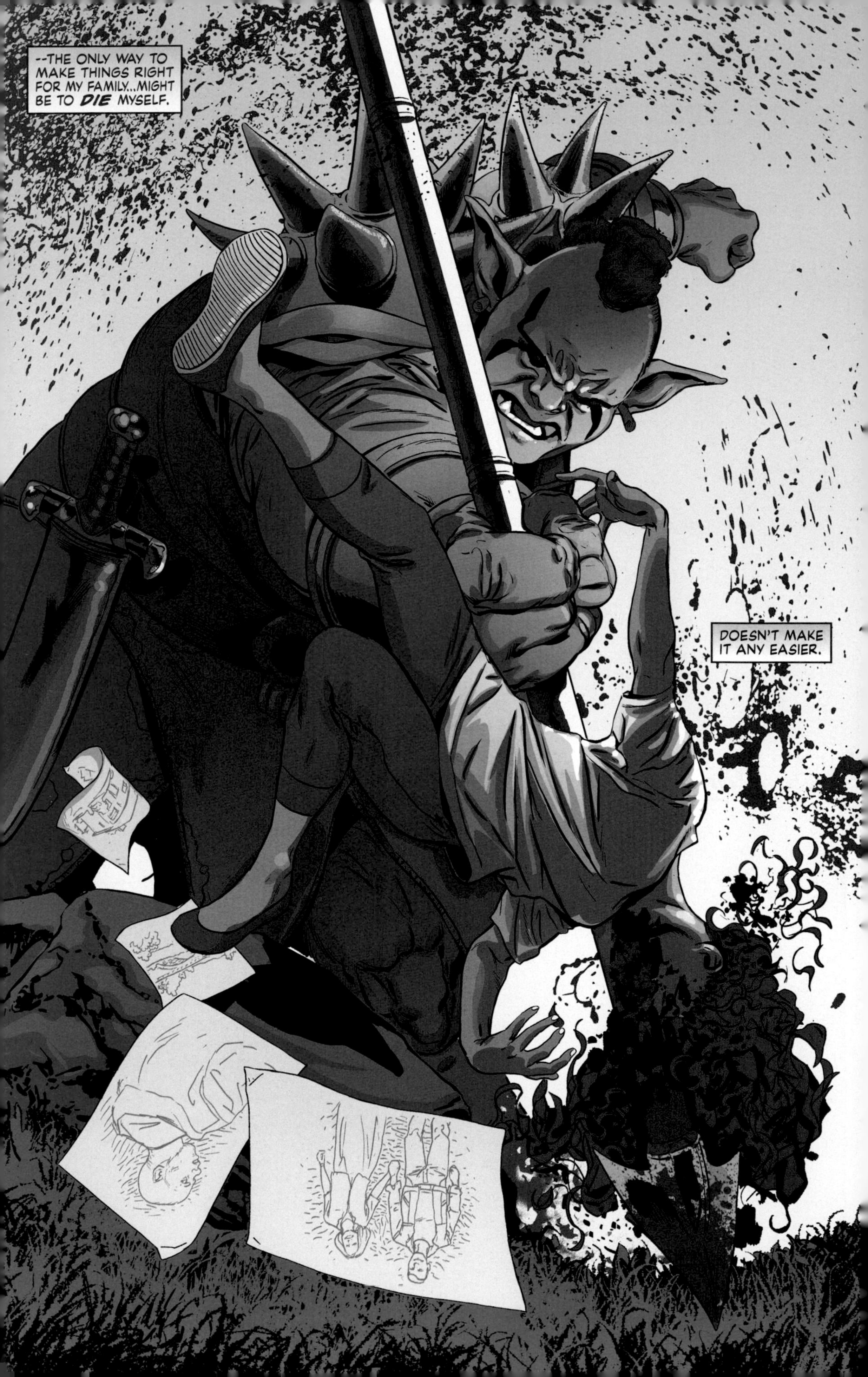
--THE ONLY WAY TO MAKE THINGS RIGHT FOR MY FAMILY...MIGHT BE TO DIE MYSELF.
DOESN'T MAKE IT ANY EASIER.

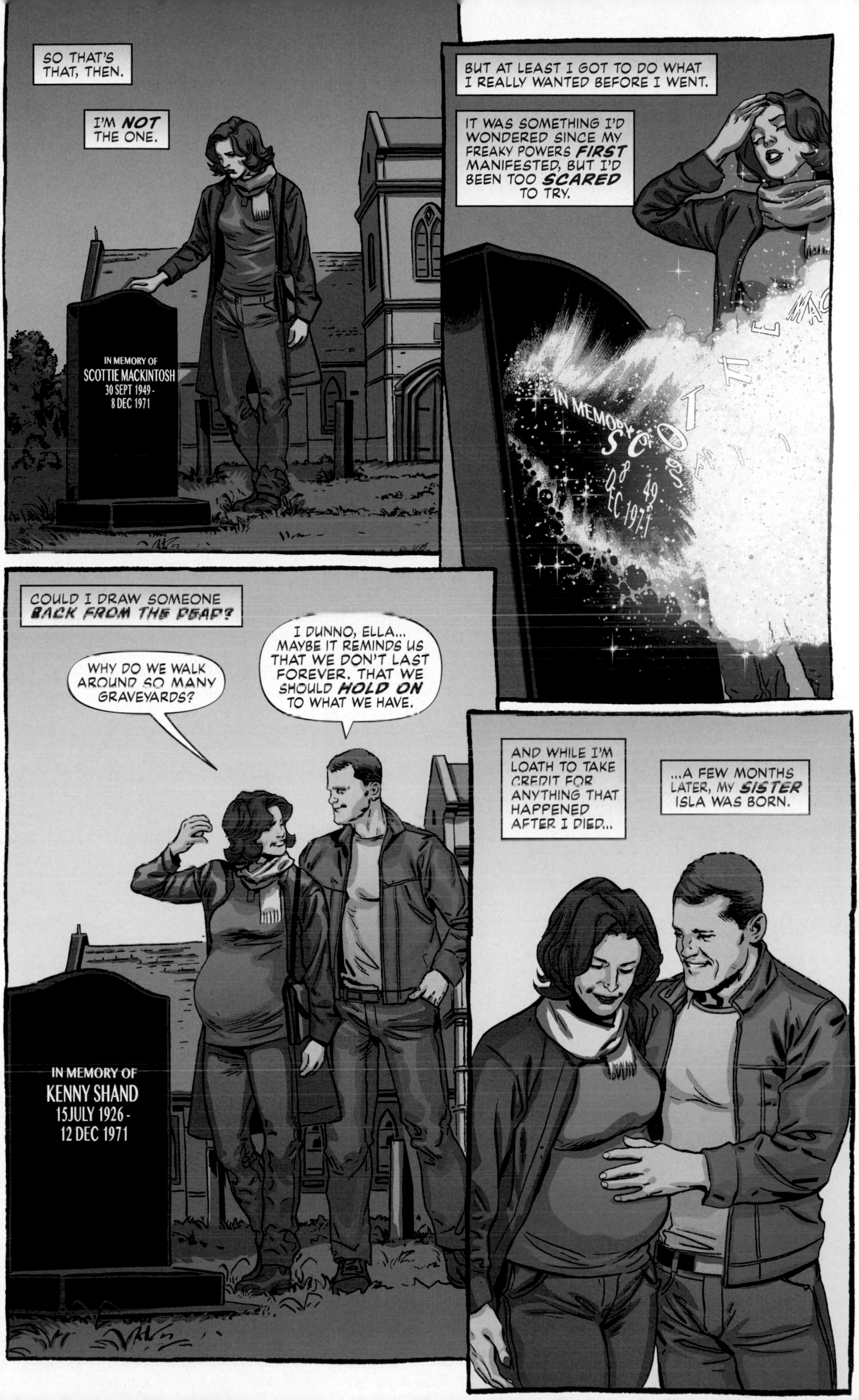
SO THAT'S THAT, THEN.
I'M NOT THE ONE.
IN MEMORY OF SCOTTIE MACKINTOSH 30 SEPT 1949 - 8 DEC 1971
BUT AT LEAST I GOT TO DO WHAT I REALLY WANTED BEFORE I WENT.
IT WAS SOMETHING I'D WONDERED SINCE MY FREAKY POWERS FIRST MANIFESTED, BUT I'D BEEN TOO SCARED TO TRY.
COULD I DRAW SOMEONE BACK FROM THE DEAD?
WHY DO WE WALK AROUND SO MANY GRAVEYARDS?
I DUNNO, ELLA... MAYBE IT REMINDS US THAT WE DON'T LAST FOREVER. THAT WE SHOULD HOLD ON TO WHAT WE HAVE.
IN MEMORY OF KENNY SHAND 15JULY 1926 - 12 DEC 1971
AND WHILE I'M LOATH TO TAKE CREDIT FOR ANYTHING THAT HAPPENED AFTER I DIED...
...A FEW MONTHS LATER, MY SISTER ISLA WAS BORN.

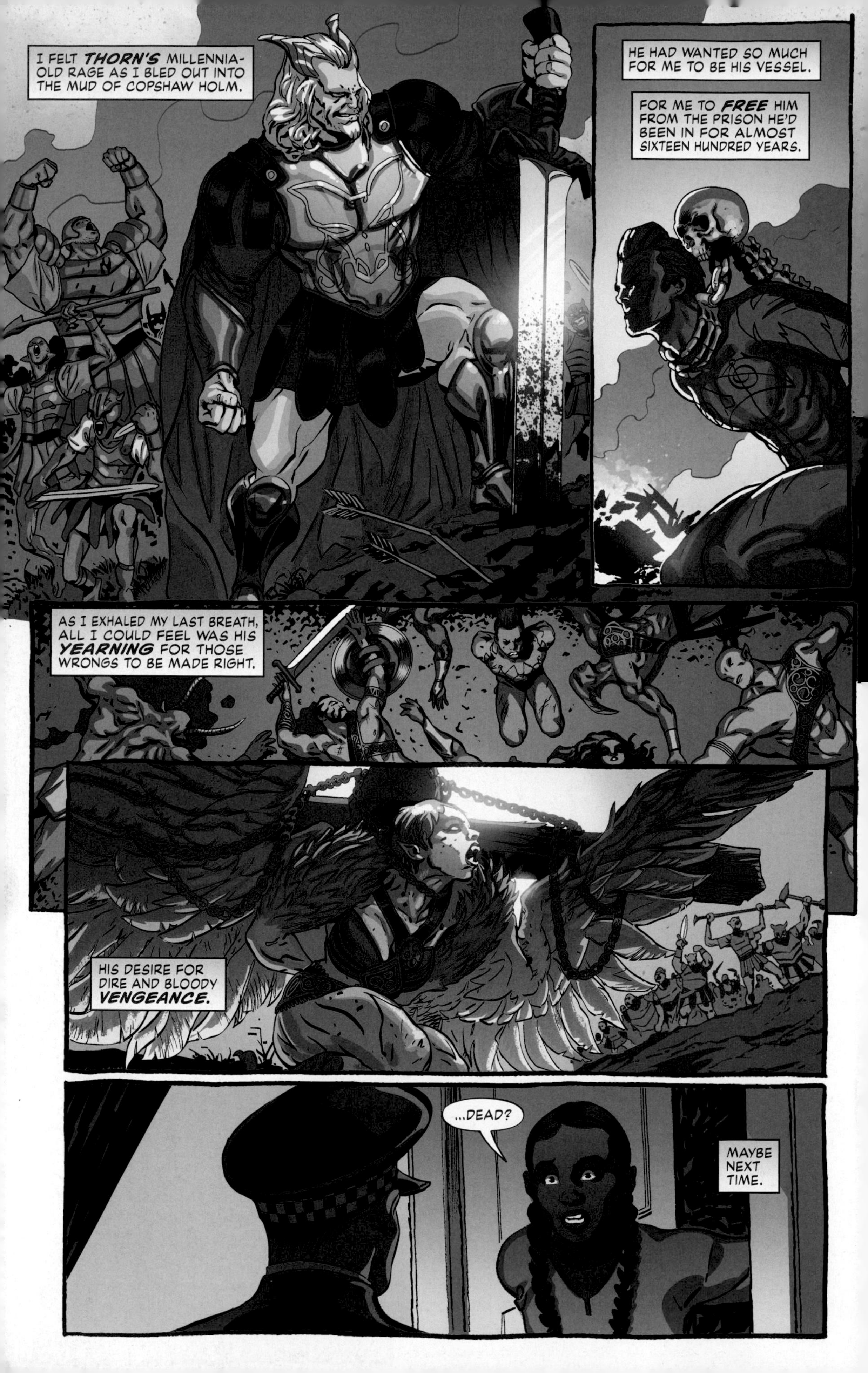
I FELT THORN'S MILLENNIA-OLD RAGE AS I BLED OUT INTO THE MUD OF COPSHAW HOLM.
HE HAD WANTED SO MUCH FOR ME TO BE HIS VESSEL.
FOR ME TO FREE HIM FROM THE PRISON HE'D BEEN IN FOR ALMOST SIXTEEN HUNDRED YEARS.
AS I EXHALED MY LAST BREATH, ALL I COULD FEEL WAS HIS YEARNING FOR THOSE WRONGS TO BE MADE RIGHT.
HIS DESIRE FOR DIRE AND BLOODY VENGEANCE.
...DEAD?
MAYBE NEXT TIME.

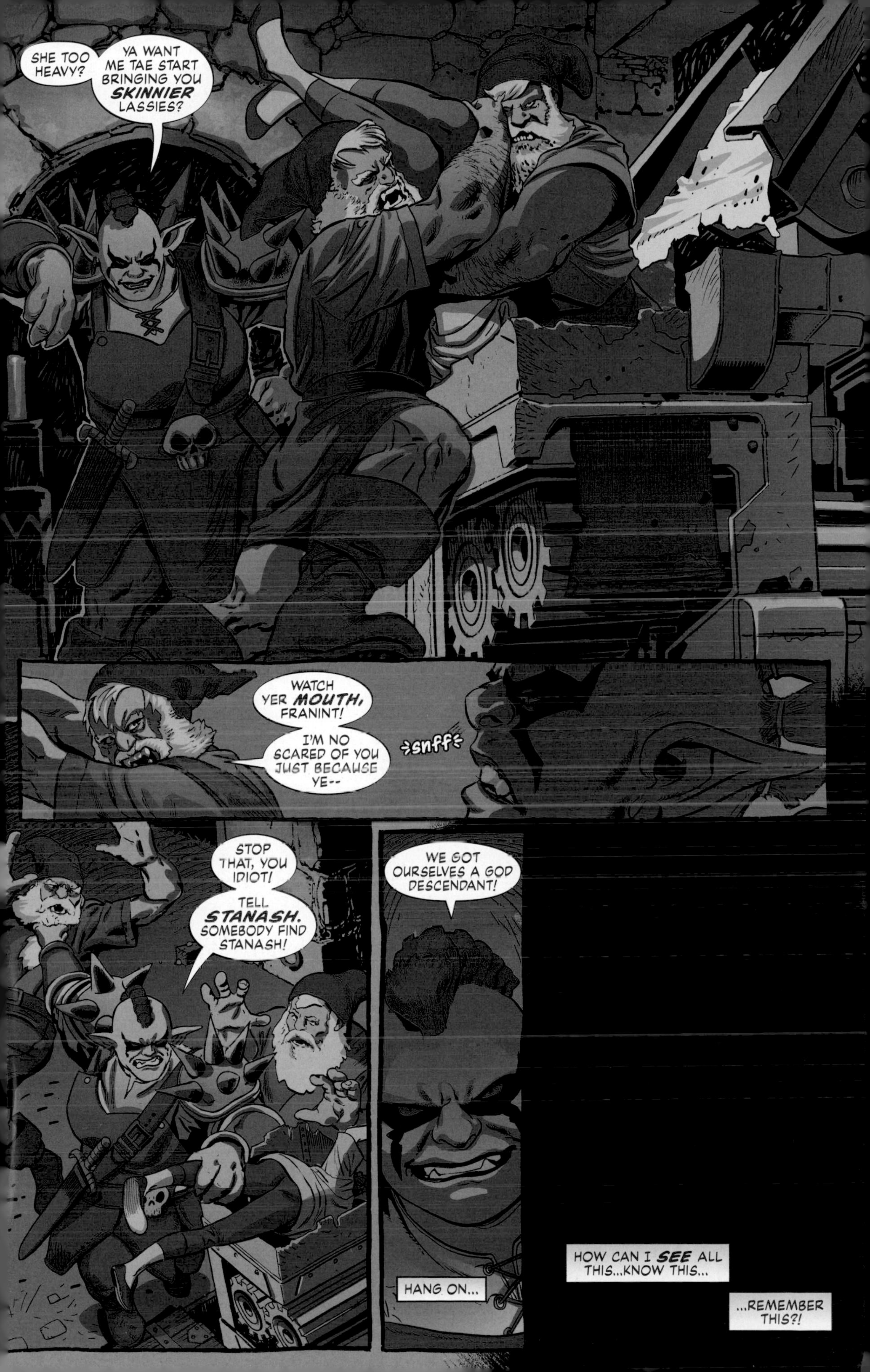
SHE TOO HEAVY?
YA WANT ME TAE START BRINGING YOU SKINNIER LASSIES?
WATCH YER MOUTH, FRANINT!
I'M NO SCARED OF YOU JUST BECAUSE YE--
snff
STOP THAT, YOU IDIOT!
TELL STANASH. SOMEBODY FIND STANASH!
WE GOT OURSELVES A GOD DESCENDANT!
HANG ON...
HOW CAN I SEE ALL THIS...KNOW THIS...
...REMEMBER THIS?!

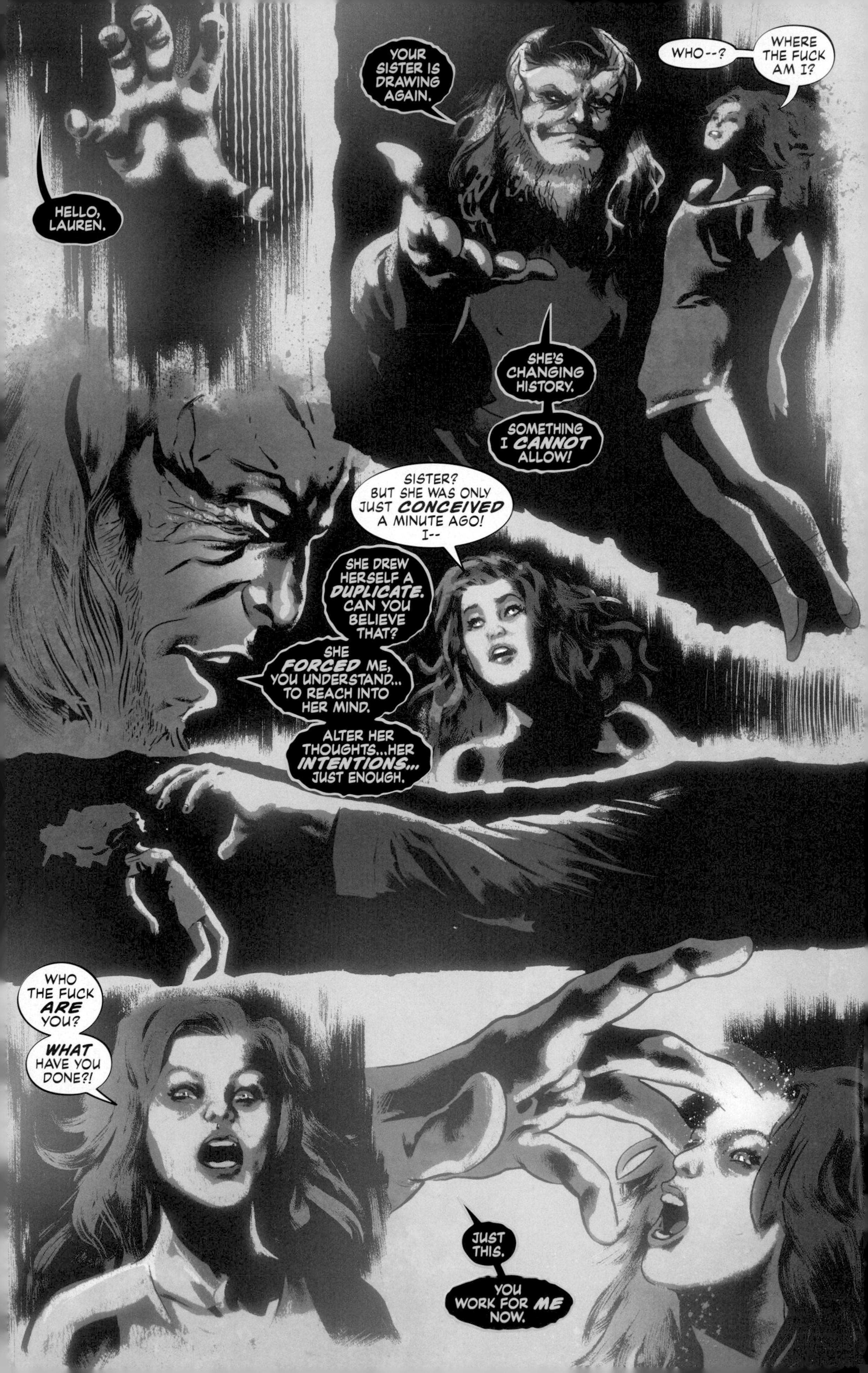
HELLO, LAUREN.
YOUR SISTER IS DRAWING AGAIN.
WHO--?
WHERE THE FUCK AM I?
SHE'S CHANGING HISTORY.
SOMETHING I CANNOT ALLOW!
SISTER? BUT SHE WAS ONLY JUST CONCEIVED A MINUTE AGO! I--
SHE DREW HERSELF A DUPLICATE. CAN YOU BELIEVE THAT?
SHE FORCED ME, YOU UNDERSTAND... TO REACH INTO HER MIND.
ALTER HER THOUGHTS...HER INTENTIONS... JUST ENOUGH.
WHO THE FUCK ARE YOU?
WHAT HAVE YOU DONE?!
JUST THIS.
YOU WORK FOR ME NOW.

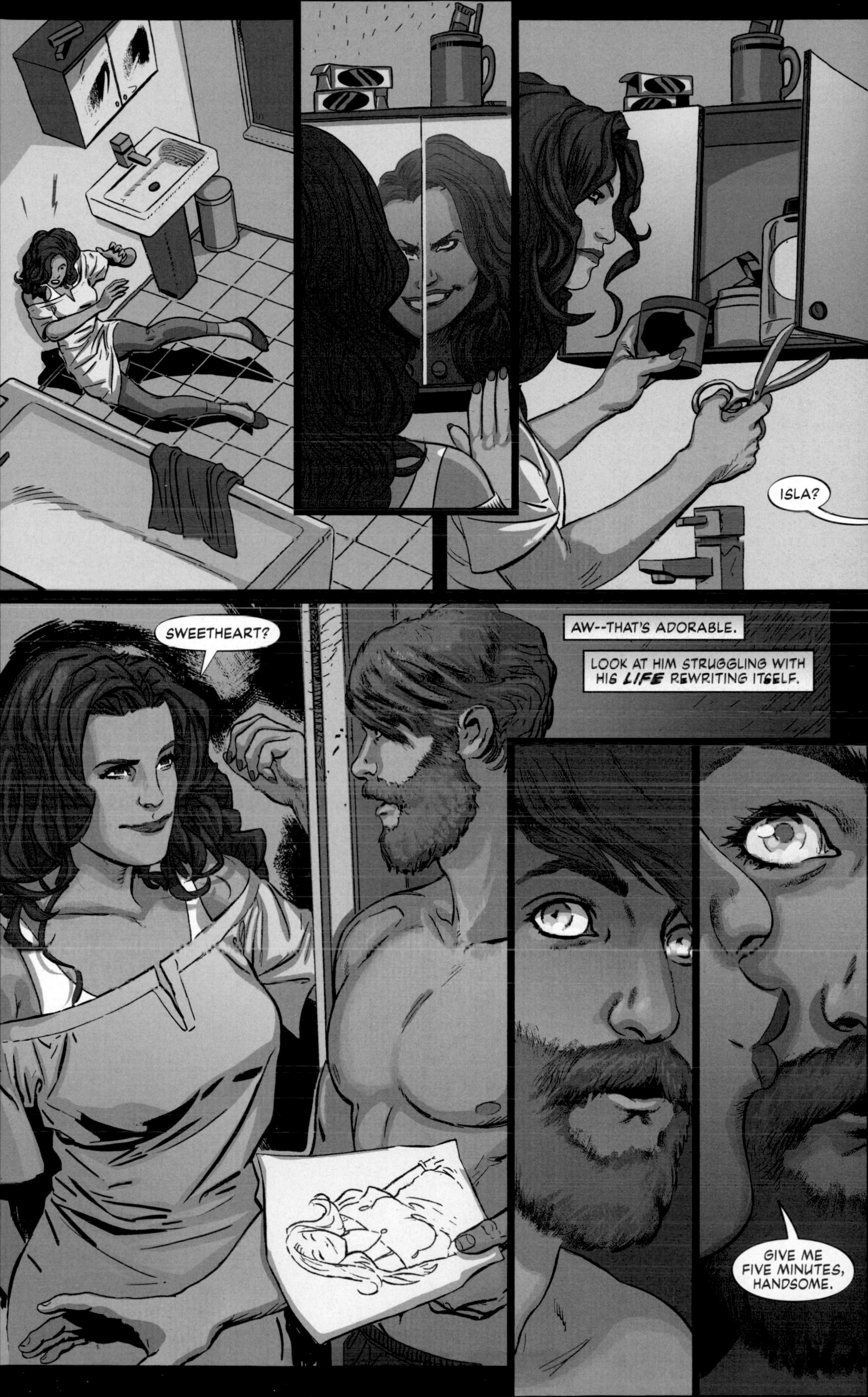
ISLA?
SWEETHEART?
AW--THAT'S ADORABLE.
LOOK AT HIM STRUGGLING WITH HIS LIFE REWRITING ITSELF.
GIVE ME FIVE MINUTES, HANDSOME.

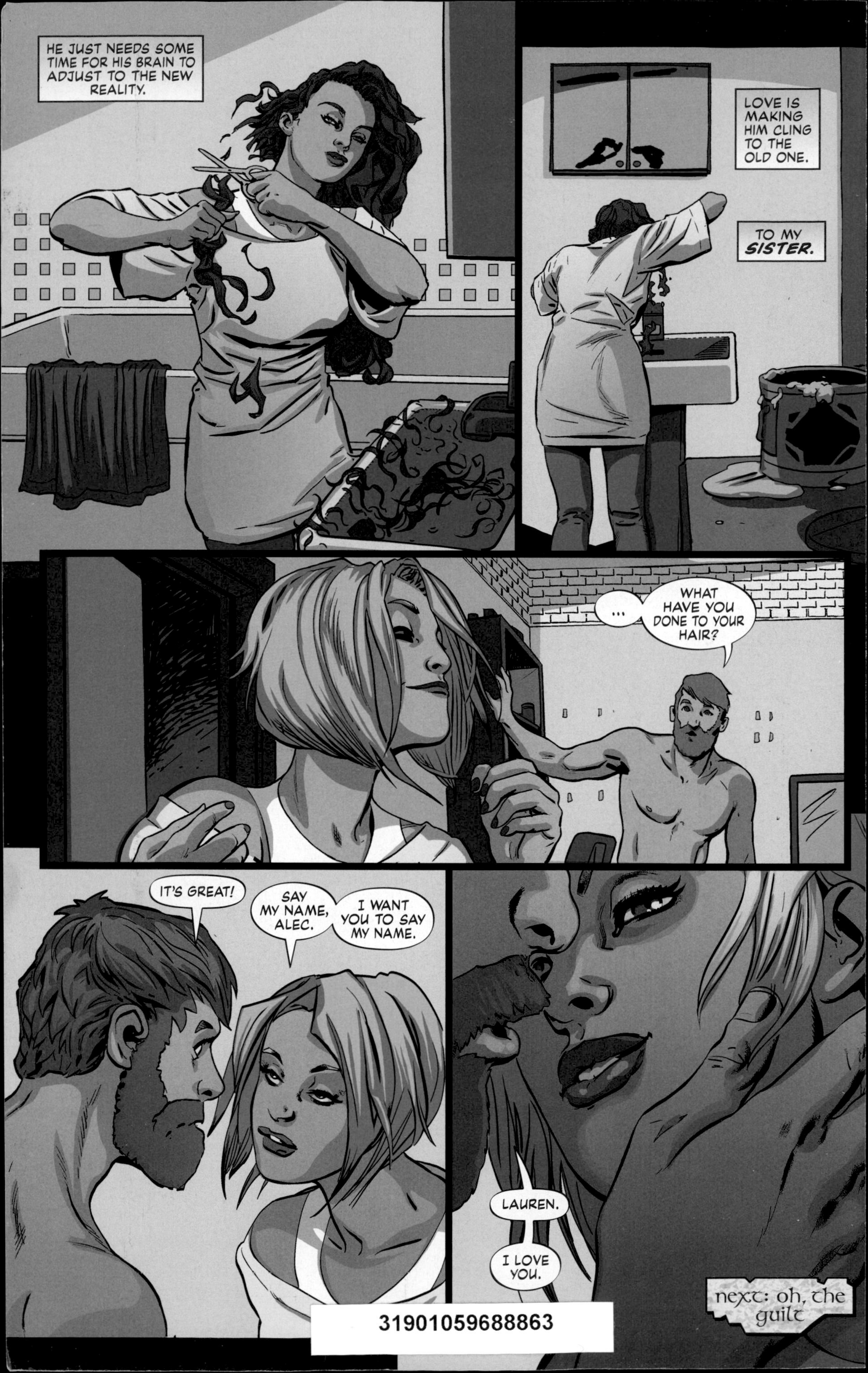
HE JUST NEEDS SOME TIME FOR HIS BRAIN TO ADJUST TO THE NEW REALITY.
LOVE IS MAKING HIM CLING TO THE OLD ONE.
TO MY SISTER.
...
WHAT HAVE YOU DONE TO YOUR HAIR?
IT'S GREAT!
SAY MY NAME, ALEC.
I WANT YOU TO SAY MY NAME.
LAUREN.
I LOVE YOU.
next: oh, the guilt